Happy Birthday Judy
With love
Mom

DAILY
Guideposts.

2002

*In every thing
by prayer and supplication
with thanksgiving
let your requests
be made known unto God.*

PHILIPPIANS 4:6

IDEALS PUBLICATIONS, A DIVISION OF GUIDEPOSTS
NASHVILLE, TN

ISBN 0-8249-4602-2

Published by Ideals Publications, a division of Guideposts

Copyright © 2001 by Guideposts, Carmel, New York 10512. All rights reserved.

Every attempt has been made to credit the sources of copyrighted material used in this book. If any such acknowledgment has been inadvertently omitted or miscredited, receipt of such information would be appreciated.

ACKNOWLEDGMENTS

All Scripture quotations, unless otherwise noted, are taken from *The King James Version of the Bible.*
   Scripture quotations marked (NAS) are taken from the *New American Standard Bible,* © The Lockman Foundation, 1960, 1962, 1963, 1968, 1971, 1972, 1973, 1975, 1977. Used by permission.
   Scripture quotations marked (NIV) are taken from *The Holy Bible, New International Version.* Copyright © 1973, 1978, 1984 International Bible Society. Used by permission of Zondervan Bible Publishers.
   Scripture quotations marked (NKJV) are taken from *The Holy Bible, New King James Version.* Copyright © 1997, 1990, 1985, 1983 by Thomas Nelson, Inc.
   Scripture quotations marked (RSV) are taken from the *Revised Standard Version of the Bible.* Copyright © 1946, 1952, 1971 by Division of Christian Education of the National Council of Churches of Christ in the U.S.A. Used by permission.
   Scripture quotations marked (TLB) are taken from *The Living Bible.* Copyright © 1971 by Tyndale House Publishers, Wheaton, IL 60187. All rights reserved.
   "A Grand Canyon Journey" was written by Rhoda Blecker.
   "A Time for Giving" was written by Rick Hamlin.
   "A Worrier's Way to God" was written by Marci Alborghetti.
   "At the Point of Our Pain" was written by Roberta Messner.
   "For Every Season" was written by Roberta Rogers.
   "Island Pilgrimage" was written by Marilyn Morgan King and Robert King.
   "The Practice of Prayer" was written by Pam Kidd.
   "The Prayer That Is Always New" was written by Elizabeth Sherrill.
   "Reader's Room" by Sandy Mitchell, Mary Yoder, Kathy Wolking, Beverly Zambito, Wendi Frantz, Sharon Howard, Josephine McConnell, Beverly Ann Sharpf, Janet Lohr, Betty Haughin, Ann Huber, and C. Donn Tipton are reprinted with permission from the authors.
   "What God Has Joined Together" was written by Eric Fellman.
   Edward Grinnan's photo is by Julie Skarratt.

www.guidepostsbooks.com
Cover designed by Eve DeGrie
Cover Photograph © William H. Johnson/Johnson's Photography
Text designed by Holly Johnson
Artwork by Edgar Jerins
Indexed by Patricia Woodruff
Typeset by Allentown Digital Services Division of R.R. Donnelley & Sons
Printed in the United States of America

TABLE OF CONTENTS

INTRODUCTION

Whether we pray in church with a community of believers, at home with the members of our family, in a small prayer or Bible study group, at the bedside of an ailing friend, with a longtime prayer partner, or by ourselves in the quiet of our own hearts, we never pray alone. Our own prayer is nourished and sustained by the prayers of so many others—the parents and grandparents, pastors and teachers, neighbors and friends who, throughout our lives, have lovingly brought our needs before the Throne of Grace. And as Paul reminds us in Romans 8:26, when we pray—no matter how tired or distracted or overwhelmed with our needs we may be—God's own Spirit prays with us and for us, far better than we could for ourselves.

Our theme for *Daily Guideposts, 2002* is "Praying Together." Our fifty-eight writers will show you how prayer can be a source of comfort in times of trouble, healing in times of need, thankfulness of heart in times of joy and peace and contentment in the events and challenges each day brings.

If you've joined us before, you'll find many old friends who've come back again to share their lives with you—and if you're a new member of our family, you'll soon come to love them as we do. And we've invited three new friends to join our *Daily Guideposts* family: Fulton Oursler, Jr., of Nyack, New York, former editor-in-chief of *Guideposts* magazine; Tim Williams, an emergency medical technician and father of two from Durango, Colorado; and Billy Newman, a businessman and father from Atlanta, Georgia.

Each month of 2002 begins with Elizabeth Sherrill's reflections on "The Prayer That Is Always New." She'll share the ways God has used her life experiences to charge the familiar words of the Lord's Prayer with new and often unsuspected meaning as she's prayed them through the years. And in the middle of each month, Pam Kidd's "The Practice of Prayer" will show how prayer has transformed her own life, and how you, too, can become the person God means you to be through a life-changing habit of prayer. In "For Every Season," Roberta Rogers begins each of the four seasons with a special story about her own prayer-journey. Eric Fellman and his wife Joy celebrated their twenty-fifth wedding anniversary last year, and throughout the year, Eric will share some of the ways that he and Joy have grown together in love and faith.

In January, Marci Alborghetti will show you how, by praying through her anxieties, she's discovered "A Worrier's Way to God." Join Roberta Messner during Holy Week and Easter to learn how God uses illness and adversity to reveal the victory of His Cross and Resurrection "At the Point of Our Pain." In July, Rhoda Blecker takes you on "A Grand Canyon Journey" to discover the glory of God revealed in one of His most spectacular creations. In October, Marilyn Morgan King and her husband Robert set out on an "Island Pilgrimage" to Iona, the island off the west coast of Scotland that has been a beacon of prayer for pilgrims for more than a millennium. Then spend Advent and Christmas with Rick Hamlin and his family as he explores the many ways God gives to us and through us during "A Time for Giving."

In the life of every family, joy is inevitably mixed with sorrow. During the past year, our *Daily Guideposts* family has mourned the loss of two old friends. Kenneth Chafin of Fort Worth, Texas, died on January 3, 2001, after a brief illness. Kenneth was a fine writer, an inspiring teacher, an unselfish and compassionate pastor, and a devoted husband and father whose whole life was lived in the service of God's people. And after a long battle with melanoma, which she shared courageously with the readers of *Daily Guideposts,* Mary Jane Clark of Durango, Colorado, died on March 31, 2001. You'll find Mary Jane's last reflections in this edition of *Daily Guideposts.* Please keep Kenneth's and Mary Jane's families in your prayers.

All families have secrets, and our *Daily Guideposts* family is no exception. Our secret, though, is one that we proclaim joyfully for everyone to share. Our secret—what makes us a family—is prayer. Many of you write to tell us that you pray especially for the writer of each day's devotional and for the readers whose letters appear in the "Reader's Room." And our writers want you to know that they, too, are praying for you and for all those whose lives are touched by the ministry of Guideposts. Every day, in every state and country in which *Daily Guideposts* is read, through this book or on the World Wide Web (www.guidepostsbooks.com), people whose names you may never know are praying with you and for you. Every working day, your letters are prayed for, by name and need, by Guideposts Prayer Fellowship. Every Monday morning at 9:45, in all our offices, we pray for the needs of our readers and for the fruitfulness of our ministries. So remember, dear friend, that we are—all of us—praying together. We never pray alone.

—*THE EDITORS*

January

My voice shalt thou hear in the morning,
O Lord; in the morning will I direct my
prayer unto thee, and will look up.

—*Psalm 5:3*

S	M	T	W	T	F	S
		1	2	3	4	5
6	7	8	9	10	11	12
13	14	15	16	17	18	19
20	21	22	23	24	25	26
27	28	29	30	31		

<table>
<tr><td>TUE</td></tr>
<tr><td>1</td></tr>
</table>

TUE
1 This grace was given us in Christ Jesus before the beginning of time. —*II TIMOTHY 1:9 (NIV)*

1/1/2002. I look at the calendar and realize it is the first day of the second year of the third millennium. Every New Year's Day makes me think of the mysteries of time, the inexorable procession of this invisible force that rules our lives.

How much time has passed since time began? I wonder. Can our minds begin to grasp the strange things we have learned about the role time plays in the universe? I know the seeming exactitude of dates, hours and seconds is an illusion. Time, we now understand, is linked to space, and its measurement can be changed by velocity. Einstein and other great minds assure us that time is relative; under certain conditions of spaceflight, a traveler could return to earth only to find that his family and friends are long gone.

If time is one of the great puzzles God has given us, relativity is often seen as a threat to common sense. It seems to turn the world upside down. But is it any more startling or revolutionary than the principles our Lord brought to us during His brief time on earth? "Love your enemies." "If someone strikes you on the right cheek, turn to him the other also." "Unless a man is born again. . . ."

Jesus, Whose grace was given us before time began, spoke of the last days when earth's time will stop. And in the few seconds it took to write that sentence, I have had thoughts that span the entire arc of time. For an instant, the great puzzle seems clear. Everything— from the first nanosecond of time, through what we call the past, the present and all that is to come—happens at a pace no clock can measure. It happens in God's good time.

And in the new creation to come—in God's ever present eternity— there will be no need for calendars.

Lord, Who made all time for us, help us to make more time for You!
—*FULTON OURSLER, JR.*

WED

2

Thou hast beset me behind and before, and laid thine hand upon me.   *—PSALM 139:5*

Something delightful interfered with my agenda for New Year's Day 2001. I had been up way too late the night before, so I thought that I would settle in for a relaxing day of snacking and watching parades and college bowl football games. Our daughter Kelly and her husband Brett planned to come over. I wanted a Scrabble rematch with Brett; I had lost to him at Thanksgiving and I don't give up easily where Scrabble is concerned.

When they arrived in the afternoon, Kelly had a set of borrowed cross-country skis with her. It was a brilliant day to be outdoors. Under a crisp blue sky, dazzling ice crystals caught the sun across the snowy fields. There was nothing to do but bundle up and join my daughter for my maiden voyage on my new snowshoes!

As we made our way side by side through the unmarred glittering snow, I glanced back at our tracks and called to Kelly, "Hey, look! Yours are smooth and straight and dainty on skis, and mine are chunky and clumpy and uneven with my snowshoes." She smiled as we resumed our gliding and trudging up a slight incline, faces toward the sun.

"We're breaking trail into the new year!" Kelly exclaimed.

Yes, we were, this frisky daughter of mine and I. She was twenty-three; I was forty-eight. Of course our "tracks in the snow" would look different. Maybe at some spots in our lives we'd even cross over, and I would be the graceful glider and she the slower plodder. We all break trail differently, some with more ease than others. But the thrill of it is, with Jesus Christ—the Beginner and Finisher of our faith—the job gets done.

I took another look back at our double trail in the snow. I'm sure I saw a third set of tracks.

Jesus, Lord of time and space, You go behind and before and beside me as I enter this new year. Thank You.   *—CAROL KNAPP*

THE PRAYER THAT IS ALWAYS NEW

"Teach us to pray," Jesus' disciples asked, and from that day to this the Lord's Prayer has been the mainstay of Christian worship. Yet, familiar though the prayer is, Elizabeth Sherrill points out that it's also ever new. "The prayer is as different each time I say it as my needs are different each time." Individual words stand out, as though God is saying, "Pause here. This is where your prayer emphasis should be today."

At the start of each month, Elizabeth will share some of the words God has highlighted for her, in the prayer we know by heart yet never exhaust. —*THE EDITORS*

THU

3   *Our* Father . . .   —*MATTHEW 6:9*

Three weeks had passed since some driver at the train station had smashed in the passenger side of my parked car. No note left, no phone number. The repairs had been done, our insurance would pay for it and, except for some lost time and a week of imposing on friends for rides, no real harm had been done. Still, I raged at the person who could do such a thing and simply drive away.

"You have to let it go," said my husband John, who was tired of hearing about it. "Staying angry will hurt you lots more than a damaged car."

Of course, I knew that—in principle. For our souls' health, Jesus commands us to forgive far worse things than this! Since I didn't yet feel forgiving, I turned to the Lord's Prayer. Perhaps when I reached "as we forgive those who trespass against us," the transformation would happen.

I didn't get that far.

Our Father. Mine and this unknown individual's. The same Father watched over us both with equal love, knew every circumstance of that other life. Who was it? A harried mother distracted by a child? A teenager with more horsepower than experience? A commuter handling work pressures with alcohol?

Whatever the person's problems, this was my brother or sister for whom I could not help praying with the first word of the Lord's Prayer and all those that followed. "Give *us* our daily bread. . . . Forgive *us* our trespasses." My own needs and that driver's needs, lifted together to God.

Years ago I'd clipped some anonymous lines from a mailing from the Omaha Home for Boys. I dug them out now and posted them on my refrigerator door:

> *You cannot pray the Lord's Prayer and even once say "I."*
> *You cannot pray the Lord's Prayer and even once say "my."*
> *When you pray the Lord's Prayer you pray for one another.*
> *And when you ask for daily bread, you must include your brother.*
> *For others are included in each and every plea.*
> *From beginning to the end, it does not once say "me."*

Our Father, as I say the Lord's Prayer each day of this year, remind me that I never do so alone. *—ELIZABETH SHERRILL*

EDITOR'S NOTE: This year, please take time to jot down some of the ways God has helped you to grow in prayer. You'll find a place for brief daily reflections in "My Days of Prayer" at the end of every month.

FRI
4

He hath made every thing beautiful in his time. . . .
—ECCLESIASTES 3:11

The scale didn't lie. Holiday indiscretions—the Christmas cookies, the fudge, a candy cane or two (or ten)—piled upon years of self-indulgence had pushed my weight well over what the optimistic height/weight charts recommended. Time and gravity had also begun their dirty work: Wrinkles and ripples surfaced where there had been none five years before.

My gray mood matched that January morning as I set off to cover my beat as a reporter for the *Wyoming State Journal*. Today I was scheduled to cover an appearance of Miss Wyoming at a local elementary school. From the press release, I knew that she would perform on the piano and speak to the children about resisting drugs. I would be sure to recognize her by her slim figure, brunette curls and trademark tiara.

Arriving at the school a little early, I snapped the top fastener on my bulky parka and pulled my woolly hat low over my ears for better protection from the bitter chill. The kindergartners were lined up by the front door. I hesitated for a moment, trying to determine whether the children formed a welcoming committee for the beauty queen or were simply waiting to go inside. Suddenly a little girl broke rank, clasped me around my legs and arched her back, the better to smile into my startled face.

"Are you Miss Wyoming?" she inquired sweetly. I nearly dropped my camera bag.

"No, honey, I'm from the newspaper."

"Oh." She continued hugging me and smiling until her teacher shepherded her back into line.

That afternoon, I smiled more, too, and walked a little taller as I completed my assignment.

Lord, thank You for the people who see past the physical wear and tear and help me to rejoice in my true beauty.
—*GAIL THORELL SCHILLING*

SAT

5

Mine arm also shall strengthen him. —*PSALM 89:21*

It wasn't working. In spite of the fact that my daughter Joanna was wearing ankle braces and high-topped basketball shoes, every few games she'd hurt one ankle or the other again.

We took Joanna to a physical therapist, who suggested ankle strengthening. He told us something odd: Joanna's ankles needed to be "retrained" to land correctly when she jumped. Each ankle had been sprained so often that her foot came down off center, making the foot roll and thus reinjuring the ankle. To our amazement, Joanna's exercises strengthened and "retrained" her ankles, and she was injury-free the entire season.

Since then, I've begun noticing in how many ways I "brace" my life instead of strengthening and retraining my character. So in this new year, I've begun spiritual therapy. Rather than just apologizing for the hurtful things I've said, I'm determined to exercise the discipline of tongue control. Instead of occasional spurts of organizing closets and drawers, I've resolved to keep them tidy. Along with my emergency support of quick prayers, I'll work on the daily exercise of Bible reading and quiet time. With my thoughts centered on God, I'm bound to land right!

Father, help me in this new year to dispose of braces that weaken me, and strengthen and retrain my spirit instead.

—MARJORIE PARKER

SUN
6

"While I was musing the fire burned; Then I spoke with my tongue: Lord, make me to know my end, And what is the extent of my days, Let me know how transient I am. . . . My hope is in Thee." *—PSALM 39:3-4, 7 (NAS)*

My family has gone to bed. I am alone in the darkened den, staring into the embers of this evening's fire. Sprawled in my easy chair, I have turned off the last light. It is time to reflect and remember, to be lulled into sleep.

Drifting into reverie, I am entranced by the glowing oak coals, their dry warmth radiating and soothing. For a moment I think of the generations of men and women who have finished their day this way: alone, draped in darkness, entranced by radiance, pondering the meaning of life.

I remember the years of my childhood, tucked away in the high, remote mountains of the Philippines. In the rainy season it grew cold and damp. Battered by fierce typhoons, our only heat came from a stone fireplace. I remember my father walking out of the night and through our front door, a load of split wood in his arms, pine kindling grasped in his hands. Dad would always light the family hearth, the place for our family to gather, to commune, to be.

And now, out of the same darkness comes a yearning for another Father. The embers of this night kindle a longing for God, a timeless longing that I share with the whole human race. As I slip toward sleep, my eyes closing, a blanket drawn around me, I know God is near. I don't know how I know: I just know. I believe, and I am a child again.

Father, in the darkness of this world, enlighten me with the radiance of Your love. Amen. —*SCOTT WALKER*

MON
7

May grace and peace be multiplied to you in the knowledge of God and of Jesus our Lord. —*II PETER 1:2 (RSV)*

By January 7, Christmas seemed a dim memory. My husband Alex had left for a conference overseas. Exhausted from out-of-state holiday visits, then the flu, I dreaded the lonely week ahead and the dark months of winter. But it's a family tradition to join our friends Bill and Melanie, Serbian Orthodox Christians who observe Christmas today, so I bundled up the children and headed to their Victorian farmhouse in rural Williamston, Michigan.

Driving there, I remembered our evening together last year. Alex, as the first male guest to arrive, represented the Christ Child and scattered wheat, nuts and coins in the four corners of the room, wishing the family good health and prosperity. Later we talked by the fire, sipping hot spiced cider while the children quietly played.

This year the house bustled with people I didn't know—farmer neighbors and university students from former Yugoslavia. After helping in the kitchen, supervising the kids sliding down the banister of the grand staircase and catching snatches of conversations, I felt frazzled by the time dinner was served.

As we gathered around the "manger"—the long mahogany dining-room table with straw scattered underneath—quiet descended. Melanie lit a candle, symbolizing the coming of the light of the world. We sang a beautiful old hymn, first in Serbian, then in English, proclaiming the glory of Christ's Nativity. Listening to the young man next to me heartily singing, I no longer heard a thick-accented immigrant, but my brother in Christ.

Passing around a common cup, each person said to the next, "Peace from God. Christ is born." As we gently spoke those words, the Prince of Peace Himself seemed present with us.

Later, as I loaded the car and drove slowly home through freezing rain, I no longer dreaded the days ahead. The message echoed softly in my heart: "Peace from God. Christ is born."

Oh, Lord, how quickly I forget You! Please help me continue to rejoice in Your coming, to see You among us and find Your peace within me each day this year.   —*MARY BROWN*

TUE

8   Therefore will I give thanks unto thee, O Lord. . . .
                                        —*PSALM 18:49*

My wife Ruby and I purchased our home in June 1965. After the closing, Mrs. Berry, the former owner, said, "I feel so bad. I'm afraid your furnace won't last the winter." But it did.

"Our home is so warm, we can grow tomatoes in January," I teased Ruby.

The end came on Tuesday, January 10, 1989, when water surrounded our furnace. The repairman came, watched the water trickle down and said, "You need a new boiler. It'll cost five thousand and twenty-five dollars."

"Can't the old one be patched?" I pleaded.

He shook his head. "Besides, you have a lot of asbestos that's got to be removed. It'll be three weeks before you can get an appointment, and that's another one thousand five hundred and twenty-five dollars cash!"

I gulped. It was below zero, and Ruby was ill. I could see our home freezing and our pipes bursting.

Unexpectedly, I managed to get an appointment to remove the asbestos the next day. By that afternoon, the job was completed, and we received a clean-air certificate. Early the next morning the new furnace arrived, and by early evening it was up and purring. Our home never cooled down.

The following morning I called the furnace company to express my delight. I asked where I could send a thank-you note. There was a long silence. Then my call was transferred from department to department. Finally, I was told, "Mr. Greene, we don't know where you can send that letter. All we receive are complaints. Why don't you try our president?" I did, and he was elated.

For some reason, we're more likely to let people know when we think we've been poorly served than to show our appreciation for a job well done. Writing a letter takes time, but it's worth making the effort to say thank you.

Heavenly Father, remind me to show my appreciation today to someone who's helped me. —*OSCAR GREENE*

WED

9

"Let them construct a sanctuary for Me, that I may dwell among them." —*EXODUS 25:8 (NAS)*

Years ago, a newcomer arrived at our church in Stone Mountain, Georgia. Dawn smiled a lot, and was more excited about prayer than anyone I'd ever known. One day she told my friend Joann and me, "I believe God wants the three of us—with help—to erect a small prayer chapel here at the church. Let's pray about it." A few weeks later, Dawn said, "I believe God's spoken to me. The prayer chapel is to be an old log cabin. He'll show it to us, and then we'll move it here."

The three of us looked everywhere for a log cabin. Then one day Dawn drove Joann and me down a red dirt road we'd traveled countless times before in our search. Suddenly, she stopped in front of an old two-story pink-shingled house that leaned to the left and was nearly covered in vines. She ran to the house as though it were an old friend. Joann and I followed politely. Dawn pulled off a few shingles and exclaimed, through laughter and tears, "Look! Here's our log cabin!"

Dawn located the owners—a huge company in another state—and they decided to donate the building to our church. "We'll haul it log by log and reconstruct it at the church," Dawn explained. She prayed some more, and found an expert in reconstructing log buildings. He lived out of state, but he accepted Dawn's enthusiastic invitation to donate his time.

It took months, of course, to reconstruct the house. But the three of us were so eager to pray in this answer to prayer that we met there one wintry Wednesday morning. The roof wasn't on yet, and it snowed on us as we prayed together, huddled close to one another for warmth.

Father, teach me again how to seek Your will in prayer.

—*MARION BOND WEST*

THU

10 Freely ye have received, freely give. —*MATTHEW 10:8*

The wind was brisk as we headed from the library to my daughter Elizabeth's music class. As we neared 57th Street, I noticed a woman sitting near the trash can on the corner. She wore a thin T-shirt and was wrapped to the waist in a black plastic garbage bag. Her body shook violently from the cold as she held out a ragged paper cup and asked for money. Even by New York City standards, this was appalling. The fistful of change in my pocket was in her cup before I even thought about it.

Then the light changed, and I herded the children across the busy intersection. Halfway there, I turned the stroller around and headed back.

"Where are we going, Mommy? Why are we turning around?" clamored the children.

"We're going back to help that lady."

Back at the street corner, I pulled Mary's baby blanket out of my backpack. It was a pretty white wool blanket, thin but large. As I began to put it around the beggar woman's shoulders, a passerby stopped me.

"Don't do it," she advised. "She's a fake!"

"It doesn't matter what she is," I replied, "she's cold!"

In a moment, we were back on our way. After a block or two, John asked, "What's a fake?"

I explained.

"Why did you give that lady the blanket, then?" Elizabeth wanted to know.

I wasn't completely sure, though I tried to explain. "Jesus asks us to help people in need, and when we give to them, we are giving to Him. To me, it's better to be cheated than to judge someone's motives and be wrong. That lady was cold. We were able to help. Even if she only kept the blanket on for a few minutes, she needed it more than we did. Whatever she did after that is between her and God."

I've never seen that woman again, nor do I have any idea what happened to the blanket. Whatever took place, I know at least one thing is different about her: Someone has been praying for her. Me.

Jesus, remake my heart in the image of Your generosity.

—*JULIA ATTAWAY*

FRI

11

Hear thou in heaven their prayer. . . .   *—I KINGS 8:45*

Some of us were discussing the power and mystery of prayer, how sometimes it seems to bring about great change, and sometimes not. Often discussions like this fade away like a summer breeze, leaving nothing behind. But this time, I remember the words of a young minister who happened to be with us.

"I'm sure," he said, "that the warehouses of heaven are bursting with wonderful answers to prayer that never get delivered because requests for them never come in. The people with the problems don't ask for help because they don't really believe they can be helped, or that they deserve to be helped, or that the mighty power that created the universe could possibly be concerned about their human difficulties. So the prayer-answer sitting up there in heaven may be blocked by doubt, which after all is the opposite of faith."

He looked at us with a smile. "Think about this the next time you have a problem and hesitate to pray about it. The shipping department up in that heavenly warehouse may just be waiting to hear from you."

I have thought about it. And it does make a difference.

Father, when I send You my prayer requests, remind me of the postage stamp of faith.   *—ARTHUR GORDON*

WHAT GOD HAS JOINED TOGETHER

Last year, Eric Fellman and his wife Joy celebrated their twenty-fifth wedding anniversary. Throughout this year, Eric will tell us some of the things the past quarter-century has taught him about marriage—and about life.   *—THE EDITORS*

SAT

12

Many waters cannot quench love; rivers cannot wash it away. . . . —*SONG OF SOLOMON 8:7 (NIV)*

Joy and I celebrated twenty-five years of marriage last year. The way we met has become family legend.

We were part of a group of college students from around the country in training to be summer-camp counselors. A buddy of mine thought it would be fun to meet this cute blonde from California by pretending to show her how to use a canoe, but then tipping it over and dumping her into the water. I was from Minnesota and practically grew up in a canoe, so I knew this was a stupid idea. I did the smart thing and waded out to rescue both Joy and the canoe. Obviously, I did the right thing.

Ever since then, water has been a metaphor for our relationship. There have been the peaceful waters of quiet walks and the deep waters of lasting commitment; the turbulent waters of disagreements and the swamp waters of hurts, small and large. There have been troubled waters of anguish at times in raising our sons and the powerful, energetic waters of shared dreams and goals. There have been the dark waters of uncertainty during tremendous change and the sparkling waters of new horizons and wonderful friends. But in it all there has been one constant: the living water of Jesus Christ holding us up and strengthening our love even on days when we didn't exactly like each other.

As we embark on our second twenty-five years, we'd like to tell you what we've learned: If you nurture a relationship like a garden with the living water of Jesus, it will survive storms, heat, cold and dark to bear a lifetime of sustaining fruit.

Lord, thank You for each other, and for the presence, power and promise of Your Son in our lives. —*ERIC FELLMAN*

SUN

13

And all the tithe of the land, whether of the seed of the land, or of the fruit of the tree, is the Lord's: it is holy unto the Lord. —*LEVITICUS 27:30*

"Stewardship," a farmer friend once told me, "is leaving my place in a little better shape than I found it." Put another way, that means giving back more than one receives.

Not long ago, I heard about a rural Midwestern church that was having trouble meeting its obligations. In fact, the deficit was so serious that some members recommended closing the church's doors. The treasurer agreed, saying the situation was hopeless, and resigned.

Then a man named Thomas, the owner of the town's grain elevator and a longtime member, stepped forward. He would agree to handle the church's finances for one year, with one proviso: No accounting would be made until the end of the year. Though quarterly reports had been the custom, the church trusted Mr. Thomas, and he was given the job.

The church focused on its ministry instead of on finances, and there was more harmony than old-timers ever remembered. At the end of the year, Mr. Thomas issued his financial report. All obligations had been met, including mission commitments at home and abroad, and the church bank account showed a balance of more than ten thousand dollars.

"How in the world did you do it?" the moderator asked.

Mr. Thomas at first seemed reluctant to reveal his secret, but then he spoke. "When you brought your wheat and corn to the elevator, I paid you what you were due, less ten percent, which I gave to the church in your name. I did it to show that you wouldn't miss your unknown tithe. But if you want your money back, I'm prepared to repay you right now." At first, there was some mumbling among the members, then laughter, then applause.

Mr. Thomas's object lesson had proven an old spiritual law that is timeless and immutable: Try as you may, you can never outgive the Lord.

> Remind me, Lord, when my purse I hold tight,
> That I've never come close to the widow's mite.

> —*FRED BAUER*

THE PRACTICE OF PRAYER

Are you looking for a more fulfilling prayer life? Do you need to make more space for communion with God in your crowded, busy days? Are you facing problems in your life that are getting in the way of prayer? *Daily Guideposts* regular Pam Kidd has lived through those same challenges, and in the middle of every month this year she'll share some of the ways in which a disciplined, deeper prayer life has changed her life, and how it can change yours. Whether you're a novice prayer warrior or an experienced prayer veteran, join Pam for some practical pointers to a closer walk with the Lord.

—*THE EDITORS*

MON

14   *The Decision to Pray*
And, behold, it was very good. . . .   —*GENESIS 1:31*

Winter has frozen out the last trace of green on the little Alabama is-land where our family cabin stands. All is silent on this frigid morn-ing as I move toward the causeway.

Last summer the lush forest that surrounded our cabin was felled by the power company's decree. Across the now-barren landscape, only a few trees are left, rejected by the woodsmen because of their imperfections. On this predawn pilgrimage, I am struggling to make sense of a world that seems, from this particular vantage point, lost and lonely.

I shake my head, recalling words that my husband David says are some of the least appreciated in the entire Bible: "And God saw every thing that he had made, and, behold, it was very good" (Genesis 1:31).

"Well, maybe it started out very good," I say out loud to the poor lost woods and the gray sky, "but from where I'm standing right now, good is nowhere in sight."

I jam my hands deep into the pockets of my fleece jacket and walk ahead quickly with my head down. I am halfway over the causeway before the dawn catches my eye. The sun has broken over the edge of the somber sky, splashing the morning with liquid gold. Ahead, the sunrise cuts a shimmering path all the way across the lake to the very spot where I stand.

"Okay, God, point well taken," I say, planting my feet in the new light of day. He's offering me a choice: I can wallow in misery, or I can move forward and claim the good. The practice of prayer is the one sure vehicle that can take me there. Ahead, God waits.

Father, I'm ready to live a better way. Help me practice praying until I find my way to You and the good life You promise me.

—PAM KIDD

READER'S ROOM

I receive *Daily Guideposts* as a gift from a very dear friend, Barbara. On my birthday—January 4—Susan Schefflein had written a devotional about the Lord leading in new ways. It was so appropriate to my situation at the time that all I could say was "Wow!"

Above the devotional Barbara had written, "Happy birthday, Sandy," with a smiley face next to it. We have been friends for years—we've laughed, cried, prayed and experienced so much together. Barbara has moved away, but we still stay in touch. When we call or write one another, we often include something about a *Daily Guideposts* devotional that has blessed us in some way. *Daily Guideposts* has been a great tool to keep our friendship thriving!   *—SANDY MITCHELL, EUGENE, OREGON*

TUE
15

Each one should use whatever gift he has received to serve others, faithfully administering God's grace in its various forms.
—I PETER 4:10 (NIV)

I am a child of integration. My elementary school days consisted of reading, writing and breaking color barriers—which included being one of the first African American children on *Romper Room* in the St.

Louis area. In 1963, my family moved to a beautiful neighborhood with groomed lawns and abundant fruit trees, a neighborhood that was not accustomed to Negroes, as we were called then.

There were just a handful of us, and we often felt unwelcome. Though we were in braids and ankle socks, and played jacks and hopscotch, we were keenly aware of Dr. Martin Luther King, Jr. Even in second grade, my friends and I pinned our hopes and dreams of equality—and our safety—on Dr. King's efforts. We knew that he wanted to make life better and more joyful for children like us.

So much has changed since 1963. When I look back, I have a better understanding of the magnitude of Dr. King's sacrifice and of his personal commitment to justice and to serving God. He was an intelligent and charismatic young man, only thirty-four years old the year he gave the "I Have a Dream" speech, and only thirty-nine at his death. His was greatly gifted; certainly, he could have had a career that earned wealth and comfort for his own wife and children. No one would have blamed him, and many might have cheered, had he chosen a more self-serving vocation. Instead, he committed himself to serving God, his entire nation—and us children in St. Louis.

Lord, thank You for the example of Dr. Martin Luther King, Jr.'s gentle words and peaceful actions, and his legacy of unselfish service. —SHARON FOSTER

WED
16
Let your face shine on your servant; save me in your unfailing love. —PSALM 31:16 (NIV)

We all have memories of embarrassing moments, and I experienced one recently that still makes me cringe. The story starts with my volunteering to go to California to represent MOPS (Mothers of Preschoolers) International at a dinner and present a gift of appreciation to a company that helped us create a picture book about the significance of mothering. The gift was a unique, twelve-inch statue of a mother and child, specially engraved, and I carried it, securely bubble-wrapped and boxed, onto the plane.

When I got to California, I took the statue out of the box, loosened the bubble wrap and placed it in a more festive gift bag, so that I could lift it out easily when I made the presentation. Off I went to the dinner, where I carefully propped the bag beside my chair. During the evening, other people got up to honor this company, and finally my turn came. I walked to the podium, placed the bag on a table just behind me and turned to address the room full of people. I'd only said a few words when I heard a strange rustling of paper and then a tinkling crash.

I froze. Without looking I knew what had happened, and, sure enough, there was the bag on the floor, filled with the broken pieces of the statue. I then began what my children call "an out-of-body experience," in which I commanded the dazed person at the podium to carry on and keep talking, and scolded her for being such a total klutz. I said something about mothers feeling discouraged and "broken" and in need of God's mending messages of love and encouragement. I then made the presentation of the bag of broken pieces and sat down, wanting to cry.

Afterward several people commented about the meaningful presentation, but their words hardly consoled me. Before leaving, I retrieved one of the broken pieces to use in trying to replace the statue. So far I haven't found a replacement, but I still have that broken piece. It reminds me of my own need for God's love and grace to mend and comfort me in my own places of brokenness.

Father, I praise You for Your unfailing love and grace.

—*CAROL KUYKENDALL*

THU
17

He has hedged me in so that I cannot get out; He has made my chain heavy. Even when I cry and shout, He shuts out my prayer. —*LAMENTATIONS 3:7-8 (NKJV)*

Lord, this is to thank You for all the times You've answered my prayers with a "No!"

Remember that girl in high school whom I wanted to marry? She was a beauty, and all the guys were in love with her. That should have been a tip-off. I hear she's on her third husband now, and I cringe to think what my life would have been if I had married her. I'm grateful for my faithful and godly wife Sharon.

The other day I passed the old house that Sharon and I wanted to buy when we first moved to town. You know, the three-story Gothic mansion, with the beautiful pine trees and the cobblestone drive? We were into antiques back then, and desperately wanted that house, but

You said no. I never noticed how completely impractical and odd the house is. The pines all died, leaving it naked. It just stands there, like the ruins of Troy. It would have cost us a fortune to fix up and maintain. Thanks for steering us to Logan Street instead.

This one comes hard, but thank You for my teaching job. After eighteen months in it, I wanted out! It was a hundred times harder than I had dreamed, but You built a wall around me and have kept me here for three decades. It gets harder every year, but I know now that all worthwhile jobs are difficult. When I think of all the good times I've had with students, and all the friends I've made, I'm glad You ignored my pleas for mercy.

You know, I never realized how much love could be in that little two-letter word *no*. I'm sure You wanted to say *yes*, but You were too wise and loving to put Your own popularity above my needs.

While I'm here, I was just wondering if You could work out an early retirement for me, and . . . well, never mind.

Lord, thank You for being wiser than my wants.

—DANIEL SCHANTZ

FRI
18

Then they sat upon the ground with him silently for seven days and seven nights, no one speaking a word; for they saw that his suffering was too great for words.

—JOB 2:13 (TLB)

I recently read about a method used by the Quakers in the 1600s to help members of their meetings who faced difficult decisions. Since they had no professional clergy to give counsel, they established Clearness Committees. When a person came with a problem, several hours were set aside to help the seeker quiet interference and release his or her own inner wisdom. Members of the Clearness Committee didn't give advice or try to fix the problem. They simply listened, sat together in silence, prayed and helped the seeker hear God's voice more clearly. The process was totally confidential and provided a means of drawing on others' wisdom without going public about sensitive or troubling matters.

Today the custom is being revived in some circles. Members of the "listening group" sign pledges of confidentiality, meet for a specified number of hours and abide by a set of rules to protect the seeker as well as themselves. These groups are good for many people, but the process seems too formal for me. Instead, I've learned to seek clarity for difficult decisions from friends, family and co-workers.

As I've relied on others for help, I've been blessed by their abilities to help me focus on God's solutions. My confidences have never been broken, and I've avoided some serious mistakes. I guess I shouldn't be surprised. After all, Jesus promises, "For where two or three are gathered together in my name, there am I in the midst of them" (Matthew 18:20).

Who needs my help, Lord, in hearing Your voice?

—PENNEY SCHWAB

SAT

19 May the Lord give you increase, you and your children!

—PSALM 115: 14 (RSV)

People often ask me how I managed to raise three children on my own. Last week when my older son Phil, his wife Katie and I went down to the Seattle Center in Washington, I was reminded again about the "how." We stopped by the Food Circus to get a Seattle-famous frankfurter, and while sitting at a table amidst a sea of people, I happened to glance up. High overhead, a helium balloon was caught in the scaffolding.

"Hey, Phil," I said, pointing up, "look!"

A slow smile came over his face as he told the story to Katie.

When he was little, my sister Tresa and her husband Bruce had taken Phil and his siblings to the Center one day. They spotted some lost balloons and decided to go "balloon hunting." But how?

"Uncle Bruce bought one balloon," Phil explained, "and a penny gumball for each of us. While we chewed our gum, he attached a long, long string to the balloon's tail. Then he told us to stick our gum to the top of the balloon. Voila! We ran out the string, our balloon skittered up and stuck to the first balloon it bumped into. We pulled them both down!"

My children had whooped and shrieked and leaped about, each begging their turn to bring down yet another balloon. They went all over the Food Circus, bagging every last one.

Munching my hot dog, I was happy for this reminder of how I "managed." The fact is I hadn't: I'd had help. Not only from my sister and her husband, but from neighbors and friends, schoolteachers and dedicated church youth group leaders.

Yes, we had a few hard, discouraging times. But we always had Uncle Bruce—or someone like him—adding so much to our lives.

Truly You give us increase in the most astonishing ways.

—*BRENDA WILBEE*

A WORRIER'S WAY TO GOD

Throughout her life, Marci Alborghetti has been a worrier, and for years, she let her worrying get in the way of her relationships with others—and with God. If you've struggled with worry in your own life—and all of us have, at one time or another—you'll want to join Marci this week as she shares the ways that God has enabled her to face her fears.   —*THE EDITORS*

SUN
20

Day 1: Winter Worry
Open the door, and flee, and tarry not.   —*II KINGS 9:3*

New Englanders are supposed to love winter. Not me. Born in Connecticut—in the summer, naturally—I dread winter. I worry about storms; I worry about losing power; I worry about driving in icy conditions; I even worry about *walking* in icy conditions! Of course, the same goes for summer and fall: I worry about hurricanes; I worry about losing power; I worry about driving . . . well, you get the idea.

I get little sympathy. One friend, Julia, parrots a constant refrain: "Give it to God."

Easier said than done. I've tried "giving it to God" when it comes to anxiety, but I've never succeeded, probably because the idea just doesn't make sense to me. But recently, a visiting priest at my church offered a solution that does. He told this story to our community of shoreline stalwarts:

A man living on the Atlantic Ocean heard from the meteorologist on TV that a massive hurricane was roaring up the coast. "I'm not moving!" he declared. "I'm giving this problem to God!" The storm approached. His town was evacuated. He told the evacuators, "I'm staying. I'm not worried. I trust God." The wind blew, rains came, streets flooded. A National Guard helicopter hovered over his house, dangling a harness rope for him. "Go away!" he shouted over the roaring waters. "I've given this to God. He'll take care of me." Minutes later, the man drowned. When he got to heaven, he whined to God, "I gave my worries to You! I trusted You! How could You let me down?" God replied, "I sent you a meteorologist, an evacuation team and the National Guard. What are you doing here?"

I learned that Sunday that trusting God doesn't mean being unprepared. In fact, sensible preparation is a way both to trust God and address my worries. So I bought a small generator and had it installed. Now, every time a storm threatens, I'm thankful God sent me a preacher, Sears and an electrician.

Father, help me remember that Your lessons aren't always accompanied by lightning and thunder! —*MARCI ALBORGHETTI*

MON
21
Day 2: Fleeing to God
Let us draw near with a true heart in full assurance of faith.... —*HEBREWS 10:22*

Some days anxiety looms up out of the blue and snatches me. Sometimes I can't even describe my fear. It could be anything: My mother is having tests for an ulcer; I haven't allowed enough time for groceries so I'm stuck in line, late for my next appointment; the car keeps stalling; a friend hasn't called in a while, so I'm convinced he's angry with me.

During these frightening episodes, only one thing is sure to help: prayer. Not reciting familiar words or reading the Psalms or talking; my "anxiety prayer" has no words at all. I curl up in the corner of my sofa, facing the pretty stone gazebo on the small square of green separating me from Connecticut's Stonington Harbor. I close my eyes and imagine myself opening the sliding glass door. God stands in front of the gazebo, His arms open to me. I start walking, then running, to Him. He lifts me like the terrified child I am and swings me around through the air like the loving Father He is. Then He sits in the gazebo facing the water, holding me in His comforting arms until my breathing slows and my anxiety lessens. I feel His love, forgiveness and grace just as surely as I hear the gentle waves and tinkling wind chimes.

I stay there with Him as long as I need to. I don't beg Him for help or tell Him my troubles. He knows. And when I open my eyes to my familiar living room, I'm always calm.

Father, never let me forget that You are just that: loving, forgiving and comforting. —*MARCI ALBORGHETTI*

TUE
22

Day 3: Walking Away from Worry
And when Peter was come down out of the ship, he walked on the water, to go to Jesus. —*MATTHEW 14:29*

Although Hooded Mergansers are among the smallest ducks, they look quite majestic. I see them just about every day during the winter on my daily walk. Most people walk to get from one place to another; I walk to get away from worry. And the Mergansers help.

My route follows the harbor and the inlets where the ducks winter. As I stride along, they glide by royally, proud hooded heads in the air, bent on getting somewhere. Occasionally they dive deep to procure a small fish for dinner, though I believe they sometimes dive just to prove how strong and adventurous they are. They are everything I want to be: brave, independent, self-sufficient—everything worry can prevent me from being.

These tiny ducks aren't afraid of anything. One day last winter I saw several large, raucous seagulls try to chase them off. There must have been some bait fish close to the surface of the water, and seagulls are not renowned for their willingness to share. They dove at the pair of Mergansers, flapping their comparatively massive wings and screeching loudly. The Mergansers studiously ignored them and swam around in tight circles, protecting their patch. Eventually, the seagulls abdicated the battle, but I was the one who learned the lesson: When anxiety flies at me, shrieking and flapping its feathers, I'm not going to panic. Indeed, I think I'll just ignore it and keep walking.

Lord, thank You for showing me Your plan for my life in the glory of nature. —*MARCI ALBORGHETTI*

<hr>

WED
23
Day 4: Sharing
One day is with the Lord as a thousand years, and a thousand years as one day. —*II PETER 3:8*

My favorite restaurant offers more than excellent cuisine. It also has the Worry Club. Conveniently located around the corner from my house, this little café provides the opportunity to share great food, and sometimes greater worries. Caroline, the café's co-owner, and Suzanne, a waitress, form the Worry Club. Along with me, of course.

It didn't take long for us to discover we were kindred souls, and I was a regular by the time the big millennium celebration came around. While everyone else spent December excitedly anticipating the biggest New Year's celebration of our time, the three of us were worrying about every possible disaster known to man, and some that were probably impossible. As people around us made festive Christmas and New Year's plans, we huddled together sharing our fears. I worried about the local power grid. Caroline reported that some survivalists were claiming there'd be a nuclear accident. Suzanne worried about friends headed to New York City for the celebration—it would surely be the perfect place for a terrorist strike.

After a few nights of this, we'd scared each other silly—literally. Some of our worries were so absurd, they were actually funny, even to us. Our shared laughter was a blessed release. And when the millennium swept across a world steeped—at least for this one twenty-four-hour period—in peace and joy, we, too, were able to celebrate.

Lord, thanks for teaching me that a worry shared is a worry diminished. —*MARCI ALBORGHETTI*

THU	*Day 5: Friends*
24	Live in harmony with one another; be sympathetic, love as brothers, be compassionate.... —*I PETER 3:8 (NIV)*

I first knew anxiety was going to be a problem when I got to college. By October of my freshman year, I knew I'd chosen the wrong school. Ironically, I'd selected a small denominational college because I felt anxious about attending a larger, less restricted university. But within weeks, I felt stifled and unhappy. Then, like every freshman, I got sick. Recovery took many days; I missed classes and lost my campus job.

At home for Thanksgiving, I begged my parents to let me quit. I hated college! I was behind in classes and still physically weak enough to make myself sicker with worry. Mom insisted I finish the term. Grumbling and trembling, I returned to my dorm.

Sue, the resident counselor for our dorm, was a quiet, tactful nursing school junior. I was surprised, and a little annoyed, when she invited me to her room. *Great,* I thought, *I must be a real basket case to be getting this invitation.* But there was no lecture or pep talk waiting for me. Instead, we just sat together and listened to music from her record collection. I hadn't thought anyone at this college would even recognize the name Bruce Springsteen, never mind have every song he'd ever recorded! For the first time since school had started, I relaxed for an hour or two.

Twenty years later, Sue has seen me through fears about melanoma, my career and loneliness. She still doesn't say much. She doesn't need to.

Jesus, You were too busy caring for others to worry about Your own agonizing future. Help me in my own small way to do the same.
                                                    —*MARCI ALBORGHETTI*

FRI	*Day 6: The Comfort of Praying Together*
25	And the people of Israel said to Samuel, "Do not cease to cry to the Lord our God for us, that he may save us...." —*I SAMUEL 7:8 (RSV)*

"Why do the people I love have to travel?" I grumbled, getting into the car after church. My friend Charlie was, at that moment, flying back to Connecticut from a Los Angeles business trip. It was mid-January, and the weather was miserable. Of course, in L.A. it had been beautiful. Knowing Charlie, I doubted he had bothered checking the weather report. "Oh, no," I told myself, negotiating the slick roads on the very short trip to the deli, "I'm the one glued to the Weather Channel and calling the airline every hour."

I parked in front of the deli, put on the emergency break—though there was not the slightest incline—and slammed the car door. Every Saturday evening we went to church and then stopped in here for some food. When I walked in that evening, the cheerful proprietress immediately said the wrong thing. Accustomed to seeing us arrive together for Saturday-night takeout, she chirped, "So where's Charlie tonight?"

My eyes filled with tears, and I collapsed into one of the café chairs. "Flying in from L.A.," I mumbled as she watched me, first with alarm and then with sympathy. Knowing my worrying ways, she didn't bother with useless platitudes. Instead, she selected our favorite items and packed them up. An astonishing peace came over me as I watched her. When I met her at the register, she took my hand, smiled gently and said, "He'll be fine. We'll pray. And we'll see you both next Saturday."

He was. We did. Many Saturdays have passed, and we've forged a fast friendship, she and I. After all, God gave her the gift of peace . . . for me to take out.

Father, thank You for showing me that a shared prayer eases worry and is pleasing to You, to me and to my prayer partner.
— *MARCI ALBORGHETTI*

<table>
<tr><td>SAT
26</td><td>Day 7: Perspective
"For I know the plans I have for you, says the Lord, plans for welfare and not for evil, to give you a future and a hope."   —JEREMIAH 29:11 (RSV)</td></tr>
</table>

Everything had gone wrong today. The vacuum broke in the middle of my housecleaning frenzy. The wraps I'd planned for dinner hadn't curled snugly around the too-bountiful fillings, and the result was an unappetizing mess. I'd pulled a muscle in my shoulder and was worried about it stiffening overnight. The VCR was on the fritz, so I couldn't watch the movie I'd made a special trip to rent. My mother called to express her displeasure at the infrequency of my visits. A trip to San Francisco loomed, and I hadn't begun to pack. It was just one of those days.

It took all my willpower not to shriek with the tension that pressed down on me as I darted around the house picking up the lint that the fractured vacuum cleaner had missed. Then my friend Charlie shouted at me from outside to come and see the wondrous sunset. "Hurry up, Marse, or you'll miss it!" he yelled. I gritted my teeth and trudged outside.

Charlie took me out to the dock that extended into the harbor. I looked up and caught my breath. The western horizon was vivid with streaks of magenta, rose and indigo that lit the entire sky as twilight crept up to meet the intense colors. I was mesmerized. And then I remembered an old saying: "Red sky at night, sailor's delight." Tomorrow would surely bring smoother sailing.

Father, help me remember that Your constant gift is tomorrow.

—*MARCI ALBORGHETTI*

SUN

27

And in him you too are being built together to become a dwelling in which God lives by his Spirit.

—*EPHESIANS 2:22 (NIV)*

I'm an emergency medical technician, and a friend of mine once asked me if I had gone to a recent car accident. "Yes," I said, "but by the time I got there, our fire department had already loaded the patient into the ambulance. I just helped with traffic control."

"Good," my friend said. "You've got common sense. I'll bet you kept things moving. I've been stuck at some of those accidents and have had to wait twenty minutes to get through."

While I appreciated his compliment, I was amazed that he missed the point. I don't care at all about the impatient motorists. They aren't hurt, and they aren't going to get hurt while they are waiting to "get through." I don't allow anyone to drive through an accident scene unless I'm absolutely sure that no paramedic or firefighter will be endangered by opening up traffic.

I went to church almost every Sunday when I was younger, but I missed the point back then. A short sermon was always better than a long one, because I just wanted to "get through." It never occurred to me that I could use the time in church to get closer to God.

My friend's view of the accident scene was a blessing of sorts. Because now when I go to church, I don't just show up, waiting to get through. I'm part of the service, helping to plan and work it. And I prefer it that way.

Dear God, help me to build a church where everyone works together to get closer to You.
                                                                 —*TIM WILLIAMS*

MON
28 He retaineth not his anger for ever, because he delighteth in mercy.
                                                                 —*MICAH 7:18*

"Linda, if beating yourself up were an Olympic sport, you'd win a gold medal!"

Annabel, my close friend, stunned me with that blunt observation after I told her how I had mishandled a situation with a student in a third-grade class where I was substituting. "I should never have let him go to the boy's room without a pass! It was my fault he got into trouble with the hall monitor! I'm so stupid!"

My friend burst out laughing, and then made her "Olympic" comment. After a brief period of reflection I had to admit that she was right. I did put myself down an awful lot. Why, just during the previous day I had called myself "a slob" for having some papers spread out on my desk, "ugly" when I left the house without makeup and "an idiot" when I left the house for an emergency substitute job without my emergency lesson plan.

In a more reflective tone, Annabel said, "I once took a workshop at church where the woman in charge had us list all the mean things we say about ourselves."

"How many did you have on your list?" I asked.

"Fifteen," she confessed. "But then the teacher said, 'Now turn to the person next to you and say all the items on your list as if you were speaking to that person!' "

My jaw dropped. "What did you do?"

"Nothing. Nobody did. We all just sat there, until I said, 'I could never say these things to anyone else!'

"And our teacher replied, 'Well, if you can't say them to anyone else, then don't ever say them to yourself!' "

My friend had a point. I would never insult a child of God—and I'm God's child, too!

God, today let me be as kind to myself as I would be to another of Your children.   —*LINDA NEUKRUG*

TUE

29

Children's children are the crown of old men. . . .
                                        —*PROVERBS 17:6*

Please, do come into my apartment. It hasn't changed much in the twenty-eight years since I moved in.

There's my bedroom to the right and the door to the kitchen on your left. In the distance is what was supposed to be a dining room, but it was too small, so it became a kind of den with a sofa bed. A good thing, too, if you tally up the number of people who have slept there. Many times I've had five or six, with the kids spilling out into the front room.

The living room, now, is filled with the things that interest me most. What? That chair with the four Teddy bears? My favorite is the professorial one with glasses, or maybe—oh well, the kids grab them when they first come in. Kids? Why, the children and grandchildren of my friends, but as I was saying—

That pile of books and pull-'ems and assorted toys tucked away in the corner? Why, the kids again, if they don't ask for paper to draw on. You'll see examples of their creativity on the door of the fridge. Getting back to the really important items here—oh, you've found the ride-a-cock horse. He whinnies, you know, just pull an ear. He's not as popular as the large walrus hiding under a bedroom table. The fun we've had with him, rolling over and pulling at his tusks. Which reminds me: I've got to sew a tusk back on.

Why, yes, the table against the wall? *Hmm.* It's crowded with photos of people close to me. Take a look at this one of Valerie and David as six-year-olds. How old now? My gosh, they're deep into their forties and have kids of their own. Did I say the apartment hadn't changed in twenty-eight years? Well, it hasn't, but I have. And the kids, they too have changed, but more kids keep coming.

You have to leave? I'm sorry. Too many interruptions about kids. I'll do better next time you come. Which I hope will be soon.

The young ones are the hope of tomorrow. Please, Father, guide them. —*VAN VARNER*

WED
30   This is the Lord's doing; it is marvellous in our eyes.
—*PSALM 118:23*

As I write this, a soft, white snow is falling on eastern North Carolina. Here along the coast in Richlands, we seldom see snow. It's an unusual event, one we are ill-equipped to handle. We have no plows to clear the roads and no chains for our tires—and we Southerners are notoriously poor drivers in the snow. So the area schools close, and most of the businesses, too, and we find ourselves with the unexpected gift of a day at home.

In my excitement over this unusual turn of events, I'll keep the phone lines busy, calling friends and neighbors, sharing my joy and amazement at having been caught unaware by the beauty of it all. I don't have boots or proper clothes for snow, but that won't keep me indoors. With old socks on my hands and plastic bags over my sneakers, I'll take advantage of the chance to build a snowman in the yard. Later, as the gray day fades into darkness, I'll scoop clean snow from the tops of cars, stir it together with eggs, sugar and cream, and eat it by the warmth of the fire. I'll savor every mouthful of the special homemade concoction, even though my head will throb with the chill of it.

It won't last long, this snow. It will probably melt by morning, and we'll go back to business as usual. But today, this unexpected gift of a day, I'll play—and give thanks. Maybe that's what God had in mind when He sent it.

My heart overflows with gratitude, Father, when I remember all the unexpected gifts You've sent my way. May I never take them for granted. —*LIBBIE ADAMS*

THU
31   The memory of the righteous will be a blessing. . . .
                                    —*PROVERBS 10:7 (NIV)*

I am driving along the highway at a reasonable speed, practicing a talk I am to give at a memorial service for a dear friend. The other drivers stare as I zoom along talking, trying to enunciate, experimenting with pitch and timbre. One woman passes me with a gaping stare, but I keep practicing. I have a few miles to go yet, and I want to get this by heart. I don't want to talk from notes—that's important, for some reason. I don't know why.

With about ten miles to go, I get to the point where I can talk without weeping. The trick is to stop talking when the tears start coming. So I drive—talking, stopping, starting over.

Finally, I get to the church, and near the end of the service, give my talk—talking, stopping, starting over—and then drive home, and that night, after dinner, I sit by the fire and pull out my notes and feed them to the fire as a sort of Old Testament prayer and offering. It's important to sacrifice the notes, for some reason. I don't know why. But I have the words in my heart.

Dear Lord, thanks for dear friends, and thanks for letting dear friends live in our hearts when they die, and thanks for prayers of all shapes and sizes, even, and maybe especially, ashen prayers.
                                    —*BRIAN DOYLE*

My Days of Prayer

1 _____

2 _____

3 _____

4 _____

5 _____

6 _____

7 _____

8 _____

9 _____

10 _____

11 _____

12 _____

13 _____

14 _____

15 _____

16 _____

17 _____

18 _____

19 _____

20 _____

21 _____

22 _____

23 _____

24 _____

25 _____

26 _____

27 _____

28 _____

29 _____

30 _____

31 _____

February

Bear ye one another's burdens, and so
fulfil the law of Christ.

—*Galatians 6:2*

	S	M	T	W	T	F	S
						1	2
	3	4	5	6	7	8	9
	10	11	12	13	14	15	16
	17	18	19	20	21	22	23
	24	25	26	27	28		

THE PRAYER THAT IS ALWAYS NEW

1 Our *Father.* . . . —MATTHEW 6:9

Today I was stopped by the second word of the Lord's Prayer . . . and a memory of nearly forty years ago. Marilyn (not her real name) led the Wednesday-night prayer meeting my husband John and I attended during the year we spent in Uganda. A missionary for most of her sixty-some years, Marilyn, we noticed, never called God "Father."

Always bolder than I when he senses a need, John asked her one Wednesday about her childhood. The seemingly casual question brought on perhaps five minutes of wordless sobs.

Nothing more came out that evening, but the following Wednesday Marilyn made a halting allusion to emotional and physical abuse. Week by week, specifics emerged, scarring memories of a mother beaten until she had to be hospitalized, a father's lust. As the agonizing scenes crept from the dark recesses where they'd hidden for half a century, and we lifted them to God's light, we watched Marilyn's whole posture literally straighten. *No wonder,* I thought, *with such a history, she couldn't see a loving God as a father.*

Then one night a member of the group began describing his own very different father. Paul's dad had always had time to listen or play a game of catch. Why would Paul rub in the contrast so hurtfully? I could see the same question in Marilyn's eyes as Paul crossed the room to stand in front of her. "You see, Marilyn," he said gently, "I was adopted. I don't know anything about my own father," he went on, "except that neither he nor my mother wanted me. But I was given a new family, and later I went forward at a church service— adopted by my true Father. The same Father Who wants to adopt you, too, Marilyn."

A month later, Marilyn let us hold an "adoption service" for her.

We even contacted a Kampala orphanage to find the proper procedure. It was a glorious celebration, not only for this dedicated woman of God, but for all of us who "have received the Spirit of adoption, whereby we cry, 'Abba! Father!' " (Romans 8:15).

Abba! Father!

—ELIZABETH SHERRILL

SAT

2 The people read it and were glad for its encouraging message. *—ACTS 15:31 (NIV)*

I was waiting anxiously at the repair shop while a mechanic checked out my car. The estimate for repairs I'd received from another mechanic was more than nine hundred dollars. It was more than I could afford, so I was getting a second opinion.

But how would I know this mechanic was telling the truth? I was clueless when it came to cars. *God, please guide me*, I prayed.

I tossed aside the magazine I'd been reading and scanned the bulletin board directly in front of me. One small note caught my attention. "Dear manager," it read, "thanks to your mechanic Jim, my 1978 Nova is in excellent running order once more." My heart did a double take. Jim was at this very moment looking at my car! With peaked interest, I continued to read. "I appreciate that Jim is not interested in involving me in needless repairs. He does only what's essential for the efficient operation of my car." It was signed, "Ed, a grateful customer." I had seen Ed's signature in our local newspaper at the end of many letters to the editor. He was an octogenarian whose judgment I respected.

When Jim returned to give me his verdict on my ailing car, I met him with a confident smile. Thanks to Ed's note, I knew I could count on Jim to tell me the truth and to give me a fair price.

What a beautiful service Ed did for me, I mused. *I must tell him.* At home I wrote a thank-you for his thank-you note. In a few days his wife phoned me. "You have no idea how your note encouraged my husband," she said. "He so often feels that his days of service are over."

As long as we're here, there's always something we can do.

Father, help me to be alert to people who need a word of encouragement today.

—HELEN GRACE LESCHEID

SUN

3

If we have been united with him in a death like his, we shall certainly be united with him in a resurrection like his.
—*ROMANS 6:5 (RSV)*

Last Sunday, I went to Calvary.

No, I haven't yet had the blessing of a pilgrimage to the Holy Land. And although there are many churches named Calvary, I wasn't attending services at one of them. This Calvary is a hospital, the only hospital of its kind in the country. All of its patients have cancer. And all of them are dying.

Calvary is not a depressing place. The corridors are painted in bright, vibrant colors; the staff is cheerful and caring; and the patients are provided with everything they need to make them comfortable and to know that they are loved. And the heart of Calvary is its chapel, where patients, brought in their beds if they are unable to walk, can hold the hand of a loved one or staff member and rest in the presence of God.

The fraternal organization I belong to holds a prayer breakfast at Calvary every year. Last year the hospital's director had a disturbing story to tell: In the world of HMOs and managed care, there didn't seem to be room for Calvary. The care it provides was just too expensive, and besides, the patients were going to die anyway. Couldn't they do it more cheaply?

This year, though, the director had good news: The mother of a prominent local politician had gone to Calvary, and when the politician heard that the hospital was in trouble, he was incensed. So he made a few calls, and soon both houses of our state legislature had passed a bill to protect patients' rights at the end of life. The governor signed the bill, and now the future of Calvary seems assured.

Like most people, I don't like to think about the end of this earthly life; I'd prefer to skip the Cross and go straight to the Empty Tomb. But when the time comes, I pray that faithful, compassionate people like those at Calvary Hospital will be God's instruments to make my dying holy.

Lord Jesus, be with me in life, in sickness and in death. And help me to always be willing to protect the weakest among us.
—*ANDREW ATTAWAY*

MON
4

Seek ye first the kingdom of God, and his righteousness; and all these things shall be added unto you.

—*MATTHEW 6:33*

I was taking my younger son Timothy to school. He was worried about a test that day, and as we rode on the subway, I quizzed him on famous names from the Revolutionary War, such as Molly Pitcher, Samuel Adams, Nathan Hale. I was impressed by his knowledge. If I'd been tested, I would have struggled to come up with a definition of Thomas Paine's *Common Sense* or what battle General Burgoyne lost.

My quizzing over, I took out my pocket New Testament to do some of my own studying. In the back of my mind, I was wondering how we would fill a position at work. "Look," I said to Timothy after I had read a couple of verses, "here's a passage you know well." *Seek ye first the kingdom of God, and his righteousness.* He smiled. We both knew a song from church with just those words. So as the subway car was hurtling through the tunnel, stopping to let passengers on and off, both of us started singing to ourselves, "Seek ye first the kingdom of God. . . ."

"Eighty-sixth Street," the conductor called out. Time to get off. I would drop off my son at P.S. 9, where he would define the difference between the Tories and Patriots, and I would continue on to the office, where I had to look through a pile of résumés for the right job candidate.

"Do well on the test," I said in parting.

"Do well at work," he said. We would both do fine, I decided. Our priorities were in just the right order.

Keep me focused on what is good and just and true, Lord.

—*RICK HAMLIN*

TUE
5

" I will whistle for them to gather them together, for I have redeemed them. . . ."   —*ZECHARIAH 10:8 (NAS)*

A TV reporter was interviewing some parents who had ten children. "When you go on an outing," he asked, "how do you manage to keep track of everybody? Have you never lost one of the kids in a crowd?"

"Oh, just temporarily," the father said with a laugh, "but he soon found me."

"You mean you didn't even go looking for him?"

"Well, not really. You see, the children have been taught from a very young age that they are to come to me when I whistle like this." He let out an ear-piercing whistle that I recognized at once as the first four notes of the children's hymn, "Jesus Loves Me."

"So you just keep walking around and whistling and the kids find you?" asked the reporter incredulously.

"Oh, no. That would be like trying to hit a moving target. I just stand still and whistle."

Today I was the one who felt lost in the crowd. I have enjoyed a long business relationship with a certain company, and this morning's mail brought a letter from them, informing me they were changing direction and no longer needed my services. I felt so inadequate seeking out new opportunities that I really didn't know which way to turn. To add to my mental anxiety, I had to drive through an unfamiliar part of the city in rush hour, when drivers were jostling each other for every possible advantage. I could feel a sense of panic starting to well up within me. *Father God, where are You?*

Just then traffic stopped for a red light.

Listen! God is whistling!

Not really, but the bells of the big old stone church nearby were pealing out their message of His presence. It reassured me that in whatever direction I choose to move in the future, God will always be the one constant, "the same yesterday, and today, and for ever" (Hebrews 13:8).

I drove home humming, "Yes, Jesus loves me."

Father God, wherever I may be, attune my heart to hear You.

—*ALMA BARKMAN*

WED

6

Call unto me, and I will answer thee. . . .

—*JEREMIAH 33:3*

When our daughter Amy Jo's marriage ended, she moved back in with us. She enrolled in a full-time master's program at a nearby university, but was feeling restless and unsure about the future. "You know," she said one night as she was setting the table, "I used to talk about going to law school. Remember?"

I did remember. She had only been about ten when she first

brought it up. And although she'd mentioned it a few times during the years, it somehow had fallen by the wayside as she got a degree in communications, took a job and got married. Now it was surfacing again. "I remember," I said, "but I'm not sure if that's what you should do now or not." Silently, I wondered where she would get the money. "Just pray about it, honey," I said, turning back to the stove. The words sounded frail. Wasn't there something else she should be doing?

A few minutes later, Amy Jo came back into the kitchen, beaming. She spread out the *Chicago Tribune* on the table and pointed to a classified ad: "Wondering if law school is right for you? Work for us and decide!" It was a large law firm in Chicago, an easy train ride from where we lived. So Amy Jo took the job, working for a year as a court runner. She loved it! Then she took the admissions test and enrolled in Valparaiso University, where she's currently studying law.

I've always believed in answered prayer. But these days I'm looking for those answers in lots of places. My Bible, of course. But also in the "thought for the day" that appears on my e-mail. Or in the overheard wisdom of an older woman in line at the grocery talking—on a cell phone—to her daughter. And, yes, even in the newspaper. As for the financial problem of law school—Amy Jo is on full scholarship, which is something we *both* prayed about!

Open my eyes, Father, to the unique avenues You use to let Your answers reach me.   —*MARY LOU CARNEY*

THU

7

In every thing give thanks: for this is the will of God in Christ Jesus concerning you.   —*I THESSALONIANS 5:18*

I've never been one for making New Year's resolutions. They always seem about as lasting—in my case, at least—as a Christmas tree. But this year I vowed to try to stick to one that I thought was important: Every day I would thank God for one specific thing in my life for which I was grateful.

At first it was easy. I was thankful for my family, my friends, my work, my new house in the hills, my wonderful dogs. I could thank Him for a beautiful day or even a good night's sleep. I was rolling along quite nicely with my resolution when I hit a wall—the gratitude wall.

I don't know if it was the prolonged dreariness of winter or just that I was running out of ideas, but by February I found myself floundering and unable to come up with something to be thankful for. Then my friend Charlie came to visit me one wet, miserable day. Charlie is a good deal older than I am, retired and in pretty good health except for the arthritis that gnarls his fingers and stiffens his gait, especially on cold days.

He came into my office all bundled up and took a seat on the couch. *Fffrrip, frrip.* Off came his rubbers. *Fffrrip* went the chinstrap to his hat. *Fffrrip frrip,* and Charlie was out of his mackinaw. He smiled broadly at me. "Thank God for Velcro!" he declared.

Thank God for Velcro? I hadn't thought of that! Yet here was Charlie, for whom something as absolutely commonplace as Velcro made his struggle with arthritis so much easier. Charlie knew how to be grateful. He saw in even the smallest details of his daily life the greatest reasons to praise God. That's what I'd have to learn to do— starting right now:

Thank You, Lord, for Charlie, who opened my eyes to the little miracles of life You provide . . . especially Velcro. —*EDWARD GRINNAN*

FRI

8

"The Lord our God is merciful and forgiving. . . ."
—*DANIEL 9:9 (NIV)*

When my son John and I arrived at the dentist's office at 8:15 A.M. for his 8:30 appointment, the office was locked up tight. We waited until 8:40; not a sign of life. I finally phoned the office's other location on the far side of town. I got through to a young-sounding woman in scheduling named Calley, who said, "Oh, I'm sorry. We've been trying to get in touch with you to tell you we changed the days that office is open. Your answering machine must not be working. I apologize. We can reschedule John tomorrow morning at the same time."

"I don't have an answering machine, and I don't want one," I answered icily. "And I've already taken John out of school this morning."

I hung up fuming. *What did she think was going to happen if she didn't reach me? She knew I was going to end up at the wrong place at the wrong time. Anybody with any decent common sense would have kept on calling until they reached me.* I even imagined getting an answering machine: *"Hello, you've reached Karen Barber. I hate answering machines, but I've been forced to get one because of the dental appointment clerk who didn't know how to call a person back when they weren't home."*

I dropped John off at school, his teeth still in need of a cleaning and mine still clenched. Calley had thrown my whole morning off-schedule, and I had thirty minutes to kill before my appointment with a woman from church whom I had been helping through a crisis. I pulled into a grocery store parking lot and began to pray for her and the very difficult home situation she was dealing with—struggling to forgive people who had deeply hurt her. Suddenly, the Holy Spirit seemed to say, *Karen, you need to forgive Calley. She said she was sorry and apologized. What more do you want?*

It was easy for me to counsel my church friend to apply forgiveness to the wrongs she'd suffered, but it was much harder for me to apply it to the everyday irritations of my own life. "Okay," I reluctantly prayed as I slowly let go of my irritation, "I forgive her."

This grace of small forgiveness keeps families and marriages, friendships and clubs, neighborhoods and churches, businesses and countries running without falling apart one irritation at a time. I picked up the phone and called Calley. "Tomorrow morning would be fine for John's cleaning," I said pleasantly.

Lord, this thing that has been gnawing at me is a small matter, but it's not too small to forgive. Please unlock the irritation and resentment from my heart so that my life might run a little more gracefully today.
                                                            —*KAREN BARBER*

SAT

9

The years of our life are threescore and ten. . . .
                                                            —*PSALM 90:10 (RSV)*

I just attained the biblical threescore years and ten. I've always known my days are numbered, but a seventieth birthday somehow drives home the point!

And my body does throw in occasional reminders, too. It's getting harder to climb to my favorite place on the mountain; sometimes I have trouble sleeping; aches and pains are often drop-in guests. I sometimes find myself at the grocery store without my list and come home without the lettuce, or read a whole chapter and forget what I've read.

And yet . . . here I am, alive today! Knowing that my years are dwindling has made me value each day more. And age has its own gifts: Now that a job no longer dictates where we live, my husband Robert and I have chosen to live in the place we love most. We are carefully choosing what activities we want to devote time to—and which we can leave to others. The next generation can take over the family holiday meals, while we oldsters bring a salad or pie and enjoy our grandchildren. But most important of all, these later years offer us time to devote to spiritual growth. How good life is at seventy!

Did you know that in China, sixty years is considered a life span? So if one lives longer than that, the sixty-first birthday is celebrated as the beginning of a new life! It's a time for those who have carried responsibility for work or home life to pass it on to another generation and spend their time cultivating their relationship with God. What a luxury and very great opportunity we seniors have! For most of my adult life, I've wished I had more time for growing in intimacy with God. Now I have it! The few physical and mental annoyances I put up with are a small price to pay for this gift of time in which to grow in grace, walking toward home in awareness of God's presence.

Realizing the shortness of life, Holy One, I hold each day's gifts in my heart with joy. —*MARILYN MORGAN KING*

SUN
10

Blessed be the name of the Lord. —*JOB 1:21*

"Let's go, sweetie," I said, as I herded our daughter Maria through the parking lot toward church on Sunday morning.

"C'mon, peanut," my husband chimed in. "You don't want to be late for Sunday school."

Maria took my hand and looked up at me, smiling. "Why do you and Daddy have so many names for me?" she asked.

"I guess because we love you so much," I said, stopping to kiss her on the forehead.

Later, as we sat in church, I studied the banner that hangs on the wall behind the altar. This large piece of midnight-blue fabric is filled with cut-out letters spelling more than a dozen different names for God, such as Messiah, Savior, Lord, Teacher, Creator, Redeemer and Father. As I thought about it, I realized that I most often think of God as a loving Father to Whom I can bring all my worries, seeking comfort. But what about His other names? Do I see Him in those ways, too?

My thoughts became a kind of prayer:

Father, I come to You as Your child, yet I wonder.
Teacher, am I learning all I can from You?
Good Shepherd, do I follow the path where You lead?
Counselor, when I ask for help, do I listen to Your wise words?
Lord, do I obey the laws You've set before me?
Prince of Peace, do I act as You would?
Lamb of God, do I show my thanks for Your great sacrifice?
Savior, do I truly comprehend what You have done for me?

Perhaps God has many names because He loves us so much.

Great God, help me to know You by each of Your names and be thankful for Your all-encompassing love. —*GINA BRIDGEMAN*

MON
11

And there were certain Greeks among them that came up to worship at the feast: The same came therefore to Philip . . . and desired him, saying, Sir, we would see Jesus.
—*JOHN 12:20–21*

If you're under fifty, you'll probably not recall the poignant painting of "Nipper," the little white dog with black ears, standing, head cocked, beside an old gramophone listening for "his master's voice."

I remembered the picture recently while waiting in the car at the market because rooted outside the store was an intently waiting and listening Nipper-looking terrier. Hundreds of customers went in and out, but the dog ignored each, obviously looking for one particular person. When that person did appear, the dog's delight left no doubt about it. If dogs can laugh, this one did—his tongue lolling in his wide-open muzzle while he made pogolike jumps. He happily trotted alongside his master, then leaped into the car beside him.

Recently I experienced some of the feelings that dog must have had while I was waiting at the airport in Syracuse, New York. When the expected plane finally arrived and its passengers began swarming up the jetway and into the lobby, I looked for one among the exiting hundreds: Lawrence, my husband, who'd been on an extended trip. Had anyone noticed either of us, our delight in seeing each other would have been obvious.

The Scriptures talk about Zacchaeus, a much-shorter-than-average man who was so eager to see Jesus, he climbed a tree to get a good view. There was a tremendous crowd, but Zacchaeus, too, was looking for one face only among the many hundreds: the Master's. When the men met, Zacchaeus "came down at once and welcomed him gladly" (Luke 19:6, NIV).

How it must please You, heavenly Father, when Your children's attention is focused on You.   —*ISABEL WOLSELEY*

TUE

12

For where your treasure is, there will your heart be also.
                                                —*MATTHEW 6:21*

Why is this so uncomfortable? I wondered. I was sitting in a prayer meeting and I just couldn't do it. While others around me were praising the Lord by raising their arms in prayer, the most I could do was pray with my hands resting in my lap. I looked at the others, so at ease. *Help me, Lord, to be comfortable in my praise of You with others.* I left the meeting that evening determined to overcome my self-consciousness while praying.

The next week was Mardi Gras, the gala celebration in New Orleans that precedes the forty days of Lent. On Fat Tuesday, Mardi Gras day, businesses and schools were closed; the parades would roll all day, and formal balls would be held that evening. We went to the city early to stake out a good spot along the parade route. Stepladders were set up to give children a better vantage point to see the hundreds of floats and catch the plastic beads, doubloons and colorful trinkets thrown from them.

The parade began. I reached my arms into the air to catch the beads being thrown my way. Then I climbed up a ladder quickly for a better view of the carnival scene. It wasn't the colorfully sculpted floats or elaborate costumes that caused me to gasp; it was the sea of hands, all reaching toward the sky. I blinked and looked again. *Why, Lord,* I thought, *surely if I can fling my arms into the air for some plastic beads, I can praise You in the presence of others.*

At the prayer meeting the next week, I sat in a pew, enjoying the quiet after the busy carnival season. But when the prayers began, I, too, lifted my arms into the air to praise the Lord.

Lord, You are my real treasure. Give me the courage to always show my love for You.   *—MELODY BONNETTE*

READER'S ROOM

During the 1980s, we had three teenagers—two girls and a boy—all avid readers, all involved in different activities and all with different personalities. With teenagers, you do your very best every day to raise them in the way of the Lord, but you never know if you are reaching them.

On our kitchen table I had a clear plastic cookbook holder with that year's *Daily Guideposts*. I never had to turn the page. Every day it was on the right page after the kids had gone off to school. I never found out which child did it, but the book continued to be open to that day's page until our youngest daughter left for college! I felt reassured that somehow, if they read that one daily inspirational message, they'd be all right.

—MARY YODER, OLATHE, KANSAS

WED
13

David said to Nathan, "I have sinned against the Lord." And Nathan said to David, "The Lord also has put away your sin; you shall not die."   *—II SAMUEL 12:13 (RSV)*

In 1976 my wife and I were divorced. What made it worse was that it was my fault. I walked the beaches of Mustang Island, Texas, wept and cried out to God, confessing my sin and my powerlessness. I was a professional speaker and writer, but suddenly not many Christians wanted me to come and speak or read my books.

Then I recalled a visit years before with a minister from England. After hearing my story, he said, "Keith, it sounds like you want to climb the spiritual mountain and call warnings about the terrain back down to the other pilgrims. But there's another way to get them to the other side of the mountain. Dig a tunnel through it. Then even someone in a wheelchair can reach the other side."

I was stunned. "That's amazing. Why don't more people 'dig a tunnel'?"

"Because," he answered, "to dig a tunnel, you have to disappear from public view for a long time—and not many Christians are willing to do that."

I decided to start tunneling. I quit worrying about what I'd lost and began quietly to get my life in order. I learned to listen for God's guidance and read the Bible in a different way, and I met several times a week with other people who wanted recovery and God. And I tried to learn what God has given us to deal with our fear and pain, and with our bruised and broken relationships.

Then one day, after many years, I got an invitation to speak to a minister's conference. Coming out of the tunnel after all those years, I wasn't the same somehow. I wasn't interested in being something "big." I just wanted to tell people who were tired of their fear and loneliness and discouraged about their relationships that there really was peace in the midst of it all.

Lord, thank You for the grace of repentance. Help me to reach out to those who have come back to Your church—and to those who would like to. Amen. —KEITH MILLER

THU

14

Behold, what manner of love the Father hath bestowed upon us. . . . —I JOHN 3:1

My wife Nicole and I had been having a terrific time when we were at home with the kids. We talked when we could and laughed a lot. It was when we were alone that things became a little awkward. Not bad, mind you; it's just that out of the situation we were most used to, we were a little out of step with each other.

Then we found out that the new church we're attending provides child care once every couple of months and gives all the parents a night alone. We jumped at the chance. It had been months since we'd been alone together.

We dropped the kids off at the church that night. I was heading back to our car when Nicole told me that the church had provided a speaker for the first hour of our time. I was angry: This was *our* time to be together, and they wanted to take up some of it. How dare they!

The speaker was a comedian; he was funny and, I have to say, I enjoyed listening to him. He ended his talk by saying, "Tonight, as you go out with your spouse, you are not allowed to talk about the kids, plans for the future, schedules or anything un-fun. You may only talk about your love for each other or reminisce about great times you've had. That's it. Now go."

We did just what he suggested, and an amazing thing happened: The awkwardness we had been feeling disappeared. Looking at and remembering all that was good about each other brought back all the feelings that had made us fall in love in the first place.

When I'm feeling out of step with God, I have found this same remedy applies. If I open my Bible and read about all the wonderful, tenderhearted things God has done for me, I can't help but love Him in return.

Lord, on this Valentine's Day, remind me to take the time to rediscover Your love in the people who are dear to me, and in Your Word.
—*DAVE FRANCO*

THE PRACTICE OF PRAYER

FRI
15
Focusing on the Future
His love is perfected in us.   —*I JOHN 4:12*

The kitchen was filled with the scent of fresh-baked sugar cookies. Four-year-old Brock sat on a stool as I coaxed scalloped hearts from a round of rolled-out dough. His assignment was to add the little candies that would turn each cookie into an edible Valentine.

"Mom," he said, without glancing up, "you know what I'm gonna be when I grow up?"

"No, Brock, what are you going to be?"

"I'm gonna be a turner."

"A turner? What's a turner, honey?"

"Oh, first I'm gonna be a football player, then I'm gonna turn into a baseball player, then I'll turn into a fireman, then a cowboy. You know, Mama . . . a turner!"

In his book *Prayer Can Change Your Life,* written with Elaine St. Johns, Dr. William R. Parker says we are all moving in one direction or another, becoming the persons we will ultimately be. Some of us are focused on a life of good and move in that direction, others are "turners" and have no set focus, no destination. So, now, let's define our focus. Think far ahead, one generation, then two into the future. Imagine your grandchildren or your earthly heirs in their middle years, sitting around a table at some happy homecoming. For me, it sounds like this:

"And what was your grandmother like?" one of my great-grandchildren asks.

The answer to that question is the person I want to become: "She loved without condition, laughed a lot, relished life. She had a way of making you feel you were the most important person there ever was."

In the weeks ahead, let's begin our prayer practice by spending at least five minutes a day openly and honestly describing this best self to God. Share your dreams with God. There's nothing a Father would rather hear!

Father, I offer my best self to You. Use me to reflect Your love to others. *—PAM KIDD*

EDITOR'S NOTE: The practice of prayer changed Pam Kidd's life, and it can change yours, too. You can read about the topics Pam discusses in more depth in the Christian classic *Prayer Can Change Your Life* by William R. Parker and Elaine St. Johns. If you'd like to order the book, please write to Guideposts, EK# 11/201629565, 39 Seminary Hill Road, Carmel, NY 10512. The cost is $16.95, plus postage and handling.

SAT
16
Behold, how good and how pleasant it is for brethren to dwell together . . . ! —*PSALM 133:1*

Whump! Tim's landing was perfect, just below my ribcage, an accidental Heimlich maneuver. As I struggled to catch my breath, he hopped onto my pillow, looking annoyed that I had ruined a perfectly good sleeping spot. I glared at him and rolled over. I still had another hour before my alarm was set to go off, and I intended to enjoy it.

I had just gotten back to sleep when Nickel launched her attack, sticking a paw in my ear. A shake of my comforter sent both cats scrambling. A moment later, I heard the toilet flush.

Not again! I had asked the cats very nicely not to drink out of the commode, but when they refused to listen, I closed the lid. Now, every few days, they have voiced their protests with toilet-flushing sprees. I abandoned my last hour of sleep and marched to the bathroom. There they posed, completely still, jet-black bookends. Tim was perched on the tank, looking angelic. Nickel faced me, her ear-probing paw poised on the handle, waiting for me to make the first move.

I struck quickly, scooping one cat in either arm, and dashed for the bedroom. I dropped the cats on the bed and hopped up myself. Then I pulled the comforter up over my head, trapping the three of us in a striped, downy tent. Slowly, Tim climbed into my lap and reached up with one paw to bat my nose. I scratched his nose. He pawed my stomach, so I tickled his. Satisfied, he curled up in my lap and began to purr. Nickel slithered into my lap and used Tim as a chaise longue, stretching out so I could tickle her stomach, too.

Quite suddenly, I opened one eye to the muted but insistent beeping of my alarm. I was curled in a ball around my two roommates.

Father in heaven, thank You for my extended "feline family." They are my friends and guardians and my foot-warmers, too. What a special gift! —*KJERSTIN EASTON*

SUN
17
And Samuel said, Gather all Israel to Mizpeh, and I will pray for you unto the Lord. —*JUDE 2*

In 1988 I worked as a volunteer just outside Freetown, the capital of the West African nation Sierra Leone. It began when a construction foreman said to me, "You're a dentist. You should know how to handle cement and putty." So for eight days I packed cement around steel window frames and puttied in panes for a new library building at Sierra Leone Bible College.

On the last day, I puttied in the last pane and stepped down from the ladder to find the smiling Pa Fona, our kitchen supervisor, watching from the shade of a tree full of weaver bird nests. "You'll be leaving soon," he said.

I stepped into the shade of a tree and said, "Yes, Pa. Our job is finished, and we'll return to our families."

Pa's dark eyes sparkled. "We have pictures of your group in our chapel," he said. "Each morning we will pray for you."

There was a lump in my throat as I said, "I'll put you on my prayer list, too, Pa."

Civil war has devastated Sierra Leone over the past few years, and I don't know what has become of Pa Fona. But there are times when I picture him standing in the shade of that tree full of busy weaver birds and saying, "We will pray for you." When I do, I say a prayer for Pa and his college, knowing that whether he's still on earth or has gone to be with the Lord, Pa is praying for me.

Thank You, Lord, for all my prayer partners, and hear my prayers for them as You hear their prayers for me. —RICHARD HAGERMAN

MON
18
May you be given more and more of God's kindness, peace, and love. —JUDE 2

Here it is, chilly February, and I am taking such pleasure in gently stirring up the rose petals in a crystal bowl of potpourri that wafts the fragrance of summer throughout the house. The petals were carefully plucked from our Mr. Lincoln roses, roses my husband chose and planted. John loves the aroma of roses; he often breaks the stride of our evening walks to stop, lean over a neighbor's fence and sniff. "Harrumph!" he'll say. "Pretty enough, but no scent! With all these newfangled purple, peach and whatever roses, where's the smell?"

At the nursery, he told Big Jim, "I want a rose, a proper rose, deep red and fragrant."

"Ah"—Big Jim sucked in his cheeks—"the Mr. Lincoln will do it. Can't get better than that."

It's appropriate to name a rose for Abraham Lincoln, a rose with not only pure color but long-lasting fragrance. Today, as we remember the inspiration and enduring legacy of his life, soul and thought, reflected in both his written and spoken word, I find myself recalling the beauty of his gospel of human kindness. This gentle man, who could have called for accolades of greatness, expressed this simple wish: "Die when I may, I want it to be said of me, by those who knew me best, that I always plucked a thistle and planted a flower where I thought a flower would grow."

Lord, day in and day out, help me to spread Lincoln's message of mercy and compassion.
—FAY ANGUS

TUE
19
Thou, Lord, only makest me dwell in safety. *—PSALM 4:8*

I was fascinated by the sight of a lone telephone pole standing in the middle of a plot of land surrounded by a chain-link fence. Then I saw the sign: This was a training center for telephone linesmen.

As I watched, two men, clearly an instructor and a young trainee, walked over to the pole. Both were wearing hard hats. The younger man was also wearing a safety belt and work shoes with spurs on them.

"All right," said the instructor, "let's get started."

The trainee looked up to the top of the pole, a bit fearfully, I thought. He started to wrap his safety belt around the pole, but to my astonishment the instructor stopped him. "Don't forget," he said, "you don't wear the harness except when you're working on a line." So the trainee hooked the belt around his waist again, circled the pole with his gloved hands, dug his spurs into the wood and climbed to the top of the pole. Only when both hands were occupied splicing wires did the trainee use his safety gear.

When the instructor signaled the trainee to come down, the young man once again hooked his belt around his waist and made his way down the pole without the harness.

"Wasn't that dangerous, climbing down without the belt?" I asked the instructor.

"No," he said. "If you slip, the belt will throw you against the pole, and you'll catch a stomach full of splinters. It's safer to hold tight to the pole."

Lord, help me learn to let go of my own safety belts and hold on to You alone. —*JOHN SHERRILL*

All the paths of the Lord are steadfast love and faithfulness.... —*PSALM 25:10 (RSV)*

"We found some spots on your lungs." With that single, stunning statement, my cancer went from Stage I to Stage IV in a single bound. Almost exactly a year ago I had been diagnosed with melanoma. After surgery and then radiation, followed by months of "clear" scans and seeming good health, we had lulled ourselves into thinking that I would be the poster child for successful early detection and treatment. Melanoma, when found and treated early, is a highly curable cancer. But the fact that it had metastasized to my lungs was disheartening news indeed.

As we discussed with our doctors the grim statistics (median survival is about six months) and the options for treatment (there aren't any really good ones), I was frightened and overwhelmed. The need to make a decision from the array of unappealing choices left me feeling like an ant trying to push around a watermelon.

At some point during those days of coming to grips with the reality of my situation, I remembered a verse from Psalm 25 I had used when speaking at a Christmas luncheon, just weeks before my initial diagnosis of cancer: "All the paths of the Lord are steadfast love and faithfulness." I told the women some of the many ways I had seen God at work in my life in the seventeen years since I was unexpectedly widowed. It was easy for me, in retrospect, to see and speak of God's faithfulness and love. But now this. *Why is this happening? Where will the journey take me, and what will be the outcome? All Your ways, Lord? Can I still trust that promise?*

Yes, Lord of our journeys, I choose to believe that even on this frightening path, Your love and faithfulness will be evident to me.
—*MARY JANE CLARK*

THU

21 Let us search and try our ways, and turn again to the Lord.
—LAMENTATIONS 3:40

Figure skater Michelle Kwan, elegant and graceful, was favored to win the gold medal in the women's figure skating competition at the 1998 Winter Olympics, but a little dynamo named Tara Lapinski exploded onto the ice in a brilliant performance that gave her the gold.

A TV reporter later asked Michelle, "How did it feel to lose the Olympics?"

Michelle looked at her in astonishment and said, "I didn't lose. I won the silver."

Way to go, Michelle! I thought, applauding her positive attitude.

Then I remembered something an elderly neighbor said to me long ago when, as a child, I cried over having lost a declamation contest that had been sponsored by our church. "Honey, you memorized your piece and you did your best. Just getting up there took a lot of nerve, but you tried your hardest and that makes you a winner even if you didn't get a ribbon. The real losers in this world are the ones who don't even try."

My neighbor's wise words have inspired me ever since to try to do my best in whatever I attempt and to respect an honest effort—from myself or anyone else—even if that effort doesn't include a prize.

Lord, please give me the words today to encourage someone who is facing a challenge. Amen. *—MADGE HARRAH*

FRI

22 Thou didst gird me with strength for the battle....
—II SAMUEL 22:40 (RSV)

God bless my seventh-grade history teacher, Mrs. Weaver, for turning the dollar-bill figure of George Washington into flesh and blood for us. She walked him into our lives with descriptive tidbits told with dramatic flair.

We knew, for instance, that Washington had red hair covered with a powdered wig; that he had false teeth that gave him fits; that his face was scarred from smallpox; that he was a farmer ahead of his time in rotating crops; that in the French and Indian War he had two horses shot out from under him; that he was shy but learned to be sociable; that he wrestled a bad temper; that during the crushing winter of Valley Forge he knelt in the snow to pray.

And we knew that when, in the throes of victory over the British, the people were ready to crown him king—King George—he penned a hasty reply from his Mount Vernon home: "Banish the thought from your minds!" Instead, he submitted to the Constitution, and with Congress launched a republic, under God, with liberty and justice for all.

On this day, Washington is rightly honored as the father of our country, a larger-than-life figure. But, as Mrs. Weaver would tell you, he was also a person with foibles and faults like all of us, whose virtues are not just to be admired; they're to be imitated.

Lord, help me to have faith in You and stay the course through wins and losses. —*SHARI SMYTH*

SAT

23

Show me the path where I should go, O Lord; point out the right road for me to walk. —*PSALM 25:4 (TLB)*

Four quotes in bright colors and varying sizes are taped to my kitchen cabinets. The first quote, on a piece of shocking-pink paper, says in huge black letters, GET OVER IT. STOP WHINING AND START WINNING. That quote wakes me up every morning and reminds me to hold no grudges and maintain a positive attitude all day long.

Quote number two is on the cabinet over the counter that holds seventy jars of tea. It says, IF YOU'RE COLD, TEA WILL WARM YOU. IF YOU'RE HEATED, IT WILL COOL YOU. IF YOU'RE DEPRESSED, IT WILL CHEER YOU. IF YOU'RE EXCITED, IT WILL CALM YOU.—BRITISH PRIME MINISTER WILLIAM GLADSTONE. That quote reminds me to be hospitable and invite my friends over for tea often. I do, and my little tea parties have enriched my life immeasurably over the years.

The next quote, the one taped to my kitchen cabinet just to the right of the kitchen sink, spells out four of the most important sentences I can say: I AM PROUD OF YOU. WHAT IS YOUR OPINION? I LOVE YOU. THANK YOU. Those four sentences nudge me to be a more affirming, affectionate, appreciative and positive person. I tried to punctuate my conversations with those four sentences when my children were growing up.

The last quote, to the left of the kitchen sink, typed on bright yel-

low paper, proclaims, IF YOU HAD FAITH EVEN AS TINY AS A MUSTARD
SEED, YOU COULD SAY TO THIS MOUNTAIN, "MOVE!" AND IT WOULD GO
FAR AWAY. NOTHING IS IMPOSSIBLE. —MATTHEW 17:20 (TLB). That's
the one that gives me constant hope, unlimited encouragement and
a daily dose of comfort, no matter what I'm trying to accomplish.

So there you have it—a whole philosophy of life on my kitchen
cabinets. And if you're ever in Oak Creek, Wisconsin, stop in for tea.
The kitchen's always open!

**Father, for the wisdom of others and the soothing comfort of Your
Word, I thank You.** —*PATRICIA LORENZ*

SUN

24

Restore, I pray you, to them, even this day. . . .
—*NEHEMIAH 5:11*

We usually hold our Mission Mississippi prayer breakfasts at an
African American church one week and a white church the next
week. Two years ago we met at Mt. Helm Baptist, an African
American church, and as we formed our usual three-to-five-person
prayer groups, I noticed that a deacon from Mt. Helm was praying
with a deacon from First Baptist. Suddenly, it hit me: I was watching history.

You see, Mt. Helm is the second-oldest African American church
in Mississippi, and it was getting ready to celebrate its one hundred
sixty-fifth anniversary. Mt. Helm was formed back in 1835 when
First Baptist allowed slaves to sit only in the balcony, in the basement
or outside during worship. Now, in this room, one hundred and
sixty-five years later, through these two men, I could see both
churches praying together, bridging the chasm created by slavery,
segregation and estrangement.

As I prayed with the deacons' group, my heart was overjoyed with
the progress we'd made. And my prayer was that these two churches
would continue to come together, knowing that although they
couldn't rewrite history, they could continue to make a new and better history now and for years to come.

**Lord, the joy of praying together and for each other is wonderful.
Help me to work at including everyone in my life of prayer.**
—*DOLPHUS WEARY*

For I will declare mine iniquity; I will be sorry for my sin.
—*PSALM 38:18*

Today is my wife Sandee's birthday. I hope this year's birthday goes better than last year's. It couldn't go much worse.

The day began with a nice shower. Problem was, I was standing downstairs. The tub upstairs was flooding. This led to several sharp words to whomever was in earshot.

I found the guilty pipe, and I tried my trusty drain snake. No luck. I tried powdered drain opener. Still nothing. Finally, I got out a hacksaw and began to cut the pipe. After much sawing, the first gentle cascade of corrosive-laden water began to fall. Lye may not harm pipes, but it's less kind to skin.

Once the water cleared, I felt around inside the pipe for the blockage. It was a doll, wrapped in a cocoon of hair and soap and little crystals of drain opener and other unspeakable items. The doll had been stuffed down the drain.

Sandee, the birthday girl, saw the look on my face and immediately sprang into action. "Kids! Time to go! Mommy's taking you for a little ride!"

I could hear my children's questions as they ran to get their coats. "Where are we going, Mama?"

"I'm not sure," Sandee said, "but it's best if we're not here." She didn't say, "Daddy's head is about to explode."

My head did explode, but with possibilities, not anger. As I seated the replacement pipe into place, my mind went into free fall. *How,* I wondered, *can a two-inch doll fit down a one-and-a-half-inch pipe? How can it cause such a mess?*

Small things—dolls, kids, words, thoughts—can have that power. I turned off my propane torch and inspected my work, all the while thinking of how my small, angry words could cut just as cleanly as my hacksaw.

That night I treated Sandee to dinner and apologies, not in that order. *Sorry* is such a small word, but it cleans up a lot of the messes you make, especially around the house.

Lord, don't let my temper cause me to stumble. But if it does, let me be quick to say, "I'm sorry."
—*MARK COLLINS*

TUE
26
But we had the sentence of death in ourselves, that we should not trust in ourselves, but in God which raiseth the dead.
—*II CORINTHIANS 1:9*

It was only February and not yet time for the King Alfred daffodils to be blooming. But there they were—the only ones in the neighborhood—in small beds on either side of my front steps, standing tall and straight and golden, with a very special message.

Two nights earlier my husband Bob had died. As we came home from the hospital, Emily commented that the daffodils had big buds on them. At that time I wasn't interested enough even to glance at them. Then, the next day, a visitor commented, "Your daffodils will be blooming soon. The buds are showing yellow." I had other things on my mind then, too.

But on the day of Bob's funeral, the first thing I saw when we turned into the driveway were the masses of wide-open daffodils filling the flowerbeds. They seemed to reach out to me.

"It's a message from God," I cried, springing from the car. My family gathered around me as I explained.

"Last year these flowers bloomed and were beautiful," I said. "Then they died. All that remained were the bulbs in the ground. But now they are alive again!" I caught Emily's hand in mine. "Your Dad had a beautiful life. Then he died, and was put in the ground. But now," I said as I swept my hand across the flowers, "he's alive again—this time in heaven! He is glowing and beautiful up there with God."

Dear Father, when the days are darkest and the pain most intense, how wonderfully You remind me of Your love and redemption.
—*DRUE DUKE*

WED
27
Everyone with one of his hands wrought in the work. . . .
—*NEHEMIAH 4:17*

During my sophomore year in college, I was appointed photo editor of the student newspaper. With a staff of five part-time photographers, it was my job to ensure that there were plenty of photos for our eight-page daily. I was proud of my new position, and I eagerly took command, changing procedures and issuing orders. I supervised every single assignment and approved every single print. The paper had always had excellent photography, and I felt I was doing a good job.

Then one day Kim, one of our photographers, was late coming back from an away basketball game and a full afternoon of photo assignments. An hour before the deadline, she dashed into the darkroom to process and print all of her exposed film. After about twenty minutes, she opened the darkroom door, several wet rolls of blank film in her hand. We had no photos for the front page, and I was furious. I slammed a notebook on the table as Kim just stood there, her tears falling.

John, the night editor, was the only other person there. He gave Kim a hug and consoled her. Then, together, they proceeded to fix the problem of the front page. In the photo file they found a shot of a large pig lying in a pile of hay. John ran the photo five columns wide across the top of the page with the caption, "Hog day afternoon."

The next morning, our student-readers were surprised and delighted by this unusual front page. That day, and for months afterward, people asked me if I was responsible for it, and each time I had to admit that I was not.

Kim graduated, and I went on to photography school. But I've never forgotten the lesson that she and John taught me that night: No matter how hard the job looks, we can get it done—if we work together.

Dear Lord, as I do my work today, let me remember that with You to help me, I need never work alone. —*BILLY NEWMAN*

THU
28
For the day of the Lord is near in the valley of decision.
—*JOEL 3:14*

For almost six years I worked as an investment consultant in the last of the grand old banks of Nashville, Tennessee, and not a day passed when I didn't feel blessed. My clients were more than customers: They were people I cared for, and I never doubted that the bank, with its emphasis on customer service, was behind me all the way.

Then the era of consolidation came calling, and my bank was bought by an out-of-state company. I was made a senior vice president in the larger bank's investment department, and my customer base was expanding. But then my concerns began mounting.

"Brock," my good friend Mr. Peterson called to say, "the people at the new bank's home office put me on hold every time I call to straighten out a mistake in my account."

"I tried your 800 number when I was out of town, Brock," an older lady reported, "and they told me I would have to talk to a broker in another state."

More calls followed and, try as I might, I couldn't shake the feeling that I was letting down my clients.

And then a headline in our Sunday paper caught my eye: "FORMER BANK EXECUTIVES TO START NEW FINANCIAL SERVICES COMPANY." Two highly respected executives from my original bank were opening a new company with a focus on superior service.

As I sat in church later that day, it was difficult to focus on the sermon. I knew I had a chance to be a part of this new business, but what if the new company couldn't make it? Even worse, what if I couldn't make it at the new company? After all, I had a family to support.

My thoughts were interrupted by organ music; I had completely missed the sermon. The minister was lifting his arms and pronouncing the benediction: "Now, go out into the world and fear nothing!"

It was all the sermon I needed to hear. I went straight home and called the chairman of the new bank.

Father, help me to fear nothing as I decide daily to serve You through serving others.   —*BROCK KIDD*

My Days of Prayer

1 _____

2 _____

3 _____

4 _____

5 _____

6 _____

7 _____

8 _____

9 _____

10 _____

11 _____

12 _____

13 _____

14 _____

15 _____

16 _____

17 _____

18 _____

19 _____

20 _____

21 _____

22 _____

23 _____

24 _____

25 _____

26 _____

27 _____

28 _____

March

That they all may be one; as thou, Father, art in me, and I in thee, that they also may be one in us: that the world may believe that thou hast sent me.

—John 17:21

S	M	T	W	T	F	S
					1	2
3	4	5	6	7	8	9
10	11	12	13	14	15	16
17	18	19	20	21	22	23
24	25	26	27	28	29	30
31						

THE PRAYER THAT IS ALWAYS NEW

1

Our Father *who art in heaven....* —*MATTHEW 6:9 (RSV)*

When I first learned the Lord's Prayer, "heaven," to my young ear, had a faraway sound. It was a remote, fairy-tale kind of place where very good people went after they died. A Father "in heaven" wasn't much help right now!

Since then I've come to feel just the opposite. Heaven, to me, means a reality closer and truer than anything I can see and touch. It means this commonplace earthly life caught up in God's eternal plan.

The Dutch evangelist Corrie ten Boom had a visual aid that expressed this well. Corrie had arrived for a visit, and my thirteen-year-old daughter Liz and I were helping her unpack. From the bottom of Corrie's suitcase, Liz lifted a folded cloth with some very amateurish-looking needlework on it. Uneven stitches, mismatched colors, loose threads, snarls.

"What are you making?" Liz asked curiously.

"Oh, that's not mine," Corrie said. "That's the work of the greatest weaver of all."

I probably looked as dubious as Liz did.

"But you're seeing it from the wrong side!" Corrie went on. Shaking the cloth open with a flourish, she turned it around to display a magnificent crown embroidered in red, purple and gold. "You have to look at things from heaven's viewpoint!"

Heaven's viewpoint . . . when I pray to my Father in heaven, I speak to the One Who can make something beautiful of the tangled threads of a lifetime. I am asking Him to help me see the perplexities of daily life "from heaven's side."

Our Father in heaven, give me eternity's perspective on the small activities of this day.
—*ELIZABETH SHERRILL*

WHAT GOD HAS JOINED TOGETHER

SAT
2

You have stolen my heart, my sister, my bride; you have stolen my heart with one glance of your eyes. . . .
—*SONG OF SOLOMON 4:9 (NIV)*

As Joy and I approached our twenty-fifth wedding anniversary, I did a lot of reflecting on our marriage, especially on how we could grow and improve.

It was not long before I came to the conclusion that the toughest times were caused by my selfishness. As a husband and father, insisting on what *I* wanted—*my* comfort, *my* priorities, *my* schedule, or just watching *my* TV program—often became the needle that burst the bubble of happiness. Figuring out how to change that was uppermost in my mind as we left on our anniversary gift to each other—a seven-day sailing trip through the British Virgin Islands.

Our trip was like a fairy tale. We sailed aboard a fifty-eight-foot yacht with just two good friends and our captain and first mate. The balmy weather was perfect, the turquoise water was stunning, the islands were beautiful, the snorkeling was wonderful, and the first mate was a gourmet French chef. Even with all that, I found myself selfishly annoyed one afternoon as Joy called to me from the water to come swimming.

As I drew a breath to remind her we'd already been swimming and *I* wanted to read a book, I watched her floating in the cove. The sun danced off her hair, and the water sparkled off her face, and those bright amber eyes grabbed me by the heart and pulled me overboard.

Swimming over to her, I remembered that first time, when I swam out to help her with an overturned canoe in front of twenty laughing college students. Then, as now, my heart was leading me, and selfishness loses to love every time.

Lord, in all my relationships, keep me thinking and choosing from my heart.
—*ERIC FELLMAN*

SUN

3

Seek ye me, and ye shall live.　　　　　—*AMOS 5:4*

Pastor Al's church is three blocks from our door, and I often met and chatted with him at the supermarket or on the street corner. Late in June 1996, Al retired from his pastorate after years of service. I attended his retirement party, and I was warmed by the fellowship. The parishioners gave Al the computer he had always wanted. He said joyfully, "I have all the sermons of Dr. Dolloff, who served this church during the nineteen thirties and forties. I'm going to put them on the computer and perhaps into a book!"

I met Al again at a Lenten service the next March. He was quiet, and his enthusiasm seemed to have vanished. "How's retirement?" I asked.

Al paused and said, "I don't know. I miss the church and the people. Our home is too quiet, and sitting at the computer all day long isn't for me. My life seems disconnected. I feel out of step."

Months later we met at a band concert. We hugged warmly, and Al handed me his new card. He was the pastor of another church in the greater Boston area. "Things are going great!" he said. "I've started a youth group, and the church is growing by leaps and bounds. Maybe I was too young to retire. Maybe I had too much energy. Maybe God had another mission for me."

Pastor Al's new life seemed to say, "You're never too old to serve God and His people."

Gentle Lord, remind me that no matter how old I am, there's always a way that I can be useful. And what better place than in Your house?
　　　　　　　　　　　　　　　　　　　　　—*OSCAR GREENE*

MON

4

And I am sure that he who began a good work in you will bring it to completion at the day of Jesus Christ.
　　　　　　　　　　　　　　　　　—*PHILLIPIANS 1:6 (RSV)*

Michelangelo's *Six Prisoners*, commissioned by Pope Julius II, were never completed. Four are housed in the Academy of Fine Art in Florence, Italy, and when I stood in front of them, I knew instantly why they were called "prisoners." In their unfinished state, these apostles of Christ twist spasmodically out of their marble in a useless effort to transcend the heavy stone. They *are* prisoners, stuck between chaos and completion.

I wandered on down the corridor to the rotunda where Michelangelo's most famous sculpture is positioned under a high dome. The *David* stood before me—huge, gleaming, brilliantly white. I circled in awe, stunned by its sheer beauty and vitality. Here the artist had been allowed to finish the task. Here was perfection, completeness.

I looked back to the four *Prisoners*. The *David*, too, had once been imprisoned—until the finishing touch of his master's hand had transformed him. Michelangelo had died before completing his apostles, and they're left forever caught in the struggle. But the touch of my Master's hand will never die. Even now He is at work transforming me.

Lord, Your Master's touch will transform me after Your likeness. Help me to be mindful of the goal of Your work in me.

—*BRENDA WILBEE*

TUE
5

Let us therefore come boldly to the throne of grace, that we may obtain mercy and find grace to help in time of need. —*HEBREWS 4:16 (NKJV)*

A discussion about prayer broke out in one of my college classes awhile ago.

"I'm afraid to ask God to bless the poor in Mexico," one young man admitted, "because I know how God works."

"What do you mean?" another student asked.

"Well, if I pray for them, then God will want me to go there and help them!"

I laughed, having had the same thoughts myself.

"I know this sounds crazy," a young woman said, "but I'm afraid to thank God for the things I have, because I'm afraid the devil will hear me and take away the things I love. You know, the way he did with Job in the Old Testament?"

A new student spoke with a strained voice. "Sometimes I'm afraid to pray because I know I have sins in my life, and I don't think God will hear me until I clean up my act."

"Me, too!" said a classmate.

"I would pray more," a smartly dressed young woman said, "but

I'm one of the rich Americans. I'm afraid God is more concerned about people who are sick and hurting. I feel guilty praying when I have so much."

"I would be glad to take some of your money," a young man volunteered.

I was ready to jump in with my great wisdom, but a senior student saved me.

"Hey, you guys, listen to us! We're trying to tell God what to do. Maybe we should just concentrate on praying, and let Him worry about answering."

We had a good laugh, and the discussion ended with a prayer session. One of the prayers went something like this:

Father, teach me to trust You, like, totally, because I know You are a perfect Dad and will always do what's best for us. Amen.

—*DANIEL SCHANTZ*

WED

6

The Lord, your God, is in your midst. . . .
—*ZEPHANIAH 3:17 (RSV)*

Not long ago I received an e-mail from my brother Steve, who does a great job of keeping us out here in Arizona up to date on his family back in Michigan. After filling me in on some news about his job, he began the report on his family with this hastily typed sentence: "Everything is god around here." I'm sure he meant to type *good,* but after I finished reading his letter I couldn't get that little typing mistake out of my mind.

Everything is God around here. How often can I report that about my life? Sunday mornings for sure, with teaching Sunday school and both my husband Paul and I singing in choir. But I thought about some other recent days. Yesterday I spent an hour catching up on the newspaper, yet I'm still behind in my reading through the Old Testament. I seem to be able to schedule a monthly night out with my friends, but can't make it to a regular Bible study. And while I don't like admitting it, today I passed along a bit of e-mail gossip when I could have better spent that time adding a name or two to my church's e-mail prayer chain.

Everything is God around here. I say that phrase in my mind almost every day now, then take inventory to see how my life is measuring up. No surprise, there's always room for improvement. But that little reminder has made a big difference, continually making me aware that every day, God is ready to be invited into each moment of my life.

Come, Lord, and be a part of everything I think, say, do and feel.

—*GINA BRIDGEMAN*

<table>
<tr><td>THU
7</td><td>Martha, Martha, thou art careful and troubled about many things....   —LUKE 10:41</td></tr>
</table>

My wife Pam is a very organized person. Her desk is always neat as a pin; she even knows how to file things. I'm afraid I'm just the reverse. My office is a small room in the attic with paper strewn all over the place, books lying on the floor, memos and photographs pinned up on the walls. Pam regards it with despair. "You know," she said to me the other day, "I think you *like* clutter!"

I had to deny that, of course, but perhaps there is some truth in it. Certainly all my good resolutions about clutter reform seem to get nowhere. It's almost as if there were something friendly and comforting about familiar clutter. Nobody else can find anything in it, but you always know where things are.

A few other special creatures seem to understand clutter's curious charm. I've noticed that cats, who are wise about such matters, sometimes find it a relief from boredom. Sooty, our good-humored black male cat, likes to jump up on my desk (where things are chaotic already) and bat things around with an inquisitive paw. He loves pencils and pens; they may be half buried in debris, but he knows how to make them roll. Scattered paperclips are also good toys; it all depends on his mood. An immaculate desk would never attract him, but mine is endlessly fascinating. And I like having him up there. Watching him cavort is more fun than working any day.

I don't recall reading anything about clutter in the Bible, but I do remember that warm-hearted scene in St. Luke's Gospel where Martha, surely a brisk and clutter-free housewife, asks Jesus to make her sister Mary come and help with serving dinner (Luke 10:40).

And Jesus tells her gently that Mary's interest in spiritual matters is more important than efficiency in the kitchen.

Would the Lord be tolerant of my lamentable lack of neatness? Up to a point, I like to think He would.

Dear Lord, help me to be more organized, if You really think I should be. —ARTHUR GORDON

<u>FRI</u>
8

"Be strong and courageous. Do not be terrified; do not be discouraged, for the Lord your God will be with you wherever you go." —JOSHUA 1:9 (NIV)

I recently began a spiritual walk alongside a friend who is in the midst of a painful personal crisis. It involves one of her children, and it is a crisis that will not pass quickly. As I pray for her each day, I ask God to show me the ways I can be a good friend to her in the midst of her needs. A few days ago, she told me some of the things that have helped her most, and I wrote them down so I'd remember them. I'm calling them my "Be-Attitudes."

- **Be a good listener:** When my friend told me her news, I cried. I had no answers, but I sat with her a long time and listened. The next day I apologized for not being stronger for her. "You gave me exactly what I needed," she told me. "You listened and shared my feelings." I still try to say less and listen more.
- **Be a reminder:** Every day, I search the Bible for at least one of God's appropriate promises. Sometimes I write them on yellow sticky notes and put them in places where she will find them: in her purse, on her cell phone or on her computer screen. A few days ago, I made a list of God's recent provisions for her, such as her marriage of growing strength, her recent study of the word *courage,* a calendar uncharacteristically free of immediate obligations. She says these reminders of God's faithfulness in her past give her strength in the present.
- **Be a hope-bringer:** Hope is knowing in the midst of a dark and dreary day that the sun will shine again. I told my friend that when I pray for her, I picture her walking through this dark place in little sunbeams of hope. Or I picture Jesus walking with her,

holding up His light so she can take the next step. She appreciates these pictures that fill her future with hope.

My friend's journey continues, and I continue to pray:

Lord, send Your angels to protect my friend in this hard place and let me be a finger pointing her to You. —*CAROL KUYKENDALL*

SAT

9

Tribulation worketh patience; And patience, experience; and experience, hope. —*ROMANS 5:3-4*

"At least we'll get dinner," I said rather petulantly. Marcia was driving me fifty-some miles out of New York on a rainy March afternoon to do some bird-watching.

"It's a rare event," she reminded me. "It's the whir of the woodcock."

"I know, I know," I replied, but clearly I wasn't impressed. Her friends had invited us and several others to come stand and wait in their icebox of a meadow just before dark, just before, you might say, we caught our death from the cold. There was no assurance that the bird would even appear to do his whirring, which, I understood, was part of his mating, but whirring or no, we were promised a warm supper afterward.

Hushed into silence, we stood and waited. And waited. I was becoming increasingly aware of the chill when, suddenly, a plump bird, mottled brown, with a very long bill, rose up out of the distant brush. With a fluttering of wings it flew straight upward, up, up, two hundred, three hundred feet in the air, then it began a zigzag course, spiraling downward, singing all the while, whistling, calling, until it landed close to its expectant mate.

I watched, transfixed by what I had seen. What was this strange emotion I was feeling? The woodcock had flown up until it touched, it seemed, the very fringe of heaven. Then the downward spinning and its strange music, intended, not for me, but for the female below. I felt almost embarrassed that I should hear it.

"You were right, Marcia," I said, humbled, on the drive back. "It was a rare event. Rare and wonderful."

Let me be open, Father, to the many experiences in which I find You. —*VAN VARNER*

SUN
10

The Lord bless thee, and keep thee: The Lord make his face shine upon thee, and be gracious unto thee: The Lord lift up his countenance upon thee, and give thee peace.
—NUMBERS 6:24-26

In the closing moments of the Sunday-morning service, our pastor raises his arms toward heaven and calls down the blessing of the Lord upon all of us in the congregation. I bow my head in the contemplative prayer that has become for me, a pre-blessing ritual. I am a greedy child of God—I want every blessing, every gift the Lord has for me; I want nothing within me to hinder His giving or my receiving.

All too frequently, as I put down my hymnal and turn my hands palms-up to receive the blessing, I wince; I find my hands already full. Sometimes my fists are clenched, white knuckled, in unresolved anger, as they were the week a hit-and-run driver fatally injured our small calico cat. Sometimes I find myself holding on to brooding resentments over words spoken to me in the heat of an argument; or worse, I may be holding on to the guilt of harsh words I've spoken to others. Sometimes I'm clutching habitual worries I thought I'd let go the previous Sunday, only to find that through the days that followed I've picked them up again. So I begin my weekly ritual of letting go:

In these moments, Lord, I empty my hands and open them to You.
I let go of anger; fill and bless me with Your love.
I let go of guilt; fill and bless me with forgiveness.
I let go of self-pity; fill and bless me with a grateful heart.
I let go of worries and fear; fill and bless me with trust.
I let go of the hurts of the past; fill and bless me with the promise of the present.

Bless me and keep me, Lord. Let Your face shine upon me, uphold me, and give me peace. *—FAY ANGUS*

MON
11

That I may come unto you with joy by the will of God, and may with you be refreshed. *—ROMANS 15:32*

There's a license plate rim available in Alaska that reads, "God's Frozen Chosen." I received an icy reminder of this when I flew to Alaska in March to help our good friends Jim and Janet Faiks on their alpaca farm—located in a secluded wooded area—while they vacationed in Hawaii.

Besides caring for their two children, I was responsible for a herd of thirty alpacas, along with miscellaneous other pets. I learned the feeding and watering routine for the animals, how to start the generator for electrical supply to the house, plus the quirks of the woodstove—the main source of heat.

Jim and Janet had no sooner departed when the early March weather capriciously turned clear and very cold. Every morning the thermometer was stuck at fifteen below zero. The alpacas, endowed with thick wool coats, did fine in the subzero weather, but I had to keep running inside to warm up by the fire while carrying all those fresh and frozen water buckets back and forth from the pens. The house was spacious, and the extreme cold required me to get up during the night to stoke the fire to keep us all warm. Finally, the day the thermometer plunged to twenty below, with a bitter wind blowing, I called a neighbor to help me start the wood-powered boiler in the basement. Now I had double fire duty, but at least we partially thawed.

Somehow, the kids and the animals and I survived the challenge. Of course, the day Jim and Janet returned, the thermometer climbed fifty degrees! I had a difficult time making them believe our chilly tale. And I did get a fresh Hawaiian pineapple out of the deal—absolutely nothing frozen about it—even if it did require signing on as one of "God's Frozen Chosen."

Lord, today I would like that warm and wonderful sensation of having helped meet a need for someone else. —*CAROL KNAPP*

TUE
12 "Alas, Lord God! Behold, I do not know how to speak...."
—*JEREMIAH 1:6 (NAS)*

I was thrilled when my first book was published in 1976, but my joy was short-lived when I learned that authors were expected to speak to groups. How was I ever going to do that? I used to get sick to my stomach just reading the minutes at my club.

My first speaking invitation came from my hometown church, where I'd been baptized and married. "I can't do it!" I wailed to my mother. She told me that there would only be a few ladies there: We could meet in the library and sit around a table, and I could speak very informally. Reluctantly, I agreed, but secretly I hoped there would be a terrible storm so I could cancel.

The day of my talk dawned clear, however, and a smiling lady I'd known all my life met me when I arrived at the church. She told me they had announced my talk in the paper, and a few other people had shown up. When she opened the door, I saw a crowd that looked to me like the five thousand Jesus fed! I nearly fainted right there. As I was being introduced, I prayed, *Oh, Lord, You've got to help me. I'm shaking so badly I can't even hold my notes.*

Above the loud pounding of my heart, I sensed His voice. He told me to read the first eight verses of the first chapter of Jeremiah. Then He said, *Put your notes away and listen to Me.*

I stuck the notes in the back of my Bible and desperately tried to find Jeremiah. After I read the first eight verses, I listened and began to speak the thoughts, pictures and memories He seemed to be giving me. I talked about things I had never planned to share with anyone. People nodded, smiled, laughed good-naturedly—even cried. When I finally sat down, an hour and a half had passed.

All these years later, I still don't like to speak in public. But when I have to, God still shows up to tell me what to say.

Lord, help me to trust You and enable me to share the message of Your love with others. Amen. —*MARION BOND WEST*

WED

13

Therefore we will not fear, though the earth give way . . . and the mountains quake. . . .   —*PSALM 46:2–3 (NIV)*

Recently my friend Jeri told me about a terrifying experience she had while attending a women's conference in Garden Grove, California. "I was staying on the ninth floor of a hotel when, in the middle of the night, I awoke to find the room swaying! The curtains moved back and forth, things were falling off the dresser and I could hear cracking sounds all around me." Being, as Jeri puts it, "a good Southern gal," she was totally unprepared to be in the middle of an earthquake. And that's exactly what it was, registering 5.7 on the Richter scale!

Later, she made her way to the lobby, along with dozens of other pajama-clad and terrified occupants. *Should they leave the hotel? Was it going to come crashing down on them even as they stood in the lobby?*

But the manager smiled, passed out coffee and told them that the hotel was safe. Why? "It's built on rollers," he assured them. "When the tremors come, we don't tumble down—we roll with the rhythms of the quake."

Built on rollers. What a perfect description of the life of faith! While not immune to sickness or financial difficulties, to family problems and work frustrations, to grief and loss, I can still stand firm because my faith allows me to "roll" instead of crumble in the midst of crises. Steadied by the assurance of God's help and divine plan, I, too, am built to withstand quakes. And so are you, thanks to our Divine Architect.

When storms and tremors assault me, God, sustain me with Your unshakable love. —*MARY LOU CARNEY*

THU
14

Every good gift and every perfect gift is from above. . . .
—*JAMES 1:17*

Nobody warned me that morning as I got up, dressed, ate my breakfast and walked to George Ross Elementary School that I'd get the jolt of my eight-year-old life.

It happened at the Acme Supermarket when I stepped on the old, rubbery, black doormat. The door flew open, and my mouth flew open with it. I shrieked and stepped off the mat. It was the first automated door in our city, and the first automated anything to come into my life. I stepped on. I stepped off. On and off, again and again, laughing out loud. Finally, the annoyed clerks threatened to call my mother while the school bell in the distance rang my lateness. Reluctantly, I left.

If it could have spoken, the door might have said, "Welcome, little girl, to the age of automation. In the future all kinds of things will happen at the push of a button. You will become immune to wonder, your senses dulled at the conveniences thrown your way. You will yawn in the face of technological novelties. So remember this moment of astonishment. May its memory return to you on a day when you need it."

That day is now. It finds me in a whiny, hurried moment when the push-button garage door is opening too slowly for my taste. My finger finds the button, stopping everything. And while I sit in my spacious van, in the dark, warm garage of my thoroughly modern home, I remember what it was like to be given the gift of something new and wonderful.

Lord, forgive me for taking for granted what ultimately comes from Your hand. —*SHARI SMYTH*

THE PRACTICE OF PRAYER

FRI

15

Truthful Prayer
Little children . . . ye have known the Father.
—*I JOHN 2:13*

"Keri, where are you?"

I wandered about the house in search of our three-year-old daughter.

"I'm in here, in the kitchen, under the table," she answered.

"What are you doing under the table?"

"Oh, me and God . . . we're just talking."

How is it that we adults manage to make something as simple as talking to God so infinitely complicated?

Many roadblocks separate me from the God Keri visited with so naturally under the kitchen table. First, there's my dark side: Sometimes I feel inferior to other people and, in retaliation, I say mean things about them. At other times, I'm afraid that God really isn't out there or, if He is, He doesn't have time to listen to me. Then there's my lazy side: I put off the effort that's required to build a solid relationship with God.

I'm sure you have your own list of obstacles that keep you one step removed from a free and open dialogue with God. And yet, because of them, we can discover the single most important thing there is to know about the practice of prayer—Dr. William R. Parker and Elaine

St. Johns call it "the Key to the Kingdom"—honesty. For me, it sounds like this:

> *God, You know the person I want to become. But when I find myself around Mae, with her money and her important job and her perfectly decorated house, well . . . I say mean things about Mae. I'm sorry I do that, God.*

This month will be honesty month. Take at least ten minutes every day to talk honestly with God. Tell Him who you are and who you want to be. Don't be afraid to tell Him the whole truth. You are His beloved child. He already knows every single thing there is to know about you. But like a good Father, He's hoping to hear it straight from you!

Father, I want to come to You as pure and honest as a child.

—PAM KIDD

SAT

16

Every valley shall be exalted, and every mountain and hill shall be made low: and the crooked shall be made straight, and the rough places plain: And the glory of the Lord shall be revealed, and all flesh shall see it together. . . .

—ISAIAH 40:4–5

I love antique stores because I never know what I'll find in them. Each antique, regardless of its worth, has its own story to tell. Many times as I wander down the crowded aisles of an antique mall, I'll see an item that would be a perfect gift for a friend.

Recently, I spotted a carpenter's wooden plane, nearly a century old. It was the same kind of plane that my grandfather used when he built his house and barn on the barren plains of northeastern Colorado. In those pioneering days before electricity, it required a lot of physical strength and practiced skill to plane smooth a rough pine plank or a stout oak beam.

Staring at the golden burnished patina of the wooden plane, I thought of my friend Pat Hambrick. Pat is a contractor and a builder of fine houses. He probably hasn't used a manual plane in years, if ever. But somehow I sensed that this old plane had Pat's name written all over it.

As I picked up the plane and held it in my hands, the words of Isaiah 40:4 flashed through my mind: "And the crooked shall be made straight, and the rough places plain." Suddenly I knew why I wanted to buy the plane for Pat. Quite simply, Pat is a peacemaker. A deacon in my church, Pat is always seeking to straighten out crooked situations and to make smooth rough areas of personal conflict.

I walked to the checkout counter with a broad grin on my face. There's nothing more enjoyable than finding the perfect gift for a friend. And there's no better friend to have than one who is a master craftsman at making relationships peaceful, smooth and straight.

Lord, may I be one who makes the crooked places straight and the rough places plain. Amen.   —*SCOTT WALKER*

READER'S ROOM

There's an old rocker in my bedroom. It belonged to my aunt, then to my sister. The seat has been covered and recovered from lime green to beige floral. But it still offers the same comfort . . . a place to gaze out the window, to rock babies, to have a morning cup of coffee and to read *Daily Guideposts.*

I have little time for window-gazing these days, and the babies are grown and gone, but the coffee, prayer and *Daily Guideposts* still anchor my day. It's hard to say which author or story over the years has most touched my life. I only know that this is when God speaks to me. I have only to be still and listen. For in the everyday stories of everyday life of everyday people, He teaches me.   —*KATHY WOLKING, HUDSON, OHIO*

SUN
17

As it is written: "No eye has seen, no ear has heard, no mind has conceived what God has prepared for those who love him."   —*I CORINTHIANS 2:9 (NIV)*

My husband Roy and I visit New York City often now that our daughter and her husband are living there. And when we do, we always stop by St. Patrick's Cathedral. Inside its doors, the cool and quiet is a sharp contrast to the hustle and bustle of Fifth Avenue.

On our most recent visit, we stepped inside and walked down the aisle toward the front of the church and sat down to pray. I looked back over my shoulder at the long aisle we'd just walked down and said, "Can you imagine what it must be like to get married here? What a walk down the aisle that would be!" Our own wedding, as beautiful as it had been, held one disappointment for us: Our pianist had missed her cue and we had walked down the aisle without any music.

Just then we heard a few chords of the pipe organ. I looked up at the choir loft in the back of the church. *It must be a rehearsal,* I thought. Standing up to leave, we faced the huge double doors at the back of the church with the long aisle before us. At that moment, as if on cue, the pipe organ began to play. Roy looked at me, "Ready?"

I looped my arm in his. "Yes."

My husband and I, arm in arm, walked down the aisle of St. Patrick's Cathedral to the most beautiful music we had ever heard. We smiled at the people in the pews, while those coming in stepped aside as we walked down the center of the aisle. When we reached the back of the cathedral, the music stopped as if on cue. We looked at each other in amazement. God had just given us our walk down the aisle—to the magnificent strains of the pipe organ at historic St. Patrick's Cathedral!

Life is a glorious journey as we walk in faith with You, Lord.

—*MELODY BONNETTE*

MON

18   Husbands, love your wives, even as Christ also loved the church, and gave himself for it. . . .   —*EPHESIANS 5:25*

The phone rang very early in the morning, and I knew it could only be my wife Julee, who had just arrived in Europe.

"My laptop was stolen!" she cried as soon as I picked up the phone. "When we landed in Zurich, it was gone. . . ." The rest of what she had to say was lost in a torrent of tears.

The words formed in my mind instantly, then leapt to my lips for immediate delivery: *I told you so.*

I had *told* Julee that it was a waste to lug her laptop on this quick concert tour, but she had wanted to be able to retrieve her e-mail. I *told* her that under *no* circumstances should she ever check the laptop, no matter how secure she believed her luggage was. Now the laptop was gone, snatched right out of her luggage, and I wanted to tell her how right I'd been. I'd given her my best advice and she had ignored it!

Finally, I said, "Don't worry, sweetheart. I think our insurance will cover it. Besides, it was time for a new computer anyway."

Did that come from me? What about the lecture I had every right to give? Besides, I was almost certain our insurance wouldn't cover this foolish loss—and the thing was practically brand-new.

"Julee, everything will be okay. Just rest up for your show tonight."

Julee's sobs soon receded to a few sniffles, and then she said, "Thanks for making me feel better. I'll call you later when I get settled."

There was a time when I would have delivered that self-righteous lecture. It would have been more important to me to be right than to be loving. Being a husband has changed me, though. I'm happy about that, and happy to say that today Julee and I celebrate fifteen years of marriage.

Thank You, God, for lost laptops and disregarded husbandly advice, and every other opportunity You give me to do something loving.

—*EDWARD GRINNAN*

TUE

19

I will instruct thee and teach thee in the way which thou shalt go. . . .   —*PSALM 32:8*

This year in our homeschool, we're learning about early American history. We've worked our way up to the mid-1600s, and yesterday we read a book about the events in Salem Village, Massachusetts. I'd remembered how striking the Salem story was to me when I was a child, but as I read it aloud to my children, I wondered if maybe it was too much for a six- and a four-year old. Our dinnertime conversation certainly revealed a lot.

"Was the story real?" "Why didn't all the girls admit that they had lied?" "Are there really witches?" "Is witchcraft a sin?" "What happens to witches today?" John and Elizabeth were keenly interested and had a ton of questions. After a pause, Elizabeth said, "I think it was kind of scary."

"Yes, it is kind of scary. But, you know, we must never be afraid of evil. Can you figure out why?"

The children thought. John was the first to come up with an answer. "Because Jesus died on the Cross."

"Yes. But why does that mean we don't have to be afraid of evil?"

No answer.

"Because God has won," I said.

The children were silent as they absorbed this. Their big eyes told me that they were thinking hard.

"That doesn't mean that the devil isn't going to try to fight against you, does it? No. He most certainly will! What it means is that as long as you trust in God, as long as you follow Him, as long as you seek to do His will, the devil won't win. He can't. Because Christ has triumphed over sin and death."

I started to hum the "God Is Bigger Than the Boogey Man" song from the kids' *Veggie Tales* video. They smiled and began to sing along. That's our school: Start in the seventeenth century, work your way back to the Cross, and end up with singing vegetables. What a wonderful way to learn!

Teacher of all, no matter who I'm talking to, guide my words so that they convey Your truth.   —*JULIA ATTAWAY*

FOR EVERY SEASON

God works in special ways in the seasons of the year. And as days lengthen, then shorten, and as leaves bud, flourish, burst into spectacular color and fall to leave the branches bare, so, too, does God's way with us vary with the seasons of our lives. This year, Roberta Rogers joins us to share a special experience of prayer at the beginning of each season.   —*THE EDITORS*

WED

20   Turn your ear to me; when I call, answer me quickly.
                                          —*PSALM 102:2 (NIV)*

It's here! The first day of spring! When I was a child and living in a northern climate, this meant that outdoor recess was not far behind.

Even now, I look forward to the freshening of the air, open windows every day and the sun warm on my back when I walk.

Because my faith-life began one spring, I always associate the early days of my prayer life with this season. The presence of the Lord was so close, the spring breezes seemed to waft prayers right up to His feet. Often "yes" answers came quickly. Then as I grew in faith and prayer, those quick answers more often became long waits and sometimes even "no's."

Yet just when I need it most, the Lord still gives me a springtime quick answer. When "Big Orange," the truck that belonged to my prayer partner Ellen's husband, disappeared from their driveway on a Monday night, Ellen and I met the next evening at eight o'clock for prayer. We had little faith that the truck would be found intact because joyriding teens had been stealing vehicles, driving them to the back woods and then setting them afire. With big, deep-treaded tires and bright orange paint, even a twenty-year-old truck was a target for the mischievous thieves.

In our desperation we became very specific. "Oh, Lord," we prayed, "please, please, if Big Orange is still intact, let the police find it. Roger really loves that truck. Lord, if someone is driving it now, let it run out of gas and let it be found!"

The next morning the police called Roger. "Big Orange" had run out of gas in a field not far from the woods where the other vehicles had been found. The police apprehended both the truck and the teens around 8:30 the evening before. Big Orange was intact . . . except for a broken gas gauge.

Lord, thank You. I rejoice in the newness of the season and in the freshness of answered prayers. —*ROBERTA ROGERS*

THU
21
And I will send hornets before thee, which shall drive out the Hivite, the Canaanite, and the Hittite, from before thee. —*EXODUS 23:28*

"How big is it?" the bee man at the other end of the line wanted to know. "As big as a basketball?"

"More like a breadbasket," I replied.

"That's a big hornet's nest, I'll come down and get it tonight." And that night, my wife Shirley and I watched as the man did his job, gathering approximately five hundred bald-faced hornets for their venom, which his company will turn into an antidote for people who suffer allergic reactions from stings.

It was while doing some yard work that I had noticed them, buzzing up under the eaves and then disappearing into a huge gray paper nest. The bee man waited until night, when all the hornets would be inside. He anesthetized them with carbon dioxide, which he sprayed into their colony. Then he dislodged the nest and placed it in a paper bag, which he secured with tape. Amazingly, he didn't suffer a single sting from the hornets, or from a yellow jackets' nest he had captured at another place earlier.

"What were hornets and their yellow jacket cousins put here on earth for?" I asked as he prepared to leave. "Do they serve any particular good?"

"Oh, yes, indeed," he answered with a laugh. "Hornets are predators at the top of the insect food chain. They help keep the population of such things as termites, carpenter ants, gypsy moths and grasshoppers under control. Yellow jackets are scavengers. They clean up all kinds of messes."

Maybe you already knew what the bee man told me and didn't need a lesson in Entomology 101, but I did. I'm always fascinated to learn how everything put here by the Designer of the Universe has a place and a purpose—and that includes you and me.

> Open our eyes, dear God,
> Sustain our childlike wonder,
> Give us reverence for every living thing
> Above Your earth, upon Your earth and under.
>
> —*FRED BAUER*

FRI

22 The children whom the Lord hath given me are for signs and for wonders. . . . —*ISAIAH 8:18*

The little boy had been tossed from a second-story window; he had no name and no birth certificate. The folks at the orphanage called him Moses, because they discovered him alone and abandoned. Patrick Klein, the director of Asian Vision, met Moses when he visited Tibet. Pat was carrying several large duffel bags stuffed with the sweaters knitted or crocheted by Guideposts readers. Moses was allowed to pick one out for himself, the first garment he had ever owned.

I hear every day from the army of sweater-makers, who create colorful, warm garments from our simple pattern. They often ask, "Where did my sweater go? Did the child like it? Do you think it saved a life?" Usually there are no specific answers to their questions, because we ship the sweaters, one hundred to a carton, through agencies like World Vision and Heart to Heart that know how to get them where they are needed.

But Pat has hands-on stories to tell about the children. He carries our sweaters with him when he visits missions and orphanages in Asia. On his last trip to Laos and Nepal, he met a group of more than three hundred children clad in T-shirts, which would have been fine if the temperature hadn't been forty degrees.

Melissa Hults volunteers at the Baltimore Pediatric Hospital. Her voice quivers a little as she remembers three-year-old Angelina, who picked out a sweater, then, hesitantly but with pride, pointed to a cow, chicken and pig that were knitted into the design. Melissa's volunteer work also takes her to Central America, Costa Rica and Guatemala. She crams sweaters into her luggage, and wherever she goes she sees the same message in the children's eyes: *Why would someone care enough to make me this sweater?*

More than a hundred thousand children have felt this caring from Guideposts readers, and that in itself is no less than a miracle.

Lord, bless those who use their hands and hearts to help and comfort Your children. —*BRIGITTE WEEKS*

EDITOR'S NOTE: For a free copy of our sweater pattern, send a self-addressed stamped envelope to Guideposts Sweater Project, 16 E. 34th St., New York, NY 10016.

AT THE POINT OF OUR PAIN

For most of her life, Roberta Messner has lived with a chronic illness, neurofibromatosis. While this disorder can take many forms, for Roberta it has meant a lifetime of pain from recurring tumors. For many years, Roberta thought of her plight as a cruel life sentence. Yet hidden inside her illness was a secret she nearly missed: At the point of her pain, the Christ of the Cross was waiting to meet Roberta in a most intimate way. This Holy Week, discover how the very circumstances that threaten to distance us from the Lord can actually bring us closer to Him.   —*THE EDITORS*

SAT
23

Saturday before Palm Sunday

Since the children have flesh and blood, he too shared in their humanity so that by his death he might destroy him who holds the power of death.... —*HEBREWS 2:14 (NIV)*

In 1969, at the age of fifteen, I was diagnosed with neurofibromatosis. Only a handful of people, even among the medical professionals I encountered, had even heard of this baffling disorder. Fewer still could pronounce it, adding to the aloneness and shame I felt. Throughout my teenage and young adult years, I never met anyone who could understand the pain, disfigurement and uncertainty I faced.

Then, thankfully, public-awareness campaigns began to change things. I'll never forget the fall afternoon when I was waiting at the baggage-claim area at the Detroit airport and a billboard with bold white letters printed against a black background caught my eye. "NEURO-FIBRO-MA-TO-SIS," it read. "THINK IT'S HARD TO SAY? TRY LIVING WITH IT."

All at once the fear and isolation that had been my lifelong companions were replaced with the most incredibly comforting feeling: Someone had walked in my shoes and knew exactly how I felt.

For me, that's one of the most compelling messages of Holy Week. The Savior of the world became man so that He could identify with the trials and temptations and, yes, even the questions, of us human beings. When we're burdened with sorrow, care, pain or guilt, He's there with a compassion our earthly loved ones can never equal, waiting to carry our load.

Your struggles are likely very different from mine, but His promise is for you as well: Christ wants to meet you at the point of your pain. Please join me in the week ahead as I recall some of the times He's done just that for me.

Lord, no experience in my life is beyond the reach of Your love. Help me to cast my cares on You.   —ROBERTA MESSNER

SUN   *Palm Sunday*
24   When he came near the place where the road goes down the Mount of Olives, the whole crowd of disciples began joyfully to praise God in loud voices for all the miracles they had seen.   —*LUKE 19:37 (NIV)*

The healing service had been advertised for weeks, and I just knew I was going to find Christ there. I needed Him in the worst way. The tumors in my head were growing fast, making my eyes and face bulge and blurring my vision. The pain was so intense that all I could do was retreat for hours on end to a dark room with an ice pack over my eyes.

I'm not very good public relations for You, God, I prayed as I settled into a pew down front. *Just think, if You would heal me—and I know You can—people would see how mighty You are and be drawn to You. No one sees You in my pain.*

The choir led the crowd in glorious music as a parade of people carrying velvet banners heralding Christ as king marched toward the front of the sanctuary. It reminded me of Jesus' triumphant entry into Jerusalem on that long-ago Palm Sunday, and my heart joined in the celebration. As the expectant crowd raised their hands and voices in praise, I rejoiced in the healing a friend had recently experienced and anticipated the miracle that was sure to take place soon in my own body.

But I wasn't healed, physically speaking, and the inner accusations closed in on me. *You've sinned, Roberta—that's why your tumors keep growing back. You don't have enough faith. Just look at you—you've even failed at being healed.* Angry, I hurled questions at God: *Why me, Lord? Why won't You heal me?*

But even in the heat of my anger, I had a growing sense of His power and presence. And as I began to trust that God knew exactly what I needed, the answers to my questions no longer seemed so important. It hadn't happened the way I hoped it would when I walked into the service, but I had found Christ there after all.

King of Glory, You have always been there, working Your wondrous miracles in my life.   —*ROBERTA MESSNER*

MON
25
Monday in Holy Week
"It is written," he said to them, " 'My house will be called a house of prayer,' but you are making it a 'den of robbers.' "   —*MATTHEW 21:13 (NIV)*

It was the most unlikely place to learn a lesson about Holy Week. I was shopping at an outdoor flea market, admiring what I thought was an antique cast-iron doorstop—a stately colonial lady holding a bouquet of flowers in her pristine gloved hands. But as I ran my fingers over her blue antebellum dress, something didn't feel quite right. The edges of her dress were too rough, not worn smooth by the passage of time. She wasn't as heavy as the old pieces I'd examined before. And her paint job was nearly perfect—too perfect, it seemed, to have survived nearly a century of slamming doors.

I left the doorstop and resumed my stroll through the market. As I made my way through the booths, I overheard a conversation between two antique dealers about the growing problem of reproductions infiltrating the antiques market. Cast-iron toys and doorstops, pottery, graniteware, advertising signs—you name it, and there's a fool-the-eye imitation to trap the unknowing. But there is a way to avoid being taken in by con artists, I learned as I listened more closely: Study the *real* thing, not the fake.

Looks can be deceiving, but as I seek to understand, Jesus will surely purge my life of all that isn't His, just as He drove those money changers from the temple. Today, I'm asking Him to rid my heart of the lies that separate me from Him, the doubts that tell me there is no purpose to my suffering. The way to victory is not to learn everything I can about the den of robbers in my path. It's to get to know God—through the reading of His Word and prayerful communion with Him—so I can always recognize the real thing.

Dear Lord, yesterday, today and forever, You are "the real thing." Help me to discern Your truth in the midst of the counterfeits.
—ROBERTA MESSNER

TUE
26
Tuesday in Holy Week
"I tell you the truth," he said, "this poor widow has put in more than all the others. All these people gave their gifts out of their wealth; but she out of her poverty put in all she had to live on." —LUKE 21:3-4 (NIV)

It took every ounce of energy I had to fill the basket. My out-of-town friend was going through a rough time. Her husband had recently left her and she admitted to me that lately she'd never felt more unloved and unlovely. When I prayed about it, the idea came to me to make her a "Tea Party" basket. I found a pretty little teapot and cup and saucer, some herbal teas and cookies, and wrapped it all up with a phone card and instructions to call me whenever her heart needed a lift and we would have "tea for two" by telephone.

To find just the right things, I had to shop at several stores. If I hadn't been in so much pain, it would have been pure pleasure, but by the time I finished up at the mall, I was so weary that I found myself stopping every few feet to rest. I couldn't stop comparing myself to friends who were strong and healthy, who juggled a full-time job, children, church and community work, and still managed to have fun, when I could sometimes barely make it through another day.

A few days later, my friend telephoned, eager to begin our tea party. "This is the dearest thing anybody ever thought of," she told me. "You never complain, but all I could think about was how you must have gone from store to store to find all these things, then waited in line at the post office with your head throbbing. It meant even more knowing that you did this for me when you feel so bad yourself."

Lord, when I reach the end of myself, You do Your very best work. Take everything I have—including my weakness—and use it for Your glory.
—ROBERTA MESSNER

WED
27

Wednesday in Holy Week
Then Mary took about a pint of pure nard, an expensive perfume; she poured it on Jesus' feet and wiped his feet with her hair. And the house was filled with the fragrance of the perfume.   —*JOHN 12:3 (NIV)*

On my fortieth birthday, I was scheduled for surgery to remove a large tumor growing in my left eye socket. The day before the operation, as I was scrambling to tie up loose ends at work, I got a phone call: "We need you right away in the conference room to finish writing up the Management Briefing."

To my great surprise, as I elbowed the conference room door open with an armload of bulging files, I was greeted by a standing-room-only crowd shouting, "Happy birthday!" My co-workers had orchestrated a lavish lunch buffet and now showered me with presents.

I received a mug with my name on it, a robe and slippers to take to the hospital, and many other "I love you" gifts. And then I got a totally frivolous present—an autograph dog, just like the one a childhood friend had received when she was ten and had her tonsils taken out. When we played jacks in her bedroom, I'd often pick it up and study all those scribbles, wondering what it would be like to be the recipient of so many get-well wishes.

There was no escaping the major surgery that was ahead of me the very next day. Yet for a blessed one-hour reprieve, I didn't have to dwell on the surgery, the pain and the possible complications; I could simply bask in the extravagant love of my friends.

Lord, help me always to give with abandon.

—*ROBERTA MESSNER*

THU
28

Maundy Thursday
And he took bread, gave thanks and broke it, and gave it to them, saying, "This is my body given for you; do this in remembrance of me."   —*LUKE 22:19 (NIV)*

Shortly after I moved into "The Leaning Log," the cabin I was renovating, I visited the Sunday-morning service at a nearby church. The sermon was titled "Gratitude: the Heart's Memory," and the minister reminisced about his walk with the Lord—his conversion, the cool waters of his baptism, people who had believed in him and how God was with him when he entered the ministry and was still unsure that God could use such an ordinary man to do His work.

That last part really got to me because I was certain I could no longer be of any use to God. I was recovering from an injury, and there didn't seem to be any prospect of my returning to work. Add to that the daily pain of my chronic illness, and I had a prescription for failure.

When I made my way down to the front of the sanctuary to participate in Communion, the pastor handed me the cup and bread symbolizing Christ's blood and broken body, and simply said, "Remember." Back in my pew, that single word consumed me, and I began thinking about some of the things that had happened in my life: the fall that could easily have broken my neck had I not landed on a thick pile of carpeting and foam padding; the countless spiritual falls into sin and selfishness—Christ had been there, too, offering forgiveness and endless new beginnings; and how Christ had always been with me during my years of chronic pain. Surely He wasn't finished with me yet; surely He still had a plan for me.

Do this in remembrance of me. I lifted my cup and whispered a hundred thank-yous.

Savior, on this day and always, help me to remember all You've done for me.
—ROBERTA MESSNER

FRI	*Good Friday*
29	Then said Jesus, Father, forgive them; for they know not what they do. . . . —*LUKE 23:34*

My doctor had ordered a new pain patch that had amazing results. The fun-loving Roberta was back, full of pep and planning, and when I decided to go on a weekend shopping extravaganza, I asked my sister and a new friend to come along.

We had a great time, but on the dark, rainy drive home, my new patch fell off. Not realizing it would lessen its effectiveness, I secured the old (and very expensive) one to my arm with some adhesive tape. It wasn't long before I had a violent headache and was pulling off the side of the road. My sister took over the driving and I curled up in the backseat.

Soon I heard my friend remark to my sister, as if I wasn't there, "We're never going to get home at this rate. Does she get any worse than this? I don't know how you stand it." Her words hurt me in a place down deep that I didn't know existed. I'd planned our trip down to the tiniest detail, tiptoed to the hotel kitchenette each morning to brew a pot of coffee and brought a cup with a cinnamon roll to my friend's bedside, carried her packages when her arms got tired.

Then seemingly out of the blue, Jesus' words, spoken from the Cross, flashed into my mind: "Father, forgive them; for they know not what they do." It was as if I were hearing them for the first time. Of course! My friend couldn't know what I was going through—she'd never been ill herself. And maybe she hadn't meant to be unkind but was just frustrated, or even scared.

When I got back to work, I printed that Scripture on an index card and taped it inside my desk drawer. It never fails to take my eyes back to the Cross, to a forgiveness beyond my understanding.

What freedom there is, Lord, in Your model of forgiveness in the midst of pain.   —*ROBERTA MESSNER*

SAT
30

Holy Saturday
So they went and made the tomb secure by putting a seal on the stone and posting the guard.
—*MATTHEW 27:66 (NIV)*

I was waiting for the results of my MRI that Saturday, worried that the doctor's grim prediction was right and I had a new tumor. I couldn't abide the waiting; doubts tormented me at every turn and my fate seemed sealed beyond hope. *Is Jesus really Who He says He is?* I wondered. *Is there really a plan to all of this?*

It was then that a call came from the hospital where a nurse-friend of mine works. A young lady I'll call Joan, who also has neurofibromatosis, had tried to commit suicide, and my friend had thought I might be willing to talk with her. I couldn't imagine what good I could possibly do, but I agreed.

When I met with Joan, the first thing she asked was to see all my scars. Like battlefield veterans, we were soon sharing war stories of the loneliness, the pain and the surgeries that had left scars both visible and hidden. Joan, whose speech was garbled because of the tumors growing in her mouth, reached for my hand and said, "You understand my every *hurt*-felt need." Her words may not have come out exactly as she intended, but they spoke volumes to my waiting heart.

In my time of waiting, when I was convinced nothing was happening, God had used me—and my pain—to comfort someone else. It's just as Paul says in II Corinthians 1:3-4 (NIV): "Praise be to the God and Father of our Lord Jesus Christ . . . who comforts us in all our troubles, so that we can comfort those in any trouble with the comfort we ourselves have received from God."

Lord, thank You for the precious scars You bear as witnesses of Your love for me. Help me to use my scars to share the good news of Your love.

—*ROBERTA MESSNER*

SUN
31

Easter Sunday
Greater love hath no man than this, that a man lay down his life for his friends. —*JOHN 15:13*

I was nine years old when I asked Jesus to be my Savior. I couldn't get over that fact that someone had died for *me*—the one with the pigtails and ugly Coke-bottle glasses who was always the last one chosen for any game at school—and that He had a special plan for my life.

That feeling stayed with me through many years and difficult circumstances, but my mother's death in April 1999 virtually drained my joy. Living with chronic pain seemed too hard, and I wished God would take me home.

One morning as I was getting ready to help my sister Rebekkah move some furniture, I asked God, "Don't You think I've done this long enough? I'm not a good witness for You as I used to be." Later that day, the white pickup we'd rented was parked with the driver's door open when it began to roll down a hill, headed for some houses and a cliff. I panicked and tried to save the day by jumping into the truck. The next thing I knew, I was on the ground with a huge tire barreling toward my head. Rebekkah knocked me out of the way, putting herself in the path of the truck.

When we both crawled out from under the truck alive, I overheard onlookers marveling at how my sister had saved my life. The thought of it consumed me: *Someone was willing to give her own life so I might live.* Suddenly, I was nine years old again, remembering the One Who on Calvary's Cross gladly suffered in my stead, the One Whose power over death promises victory even when it seems I can't possibly make a difference. And, suddenly, I wanted to live—really live.

Precious Savior, thank You for the abundant life You promised me by Your Resurrection. —*ROBERTA MESSNER*

My Days of Prayer

1 _____

2 _____

3 _____

4 _____

5 _____

6 _____

7 _____

8 _____

9 _____

10 _____

11 _____

12 _____

13 _____

14 _____

15 _____

16 _____

17 _____

18 _____

19 _____

20 _____

21 _____

22 _____

23 _____

24 _____

25 _____

26 _____

27 _____

28 _____

29 _____

30 _____

31 _____

April

Where two or three are gathered together in my name, there am I in the midst of them.

—*Matthew 18:20*

S	M	T	W	T	F	S
	1	2	3	4	5	6
7	8	9	10	11	12	13
14	15	16	17	18	19	20
21	22	23	24	25	26	27
28	29	30				

AT THE POINT OF OUR PAIN

MON
1

Easter Monday
Mary of Magdala went to the disciples with the news: "I have seen the Lord!" —*JOHN 20:18 (NIV)*

Back in my office at work the Monday after Easter, I'm playing one of my favorite CDs, "Songs of the Resurrection," by pianist Stan Whitmire. I find myself listening again and again to his beautiful rendition of "I've Just Seen Jesus." I think of how, in my human reaction to pain, I fail Christ every single day of my life. When I'm shaken by fear, anger, doubt or defeat, He's there at the very point of my pain, understanding every emotion and sharing every struggle I face.

This morning, I walked into work with a co-worker who told me about her father's cancer and inquired about my own health. "You've been through all that and you still trust the Lord?" she asked, shaking her head.

My heart overflowed with the promise of Easter and I assured her, "Jesus will be there for your father. Always. No matter what lies ahead."

At long last, I'm beginning to understand that there are many levels of healing. While my human nature longs for a permanent physical touch of Christ's healing hand, I'm trusting more in His will and special purpose for me. If people are listening to my life, I want them to hear the message of Easter, a promise of hope despite outward circumstances. I want them to know I've seen the Lord.

My journey toward Easter has been long and circuitous, and it continues today. The process is anything but precise and predictable, yet the outcome is always victory when I place my trust and hope in the One Who is the Victor.

Each time I enter Your presence, victorious Savior, I get a glimpse of Your Easter glory. Thank You. —*ROBERTA MESSNER*

THE PRAYER THAT IS ALWAYS NEW

TUE

2   Our Father . . . *Hallowed* be thy name.   —*MATTHEW 6:9*

My flight had been delayed yet again, and the boarding area at JFK was filled with disgruntled travelers. In a corner, two young men in long black coats and wide-brimmed hats bowed rhythmically toward a wall, rapt in worship. I didn't know the words the young Hasidic Jews were saying, but because they prayed I suddenly saw, not a noisy airport corridor, but a hallowed space.

When I first learned the Lord's Prayer years ago, I puzzled over the words "hallowed be thy name." "To hallow," says the dictionary, "is to make holy." How could the name of God be "made" holy! Wasn't it already holy—the holiest thing I could imagine?

Jesus must be telling us, I realized, not that our prayers create holiness, but that prayer opens our eyes to the Father's holiness inscribed on everything around us: people, trees, skies, airports.

In a crowded terminal, two young men invoked God's presence among fretful travelers and blaring loudspeakers. Silently I joined in with the Lord's Prayer. "Our Father. . . ."

And at the word *hallowed*, I did indeed see differently. I saw the overhead monitor screens and the plastic chairs bolted together in rows in a new light—the light of His infinite love for everyone there: the tired-looking Arab family with the crying baby, the harried clerk at the check-in counter.

God's arms are over and around and beneath us every moment of our lives. To hallow His name is to open our eyes and look.

Our Father, show me Your holiness in unexpected places today.
                        —*ELIZABETH SHERRILL*

EDITOR'S NOTE: How has God been renewing your life through prayer this year? Please take a few moments to look back at what you've written in "My Days of Prayer," and let us know how your prayers have changed your life. Send your letter to *Daily Guideposts* Reader's Room, Guideposts Books, 16 E. 34th St., New York, NY 10016. We'll share some of what you tell us in a future *Daily Guideposts*.

WED
3

Be completely humble and gentle; be patient, bearing with one another in love. —*EPHESIANS 4:2 (NIV)*

I struggled to adjust to our new pastor, whose strict, follow-every-letter-of-the-law approach drastically differed from that of his easygoing, jovial predecessor. I'm ashamed to admit it, but I learned a jolting lesson last week.

During Holy Week, our pastor seemed short, even angry. At first I figured that his grouchiness was due to the busy schedule of Holy Week services. Then I formed a negative judgement: *Instead of being in the true spirit of the week, he's obsessed with trivial details.*

At the Holy Saturday midnight service, he was still grumpy. Again, I let the mental criticisms flow. I compared him with his predecessor, who simply radiated joy at Easter. At the end of the agape meal after the Easter Liturgy, everyone departed hugging each other and joyfully shouting, "Christ is risen! He is risen indeed!" But our pastor barely returned our greetings, and I thought, *He hasn't smiled once today. What a sourpuss!*

On the Wednesday after Easter, we went to church to have our family photo taken for the new directory and learned that the pastor was in the hospital with gallstones and would be having surgery the next day. The lady in charge of the directory told us his condition and said, "I thought he was rather irritable last week, but now I know why! Here he was in intense pain all week, especially during the midnight Easter service, and he was trying not to complain."

How I wished I had given him the benefit of the doubt. Why, what I critically viewed as "his perfectionist obsession with details" can be an asset to our parish—the richer ceremonies and the beauty of the church this year were due to his oversight. I resolved to try to appreciate his new ways.

Lord, when someone near me is busy and irritated, remind me to offer help instead of judgments. —*MARY BROWN*

THU

4 Then God opened her eyes. . . . *—GENESIS 21:19 (NIV)*

For the last few years, I've been working independently for several groups on projects instead of as a full-time employee. This means I have lost the support of having an assistant, office equipment, telephone, automobile and filing system at my fingertips. One day, while trying to meet several competing demands at once, my car broke down. I was pacing up and down at the repair shop looking at my watch and figuring there was no way to get downtown to the next meeting on time.

Glancing up the street, I noticed a square black pillar with a bold M on top underlined by an orange stripe. It was a Metro stop, just two blocks away, and the trains there were capable of whisking me past rush-hour traffic and into the city in under fifteen minutes. As a newcomer to urban life, I hadn't known where to look for an alternative to my car.

Settled comfortably into my seat a few minutes later, I reflected that there were probably other resources around me, different from what I was used to, but capable of meeting my needs if I would just look up and see them. That's probably true in your life, too: Look around this week for all the alternatives God provides to help you on your journey.

Thank You, Lord, for the myriad ways You provide for me each and every day. *—ERIC FELLMAN*

FRI

5 He is not far from each one of us. *—ACTS 17:27 (NAS)*

My husband Leo and I heard footsteps as we sat at my sister Zelma's bedside, quietly visiting with her as she lay in the palliative care ward of the hospital. Looking toward the door, we recognized Sister Rose of the Grey Nuns.

She approached the bed and took Zelma's frail hands in hers. "I just came to bring you a little love. I brought some this morning, and I thought that you might've run out by this time. But, no! I see your visitors have brought you fresh love. I'll come back later."

Sister Rose peddled God's love like a door-to-door salesman giving out free samples. After a long career in nursing and several additional years of chaplaincy, she knew the loneliness and fear of terminal cancer patients. Day after day she cheerfully made her rounds, holding one patient's hands, stroking another patient's brow. Assisting the helpless, quieting the restless, praying with the anxious, soothing the fearful, she was tenderness personified.

"You must have some interesting stories to tell," I said to her one day as we shared a cup of coffee in the visitors' lounge. "What touches you the most?"

"The way God changes people," she replied without hesitation. "I have seen many a person arrive on this ward without a speck of faith, and that is sad. But I can tell you something else. When people finally realize there's no hope except in God, they find that God is enough. And He is so loving," she said, "that it takes only this much faith." She held her thumb to her index finger with only a crack between.

That's about the diameter of a mustard seed, I thought, as I returned to Zelma's bedside. Jesus said that's all the faith we need in order to move mountains, even mountains of doubt.

"Have you seen Sister Rose today?" Zelma asked weakly as I approached the bedside. "I enjoy her visits."

Her words alone told me Sister Rose had not only been peddling love, she had been planting seeds of hope.

Lord, when love seems in short supply, make me a faithful messenger caring for those who suffer. —*ALMA BARKMAN*

SAT

6

Blessed are they that mourn: for they shall be comforted.
—*MATTHEW 5:4*

I had prayed for this to be just another day, but on the first anniversary of my mother's death I awoke to a wet and windy Saturday in the Berkshire Hills, the kind of raw early April morning that makes spring seem hopelessly far off. I'd wanted to hike a favorite stretch of the Appalachian Trail, but the weather sabotaged my plans and I found myself wandering aimlessly through one of the musty secondhand bookstores for which this part of Massachusetts is known.

I needed another book like I needed a hole in my head, as Mom would have put it. I missed Mom saying things like that, missed them more than I ever imagined I would. I thought her long decline from Alzheimer's had prepared me for her death, but sometimes my feelings about losing her were unexpectedly poignant, like today.

As my eyes roamed the shelves, a title on a worn red spine leapt out at me: *The Southpaw's Secret.*

It was a boys' book, part of the relatively short-lived Mel Martin mystery series by John R. Cooper that I'd been crazy about when I was a kid. Mel Martin was a high-school baseball star, and a crafty sleuth to boot. The books had already gone out of print by the time I read the two volumes I inherited from my older brother, but I was hooked. I don't know how many hours Mom spent helping me hunt down the other Mel Martin books.

Mom was a great sleuth herself, especially when it came to finding things for me: the Beatles' first album, for instance, which sold out the Monday after their historic appearance on *The Ed Sullivan Show.* Mom was able to unearth a copy in a tiny electronics store in Walled Lake, Michigan, about thirty miles from our house. Mom spent half her life finding obscure stuff I had to have.

Except *The Southpaw's Secret,* the one Mel Martin book she never was able to track down. And now it had found me. After all these years.

You are there, Lord, to help us find what we need.

—*EDWARD GRINNAN*

SUN
7
Sing psalms, hymns and spiritual songs with gratitude in your hearts to God.   —*COLOSSIANS 3:16 (NIV)*

The scratchiness in my throat was definitely growing worse as we rehearsed Easter anthems at Wednesday-night choir practice. By the time it was my turn to launch into the triumphant Alleluia, the solo I looked forward to singing all year, I could barely whisper. Laryngitis had silenced me.

It wasn't fair! Just last Christmas another severe head cold and bout with laryngitis had prevented me from singing with the eighty-voice Community Christmas Chorale. Since I had no family for two thousand miles and worked outside of town, singing with the church and community choirs helped me to feel that I belonged somewhere. Yet here I was, sidelined again.

Easter morning seemed unusually serene without the frantic rush to church for early vocal warm-ups, sleepy children in tow. In fact, our family enjoyed a leisurely breakfast and a chance to savor my braided Easter bread—and each other. I didn't know Sunday morning could be so calm!

Even with the overflow Easter congregation, we sat in our regular pew. My children, who usually sat with friends when I sang, basked in the unaccustomed coziness. When did we last sit together as a family at Easter?

Since I had rehearsed for several weeks before the laryngitis hit, I found myself lip-synching all the anthems. The substitute soloist motioned for us to stand as she began the joyous Alleluia. Despite my regret at not leading it, I found myself singing with gusto—soundlessly. A lip-synch Alleluia? Why not? The joy begins in my heart, not in my mouth. Singing only makes it louder!

Now I noticed for the first time the sweet, tentative voices of the worshipers around me: the elderly couple, the bashful widow, the teenager. I quickly resolved to sing more softly in the future; I'd probably been drowning them out for years!

Heavenly Father, thank You for the praise that fills my heart even when my voice is still. —*GAIL THORELL SCHILLING*

MON
8
"I will bring the blind by a way that they did not know; I will lead them in paths they have not known...."
—*ISAIAH 42:16 (NKJV)*

My wife Sharon was sitting in the porch swing when a delivery truck pulled up and the driver called out, "How do you get to the junior college?"

For several minutes she struggled with street names and landmarks. Finally, in frustration, she pointed to the northwest and said, "It's over that way!"

The driver smiled and waved. "That's all I need to know!"

It was a reminder to me that there are usually a number of alternative ways to get somewhere in life. When God answers my prayers, He knows a lot of different ways to do it. I'm afraid I have a bad habit of asking Him for something, then telling Him how to do it!

"Lord, I need a vacation. Help me to sell this story, so I can afford one." I never sold the story, but my publisher—out of the clear blue—invited me on an expense-paid trip to California.

"Lord, punish that noxious student who makes my life miserable. Send him to another school, or maybe into the Marines." Instead, the student came to me unbidden and apologized for his rebellion.

When I pray, "Father, show me the way," I need to be prepared for detours and side roads, if necessary. Sometimes He may take me through a dark tunnel, up a mountainous ridge or even backward for a few miles. The God of Creation has a lot of angles.

"It's over that way," God says when I ask for greater happiness. And I will watch with interest and an open mind to see how He gets me there.

From now on, God, I'll try to let You do the leading, and I'll do the following.
—*DANIEL SCHANTZ*

TUE

9

I have written to you . . . encouraging you. . . .
—*I PETER 5:12 (NIV)*

I love e-mail! It's a casual, almost instantaneous way of communicating, especially with our children, some of who are currently living in Africa. But I also miss the special pleasure of receiving "snail-mail"—noting the stamp, slitting open the envelope, unfolding and holding in my hand words put to paper by someone who cares about me.

It seems like a lot more trouble to write a real letter—find the stamps, select some stationery, find the address and a pen that works. But we have some friends who help me keep that "inconvenience" in perspective.

Several times a year we get letters from our Tanzanian friends, the Kimambos. We've been in their home, and we know they don't have a drawer devoted to varieties of note cards and letter paper, as we have in our study. Our last letter from them was written on two sheets of paper from different school tablets, held together with a straight pin. And because they don't know English, they have to walk to a friend's house and dictate their letter to her in Swahili, which she translates into English and writes down. Then it's off to the stationer's to buy an envelope, and to the post office to buy a stamp and mail the letter. Their letters are a great gift to us, a source of encouragement and joy.

114 · APRIL 2002

Isn't there someone in your life who would appreciate hearing from you today? Find some paper and a pen. Writing a letter is a wonderful way to tell someone you care.

Lord of all things, may my words to a friend bring encouragement and love.
—*MARY JANE CLARK*

10
Thus saith the Lord, Refrain thy voice from weeping, and thine eyes from tears: for thy work shall be rewarded. ...
—*JEREMIAH 31:16*

Ten months ago, I moved to San Diego, California, to be the co-creative director of a small advertising agency, in tandem with a woman I'd worked with in New York. It didn't take me long to figure out I simply wasn't qualified for the position; my partner, however, was highly qualified, which only heightened the pressure I felt to perform. Not only did I feel that I was doing poorly, my performance was in glaring contrast to her brilliance on the job.

My passionate partner, however, misjudged our boss's ability to accept her outbursts of anger. After six months, he took me aside and said, "I'm going to fire your partner, and I want you to step up and take control."

If I wasn't able to do the job in tandem with someone else, how was I going to do it by myself? I was scared. I felt as if I were the keeper of a terrible secret: I couldn't do the job, and the task before me was to keep everybody in the agency from finding out.

As the days went by, I thought more and more about quitting. But then I read something an advertising pioneer wrote just before he left the agency he had created and turned into a giant: "I'm leaving my agency because I'm no longer scared. As soon as I walk out of these doors for the last time, I'm going to climb a tree and walk out to the end of the thinnest branch I can find."

So I've decided to embrace the fear and trust God to use it to allow me to grow into the job. Isn't that what faith is all about?

Lord, You, too, felt fear on the Mount of Olives. Help me remember that faith is stronger than fear.
—*DAVE FRANCO*

THU
11
We also thank God constantly. . . .
—I THESSALONIANS 2:13 (RSV)

I have a favorite silver choker necklace with little gold x's on it, and every time I wear it, I'm reminded of God's extravagant love.

I'd been at a MOPS (Mothers of Preschoolers) Convention in Pennsylvania for several days, teaching workshops and doing leadership training. I felt tired, and when I'm tired, I sometimes do dumb things. On the last afternoon of the last day, I ran into a distinguished-looking lady I barely knew. She was wearing a unique gold-and-silver necklace that exactly matched the gold-and-silver ring my husband Lynn had given me on our anniversary the year before.

"Oh, Barbara, I love your necklace, and look how perfectly it matches my ring," I gushed, holding up my right hand to show her. "May I have it?" I assumed my goofy grin would assure her that it was a humorous, absurd question.

Without a moment's hesitation, she took off her necklace and placed it around my neck. "I would be delighted for you to have it," she said, smiling graciously.

I scarcely heard her next words about having too many necklaces and hardly ever wearing this one. I was too embarrassed and too busy falling all over myself, trying to take back my thoughtless words.

"Oh, no, no, no, Barbara. You don't understand. I didn't really mean that I wanted your necklace. Sometimes I say foolish things like that, but I was only kidding. I'm so sorry. I can't take your necklace!"

She looked directly into my eyes. "I want you to have this necklace," she said, kindly but firmly. "So please, just accept it." Then she walked away, leaving me totally speechless and totally humbled.

I wore the necklace the rest of the day. I wore it on the plane home, and I wore it all the next day. I still wear it more than any other necklace, because when I do, it reminds me of a Savior named Jesus, Who gives me the kind of love I don't deserve, and just wants me to accept it.

Jesus, may I pass the story of Your extravagant love and grace on to others.
—CAROL KUYKENDALL

READER'S ROOM

During 1999, I took each of the verses of the Twenty-third Psalm at the beginning of the month and incorporated it into "My Faith Journey." For instance, in April I wrote, "Lord, You restore my soul as I color Easter eggs; as I believe in another human being, or as I pray under a starry sky." In July I wrote, "You comfort me, Lord, as I drive through the countryside; as I float in the pool or as I listen to a two-year-old sing." In October, "My cup overflows with being creative, watching a spider spin her web or basking in a palette of fall colors." And in December, "I dwell with the Lord as I listen to Christmas music, hold newborn twins or clean the house."

—*BEVERLY ZAMBITO, ELDERSBURG, MARYLAND*

FRI

12

The Lord seeth not as man seeth, for man looketh on the outward appearance, but the Lord looketh on the heart.
—*I SAMUEL 16:7*

It was the first warm day of spring, and my children and I headed toward the playground to exercise our winter-weary bodies. Mary, who was crawling the previous fall, now explored eagerly, deftly climbing stairs and whizzing down the baby slide. Her famous smile (famous at least in our neighborhood) grew wider and wider. I smiled, too. I love to see my kids happy. After about ten minutes, she moved over to the big kids' equipment. Up she scrambled, tiny legs stretching mightily to get up waist-high steps. Down she came on the five-foot slide. She did it many times.

Then, in a flash, Mary was at the monkey bars. I watched from a short distance away, knowing she could not get up higher than the first rung. Where she got her athletic ability I don't know. But I was proud of her, pleased with her energy and independence. Mary grinned at me, face peering over the second rung. Then, just as it occurred to me that she could slip and bash her mouth, she did. Hard.

I raced over. She was bleeding and her lip was a mess, but it didn't bother her much. In less than a minute she wriggled out of my arms and ran off to play some more.

Some time later, Mary came over for a hug and smiled gloriously, just for me. I stared in horror. Her two upper front teeth were chipped. Not badly, but each had an obvious ding.

My heart sank. My precious girl had a noticeable flaw. I mentally ran through the accidents that would have been worse, but still my foolish, worldly heart said, *Why, oh why, did it have to be her beautiful smile?*

Being closer to God than I, Mary did not share my vanity. She grinned through her imperfections, showering me with the same love she'd always exuded, and headed for the slide once more.

Father, You love me in spite of my imperfections. Help me also to see through the flaws of others as You see through mine.

—*JULIA ATTAWAY*

SAT

13

For where two or three are gathered together in my name, there am I in the midst of them.   —*MATTHEW 18:20*

I stood in the middle of the busy department store, locked in my own sorrow. My daughter had just been hospitalized for an overdose of drugs and alcohol. No matter how hard I prayed, she kept going downhill. Now her life hung in the balance. As I gazed ahead, I spied Armando Llanos and quickly turned away. I hadn't seen Armando or his wife Eva for some time, and he didn't know about my trauma.

But I didn't get away from Armando fast enough. "Shari, how are you?" he called in his heavily accented English as I tried to duck into another aisle. A native of Colombia, he'd lived a rough life. A dramatic conversion had turned him around, and now he talked about Jesus wherever he went. As he approached, I couldn't stop my tears from welling up, so I told him about my daughter.

"We need to pray, sister," he said softly, putting a hand on my shoulder. Then, to my embarrassment, he began to pray aloud right there in the bath-and-bedding department.

Armando's prayer seemed inappropriate and out of place, and I was embarrassed as I felt the stares of people rushing by. Yet, somewhere in the middle of the prayer, a warm rush of love filled me. "Jesus is going to heal your daughter," Armando said when he finished, his face glowing. "But it may take some time, like it did with me."

Jesus did heal my daughter. And it did take some time—several more years, in fact. But Armando's prayer had two immediate results: It pulled me out of my depression, and it taught me that our Lord isn't ashamed of being called on anywhere, even in a department store.

Jesus, help me to keep my pride from getting in the way of my prayer.

—SHARI SMYTH

SUN
14

Strengthened with all might, according to his glorious power, unto all patience and longsuffering with joyfulness.

—COLOSSIANS 1:11

I hadn't been to Barcelona since 1965, and I was impatient to find out what had been done to the Sagrada Familia. This is an enormous church, largely the brainchild of the architect Antoni Gaudi, who spent more than forty years of his life conceiving and shaping it. It was unfinished at his death in 1926, but construction continued, paid for, not by the Catholic Church or the government, but by people who believed in his work. Gaudi's unique structure has achieved international attention, so much so that you can't mention Barcelona without saying "Gaudi" in the same breath.

I had been awestruck when I first saw the four towers, which ascend to a dizzying height, embellished with scenes of the birth of Jesus, all done in fanciful, original, unbelievable detail. It didn't matter that Gaudi's art was not to my taste; it impressed me like the pyramids of Egypt or the Hoover Dam. This was the east front; the west would eventually depict the Passion; and the south, the Glory. The saints and angels, the twelve Apostles, Jesus Christ and God the Creator, all would have a place in a temple in which fifteen thousand people would worship.

After thirty-five years, much work had been accomplished. The entire façade of the Passion had risen, and its four towers complemented those of the Nativity, to my special delight. But I was in for a shock. "We are about at the fifty-percent point," said the guide.

"You mean that since 1890 you've only gotten halfway?" I was astounded and, as I had been on first seeing Sagrada Familia, impatient. "Why, I won't be alive to see it finished."

"Gaudi won't be, either," said the guide, and then added a quote from the very religious Gaudi that has stood me in good stead ever since: " 'My client is in no hurry.' "

You find ways to placate even my impatience, don't You, Lord?

—*VAN VARNER*

MON
15

And Ruth said, Intreat me not to leave thee, or to return from following after thee: for whither thou goest, I will go.... —*RUTH 1:16*

The cavernous Union Depot in St. Paul, Minnesota, was the first scheduled stop for the traveling *Titanic* exhibit. I waited patiently in line for the chance to see what haunting mysteries the sea had yielded after more than eighty years. Wandering by each display case, I felt one poignant stab after another as I gazed at a child's marbles, some of them cracked in two; a broken clarinet, corroded an eerie green; a man's safety razor and blades, laid out ready to use; the backs of a woman's mirror and brush set; a deck of playing cards, fully restored by freeze-drying them; and a jar of fat olives, meant for the dining room.

As if this weren't enough, every so often a recording of the *Titanic*'s magnificent whistles blew through the crowded, subdued room. It was easy to imagine how that sound must have thrilled the passengers leaning over the rails. The whistles could be heard for eleven miles.

But the most impressive discovery for me was the account of the matronly, gray-haired Ida Straus. According to the story, she stepped back out of the lifeboat about to carry her to safety, allowing her maid to take her place, and calmly told her husband, "We have been living together for many years and where you go, I go." Together they went down with the ship.

Ruth's statement to her mother-in-law Naomi, "Where thou goest, I will go," has been repeated by brides and grooms in many modern-day weddings. But I never truly understood it until I stepped on board the *Titanic* eighty-seven years after it sank, and overheard Mrs. Straus.

Timeless Lord, thank You for great examples from the past that help me to live my present more fully for You. —*CAROL KNAPP*

THE PRACTICE OF PRAYER

TUE
16

Trusting Prayer
"This is how you should pray: 'Our Father. . . .' "
—*MATTHEW 6:9 (NIV)*

When I was four years old, my family went on an outing to Dale Hollow, a crystal-clear lake near the Tennessee-Kentucky border. One minute, I was lolling in the bow of the boat as we floated along; the next minute, I was being lifted up in my daddy's arms and tossed out into the water. I trusted my father completely, so I was not alarmed. I sank deep into the water, than swam straight up. As I broke the surface gasping for air, I sputtered, "Next time you do that, Daddy, tell me first."

A hundred such stories are stored in my memory: clinging to Daddy's back as he dove off a rocky cliff; jumping from a high tree limb straight into his arms. He wanted me to be confident. He didn't want me to be afraid. And because he was my daddy, I never was.

As I delve deeper into the practice of prayer, intent on developing an open, honest relationship with God, I find a particular strength in the way Jesus taught His disciples to pray. When Jesus tells us to call God our Father, He's telling us that God loves us, accepts us, wants to be with us. We can do nothing to make God love us more; we can do nothing to cause Him to love us less.

So when you pray, don't hide your fears and gloss over your feelings. Talk with God as though you trust Him enough to jump out of a tree and straight into His arms.

It's me, Father, your daughter Pam. My day has turned chaotic. Earlier, I put my trust in a colleague and instead of doing what was right, she did what was easy and I was the one who lost. Now images of revenge are creeping into my thoughts. I crave a calm heart, a peaceful demeanor, a kind attitude. Help me, today, to remember to believe in my best self.   —*PAM KIDD*

WED

17

Therefore all things whatsoever ye would that men should do to you, do ye even so to them. . . . —*MATTHEW 7:12*

When I was in college, I worked as a waitress in a large, busy restaurant. The owners trained the staff well, but they were not very tolerant of mistakes, and on every table there were cards for the customers to write down their comments about the food and service. Most customers didn't bother with them.

One evening, however, I brought a couple the wrong soup, and they became furious. They said they were going to complain to the manager about me, and reached for one of the cards. I fought hard to hold back my tears because I was afraid I would lose my job, but I did my best to be courteous.

Another couple at the next table must have heard the remarks, because when I took their order, they smiled and told me to take my time bringing their food because they weren't in a hurry. That gave me time to pull myself together.

Later, as we were closing, the restaurant manager said he had two comment cards for me. One accused me of being careless and stupid. The other described me as thoughtful and efficient, and said I had been attentive in spite of a difficult encounter at another table. "This second card saved your job," the manager told me.

Ever since then I have made an effort to thank people who do their jobs well, no matter what those jobs may be. I try to be specific about what they have done well. Sometimes I put my gratitude in letters. I don't know whether my efforts have saved anyone's job or made a difference in anyone's life, but they mean something to me. I know how it feels to be appreciated for something I've done, and I just like to pass on the feeling.

Dear Lord Jesus, You are so quick to applaud me, for even my smallest accomplishments. Help me to be like You with others. Amen.

—*PHYLLIS HOBE*

THU	The twenty-four Elders fell down before the Lamb, each
18	with a harp and golden vials filled with incense—the prayers of God's people! —*REVELATION 5:8 (TLB)*

My prayer life was dragging. I'd been asking God to do work in my son's life for more than fifteen years, and I'd become weary. "Give it up, Marion," I kept telling myself. Discouragement and I had become great pals.

Then one day a package arrived from an old friend whom I hadn't seen in twenty-five years. I smiled, remembering her tremendous faith, and was relieved that she didn't know about my pathetic prayer life. When I opened the package, though, I was aghast. It was a book, *Intercessory Prayer,* by Dutch Sheets.

I started to read the book, mostly because I knew my friend would ask me about it. When I got to page 208, I found something that spoke to me so clearly, I could hardly believe it!

"There are bowls in heaven in which our prayers are stored," the author wrote. "I think it very likely that each of us has his own bowl in heaven. . . . When enough prayers have accumulated to get the job done, He releases power. . . . Victory goes to the persistent." He included Revelation 5:3–8 in his powerful explanation of "Tipping the Prayer Bowls of Heaven."

I put down the book, picked up my Bible and, sure enough, I found the amazing promise. So I quietly slipped to my knees with a clear mental picture of my son's prayer bowl. It looked just like the huge green bowl he'd always used for cereal. And I prayed:

Father, help me fill that big green bowl so full of prayer that one day You'll tip it and Your glorious answer will pour forth!

          —*MARION BOND WEST*

FRI	
19	Be of good courage, and he shall strengthen thine heart. . . . —*PSALM 27:14*

Everything seemed to happen at once. First, the starter on our car tore the teeth from the flywheel. Then the hinges on our oven door collapsed. The retaining rings in our dishwasher sheared, and the upper tray came tumbling down. A pipe in our kitchen ceiling burst. Finally, our dishwasher failed altogether.

How was I going to get all of these things fixed? Repairmen are neither plentiful nor inexpensive in our area. My thoughts were a jumble as I thumbed through the morning paper. Then a familiar face seemed to leap out of a photo on page six. It was Kathleen, who sang with our church choir! I knew that she was a long-distance runner and soon would be running in the famous Boston Marathon. But why the full-page profile?

"Cancer Survivor Runs Her 16th With Vigor," the headline read. I read on and learned that Kathleen had undergone cancer therapy in March 1996 and had run in the one-hundredth marathon only forty days after her treatment. I hadn't known about Kathleen's bout with cancer. She had run that marathon feeling it would be her last; it wasn't. "I got a little tired," Kathleen said. "But I have a good attitude and that's important. I enjoy people, and I will accept whatever time the Good Lord gives me."

I folded the paper and reached for the telephone book. *I'd better get started looking for repair people,* I thought. *Attitude is everything.*

Father, no matter how difficult the task may seem, give me the courage to make my best effort. —*OSCAR GREENE*

<u>SAT</u>
20
    There is no fear in love. . . .   —*I JOHN 4:18*

For many years after my husband Larry and I were married, I was at odds with his mother. I longed for a good relationship with Laverne, but I felt she was too reserved, and intentionally kept me at a distance. I wanted the kind of closeness she had with her daughter Sherry, but it seemed I was always on the outside looking in.

I'm not much of a pack rat, but I do save all the letters we receive, and over the years I have collected thousands. When I decided to sort them, I was stunned to find that more than two hundred had come from Larry's mother. In them she had woven a tapestry of the life she had shared with Larry's dad in Michigan during the past twenty-five years. It had been a very long time since I had read the letters, and I was suddenly struck by the love and warmth expressed in them.

Laverne had shared the family's everyday activities, the younger kids' events at school, the births, deaths and marriages of mutual friends and relatives, and the many birthday and Christmas celebrations that we had missed because we were too far away in North Carolina. Time and again, in subtle ways, she had singled me out in the letters, doing her best to make me feel special.

Why hadn't I been more aware of Laverne's intentions as the letters had trickled in one by one? My answer shamed me. I had been so focused on the things I felt she was not giving me that I had missed the great bounty of love being offered each time she wrote to us.

It was hard to write the long overdue letter of apology that my wonderful mother-in-law deserved, but she was gracious and forgiving. And today, I'm thankful to report, we finally have the relationship my heart has always longed for.

Father, I give thanks that even when my perceptions are distorted, You still see me with eyes of love. —*LIBBIE ADAMS*

<table>
<tr><td>SUN
21</td><td>Christ cares for his body the church, of which we are parts.
—*EPHESIANS 5:29–30 (TLB)*</td></tr>
</table>

I awoke early in my hotel room. It was Sunday morning, and I disliked being away from home. I missed worshiping at my church—the smell of freshly waxed pews, the rich music of our vintage organ, the warm handshakes and blessings of peace. As I dressed and packed, I listened to the sounds around me: elevator dings; doors slamming; the hum of air conditioners. From outside came the honking of taxis and the throbbing of car engines.

I went to the window of the twenty-sixth-floor room, checking to see if I'd need my umbrella. That's when I heard it: music. Muted and melodic. I opened my window and listened closer. A saxophone! On this gray Sunday morning, a lone musician was playing "Amazing Grace." Its sweetness echoed up through the skyscrapers and, suddenly, I was in church. That solitary saxophone became my Sunday choir; the pedestrians scurrying along beneath open umbrellas became my pew mates. God himself gave the sermon: "If you seek for me, you will find me" (Luke 11:9). I clicked my suitcase shut with a hearty "Amen!"

You are bigger than the houses we build to honor You, O God! Help me to see Your church in all its many forms.

—*MARY LOU CARNEY*

MON
22

O Lord, how manifold are thy works! In wisdom hast thou made them all; the earth is full of thy creatures.
—*PSALM 104:24 (RSV)*

Last night I argued with a raccoon. He was the size of a pony and was gingerly punching holes in my children's inflatable pool with his claws, trying to get into the pool to drink the water. He was startled by the hissing noise from the pool's dying exhalation, and startled, too, by the hairy man suddenly growling at him from a halo of light on the porch.

I called him names in English and Gaelic, neither of which he spoke, apparently, and he ambled off cursing at me in Raccoon, which I don't speak.

The pool slowly deflated, sighing, and the raccoon didn't get a drink, so we were both annoyed and frustrated. But I walked back into the house amazed at the capacious hand of God, Who has seen fit to make, among the countless zillions of creatures from His factory, a raccoon the size of a truck. One raccoon among so many, and so well made; a pool seems like a small price to pay, all in all, for the chance to see Leviathan up close.

Dear Lord, thanks for the gargantuan, infinitesimal, extraordinary bubbling life—Your greatest gift of all—spread so widely and well among Your creatures, even unto the Tribe of Raccoon.

—*BRIAN DOYLE*

TUE
23

My mouth shall speak wisdom; the meditation of my heart shall be understanding. I will incline my ear to a proverb....
—*PSALM 49:3–4 (RSV)*

Don't get me wrong, I love dishwashers, microwave ovens and all the gadgets that make life easier, but there are times I'm nostalgic for the sweet moments during my growing-up years when Mother and I did the dishes by hand. It was an unhurried time, a time to linger. Often it was a joking, laughing time, or a time to sing lilting favorites like "When Irish Eyes Are Smiling" and "It's a Long Way to Tipperary." Mostly though, it was a talking time.

Aprons on, we would stand at the kitchen sink together. I washed, my hands tingling in foamy hot suds, while Mother dried. In between there was chatter, interspersed with the homilies by which

Mum gently guided my attitudes and developed my values. She had a reservoir of what I came to call her "dishpan proverbs." If a pot wasn't washed properly, it was handed back with "If something's worth doing, it's worth doing well!" When I got my first job, frittered away my paychecks and was constantly short of cash, I heard, "Spend more than you earn, and you're sinking your boat!" There was no gossiping with Mum. "Rise above it!" she'd say. "Say something nice or don't say anything at all!"

During my dating years, littered with emotional hurts, Mum would frequently frown and clatter the cups as she stacked them. "It takes quite a bit of sorting out to find out just whom you don't want to be with, before finding out whom you do!" she'd say. Much teary-eyed sorting out finally brought me a love, steadfast and true, that has lasted for more than forty years.

I've raised my own family on Mother's "dishpan proverbs." Pulled from the kitchen sink, they are wisdom much remembered and passed along. In a muddle? Life twisted up? Come on in, we'll do the dishes and sort it out. You wash, I'll dry.

Help me to remember, Lord, that wisdom can be found even in the sharing of a simple task.   —*FAY ANGUS*

WED
24
For God, who commanded the light to shine out of dark-ness, hath shined in our hearts, to give the light of the knowledge of the glory of God in the face of Jesus Christ.
—*II CORINTHIANS 4:6*

Spring before last, Shirley and I took our family—kids and mates and grandkids, eleven of us all told—on a motor coach trip through Germany, the homeland of our forebears. It was an unforgettable ven-ture, visiting churches and museums and landmarks that together weave a brilliant historical tapestry. I couldn't help but be moved when passing through places that were home to Martin Luther; Albert Einstein; composers Wagner, Beethoven, Brahms and Bach; writers Thomas Mann, Kant and Goethe; artists Max Beckman and Albrecht Dürer.

I got to see more of Dürer's work, hanging in Nuremberg, where he was born, and Munich, than ever before. I knew about his "Young Hare" and "Praying Hands," but had missed such masterpieces as "Adoration of the Magi" and "Martyrdom of the Ten Thousand." Yet it was his self-portrait that fascinated me most. When our guide asked us who the gentle-eyed, long-haired artist most resembled, someone volunteered, "Jesus." And others agreed. Our guide explained that Durer's five-hundred-year-old self-portrait had served as a model for many others who over the centuries have tried to depict Christ.

When I get to heaven, I want to ask Warner Sallman, who painted "Head of Christ," one of the most famous twentieth-century renderings, if Dürer influenced him. I recall a conversation I had with Mr. Sallman at the end of his life. We were discussing how every culture sees Jesus through its own lens. Asian artists have painted Him to resemble Asians; Africans, with African skin color and features; Hispanics, as Hispanic; and so forth. Mr. Sallman mused that it was good for every people to see Christ in their own image, because He died for us all. "Yet the most important thing," the artist added, "is not that we look like Him, but that we act like Him."

> Help us focus, Lord, on Christlike deeds,
> On gifts of love, not dividing creeds.

—FRED BAUER

THU
25   For Christ's sake, I delight in weaknesses.... For when I
      am weak, then I am strong. —*II CORINTHIANS 12:10 (NIV)*

I have always considered my allergies a burden, especially when a stroll in the garden on a lovely spring day sends me into a fit of sneezing and runny eyes. Medications help, but the one allergen that they can't seem to overcome is perfume. I wouldn't think of using perfume or scented soap. I often have to move out of theater seats and church pews to avoid someone seated near me doused in strong perfume. I complain to God, "Why can't I be normal? Surely there was no good reason to make me like this."

Then one spring day, a woman seated next to me on an airplane pulled off a sweatshirt, frowned and said, "This smells like perfume. It must have gotten on there when I hugged my mother. I'm allergic to perfume."

"I am, too," I commiserated, wiping my nose. "We're perfect seatmates."

The woman's tense shoulders relaxed, and she said in an uneven voice, "Then I know you'll understand. I'm on an emergency flight home because my sister has just died from an allergic reaction to a new drug."

I listened as the stranger told her story. She was struggling with many "what ifs" about her sister's death, and it was obvious that I was just the listener she needed to quietly remind her that God was watching over her. I told her, "God had a hand in making our seat assignments. He put me here to let you know that He's with you during this difficult time."

After I waved good-bye and breathed a prayer for my bereaved friend at her connecting gate, an astonishing thought came to mind: All my life I've done nothing but feel sorry for myself because of my allergies. Not once have I considered that under the right circumstances, God could actually use them. That day I was just the one He needed to reach out to a hurting person, because I understood how she felt, and I wasn't wearing perfume.

Lord, show me today how You can use the parts of me I thought were broken to minister to others. —*KAREN BARBER*

FRI

26

"Come with me by yourselves to a quiet place. . . ."
—*MARK 6:31 (NIV)*

We had just finished breakfast on a lovely spring morning when my wife Noel spoke words I did not want to hear. "It's time for us to go," she said.

I had no plans to go anywhere. I had been overworked and rushed for weeks, and there was still work waiting in my study. I started to protest, but she put a finger to my lips. Then she stood up, walked behind my chair—and blindfolded me with a bandanna!

"No peeking," Noel warned, as she carefully led me out of the house and into our car. "Just lean back and relax. You need a complete break from work, and I have a surprise for you. Try to guess where we're going."

Grudgingly, grumpily, I tried, but all my guesses were wrong. "Here's a clue," she said, as the car picked up speed. "Think of the most beautiful places we've seen." As she drove, the pictures flashed in memory behind my closed eyes: Paris under a full moon; Crystal Lake in Oregon; lightning storms and rainbows over the Tappan Zee. . . .

We began to talk about our trips and the surprises we had shared. I forgot about the long drive and the work I had left unfinished. "Now," Noel said as the car slowed and made many unfamiliar turns, "tell me your all-time favorite."

That was easy, because it was hers as well. Years before, we had been in Japan at cherry-blossom time and visited the Katsura Gardens in Kyoto—living jewels of color, carefully tended for more than a thousand years. Walking among the flowers, crossing wooden bridges above rushing brooks, we had felt we were strolling through the pavilions of paradise.

The car stopped, and Noel opened my door. Off came the blindfold—and there was the green grass of Katsura, the bridges, the brooks, and masses and masses of cherry blossoms! She had taken me to a place I had never known existed: the Japanese Hill-and-Pond Garden at the Brooklyn Botanic Garden.

Lord, when the cares of the world are too much with me, help me to remember that heaven is waiting, and that You have provided us with glimpses of the beauty to come. —*FULTON OURSLER, JR.*

SAT

27

And David danced before the Lord with all his might.... —*II SAMUEL 6:14*

My son is a dancer.

Chase is sixteen, and he is also a kickboxer, a football player, a musician and a scholar. He is very handsome and enjoys an active social life. At a time in his life when most people his age would do anything to avoid any kind of embarrassment, he is a dancer—and I admire him for it. He is comfortable with who he is, with all of who he is.

He knows that dancing is not what most people expect when they meet him—all six feet and 196 pounds of him. But, when Chase dances, he is incredibly graceful, athletic, even inspiring. In his movements, I can feel him praising God.

His talent amazes me. But mostly, I admire him because he has the courage to embrace his gifts rather than deny them so that he will fit in or make others feel more comfortable. Rather than deny a facet of who he is, he endures an occasional whisper or question.

But most times the comments are favorable, and sometimes wistful. When I've told other men about Chase's passion for dancing, they smile, nod and seem to drift into bygone days. "I used to sing," they tell me. Or they recount how, long ago, they danced or sang or painted. They have confided to me that they stopped pursuing their talent because they were afraid of what other men might say or do.

Chase's courage and commitment also makes me question myself about what I might have left behind. How often, because I fear what people might say, have I denied a little bit of who I am and what I believe? Am I all that God has called me to be? Am I singing His praises in all the different ways He has called me to sing?

God, help me to lead a life that praises You fully. Help me to dance like David—and Chase. —*SHARON FOSTER*

SUN

28 Verily I say unto you, Inasmuch as ye have done it unto one of the least of these my brethren, ye have done it unto me. —*MATTHEW 25:40*

My good friend Mary Ann Lanz had come to my house to tell me about her mission trip to Honduras. She had asked several of us to pray for the trip's success, and her face was radiant as she reported how our prayers had been answered. The team had built one church, seen hundreds of public professions of faith and rededications to God, distributed thousands of Bibles and other religious materials, and so much more.

"Over four hundred children attended each of the church services," she told me. "And in the midst of it all, God never forgot one of the least of them."

She told me about a little girl who attended one of the services alone with her sister, a toddler. As the service began, the toddler became very restless. She refused to sit in her sister's lap, slid down on the ground and became quite bothersome with her fretting and whining.

"I knew she had to be made quiet," Mary Ann said, "but I didn't know how to go about it. And then I remembered the lollipop!"

Mary Ann had dropped a lollipop into her jacket pocket the day before. The next morning she was running late and forgot to take the candy out of her pocket, so it was still there.

She managed to catch the eye of the older sister and motioned to the two of them.

"In my broken Spanish, I said to the older sister, '*Solamente uno,*' which means 'only one,' and I placed the lollipop in her hand. She gave me a great big smile and began to unwrap the candy for the little one.

"There was no more unrest," Mary Ann said. "The service continued quietly. But the greatest part of it all was that God knew there would be a need for that lollipop, and He provided it. I thank Him humbly for using my pocket to hold it."

Father God, make me ready and willing for anything You ask.
                                              —*DRUE DUKE*

MON

29

In the morning. . . . cause me to know the way wherein I should walk; for I lift up my soul to thee.   —*PSALM 143:8*

There are times when I wake up around four or five in the morning, only to find that my wife Rosie is already up, having her quiet time and praying. The first time it happened, I asked her why she was up so early. "This is the best time for me, Dolphus," she replied. "With so many interruptions from the telephone and the door bell, my household chores, driving Ryan back and forth to school, as well as my other work"—Rosie runs a small foundation from our home—"this is the only time when I can hear the Lord speaking to me through His Word and then speak to Him through prayer."

It didn't take much to convince me that she was right. When I see Rosie at her early morning devotions, I know she is praying for me, for our children, her father, her brothers and sisters, our nieces and nephews, and for many others throughout the world. She calls out their names and prays specific requests for each of them. I can face my day better because of her prayers.

I know that I'm not as faithful in prayer as Rosie is; it's too easy for me to get lost in my busy agenda. Yet her example challenges me to do better, and so I pray:

Lord, thank You for Rosie and her faithfulness, and the faithfulness of the millions like her. Help me to be consistent and fruitful in the time I spend with You.
                                              —*DOLPHUS WEARY*

<u>TUE</u>
30 Jesus shouted to the crowds, "If anyone is thirsty, let him come and drink. For the Scriptures declare that rivers of living water shall flow from the inmost being of anyone who believes in me." —*JOHN 7:37–38 (TLB)*

Water has always been a big part of my life. I grew up just a few blocks from the Rock River in Rock Falls, Illinois. Since 1980, I've lived in Wisconsin, just a couple of miles from Lake Michigan, which is as beautiful as an ocean. My dream is to live someday on the very edge of a body of water. I don't care if it's the ocean, a river, lake or pond. I just want to be able to look at the water every day.

Strangely for such a water lover, I'd never been much of a water drinker, until the summer of 2000. My son Andrew had been hospitalized a couple of times the previous two years for dehydration during his bout with ulcerative colitis. I started nagging him to drink more water, and I decided I should heed my own words. So that summer I started drinking water with gusto.

My goal was sixty to a hundred ounces a day. I bought sixteen- and twenty-ounce water bottles and kept them filled and refilled in the refrigerator, and within a week of trying to start the new habit, I was doing it. Now I never leave the house in my car or on my bike or in-line skates without a water bottle. And I drink it all day long inside the house. I'm addicted!

When I started drinking more water instead of those expensive sodas, juices, teas and lemonades, I started feeling better, lost some weight and had more energy than I'd had in years.

Water. What a simple yet marvelous gift the Lord has given us. It's the most basic ingredient for life, and if you have excellent water from your tap as we do in Oak Creek, it's practically free!

Lord, I don't often remember to praise You and thank You for the most basic things, like water and air and sunshine. Keep my mind full daily of Your amazing gifts. —*PATRICIA LORENZ*

My Days of Prayer

1 _____

2 _____

3 _____

4 _____

5 _____

6 _____

7 _____

8 _____

9 _____

10 _____

11 _____

12 _____

13 _____

14 _____

15 _____

16 _____

17 _____

18 _____

19 _____

20 _____

21 _____

22 _____

23 _____

24 _____

25 _____

26 _____

27 _____

28 _____

29 _____

30 _____

May

And when they had prayed, the place was
shaken where they were assembled together; and
they were all filled with the Holy Ghost,
and they spake the word of God with boldness.

—*Acts 4:31*

S	M	T	W	T	F	S
			1	2	3	4
5	6	7	8	9	10	11
12	13	14	15	16	17	18
19	20	21	22	23	24	25
26	27	28	29	30	31	

THE PRAYER THAT IS ALWAYS NEW

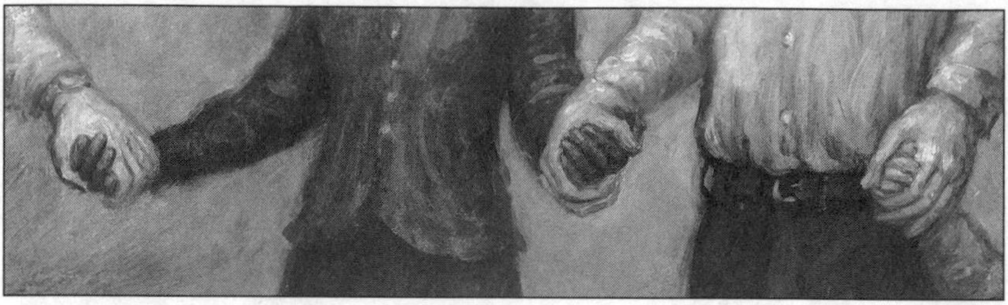

WED

1 Our Father . . . Hallowed be thy *name*. —*MATTHEW 6:9*

It wasn't until I began reading the Bible in my mid-thirties that it occurred to me to wonder about God's different names.

In Scripture, I noted, people's names stand for their characters—their origins, their history, the sum of all they are. As they change, so can their names. Abram and Sarai of Ur, as they journeyed to Canaan, became Abraham, "father of many," and Sarah, "princess." Jacob, "he who deceives," grew to be Israel, "he who wrestles with God." Saul, the narrow-minded stickler for the law, became Paul, apostle to those outside the law altogether.

What puzzled me was that God's name, too, changed over time. There was the name revealed at the burning bush, *Yahweh,* "I am," so weighted with the character of God that a Jew would never say the word aloud. "This is my name forever," He told Moses. Yet as the centuries passed and His people walked with Him into new situations, I noticed them using other names. Depending on the circumstance, they knew Him as *Provider. Defender. Victor. Healer. King. Father. Husband. Holy Spirit.* According to the need, He was their *Rock,* their *Fortress,* their *Shepherd.*

Best of all, He was revealed as *Jesus,* "Yahweh saves."

But God, of course, cannot change! Encountering His many names, I realized that what changed was people's understanding of Him, forever growing as they grasped new glories of the statement, "I am."

"Hallowed be Thy *name*" became for me a prayer that this might be true in my own daily walk. That I, too, would call Him by many names as I grasped new dimensions of His power. It happened first when my mother died, and He became my *Mother.* And again in strange settings, where He has been my *Travel Guide.* And in illness, when He was my *Health.*

Our Father, what riches of Your name will You show me today?
—*ELIZABETH SHERRILL*

THU

2

As we have therefore opportunity, let us do good unto all men. . . .
—*GALATIANS 6:10*

Our tour group had just crossed the Sea of Galilee, and we were walking up the sloping bank when our guide pointed out a low, round building being excavated in what had once been Capernaum. "They think this is Peter's house," he said. "The home that Jesus and His disciples often visited."

This was also the spot where there had been so many people wanting to see Jesus one day that no more could get inside. But that didn't stop four men who were carrying an ill friend. They simply crawled on top the structure, cut a hole in the roof and let the sick man down through the opening. Can't you just visualize that paralyzed figure on a stretcher with each of the four men having a grab-hold on one corner? What ingenuity. One, two or even three fellows could not have managed this maneuver; it took four.

I often think of this story when I learn of someone whose problems—illness, financial, mental, whatever—are so great that even "two or three who gather together in My name" are not enough. That one may be so paralyzed that he or she cannot possibly get through a problem alone, or even with the aid of two or three more. This is a time to make sure there are four, each of whom will grab one corner.

It is touching to read how the story ends: Jesus sees the faith of the four and heals the fifth, and all five share in the benefit as a result.

Heavenly Father, You have told Your children that it is a privilege, not a chore, to help one another. Help me to look out for those whose burdens are so great, they cannot possibly carry them alone.
—*ISABEL WOLSELEY*

3

He shall not judge after the sight of his eyes. . . .
—ISAIAH 11:3

When I walked into my office this morning, there was a crisp twenty-dollar bill on my desk. Puzzled, I asked my assistant Carol if she knew where the money had come from.

Carol smiled and said, "That's an interesting story, Scott. This morning when I arrived at the office, there was a nice-looking young man in the reception area. He asked if you were here. When I told him it would be an hour or so before you arrived, he reached into his pocket, pulled out a twenty-dollar bill and handed it to me. He said that you had given him some money several years ago, and that he promised he would repay you. He said to tell you he had a great job now and to thank you. Then he left."

As Carol talked, I suddenly recalled meeting that young man. Late one Saturday night, I had been leaving the church office after putting the finishing touches on a sermon. As I turned out the lights and walked toward the door, I saw the silhouette of a man standing on the steps.

I opened the door cautiously, and the man turned to meet me. For a moment our eyes met, and I heard him say, "Pastor, I need some help. My car is nearly out of gas, and I've got to get to Austin tonight. Could you lend me some money? I promise I'll pay you back."

How many times have I heard that line? I thought, and I mentally formulated my reply: *The office is closed. There's nothing I can do.* At the same time, I felt my hand reach for my billfold. Pulling out what I thought was a five-dollar bill, I realized too late that I was handing him a twenty. I wished him luck, we parted and the man melted into the night.

While I had quickly forgotten that moment long ago, he had remembered. And now I could only be thankful that God's Spirit had shut my mouth and guided my hand to my pocket.

God, may I always err on the side of grace as I give Your love to others. Amen.
—SCOTT WALKER

4

And ye shall hallow the fiftieth year, and proclaim liberty throughout all the land. . . .
—LEVITICUS 25:10

William and David have known each other since before they could speak. We were pushing our six-month-old son Will around in a stroller when we met David in his stroller, accompanied by his parents. Ever since then it's been play dates and sleepovers, football games and basketball, e-mail, phone calls and long rides on the school bus together. But one of the proudest moments for us to share was David's Bar Mitzvah.

At the service David stunned us with his reading in Hebrew from the Torah, the Books of Moses, and then we were further impressed by the sermon he gave, explaining the text from Leviticus 25:10, "And ye shall hallow the fiftieth year, and proclaim liberty throughout all the land." For a thirteen-year-old Jewish boy, this was the moment to celebrate his coming into adulthood. For years his parents had taken him to Hebrew school, sometimes two or three times a week. But what he did with what he learned . . . well, that was David. His mother hinted at it in the story she told at the reception:

On a lovely summer night when David was still in his stroller, he gazed up at the sky, pointing at the crescent moon. "Cow," he said. "No," his mother responded, "moon." "Cow," David insisted. "Moon," his mother corrected. Later as she was reading him a bedtime story and looking at the illustrations, she finally understood what he was referring to: the cow that jumped over the moon. "His mind was leaping ahead of mine," she said.

That's the way it is raising children. We lead, and they leap ahead.

Lord, make me a good example to the children in my life.

—*RICK HAMLIN*

5   Let brotherly love continue.   —*HEBREWS 13:1*

It was a warm spring day in Atlanta, Georgia. Azaleas and dogwoods burst forth from around every corner as my daughter and I drove home from church. As we passed my old neighborhood, she asked to see my childhood home. We stopped near the mailbox and looked up the steep hill. Then we drove up and around to the back, where an elderly couple was pulling up weeds.

I introduced myself, and they quickly invited us in. As we wandered through the house, I pointed out the kitchen where I had taken my first step and my brother David had said, "Now I have someone to play with!" I showed my daughter the bathroom that David and I had used more for GI Joe battles and Creepy Crawler production than for bathing. In my parents' old room, I told her how we had pinned towels around our necks and dove from the top of a wingback chair onto the king-size bed, yelling, "Superman!" The old house seemed unchanged, but when we stepped out back to leave, I noticed that a tree was missing.

On warm summer days, David and I would eat peaches while sitting on top of the brick retaining wall that adjoined our neighbor's property. After a couple of years of tossing peach pits into the rambling undergrowth next door, a tree had appeared. As I stood there looking at the vacant spot, I realized that I had never tasted a peach from that tree.

One hundred and fifty miles and the responsibilities of our respective families keep David and me apart. We rarely speak on the phone, and we hardly ever write. We aren't estranged; we haven't quarreled. We just forget.

David's birthday is at the end of August, a time of ripeness for our Southern peaches. This year, I plan on giving him a basketful.

God, in this world where so much is only temporary, strengthen the love that bonds me to my family. *—BILLY NEWMAN*

WHAT GOD HAS JOINED TOGETHER

MON
6

Look to the Lord and his strength. . . . Remember the wonders he has done. . . . *—I CHRONICLES 16:11–12 (NIV)*

During our sailing trip in the Caribbean, the captain gave us the choice of where to go each morning. One day, anchored in calm water off a beautiful island with no other boats around, we asked him just to stay there another day. The next morning he came to the breakfast table and asked gently, "May we have a change of paradise today?" As we laughed, he continued, "Remember these days are wonderful, but they will end. Cherish each one." As we looked at each other, my wife Joy and I knew he was right, and we began to take time each evening to reflect on and remember the day together, etching it in our minds before we drifted off to sleep, anticipating the next day.

Later in the year, Joy and I found ourselves in some difficult parts of the world. The islands seemed a universe away from the dust of drought and the odor of death that hung over some of the war-torn lands we visited. Our memories of paradise helped us through those hard times and increased our compassion for those whose lives have never known that kind of peace and beauty.

Now Joy and I are trying to remember always to make memories of the wonderful moments in our lives so that the tough times will seem less so. Why not try to do the same thing in your life?

Lord, thank You for the wonder and beauty You put into so many of my days. Fix them in my memory, and let me never take them for granted. *—ERIC FELLMAN*

TUE

7

Your love has given me great joy and encouragement, because you . . . have refreshed the hearts of the saints.
—PHILEMON 7 (NIV)

I don't wear a lot of makeup. But today I'm going to have brunch with my daughter and talk about her wedding next year. So, as I stood before the mirror, I reached out for a lipstick and began to put it on. As the light brown color rolled smoothly on, I realized with a sudden flash—a mix of joy and pain—where that lipstick had come from.

Months before, as I was convalescing from a long illness, a friend had encouraged me to stop hiding and to stop feeling that I couldn't manage the routine of daily life. Her idea? "Come out to lunch," she said. "We'll go to the little restaurant across the street."

Across the street seemed to me like crossing the Red Sea. But I did as I was told, put on an outfit that had hung untouched in my closet for months and crossed the street. My friend was already there, sitting at a comfortable table by the window looking out over the busy street, where people were going calmly about their daily lives. After we had ordered our lunch, she handed me a small gift bag. "Here," she said, "you need this."

Surprised, I looked into the bag. And there was a lipstick. Not a garish or brightly colored lipstick, but the one I am wearing today as I go with delight and eagerness to meet my daughter. After that lunch with my friend, I carefully put on the lipstick and began to look forward.

Thank You, Lord, for the support of friends and the grace-filled touch of a lipstick. —*BRIGITTE WEEKS*

WED

8

Whosoever shall give to drink unto one of these little ones a cup of cold water only in the name of a disciple, verily I say unto you, he shall in no wise lose his reward.

—*MATTHEW 10:42*

The walls of the house were rubble. Fallen rafters jutted out from a heap of debris on the ground, old door frames gaped in front of us, leading nowhere. I stood looking at the ruins, my heart beating rapidly as I remembered similar homes where we had so often taken shelter from enemy fire here in Italy during World War II.

In faltering Italian I spoke to a man, about sixty, who was standing nearby. "Battle damage?" I asked. More than half a century had passed since the Italian campaign, but everything changes slowly in these poor, isolated reaches of the Apennines.

The man, dressed in threadbare black, looked me over carefully before answering. "Yes," he said, and then he asked a question of his own. Was I an American? Yes. Had I been here in the war? Yes. At this reply the man became animated.

"I've been wanting to thank an American," he said, grasping my hand. "I was eight when you came to Italy. You know what I remember most? You guys gave us your chocolate. Thank you, thank you."

GIs had risked their lives in Italy, but this man remembered us for the bars of chocolate we gave him. Today, too, I suspect, it is the little kindness that is remembered by those we befriend, perhaps because the small act best speaks to the eight-year-old child within us all.

Lord, help me to share some small treasure with a stranger today.
—*JOHN SHERRILL*

THU
9   Ye shall be witnesses unto me . . . unto the uttermost part of the earth.   —ACTS 1:8

Spring in New York City is a very short season. Chilly April seems to give way suddenly to hot May. But today is beautiful, so I'm taking an after-lunch stroll down Fifth Avenue from the Guideposts editorial offices on 34th Street.

Five blocks downtown, on the corner of 29th Street, I come to Marble Collegiate Church. To the right of the entrance, there's a life-size bronze statue of Guideposts' co-founder, Dr. Norman Vincent Peale. Feeling a little guilty for being away from my desk, I duck my head and walk by, trying to look inconspicuous.

The next dozen blocks go by quickly. With a sigh, I hurry by the big bookstore on 18th Street. If I stop there, it'll be hours before I get back to work. At 12th Street, there's another church, First Presbyterian. Then, two blocks south at 10th Street, I see the open door of the Church of the Ascension. There's been a service there today, and while the sexton is putting things away, I stop in to look around.

On the wall above the altar is an enormous painting by John Lafarge of the event for which the church is named. Surrounded by a circle of angels, Jesus rises into a cloudy sky, while His disciples gaze up at Him in amazement. But there's something odd about the picture: The curving green hills in the background seem somehow out of place. On receiving the commission for the mural, I learn, Lafarge made a trip to Japan, and the Far East, not the Middle East, provided the landscape for his painting.

I take my eyes from the painting and glance at my watch. It's almost two; I'd better head back to the office. As I walk back up Fifth Avenue, surrounded by strollers whose roots are in a hundred different countries, Lafarge's odd choice suddenly makes sense: Japan and Galilee are equally close to heaven—and for the believing heart, so is New York City.

Lord, renew us in Your Spirit and make us one in You.
—*ANDREW ATTAWAY*

FRI
10

By my God have I leaped over a wall.   —*PSALM 18:29*

At a flea market I came across an early edition of the children's book *The Little Engine That Could.* Instantly I grew nostalgic over this classic tale of a little engine that could pull a train of toys and candy over a mountain by using positive self-talk.

"Hannah," I called to our seven-year-old granddaughter, "come. I want to read you an important story." She came running.

I read the story with enthusiasm and sound effects. Hannah seemed hypnotized, and I underscored the message that you can do big things if you say to yourself, "I think I can, I think I can, I think I can."

At last I closed the book. "Well, Hannah, the next time you face a problem that's a mountain to you, what are you going to say?"

She shrugged and said, "I'll say, 'Oh, brother, here we go again.' "

It wasn't the right answer, but it's what a lot of us would say. I suppose all of us have ambivalent feelings before a difficult task. "I think I can—I think I can't—I think I can. . . ."

No, positive thinking doesn't make me superhuman. I can't do everything I think I can. I once tried to water ski, but all I got for my trouble was a hernia. But I certainly can't do anything well if I have made up my mind that I can't. I've had students flunk my class because they had decided in advance that they couldn't pass my tests, so they just didn't show up for them.

Whether I'm facing my first public speech, chemotherapy or a piano recital, a good first step is for me to say, "With God's help, I can do this."

Oh, Lord, here we go again, up another mountain. I feel like I just can't do it, but if You'll walk with me, I'll give it a try.

—*DANIEL SCHANTZ*

SAT
11

Walk in love, as Christ also hath loved us, and hath given himself for us an offering and a sacrifice to God. . . .
—*EPHESIANS 5:2*

"Here's the deal on getting married," my friend Cathy said. "You're allowed three pet peeves about your husband in any given year. It doesn't matter what they are—the toothpaste top, the way he eats, where he leaves his shoes, whatever. But you're allowed only three. Anymore than that, and you'll both go crazy." It sounded reasonable to me. If I was allowed only three main irritations, then I'd have to prioritize and admit that the rest didn't really matter.

"Being married is great," wrote my college pal Bing, "though there will be mornings when you wake up and think, 'Who *is* this man, and what is he doing in my life?'" I was startled, but made a note of the possibility.

"There are ten things God wants you to do for your husband," said an article I read somewhere. "Forgive, forgive, forgive, forgive, forgive. . . . " *Gulp.* Can it be as bad as all that?

Our wedding day dawned, sunny and warm. I went over to the bakery to check on the cake, got my hair done and put on the gown that my mother had worn many years before. I was excited, but not too nervous: God was giving me Andrew, and I was utterly sure that Andrew was God's choice for me long before I made that choice myself.

As I entered the church with my father, the first things I saw were the rows upon rows of smiling faces, the friends who would witness our vows. Next I saw Andrew, looking mildly terrified (but extremely handsome) at the front of the church. And then, over Andrew's head and slightly beyond him, I saw the thing that would truly unite us, the source of more guidance and assurance than all the advice in the world: the Cross.

I took my place beside my husband-to-be, slipped my hand under his arm and we turned together toward our future—in Christ.

Thank You, Lord, for the love that bound You to the Cross for us, and that binds us together in marriage. When troubles come, keep us close to each other by keeping us close to You.

—*JULIA ATTAWAY*

SUN

12

I bowed down heavily, as one that mourneth for his mother.   —*PSALM 35:14*

I was nine, and had more baseball cards than Cooperstown.

I wanted to organize them (I know—it's hard to believe I ever wanted to organize anything), and I asked my mom for help.

I realize now what I was asking then. I was asking a woman who woke up at 5:00 A.M., made our lunches, sent us out the door, took two buses to work (as a teacher in the Pittsburgh public schools), came home, took my sister to night classes, came home for a second time, corrected papers, put us to bed and went to sleep herself around midnight. I was asking this woman, who didn't know Richie Allen from Charlie Rich, to sort through a couple of hundred baseball cards.

And she did. Of course she did. She could be nothing but kind; it was as immutable as her eye color. It was her nature—five-foot-two, Irish American, and kind.

My mother taught us the value of kindness, no matter how small the act. And when she died, when my family foundered in grief, we found out something else. We found other people who must have had the same kind of parents, people who performed those small acts of kindness when we needed them most, who reminded us of all the friends we have, the continuity of life, the Light Perpetual upon my mother's face, now and forever.

I still think about my mom. I miss the way she would laugh (quietly, behind her hand, but often); I remember her voice on the phone (always asking about us, never talking about herself); I remember that she could make sense of baseball cards and wayward socks and student papers and lives.

I remember it all. But I have no regrets. How blessed we were to have her.

Dear God, thank You for my mother. Hold her always in Your loving hands.
                                                      —*MARK COLLINS*

MON

13

By them shall the fowls of the heaven have their habitation, which sing among the branches.   —*PSALM 104:12*

On my walk in the park with my dog Shep, I approached a woman in a scraggly sort of raincoat with a pair of binoculars hanging from her neck. "What is it today?" I asked.

"Redstart," she said. "Warbler."

"Oh, yes," I replied knowingly. It was May and the warblers, I now knew, had arrived, and a mass of bird-watchers was ready for them. Central Park is a stopping point for as many as three hundred species of birds, who tarry for a short while before heading north. The bird-watchers, I'm told to my amazement, are part of an army of Americans that outnumbers all hunters and fishermen combined.

I'm ashamed to say that the "Oh, yes," I had given the lady so knowingly was a sham. I really can't tell a warbler from a chickadee. I've tried, honestly I have. I can recognize a canary or a robin, an ostrich or bald eagle or turkey, but I'm at a loss to distinguish a catbird from a mockingbird. Even the sparrows, who delight me by nesting on my air conditioner, I confuse with starlings. I've taken professional bird walks, only to have my field glasses give me "warbler neck." I have bird books in my library from Roger Tory Peterson's *Birds of America* to Marie Winn's *Red-Tails in Love*, and my CD collection is filled with recordings for birding by ear, but let's face it, I'll never make it as a birder.

That's sad, but sadder still are the reports of diminishing bird species in North America, which can partly be attributed to deforestation, chemicals and the spread of people's housing. I despair for these creatures whom Adam named and to whom the Lord God said, "Let fowl multiply in the earth" (Genesis 1:22). But I'm happy that there is a refuge like Central Park. I'm on the side of the birds, even if I can't spot a redstart warbler.

Lord, strengthen me to stand up for Your world and its creatures.

—VAN VARNER

TUE

14 [God] will be our guide. . . .   *—PSALM 48:14*

During a vacation to St. Charles, Missouri, the quaint town that in 1804 was the launching point for Meriwether Lewis and William Clark's history-making expedition west of the Mississippi River, I became fascinated with the courage of these adventurous men. Knowing little about what they might find, the Corps of Discovery was thrilled to head off into uncharted land, land so mysterious that even President Thomas Jefferson believed that the woolly mammoth might still have inhabited the area.

I was feeling a little like Lewis and Clark at the time, only a bit overwhelmed by another kind of uncharted territory ahead of me: special work projects; the presidency of an organization I belonged to; becoming leader of my son Ross's Cub Scout den; leading a Bible study for the first time. I wondered how Lewis and Clark were able to bridge the gap between the known and the unknown. As I learned more, the answer seemed to lie in their great faith—faith in themselves and in each other, unfailing trust in their own skills and judgment.

That's the kind of faith God wants me to have in Him, I thought. I must trust in His limitless abilities, His leadership and His judgment to know what's right for me. He created these wonderful opportunities for me: to lead an organization I care about; to spend time with my son in learning and fun; to express myself creatively in work and church. When I feel I'm in over my head, I need to turn to God in prayer, asking His guidance and direction. I can count on His infinite skill to lead me through the wilderness He sets before me.

Creator of all, guide me with Your strength and Spirit, so I may confidently explore the world You make new each day.

—*GINA BRIDGEMAN*

THE PRACTICE OF PRAYER

WED
15 *A Time for Prayer*
    Continue in prayer. . . .   —*COLOSSIANS 4:2*

Several years ago, I developed a yen to make cinnamon rolls. I chose a cookbook, gathered ingredients, sifted, stirred, rolled and baked according to instructions. The rolls smelled good baking, but . . . "We could use these to pave the driveway," my husband David said with a laugh.

Oblivious to humiliation, I located a second recipe, and soon the smell of cinnamon rolls curled through the house. "Uh, Mama . . . a little doughy. Sure you baked them long enough?" Keri commented.

Stubborn me went on to make cinnamon rolls too sweet and then not sweet enough. Finally, I got it right.

Over the next four months, we're going to commit ourselves to the four points that Dr. William R. Parker considers "inherent in successful prayer." The first point, as you've probably guessed, is: Make prayer a regular activity. Practice makes perfect, and though the point is obvious, it is also imperative. Don't fail to set aside a regular prayer time.

Without practice, I would have never known that moment when my family gathered around the breakfast table awed by my perfect cinnamon rolls. If you commit yourself, if every time you fail but get up the next morning and try again, you will at last find yourself in communion with God.

Practice praying at a set time; develop the habit of praying the last thing at night; pray the first thing in the morning. You *will* forget. You *will* lose your train of thought. You *will* think nobody's listening. You *will* fall into superficial dialogue. But after a while, Dr. Parker promises, your prayers will become "the practice of the presence of God."

Set aside a special prayer time—for me, it's an early morning walk. Go to sleep with a prayer on your lips. Say a prayer the moment you wake up. Pray, pray and keep on praying.

Make every moment of my waking and sleeping a prayer to You, my Father!
—PAM KIDD

THU
16
And the streets of the city shall be full of boys and girls playing in the streets thereof. *—ZECHARIAH 8:5*

Spring may mean flowers to you, but for a fervent contingent here at the Guideposts editorial offices in New York City, spring means one thing: softball.

Our co-ed team formed a few seasons ago on something of a whim. No tryouts, no experience necessary; just a willingness to show up at East River Park under the shadow of the Williamsburg Bridge, play hard and be entirely open to the possibility of making a fool out of oneself.

Our wise and courageous coach Stephanie made it clear that anyone who bought a uniform shirt was entitled to equal playing time. Many had never put on a glove before or swung a bat. The point wasn't to win, but to have fun.

It's a good thing the point wasn't to win. That first season, we were woeful. Other teams discovered themselves beating us so badly that they declined to finish the game. That's called the mercy rule. We required a lot of mercy that first year. Yet we took delight in the few bright moments that occurred—one of George's towering home runs into the East River or Stephanie's speedy triples or just a fluky catch.

Undaunted, we turned out again the next season and won two games. Granted, one was a forfeit because our opponents couldn't find the field, but it counted as a W nonetheless. We gained a reputation for being scrappy. And we got better. Last season, we tied for first place and went to the city playoffs—the same team that could barely win a game our first year out.

The point still isn't to win. Just coming together and playing as a team was more fun than anyone imagined, and while we were having fun we improved. To me, that's a tiny miracle.

Lord, as I dust off my glove for another softball season, keep me focused on fun. And let me not forget to be merciful, for there are games now when we're the ones who are called upon to exercise it, believe it or not. —*EDWARD GRINNAN*

FRI
17

For it is by grace you have been saved, through faith—and this not from yourselves, it is the gift of God.
—*EPHESIANS 2:8 (NIV)*

Whitney and I had been separated for eight months. Now we were on a first date, tentatively, fearfully moving toward reconciliation. We were at the Billy Graham Crusade in Nashville's Adelphia Stadium, waiting for the program to start. Side by side, we sat in silence on a hard bench, feeling the pain of our fractured marriage. Daylight thinned to dusk. The lights popped on over the football field, shining on the distant platform under the gigantic scoreboard. Empty folding chairs waited for the legendary evangelist and his team.

A memory bright as the lights flooded my mind. I was sixteen, my whole life stretching out ahead of me, sitting in a stadium in Philadelphia listening to Billy Graham. His message had stirred my devout teenage heart: I would serve God always and never stray, I vowed. And, at the end, when hundreds streamed forward to the strains of "Just As I Am," I was filled with happiness for them and for me.

Now, as a silver-haired, slightly stooped Billy Graham rose to speak, my marriage lay broken. Though I'd served God, I'd also strayed at times. Instead of the years stretching lightly ahead of me, I felt weighted by the passage of time.

The sermon ended. The crowd of thousands shifted in their seats to pray. The choir began singing "Just As I Am," and tears ran down my cheeks. How I wished I could go back and do it over! Whitney reached for my hand, his grip strong and reassuring.

As I watched the hundreds streaming forward, something stronger than happiness lifted my burden: It was the joy of second chances, the joy of a sinner saved by grace—again and again and again.

Jesus, thank You for grace greater than all our sins.

—SHARI SMYTH

SAT	We have this treasure in earthen vessels, to show that the
18	transcendent power belongs to God. . . .
	—II CORINTHIANS 4:7 (RSV)

We recently had an open house for our neighbors in the small mountain village of Green Mountain, Colorado. A couple from across the road brought their grown son Sid, who was visiting his parents. As Sid and I stood on the deck overlooking the untouched property in front of our house, he said, "Did you find my buried treasure?" Then he explained that he and his brother used to play here when it was a vacant lot full of pines. When Sid was about eight, he'd buried a coffee can full of toy soldiers, marbles and old golf balls under a tree where our house now stands. Sadly, I had to tell him that the excavator hadn't mentioned a coffee can when he used his backhoe to dig the hole for the foundation.

"Oh, that's okay," Sid said, holding his hand to his heart. "It's still in here."

I have a buried treasure in my heart, too. It's my childhood memory of swinging under the wisteria arbor in our backyard, trusting that, for that moment, the colorful tulips, the soft blue sky and the singing birds were all that mattered. I think it was my first glimpse of God's presence living in me and in all things. It's a treasure the backhoe of advancing years can never touch.

What buried treasure lies in your heart?

Help me, Beloved One, to hold sacred the hidden treasures of my heart. —*MARILYN MORGAN KING*

SUN
19

And suddenly there came a sound from heaven as of a rushing mighty wind, and it filled all the house where they were sitting.   —*ACTS 2:2*

We were still living in Alaska, and I was listening to the breeze stir the leaves in the forest of birch trees outside my open bedroom window. At the same time I was meditating on John 3:8 (RSV), where Jesus likens being born of the Spirit to the presence of the wind, saying, "The wind blows where it wills, and you hear the sound of it, but you do not know whence it comes or whither it goes; so it is with every one born of the Spirit."

Suddenly, through the wall on the opposite side of the room, I heard my daughter Kelly begin singing praise choruses she learned on her college campus. As I listened to the sound of the wind—with its intimations of the Spirit of God—and simultaneously heard Kelly's songs of holy adoration, I thought with delight, *Why, this is Holy Spirit surround-sound!* I let it envelop me and carry me to joy-filled heights, buoyed by a sense of God's presence.

Since that experience I find myself deliberately listening for more "Spirit surround-sound." It may be in the wind or waves, in church bells pealing, or in the familiar voice of a loved one. It might come from an unexpected source, such as the swish of a compassionate nurse's uniform in a hospital, or the click of computer keys in a job that the Lord has provided or a prayer of encouragement offered over the phone. It can be any sound that inspires us to glorify God and celebrate the love that Jesus Christ has for us.

Try listening intently today. The music is sure to be there.

Jesus, Your Holy Spirit is waiting to be heard. And my heart is ready to listen. —*CAROL KNAPP*

MON
20

I am bringing all my energies to bear on this one thing: Forgetting the past and looking forward to what lies ahead. —*PHILIPPIANS 3:13 (TLB)*

Because of illness, my ninety-one-year-old mother had been away from her home in Elberton, Georgia, for five years. She lived for four years with my husband Gene and me, then moved to a nearby assisted-living facility. One day she said, "Marion, you may as well go ahead and sell my house. I'm not going to be able to return."

It all happened in an amazing eight days. A buyer appeared quickly, and Gene and my children and some of my grandchildren helped me to empty Mother's house. After the closing at the lawyer's, I hurried back to Mother. "I did it," I announced, waiting for her questions. *She must have so many,* I thought. *Practically everything she owned and loved is gone. She'll want to know how I disposed of each item.*

To my surprise, she smiled and said, "Thank you. I knew you could manage."

"Don't you have questions?" I asked.

"No." She looked perfectly content sitting in her electric recliner. "I don't live in the past, Marion. I never look back. I like to look ahead."

"Okay," I said. "But I did bring you something from your house—something I couldn't part with."

"Oh, what?" she asked. She clapped her hands excitedly and her eyes shone.

I ran out to the car and came back with a huge plastic sack. In it were all Mother's hats, going back to the hat she'd worn at her wedding in 1931. While she watched with delight, I stood on her bed and hung the hats on the wall, using my shoe for a hammer. Then I sat back down, and together we silently admired the hats. Finally, Mother said, "Maybe I'll get to wear some of them again!"

Father, when the time comes, help me to relinquish the stuff in my life graciously and with thanks. —*MARION BOND WEST*

TUE
21

Heaviness in the heart of man maketh it stoop: but a good word maketh it glad. —*PROVERBS 12:25*

Change is never easy, and after almost six years with the same company, I had lingering misgivings about leaving. But I was no longer able to serve my clients as I once had, so I gathered up my nerve one Sunday afternoon and called Rob McCabe, chairman of the newly formed Pinnacle Financial Partners.

Before the buyout, Rob had been one of the top executives at the bank where I was still employed. A consummate professional, he was respected throughout the community. To my delight, he agreed to meet with me that week.

I felt totally at ease with Rob, and I guess he felt good about me, because after several more meetings, he offered me a job. After talking things over with my wife Candy, my parents and my sister, I decided to take the position. Yet, despite the excitement I felt, my heart was heavy. My manager at the bank, Gary Collier, was more than a caring, supportive boss; he was a friend. On the day I resigned, I tried to explain to Gary why I had to leave, and he tried to understand as best he could. Still, I felt I was betraying him.

That night my wife and I went over to my parents' house for dinner. My father quickly sensed my pain, and after dinner he took me aside. "Brock, you've always talked about how good Gary has been to you," he said. "If you believe that this move is best for you, don't you think that in the end, a friend like Gary will be glad for you?"

Dad's words set me right, and my sadness lifted. I had worked closely with Gary for six years, and we were good friends. Our career paths might separate, but our friendship would prevail.

Father, go with me through life's journey. Show me how to take chances and dare new ventures with a glad and trusting heart.

—BROCK KIDD

WED

22

Let us fix our eyes on Jesus. . . .   *—HEBREWS 12:2 (NIV)*

The weather was perfect as we drove through miles of green springtime, admiring the prosperous farms with their huge barns set on beautiful stone foundations, and gracious old brick farmhouses encircled by gardens bright with tulips. My husband Harry and I had gone to Michigan for an experimental cancer vaccine therapy, and during the two weeks between my treatments we decided to explore some new territory. Just over the river and across the bridge was

Canada, so we set out for the Bruce Peninsula in Ontario, that bit of land between Lake Huron and Georgian Bay.

We spent several days in the provincial parks, hiking well-kept trails through dense evergreen forests and rock-hopping our way along boulder-strewn beaches. We perched ourselves happily on the sunny high bluffs and cliffs of the Niagara Escarpment, overlooking the vast blue of one of the world's largest freshwater lakes.

Paradise . . . except for the black flies. Tiny little biting things, traveling in dark cloudlike swarms, they threatened to disrupt our idyllic vacation. Slapping and thrashing, we soon became preoccupied with the little beasts and oblivious to our beautiful surroundings.

Living with cancer is a lot like dealing with those black flies, we soon agreed: It all depends on where we focus our attention.

Gracious Creator, help me to keep my eyes on the beauty and joy that surround me rather than on the "black flies" in my life.

—*MARY JANE CLARK*

THU

23 He . . . gathered the assembly together in front of the rock. . . . —*NUMBERS 20:10 (NIV)*

I have two very small rocks on my desk. One was free; the other cost me twenty-five cents. I smile whenever I look at them because they remind me of our neighbors Evan, five, and Morgan, three, and they restore my faith that people still know what's worthwhile.

Evan and Morgan, with a huge teddy bear in a red plastic chair, had set up shop in their front yard. I thought they'd opened a lemonade stand until I read the big cardboard sign Evan was holding: ROCKS FOR SALE. I thought it was funny that these little entrepreneurs believed their pebbles were worth something, but I stopped to buy one—for eighteen cents—as I walked around the block. Evan punched the button that opened the drawer of the yellow toy cash register and deposited my quarter. He gave me my rock, and Morgan added another—free.

By my second trip around the block, three yardmen from across the street were customers. The mailman stopped, but since he had no money, Evan gave him a free rock for his bag. By my third round, a mother with a carpool from school had stopped, and the kids gathered around the rock table. Others came by, and by the end of the afternoon, Evan and Morgan had made $7.50!

Their rocks had value after all—they made lots of hearts lighter.

Father, help me to remember that love and encouragement are priceless, both when we give and when we receive them.

—*MARJORIE PARKER*

⁊

24

And there are diversities of operations, but it is the same God which worketh all in all. —*I CORINTHIANS 12:6*

"The program hosts are in there praying and said for you to join them," the receptionist told me kindly. I was at a radio station where I'd been invited to do an interview about the ministry of MOPS (Mothers of Preschoolers). I nodded and opened the door to the room, but quickly closed it behind me as soon as I saw the two people inside. Instead of sitting at a table and praying quietly as I expected, they were pacing around the room, eyes closed, arms lifted, talking directly to God—out loud, enthusiastically and both at the same time.

"Praise God! Hallelujah!"

"Come, Lord Jesus!"

"Yes, Lord! Bless us here and now, Father. You are so good. Hallelujah!"

Egad, I thought. I come from a conservative Presbyterian background and we pray differently—quietly, one at a time, hands usually folded, and standing or sitting still. Though I wanted to enter into this lively prayer time, I didn't know exactly how. So I bowed my head, feet planted firmly in one place, and began praying silently.

The program hosts continued to walk around the room, claiming God's presence and confidently asking for His blessing. After a few moments, they said, "Amen," and then greeted me warmly. The rest of the morning went smoothly, and surely we all were confident of God's presence.

Today, several weeks later, I don't remember much about the content of that radio interview, but I vividly remember the powerful, confident prayers and gestures of those two people. Their way of prayer is not my way, but my way is not the only way. I think God smiles when He sees His children gathered the way we were—diversity knit together in the unity of prayer.

Hallelujah! Come, Lord Jesus! Bless us here and now!

—*CAROL KUYKENDALL*

READER'S ROOM

May 25, 2000, saw me turn thirty, and Patricia Lorenz's January 31, 2000, devotional about her friend Alice's forty-ninth birthday celebration had touched me so much that I wanted to do the same thing. I called my special day a "Ladies Celebration of Life," and I worked on planning it for over three months!

In planning my guest list and thinking of the way each guest had touched my life, the memories just started flooding in, and I just had to write them down. I wrote a book of stories about my life called *Why I Threw Myself a Party: A Nostalgic and Inspirational Celebration of Life.* In so doing, I became a whole new person, refreshed, renewed and so much more open to the "doing" part of my life.

As for my party, it was a blessed day and a great success!

—*WENDI FRANTZ, HANNIBAL, MISSOURI*

<u>SAT</u>
25   Deliver us only, we pray thee, this day.   —*JUDGES 10:15*

My wife Rosie and I were getting ready to drive to Memphis, Tennessee, for our daughter Danita's graduation from medical school. "Make sure you've got enough tissues in your purse," I reminded Rosie with a smile. I knew that once Danita's name was called and she began to walk across that stage, her daddy was going to need a tissue or two to wipe away the tears.

That afternoon, as we settled into our places in the large auditorium, I felt my joy turning into sadness as I remembered the day I graduated from high school back in 1965. Even though I graduated at the top of my class, I knew it was impossible even to dream about being a doctor. My dreams back then were limited by race and class and poverty, but Danita's dreams were limitless—and now they were coming true.

The phrase from Judges 10:15 came into my mind: "Deliver us only, we pray thee, this day." I prayed to be delivered from my bitterness over the things I couldn't do back in the 1960s, and the pain I'd felt then dissolved in the joy of my baby girl's graduation.

Yes, the tears did flow, but they were tears of joy for Danita, and for God's victory over the pain in my life.

Lord, help me to trust in Your deliverance no matter how sharp the pain, and teach me to pray my way to the joy beyond it.

—*DOLPHUS WEARY*

SUN
26
The fear of the Lord is the beginning of wisdom. . . .
—*PSALM 111:10*

Some years ago, when a publisher asked me to write a biography of Norman Vincent Peale, I was glad to attempt it because Norman was such good company and had such a good memory.

His recollections of his Ohio childhood were still fresh and vivid. Some of those memories involved sleepy summer Sundays when his father, a Methodist minister, would be preaching at one or another of the little country churches and Norman, age three or four, would be sitting with his mother in the congregation. "I can see it all still," Norman said, "the acres of corn coming right up to the door of the church, the farmers and their wives tying their wagons outside, the horses stamping and sneezing, my father red-faced in the heat, preaching with such fervor, mopping his brow now and then with a handkerchief pulled out of his swallowtail coat.

"There was one church in particular that made a lasting impression on me because it had, painted up above the altar, a great all-observant eye. It was the eye of God, of course, and I didn't doubt for a moment that it could see every thought I had and everything I did. The painting had a very strong influence on me, not just then, but for the rest of my life. And I can't help thinking it would be a very good thing if modern youngsters could be exposed to such an experience. I really believe crime rates would drop and people would live happier lives."

"The beginning of wisdom," I murmured.

"Exactly," Norman said. "And I'm glad you still remember what the Psalmist said."

Father, thank You for these memories from the past that help us to live in the present. —*ARTHUR GORDON*

MON
27 Grace be unto you . . . from God our Father, and from the Lord Jesus Christ. —*I CORINTHIANS 1:3*

In 1998 I was selected to receive an award as Outstanding Kansas Woman. You'd think I'd be elated, right? Wrong. Previous winners included former Governor Joan Finney and university basketball coach Marian Washington. I'm not a public figure and certainly didn't deserve an honor. When people congratulated me, I changed the subject. The newspaper wrote a wonderful story, but I wouldn't let them print my picture. And I was certain our children and friends wouldn't want to drive six hours to attend the award dinner in Topeka, so I didn't invite them.

When I told my pastor how I felt, he looked at me a moment, then said, "This isn't about deserving or not deserving, it's about gratitude. Accept the honor as a moment of God-given grace in your life."

A moment of grace, God-given, in my life. Looking at the award from that viewpoint helped me to stop focusing on myself. I actually had a wonderful time at the presentation dinner, and was astonished and thrilled by the host of family and friends who came to share the celebration with me.

I'm learning to recognize and appreciate other moments of grace, both large and small: the way granddaughter Olivia's eyes light up when I walk into her house; seeing a rare morning rainbow in the western sky; and, most of all, the love of Jesus. He freely shares His grace, not requiring that I deserve it, but simply asking that I be willing to receive it.

"Come, thou fount of every blessing, tune my heart to sing thy grace!" (*Robert Robinson*) —*PENNEY SCHWAB*

TUE
28 I lie awake; I am like a lonely bird on the housetop.
—*PSALM 102:7 (RSV)*

Stuck in "empty-nest syndrome," I've often wondered how to redefine my role in life now that the children are on their own. But this spring my mother, who lives directly behind me, pulled my late grandfather's garden umbrella out of storage—and I turned a corner.

To Mum's dismay, mice had been busy chewing up Grandpa's umbrella fringe. She dragged out her shop vac but didn't realize she'd forgotten to put in a vacuum bag and was now blowing mouse droppings and tassel all over the deck behind her. When I went to sweep my own deck a few days later, I discovered some of the tassels on my back step. The next day I found more. I thought it odd: There had been no wind to carry the fringe from Mum's house to mine and the heavy growth of wisteria sheltering my deck. When my father came over, I mentioned it to him. "Do you suppose it's the mice again?"

"No," he answered, "but maybe it's birds." We both looked up. There, in the jungle of wisteria, was a robin's nest—with bits and pieces of Grandpa's umbrella fringe tucked into the twigs!

"How pleased he would be," exclaimed Dad, "to see the birds make use of his fringe."

Growing up, I'd been proud to be my grandfather's granddaughter. He was a godly man, generous and kind to friends and strangers alike. It pleased me when people patted my head and said, "Such a good man, your grandfather. And my, but don't you look just like him!" Looking up at his umbrella fringe, I suddenly realized I didn't need to redefine myself at all: I'd been a granddaughter long before I was a mother. And how many things had Grandpa taught me about who I am? Two stand out most: I am precious. And Jesus loves me.

Summer ripened, the baby robins hatched, thrived and flew away. But I'm not left behind feeling lonely. I have Grandpa's umbrella fringe: I am still his precious granddaughter, and Jesus loves me.

Jesus loves me, this I know, for my Grandpa told me so.
—*BRENDA WILBEE*

WED
29
Love bears all things, believes all things, hopes all things, endures all things. Love never ends. . . .
—*I CORINTHIANS 13:7-8 (RSV)*

"All I want to do," I said to my old friend, "is to have another chance to get to know you. It's been years since we really talked, and I miss our friendship. I've seen and confessed my controlling ways, and I've really worked on eliminating them."

I hadn't realized how insensitive I had been to him until finally he'd confronted me about my controlling behavior and asked me to back off. Every now and then I would call to try to reopen the door. I believed that my attempts to "love" this former friend would succeed in bringing us back together. But my determination only seemed to make things worse. Each time I called him to ask for reconciliation and forgiveness, I was ignoring his request for distance and reinforcing his conviction that I'm still an unreasonable controller. Miserable, I cried out to God, "I have no idea what to do! Help!"

Following the nudge I got after that prayer, I memorized the entire thirteenth chapter of First Corinthians and recited it every day. I was pleased that it said, "Love never gives up." But then another statement pierced my heart: "Love doesn't force itself on others . . . isn't always 'me first' . . . doesn't fly off the handle," all of which I had done in my attempts to get my friend to reconcile with me—so that *I* could be comfortable.

I cried out to God again, "Lord, I now see that what I have done is not Your kind of love. But what would Your kind of love have me do instead?"

Gradually, it dawned on me that if I practice God's kind of love, I'll keep loving this man *without* trying to change his feelings about me; I'll honor his need for distance and stay in the relationship at the level with which he is comfortable.

Lord, please help me learn to love other people without trying to change them or get something from them in return for my love. Amen.
—*KEITH MILLER*

THU
30
And this day shall be unto you for a memorial; and ye shall keep it a feast to the Lord throughout your generations. . . .
—*EXODUS 12:14*

We often make the trip to our lake cottage in Indiana over the Memorial Day weekend to "open up the place." It's a family tradition that dates back to around 1910. And if things follow their normal course, I'll take Mother, who still lives in my birthplace, Montpelier, Ohio, out to Riverside Cemetery where we'll place flowers on the graves of our loved ones. Homegrown flowers—peonies and irises— were the bouquets of choice when I was growing up, because they usually came into bloom about this time of year.

At my father's grave, Mama will point to the vacant space next to his, and remind me again that that is where she will be laid to rest. She won't say it forebodingly—her Christian faith is too strong for that— but matter-of-factly. I think she wants to prepare me. I'm prepared. Only a few yards to the east are some plots reserved for my family.

Not long ago I stopped in Boalsburg, Pennsylvania, and visited a cemetery said to be "the birthplace of Memorial Day." There, three young women—Emma Hunter, Sophie Keller and Elizabeth Myers—began the custom of decorating soldiers' graves in 1864, while the Civil War was still being fought. They wanted to recognize the contributions of villagers who had paid the ultimate price, and they did it with what was at hand, some homegrown flowers. The idea of decorating graves caught on, and today, because of the thoughtfulness of Emma, Sophie and Elizabeth, millions of people across the nation this Memorial Day will remember with deep affection those whose lives once touched theirs.

> Teach us, Lord,
> The best way to pay an unpayable debt
> Is to show with our lives that we didn't forget.
> —*FRED BAUER*

FRI
31
I have broken the bands of your yoke, and made you go upright.
—*LEVITICUS 26:13*

The large woven basket filled with sphagnum moss came as an anniversary gift from a son-in-law. It was a dull, dingy mess, but the directions accompanying the basket said there were bulbs under the moss that would produce gorgeous blooms if watered correctly.

In time, the promised blue crocus, purple iris and white narcissus began to bloom at the periphery of the basket. But in the center was a bulge like a miniature lava blowout in the Idaho desert. Each day it swelled more. I wondered what was happening until one watering day, I noticed a mass resembling Chinese noodles had broken through the moss and appeared on top of the bulge.

Roots, I thought. I forced my fingers under the mass and felt a bulb that had been planted upside down. I eased it out of its pot and discovered three bent white stems struggling to grow upright as God had intended. I put the bulb back in the basket right side up, tucked potting soil around the roots and waited.

The plant reached its stems to the light and produced the crop God intended—a group of delicate paper-white narcissus blooms.

Something like that happened to me when I was a teenager. I was growing in the wrong direction until a teenage Christian neighbor taught me how God could break the band that held me captive and let me grow upright. God turned me over, and I reached for His forgiveness, blossomed in His care and was able to grow as He intended.

Lord, break the bands of the yoke that keep me from You and set me upright in Your love. —*RICHARD HAGERMAN*

My Days of Prayer

1 _____

2 _____

3 _____

4 _____

5 _____

6 _____

7 _____

8 _____

9 _____

10 _____

11 _____

12 _____

MAY 2002

13 _____

14 _____

15 _____

16 _____

17 _____

18 _____

19 _____

20 _____

21 _____

22 _____

23 _____

24 _____

25 _____

26 _____

27 _____

28 _____

29 _____

30 _____

31 _____

June

And they continued stedfastly in the
apostles' doctrine and fellowship, and in
breaking of bread, and in prayers.

—*Acts 2:42*

S	M	T	W	T	F	S
						1
2	3	4	5	6	7	8
9	10	11	12	13	14	15
16	17	18	19	20	21	22
23	24	25	26	27	28	29
30						

THE PRAYER THAT IS ALWAYS NEW

1 Our Father.... *Thy will be done.* ... —MATTHEW 6:9-10

"It was God's will." The lady who said this to me at the funeral of a high-school classmate doubtless meant it to comfort. But to me, at age fifteen, it said only that God's will was harsh and unfeeling.

Since then I've heard the same words at other times of tragedy—and always spoken so sadly, with a kind of helpless fatalism. It's taken a lifetime of watching His will bring about better things than I knew to ask for, to make me see in this verse of the Lord's Prayer a wonderful promise.

Reciting it this morning, I thought of the e-mail that came to me yesterday from a woman who reads *Daily Guideposts* on the Internet in Japan. A year ago, Susan wrote, she started to pray an hour each day for God's will to be done in her life. Surely, she thought, His will included healing of a swelling in the calves of her legs.

On July 10, however, she woke to find the swelling worse. The timing was terrible! The very next day all their friends were coming to a big birthday party for her husband Takashi. Today, of all days, she couldn't take time to go to the hospital where she received her treatments.

Takashi, though, was concerned for her. Over her protests, he drove her to Tsukuba University Hospital. All the way there she chafed at what seemed to be God's unsympathetic ear.

A few minutes after they arrived, Takashi suddenly complained of feeling dizzy. A doctor did a quick EKG, put him on life support and assembled the cardiac team for an emergency triple bypass.

"Twenty minutes later," the surgeon told her after the successful operation, "it would have been too late to save him."

Our will, God's will. When Jesus prayed before the agony of the Cross, "Not as I will, but as thou wilt" (Matthew 26:39), He wasn't resigning Himself to the worst, but asking God for the very best.

Our Father, Thy perfect will be done in my life today.

—*ELIZABETH SHERRILL*

SUN

2

Therefore, as God's chosen people, holy and dearly loved, clothe yourselves with compassion, kindness . . . and patience.   —*COLOSSIANS 3:12 (NIV)*

My husband Bob was a certified lay speaker in our church, approved to preach when the regular pastor was absent. He had studied and been tested and was always proud when invited to fill a pulpit. He worked hard preparing each sermon.

One late spring, he was invited to preach in neighboring Haleyville, Alabama. On that morning I was seated, as usual, in the front pew of the church we were visiting. The service preceding the sermon went fine. But when Bob began to speak, I was horrified to realize I couldn't hear one word he was saying. We knew Parkinson's disease had affected his speech, but neither of us realized it was diminishing the resonance in his voice.

I tried to get his attention, but how? Anything I could do would only embarrass him. I could do nothing, but be quiet and pray that God would help him.

I was miserable throughout the entire sermon, imagining the congregation sitting behind me squirming restlessly. I dreaded the comments I expected after the service, such as, "I wish I could have heard what you were saying."

But not one person criticized. Instead, they moved close to shake his hand after the service and thank him for coming. Some even said, "We always look forward to your being here. You give us so much to think about."

Their handclasps and gentle hugs quieted my fears and brought tears to my eyes. These people needed no sermon that morning. They were already practicing one of Jesus' greatest commandments, "That ye love one another; as I have loved you" (John 13:34).

Lord, when people do love one another, it is beautiful to see.

—*DRUE DUKE*

MON

3 Let there be no strife . . . between me and thee . . . for we be brethren.

—*GENESIS 13:8*

I've worked as an editor at *Guideposts* magazine for more than sixteen years, and sometimes I'm asked what my favorite story has been. I have to admit that I can't pick just one, but I can tell you about the one favorite that we never printed.

A woman from a large family hurried home to say farewell to her terminally ill father. She managed to get to the hospital just as he died. In the days that followed, all his children were home, reminiscing about their father. He had been kind, witty and generous, and although he had nine children, he was able to make each of them feel special. It was only after the funeral that the daughter had a chance to tell her siblings what was on her mind. "I was his favorite, you know," she said. Her brothers and sisters looked at her, startled. Then they responded:

"No, *I* was his favorite."

"*I* was."

"*I* was."

What might have been a competition became one more shared eulogy about their dad. Each of them felt certain that he or she was the favored one. That was their father's particular gift.

It reminds me of how someone once described God: "He loves each one of us as though there were only one of us to love." If I could be as caring with my own loved ones.

There was no return address on the manuscript and the envelope it came in got lost. We could never reach the writer and therefore we could never publish the story. Perhaps someday the writer or one of her siblings will send us the story again. This time I'll be sure to save the envelope it comes in.

Lord, give me the power to see how each of Your children is favored by You.

—*RICK HAMLIN*

TUE
4

He will swallow up death in victory; and the Lord God will wipe away tears from off all faces; and the rebuke of his people shall he take away from off all the earth: for the Lord hath spoken it. —*ISAIAH 25:8*

Two of the difficult places my wife Joy and I went this year were the countries of Burundi and Rwanda in central Africa, the scenes of horrific genocide in 1993 and 1994.

A simple term like *genocide* masks the reality of whole villages wiped out in a single day or of a child who has lost every living relative. In Rwanda, the horror was magnified because churches were used as the killing grounds into which tens of thousands of people were herded and murdered by machetes, bullets and fire.

For us, it seemed that hope had been snuffed out in that land and no amount of sunshine could lighten the darkness we felt. Then we were asked to visit a memorial being created in a rural village. There, on the grounds of a ruined church, survivors tended the bones of the dead, lying scattered and lonely where they had fallen. Our group struggled to hold back the tears, and one woman who could not asked the elderly attendant how he could bear to come there day after day. Reaching up to touch her wet cheek, he replied, "I do it for the tears, the tears of those who come water the garden of our hope so that this will not happen again."

Lord, when sorrow strikes, let our tears flow, and give us hope that one day You will wipe away all tears from our eyes.

—*ERIC FELLMAN*

WED
5

I wait expectantly, trusting God to help, for he has promised. —*PSALM 130:5 (TLB)*

The wall of pictures was the focal point of the living room. It drew the eye with beauty: a glorious sunset in Bora-Bora, crashing waves off the coast of Ireland and, here in California, a quaint teahouse in Carmel. But it also held several empty frames that displayed only the soft cream wall on which they hung.

My hostess grinned as she saw my eyebrows go up. "This wall," she said, "has pictures from all the trips we've taken during our marriage."

"What about the blanks?" I asked.

"Ah, those are the most important of all! They stand for the years we couldn't afford a vacation. They're even dearer to us than the photos, because they remind us of the times we spent waiting on God. Those were tough times when illness, debts and difficulties had us up against a blank wall. Prayer was our only lifeline of hope." She paused as she reached to straighten a frame.

"And?" I asked.

"Prayer pulled us through. Moment by moment, we tugged on that lifeline and came to know the faithfulness of God as He worked His miracles through those 'in between' times. It wasn't long before we were able to take vacations again! Look"—her eyes glistened—"here's the fountains of Tivoli, from our forty-fifth anniversary trip to France and Italy."

She smiled as she pushed her walker slowly into the kitchen. "We can't get around much anymore, but we take a mini-vacation every day. We look at a picture, smell the smells, hear the sounds and feel the air . . . and once again we're there!"

That evening my husband John and I dragged out all our travel albums. We're starting a collage of travel memories and, yes, we have blank spaces for the "in between" times when we, too, waited on God, and He pulled us through on the lifeline of prayer.

Lord, give me the grace to trust You during all the "in between" times.
— *FAY ANGUS*

THU

6

My hope is in you all day long.   — *PSALM 25:5 (NIV)*

"Oh, no," I exclaimed to my husband Roy, "I forgot to give away the extra tickets!" I had received complimentary tickets to the grand opening celebration for the National D-Day Museum in New Orleans. I'd given a few tickets away, but I still had three left. I quickly made a few calls. No one could make it.

I felt awful. *How could I have forgotten something so important?* I wondered.

"I have an idea," Roy said. "Let's give away the tickets before we go in."

"And who will we give them to?" I asked.

He looked at me for a moment and said, "We'll know."

When we arrived in the city, we parked on a side street and boarded a streetcar to go to the museum. An elderly man and a young girl were sitting opposite us. Roy pulled two of the tickets out of his front pocket. "Okay," he said as he got up, "here go the first two." He sat down a few minutes later, smiling broadly. "He hadn't been able to get tickets," Roy said as he looked over at the man. "He was a prisoner of war in the Philippines during World War Two. He's taking his granddaughter."

We got off at the next stop and made our way through the crowds toward the arena for the opening-day festivities. *Well, Lord,* I thought, *who am I going to give this one last ticket to?* I handed my ticket to the lady at the gate. At that moment I noticed a commotion at the next turnstile. "What do you mean you can't find your ticket?" I heard a man say to his wife. He and their young children were already inside while the wife frantically searched her bag. Roy quickly handed her our extra ticket. Her kids cheered.

I learned some valuable lessons about courage, sacrifice and honor at the museum opening. But I also learned how a tap on the shoulder from God could lead me to just the right people.

Lord, how many times have I not heeded Your call? Help me always to respond to your gentle urgings to do right.

—MELODY BONNETTE

FRI
7

Are not two sparrows sold for a farthing? and one of them shall not fall on the ground without your Father.
—MATTHEW 10:29

For the second time that spring, a mama dove had set up house in our backyard grapefruit tree. Now she was crowded in her nest with two babies. I thought I'd take a peek as I'd done every day since she laid her eggs. But as I ducked under the tree's heavy limbs, my shoulder brushed a leafy branch. The birds startled and flew out of the nest in three directions. Mama and one of her babies flew out of the yard, but the other wasn't quite strong enough. It flapped and tumbled across the grass, coming to rest in a dazed heap. I quickly chased our dog inside to protect the stunned bird, then flopped down in a chair, distraught.

"Oh, God," I said, "how could this have happened?" I felt terrible, but not just because of the bird. That morning, I had met with a friend with whom I'd been working on a creative project for more than two years. We had to admit defeat. In spite of a lot of hard work and prayer, our idea simply wasn't going to get off the ground. I wondered if the same was true of the little bird that sat motionless in the grass.

"I thought you cared about every little bird that falls to the ground, Lord," I said, remembering a familiar Bible verse. But remembering prompted me to look up that verse from Matthew, and in reading it again, I saw it in a new way. *One of them shall not fall on the ground without your Father.* Nowhere does it say God will keep the bird from falling. Like us, it may fall, hurt, fail and even die, but not alone, not without the Father knowing, caring and loving it through all eternity.

I looked out the window and saw the little bird stir, flap its wings and fly off. In spite of my disappointment, I knew God would help me do the same.

Your unfailing love comforts me, Lord, and gives me the strength to get up and fly again. —*GINA BRIDGEMAN*

SAT

8

We look not at the things which are seen, but at the things which are not seen. . . . —*II CORINTHIANS 4:18*

I have a large collection of ties, each one carefully chosen for its color, design and significance. I have ties that mark holidays, ties that celebrate ball parks, chess, parrots, postage stamps and angels.

My son Tony is an artist. Artists never wear ties. For years, I refused to notice this: I bought Tony ties even after his mother quietly informed me that he didn't like them. Whenever I saw one that seemed exactly right, I bought it, convinced that someday he would see how perfect it was.

At Tony's graduation from the California Institute of the Arts, I proudly wore my Georgetown University tie. The ceremony, held outdoors, was unique. As each graduate's name was called, the young man or woman would rise from the audience and walk to the stage to begin a memorable performance. One young woman, dressed in a ballerina's costume, climbed up a ladder, gingerly walked across a tightrope and reached down to take her parchment from the president's hand. Another came forward leading a trained ocelot, who took the scroll in its teeth. The cheers from the audience kept rising, and I wondered what Tony would do.

But when he was called, he did nothing unusual. He simply walked forward and accepted his diploma. Yet, to my amazement, with every step the crowd's roar grew louder, ending in a crescendo of laughter and applause. *He must be very popular,* I thought.

Afterward, Tony met us with a big grin. "Did you like my performance?" he asked. *Performance?* "He didn't get it, did he?" Tony said, winking at his mother. "Dad, look at me. In honor of the occasion, I decided to dress just like you!"

I blinked. I looked hard at him, and then I saw. His performance had been what he wore. It had seemed exactly right to me, but to his friends, it was an outrageous costume: a suit, a white button-down shirt—and one of the ties I had given him.

Lord, in everyone I meet, let me see Your image, not mine.

—*FULTON OURSLER, JR.*

<hr>

SUN

9

So Abraham called that place The Lord Will Provide. . . .
—*GENESIS 22:14 (NIV)*

The day after our son's wedding in Seattle, Washington, a couple of years ago, Lynn, our daughter Kendall and I flew home to Colorado. We were exhausted, but filled with wonderful memories . . . and a few questions about how life would be different for our family on this side of the milestone.

"Does this mean I can no longer call Derek and leave dumb messages on his answering machine?" Kendall asked, tears suddenly filling her eyes.

"Of course you can," I assured her, but her question touched off a few of my own. *How will my relationship with Derek be different? How will I be a good mother-in-law? What will the holidays be like?*

In my heart, I knew this was another familiar lesson in learning to let go, which always reminds me of the story of Abraham and Isaac, so I shared it with Kendall. "The Bible tells the story of Abraham, who was called to surrender or 'let go' of his son Isaac on Mount Moriah. What a struggle that must have been! He knew what he was letting go of—the son God had promised him—but he didn't know what, if anything, God had in store for him. When he got to the place of surrender, he found that God had provided and had given him back even more than he had surrendered.

"Maybe that's how you feel now, Kendall. You know that you're losing your childhood relationship with your brother, but you don't know what you'll get in its place. That's where our faith comes in. We have to let go of the way things were in order to make room for the way they will be, and trust God to provide."

As I finished talking, I looked over at Kendall. She had fallen asleep. I could hardly blame her. Besides, the story was more for me than for her, and as I started to doze off, I began looking forward to the exciting new relationships we had ahead of us as a family.

Father, when we let go of something, You fill our emptiness with something even better. —*CAROL KUYKENDALL*

MON
10 When words are many, sin is not absent, but he who holds his tongue is wise. —*PROVERBS 10:19 (NIV)*

My small son is hunched over the typewriter. He recently learned to write his name and he's been writing it forty times a day, sometimes with a red pen on the wall in the basement, so I assume he is now typing his name forty times. But, no, he is writing a poem, he says. He shows me proudly:

ggfddfg
eee
eee
aaaaaaaaaaaaaaaahjs

'''''''''''''''''''''''''''''
d   l   t

"What do you think, Dad?" says the boy, beaming. The prim editor in me says this is nonsense, but the grace of God lets a father's love shove the cold editor out of the way. I cheerfully tell my son that I am impressed with the Welsh motif of the opening line, and the casual e.e. cummings reference in the second and third lines, and the onomatopoetic exhalation or sigh of the fourth line, and the way the fifth line looks like a line of leaping dolphins, their backs flashing in the sun, and that great closing line, which is clearly a sort of joyful math, death (d) being followed as always in this world and the next by life (l), the two flowing of course through time (t).

"That's great stuff, Joe," I say, and he proudly runs upstairs to show his mama. I stand there thinking how grace comes in a zillion forms, some of them the gift of silence.

Dear God, thanks for letting me know when to shut my mouth.
—*BRIAN DOYLE*

TUE	As the garden causeth the things that are sown in it to spring forth; so the Lord God will cause righteousness and praise to spring forth before all the nations.
11	

—*ISAIAH 61:11*

After thirty-five years in Princeton, New Jersey, my wife Shirley and I are dividing our time between a beach place in Englewood, Florida, and a stone house in State College, Pennsylvania. We acquired the latter last fall, so when we came north this spring, we got our first look at the bounty of flowers we had inherited from the previous owners. The house, built in 1933, had been home to three families before us, and each, I imagine, made a contribution to our garden.

Like clockwork, the perennials—daffodils, irises, peonies, forsythia, lilacs, lilies, bergamot, loosestrife, mountain blue, bleeding hearts, trillium, phlox, clematis, roses, turtlenecks, black-eyed Susans, chrysanthemums and other flowers whose names I am still learning—have taken turns on the stage just outside our door. Almost every day, it seems, there is a new bloom bowing reverently in our direction. But it is I who feel the need to bow—to the God Who fashioned such beauty, and to the people who planted this rainbow of color that sometimes takes my breath away.

Once again, I am the beneficiary of someone else's gift. And I am grateful to the unseen hand of our heavenly Father, Who concerns Himself with the little things of life, the fallen sparrows and the lilies of the field. Someone rightly said that we stand on the shoulders of those who have gone before us, that our very faith is built upon the words and deeds of our forebears. We pay homage to them and our

Creator when we with our lives give back beauty and love to a world that can always use a little more of both.

Remind me, Lord, of what Helen Steiner Rice once told me:

> You can't give a rose all fragrant with dew,
> Without part of its fragrance remaining with you.

—FRED BAUER

WED
<u>12</u>   "I am doing a new thing ... do you not perceive it?" ...
—ISAIAH 43:19 (RSV)

Last June, my niece Scarlett graduated from high school, and I gave a big open house for her. We began early that morning, setting up tables and chairs out in the yard. And the food! Vegetables to cut, baked beans to make and chicken to pick up at the deli. I had just finished tying helium balloons onto the mailbox when the first guest turned into the driveway.

It was a wonderful celebration, filled with presents and cake and cards and good wishes. Scarlett was the center of attention as she welcomed friends of the family and members of our church congregation. Her friends, too, came and went all afternoon. They were a diverse lot, with piercings in some untraditional spots and hair colors that rivaled those helium balloons.

I watched Scarlett as she posed for a picture with her diploma. She hadn't cared much for high school, so she was exploring several different career options, some of which would require on-the-job training instead of formal schooling. For now, she was going to work in a doctors' office as a clerk.

People shook her hand, hugged her, gave her advice. As we were cleaning up, Scarlett said, "Thanks for the party. It was great!"

"You're more than welcome," I replied. We tossed paper plates into the trash and began taking down folding chairs.

"I'm not sure what I want to do with my life," Scarlett confessed. "And everyone keeps asking me!"

"It's okay not to know," I assured her. "Just be open to new experiences. New beginnings are all around you!"

So Scarlett worked for those doctors all summer. She watched them help sick people and listened to them talk about research and the future of medicine. And when fall came, she enrolled in a local college—as a premed student.

Help me remember, Lord, that You are the Author of new beginnings. And give me the courage to imagine great things ahead!
—*MARY LOU CARNEY*

THU
13   The everlasting covenant between God and every living creature of all flesh that is upon the earth.—*GENESIS 9:16*

I was looking something up in my Bible concordance when my eyes fell upon the word *Dog*. Since dogs are a special fondness of mine, and since my Belgian shepherd Shep was at that moment at my feet (a not unusual place for her to be), I was intrigued. "Ah, Shep," I said aloud, "let's see what the Bible has to say about you and your kind." I thought I'd find some loving pictures; I even had an idea that a scraggly dog was in the crowd following Jesus. Not so.

The concordance read: "Dog—canine mammal." Underneath it continued "Described as," and then began a discouraging list, everything from "Carnivorous" to "Dangerous" and "Unclean." There followed another grouping of some thirty-two entries under the heading "Figurative of." I decided to look them all up; it consumed an afternoon. A discouraging afternoon, for I found what I took to be a pack of fierce dogs circling around David (Psalm 22:16), troublesome dogs making a racket (Psalm 59:6), dogs returning to eat their own vomit (Proverbs 26:11)—everything vile. Even in the New Testament, Luke told of a dog that licked the sores of a dying beggar named Lazarus (Luke 16:21). The only half-pleasing moments were a passage from Job in which the dogs were presumably entrusted with a flock of sheep (Job 30:1), and in Ecclesiastes, where the preacher says, "a living dog is better than a dead lion" (Ecclesiastes 9:4). That was true, but it wasn't what I had hoped to find.

Next to *Dog* in the concordance was *Doleful*, which I was feeling, and then came *Dominion*, which gave me a charge. "Listen to this, Shep. 'And God said, Let us make man in our image, and let them have dominion over—' " I didn't hesitate to add, " 'the dogs.' And you know how good I am to you. As a matter of fact, I just might take you to the cathedral when they have the next blessing of the animals."

Shep didn't disagree and I felt mollified. "Let's go out for a walk," I said. She was ready.

What is really important, Father, is that You created all living things, and left it to us humans to look out for our animal friends.

—*VAN VARNER*

14

Lord, you have poured out amazing blessings on this land!...
—*PSALM 85:1 (TLB)*

Like many "proud to be an American" citizens, I have always had the utmost respect and devotion to the American flag. Old Glory flew on the front porch of my childhood home in Rock Falls, Illinois, on every holiday and on top of my dad's pontoon boat that cruised the Rock River for many years.

In my own home I have a sturdy nylon three-by-five-foot American flag that I fly proudly near my front door on every holiday and on days when I just feel like hollering from the rooftops that it's great to be an American, like the days when my grandchildren were born, or the day my friend won a cruise and invited me to go along.

My son Michael attended the University of Wisconsin, a school known as "the Berkeley of the Midwest," where students often find something to protest. In January 1991, during the Gulf War, a group of students decided to march down one of the campus's main streets. At one point, they stopped and set an American flag on fire. Michael heard the commotion from his dorm room and followed the crowd to the burning flag. As a proud member of the National Guard Band, an organization he joined at age seventeen to help pay his way through college, he quickly pushed his way to the center of the crowd where the flag was burning and stomped it out. The protesters were furious, jeering and shouting insults. Finally, the police arrived, and Michael was quickly whisked away in a squad car. "For your own protection, son," one officer explained as Michael was driven back to his dorm by a couple of officers who were no doubt proud that the young college student had defended his flag.

Here's to all the red-white-and-blue days in our lives. May Old Glory remind us to cherish our American citizenship every day, not just on Flag Day.

Father, thank You for allowing me to be born in a country where freedom of government, religion and speech—including the right to protest—reign supreme. Help me to appreciate the freedom our flag represents. *—PATRICIA LORENZ*

THE PRACTICE OF PRAYER

SAT

15 *The Prayer of Surrender*
Thy will be done. . . . *—MATTHEW 6:10*

Because I'm perfectly capable of being a control freak, a seeker of revenge and one who hesitates to forgive, Dr. William R. Parker's second touch point of successful prayer is my ultimate test: "Make prayer an act of surrender," he says. "Pray dangerously. Let go and let God."

There is a song we sometimes sing at church on Sunday mornings, and when I find myself in a tug-of-war with my old self—trying to take back what I've struggled to give to God—I retreat to a vision evoked by it: "Lord, You Have Come to the Lakeshore."

I am walking barefoot across a beach. My self-imposed burdens are heavy. The sun is hot. The sand burns my feet. Up ahead, beyond the point where the waves lap the shore, a wooden boat floats. The boat is painted the color of the sky. There are no oars, no motor, and I know the boat waits only for me. I step into the water, wade up to my knees, then halfway to my waist. The boat rocks with the breeze. I touch its wooden side, hike myself up, fall into its bow, then right myself on its middle seat. I sit there, calm, trusting, at perfect peace.

All my worries are on the shoreline. I shiver in anticipation. God is my captain. *Thy will be done.* I am free.

"Making prayer an act of surrender" just might be the boldest venture you'll ever take. You are surrendering your old self to God. You are trusting Him to make you new.

In the month ahead, let's vow to surrender every inclination to control, every grudge, every bad thought, over and over again to God . . . until we are free.

Father, I leave behind all the trappings that hold me back. I surrender all to You. I trust.
—PAM KIDD

READER'S ROOM

Many years ago, while visiting my grandparents, I found an old copy of *Daily Guideposts* that belonged to my grandmother and read a few pages. The daily devotionals were inspiring, but it was the daily journal sections at the end of each month that really caught my attention. My grandmother had written some type of praise to God each day, thanking Him for the many blessings He had provided for them. What was so amazing to me was that her thanks and praise continued all during the time my grandfather's only sister was dying. I was much younger then and it took many more years for me to incorporate daily praise to God in *all* things. Today, I begin each journal entry with TYFT—Thank You for Today—no matter what happened that day. I don't have the time to write as extensively as I would like, but the *Daily Guideposts* journal makes it possible for me to express in writing my daily thanks to God. —SHARON HOWARD, DALLAS, TEXAS

SUN
16 Whoever sows sparingly will also reap sparingly, and whoever sows generously will also reap generously.
—II CORINTHIANS 9:6 (NIV)

The Father's Day fax from London arrived late in the day. My husband Whitney, who'd feared that Wendy, his eldest, living away from home for the first time, had forgotten his day, took it eagerly and read:

Dear Dad,

It's raining here in London. What else is new?

On days like this I think of sun and beach. On *this* day I'm thinking of a special beach the summer I was eight. It was nearing the end of the day. We were all exhausted from volleyball, football and building sand castles. You and I had just finished throwing a tennis ball (you know how we used to throw them into the waves), and had decided we'd had enough for the day. So we had a last toss and then you said you wanted to show me something.

"Sit down next to me in the sand," you said. We were standing in the water near where the waves break and shoot toward the shore.

"What are you doing, Dad?" I asked, mystified.

"Just sit here and let the water wash over you, and you can feel your feet and hands being buried in the sand."

So we sat there, not minding that we were getting lumps of sand in our bathing suits and that our skin was wrinkling like prunes. We sat there till after everyone else left. I don't know what we talked about. What I do know, what is still with me to this day, is that feeling of sitting next to you, with salt in our ears and noses and eyes, and idling away the last of the daylight, knowing that you loved me enough to take the time to sit next to me in the water and watch the world go by.

Thanks for that and all the other great memories you've given me. They're with me wherever I go.

Love, Wendy.

Lord, thank You for loving fathers—an image of Your love for us.
—*SHARI SMYTH*

MON

17 Behold, I make all things new....

—*REVELATION 21:5*

Yesterday, I traveled to a small town in the lush, green piedmont region of South Carolina to visit a friend. Here time moves more slowly. And it seems that everyone lives in a white wooden house with a broad porch and a large, shady lawn.

Needing exercise, my friend and I set off on a brisk walk around a small park. Looking ahead, I saw two elderly ladies shuffling down the sidewalk toward us, one bent over a walker, the other using a cane. As we passed, one lady muttered something I couldn't understand. I stopped and said, "Excuse me, ma'am?"

In a practiced schoolteacher's voice, she answered, "Young man, we always walk around the park in this direction."

Taken aback, I replied, "Do you mean you want us to circle the park in the same direction you're walking in?"

She nodded and said, "Folks 'round here do. Always!" Then the ladies curtly shuffled off.

Stifling our laughter, my friend and I wheeled about-face and obeyed her wishes. We didn't want to spoil her day.

I must admit that I see myself in those two ladies. I've grown accustomed to my own routine: reading before I fall asleep each night; drinking a cup of English tea every morning; never wearing lace-up dress shoes; always wearing button-down shirt collars; driving to work by the same route each day. My well-worn habits have slowly become deep ruts. Flexibility and novelty are good for me, too. I need to circle the park a different way.

Dear Lord, may I do something new today.   —*SCOTT WALKER*

TUE

18

> God . . . will not forget your work and the love you have
> shown him. . . .   —*HEBREWS 6:10 (NIV)*

While I was packing clothes for our move to a new apartment, I came across my high school yearbook in the dusty corner of a closet. I don't think I'd looked at it in at least a decade. Accustomed to seeing a few wrinkles in the mirror each morning, I was surprised to see how much we formerly mature young ladies and gentlemen looked like teenagers. I turned to read what some of my friends had written.

"Have a great summer and a great life! Luv, Lisa."

"It's been real nice getting to know you. I'll always remember the fun we had in study hall. Kathy."

Unimpressed, I turned the pages trying to recall the names and faces of some of the five hundred and forty students in my class. I found pictures from the spring musical, my favorite history teacher, an article on students who built a greenhouse that I never knew existed.

Just as I was about to close the book, I noticed a long, handwritten note on one of the end papers. "Dear Julia, You have been a terrific friend this year, and I shall never forget you. Thank you for all your help. I don't know how I would have made it through the rough water without you. Love always, Karin."

Karin? Who was Karin? I had no idea.

I looked back through the pictures, trying to figure out who this mystery person could be. Thirty minutes of searching, and I still had no clue. What I did find was a note from another mystery person: Maureen. "Julia, I can't tell you how much you helped me when I was so upset. Thanks for being there and being a friend."

Two people, each of whom were totally lost to my memory, yet to whom I'd obviously been important. *How strange!* I thought. And then, astonished, *What a blessing to have been given the grace to help someone and then forget that I'd done it!*

Lord Jesus, whenever I'm feeling frustrated because I'm forgetful, help me to forget myself. —*JULIA ATTAWAY*

WED
19
Weeping may endure for a night, but joy cometh in the morning. —*PSALM 30:5*

Nighttime has always been my time. Night is perfect for the things I like to do—write songs and stories—and it's perfect for reflection, for looking deep inside. "Up late, sleep late," has always been my motto, and I never had any reason to change it.

Until I had kids. Between their nightmares, sicknesses and inexplicable phenomena like simply popping up at five in the morning, I've had to be up early more than at any other time in my life. I can get my kids back to sleep by holding them and walking around the house, but trying to sleep while walking in a well-furnished, darkened house with one eye closed, all the while holding a child, is a recipe for disaster. I know: I've tried.

But having kids who can't sleep has brought me face to face with one of God's greatest gifts to man: sunrise. Light breaks through the dark and in the renewal of the day is the renewal of God's promises in the Easter triumph of His Son. And in the stillness before the morning rush, the Bible speaks particularly clear to the ear of faith. God's Word and the morning are a wonderfully synergistic combination.

Lord, help me to be disciplined and seek You in the morning.

—DAVE FRANCO

20

> Be ye angry, and sin not: let not the sun go down upon your wrath. *—EPHESIANS 4:26*

"What's wrong with them?"

"We've had them for twenty years!"

"So? I like them. Why do we need new dishes? These are fine."

"They don't display the food."

My husband Edward wanted new china. I didn't.

Of course, it wasn't that simple. After all, I had picked out our dishes in the first place. Edward was irritated that I would make an issue over something he considered a routine upgrade. He thought I was fussing about the cost. He liked plain white porcelain. I liked the beige-and-dark-blue stoneware already on our shelves.

Six months passed in a kind of armed truce. I would notice glossy brochures on the coffee table bearing names like Wedgwood or Lenox. When we walked up Fifth Avenue, Edward would stop and gaze wistfully at lavish china displays in store windows, while I walked briskly on, pretending not to notice. Web sites offering a hundred china designs at a discount appeared on my computer. The specter of the china stood between us at every meal.

One day I was complaining about the "china affair" to a family friend. Hearing the resentment and pique in my voice, he looked at me for a while and then said, "You know, Brigitte, I think you should give this china to your relationship."

"What do you mean?" I snapped, but I knew perfectly well what he was telling me—it was time to resolve this senseless dispute.

As I walked home that evening, I felt suddenly at peace. The message was as clear to me as a flashing neon sign. "Let not the sun go down on your wrath," Paul told the Ephesians, and although he probably wasn't thinking about white Wedgwood dishes, I understood. Too many suns had gone down on this particular wrath.

An hour later Edward came in, carrying his usual pile of books. "I've changed my mind," I said quietly. "Order the china."

Lord, open my mind to Your Word in the wise words of friends.

—BRIGITTE WEEKS

FOR EVERY SEASON

FRI
21

It was you who set all the boundaries of the earth; you made both summer and winter.   *—PSALM 74:17 (NIV)*

For fourteen years I have been a "weather watcher" for a TV station in Washington, D.C. Three to four times a day I send the current temperatures—the highs and lows and precipitation totals—via the phone or the Web. Sometimes they use the information on the air, but most of the time it is simply a volunteer service that I enjoy providing.

In the course of being a weather watcher, I've learned that it can be difficult to determine exactly when one season ends and another begins. For example, there is a meteorological summer, which starts on the first of June. Then there is an astronomical summer, which starts three weeks later. Then there are the moments when summer really arrives in each of our lives. It may be the day school lets out or the day we set off on our vacation. It may come with the first heat wave or heavy thunderstorm. Summer is a lethargic time, and its arrival matches its nature.

In my prayer life, I have summer arrival times, too. These are times when I've prayed and prayed and begun to feel that either an answer isn't coming, or it has already come and I've missed it. Then suddenly, like an afternoon thundershower, there it is. Recently, I had a deadline approaching and simply couldn't gather my thoughts. "Help, Lord!" I prayed.

Suppressing my panic, I prayed for the grace to tell the project manager I had nothing for him, a truly humbling experience. But I know well that to run ahead of the Lord is as futile as trying to make summer come before its time. Suddenly, one morning, my ideas began to gel. By the afternoon, half of the project was done!

Lord, thank You for seasons that come in life, sometimes slowly, but still steadfastly. Grant me summer-slow patience to wait when I must.
—*ROBERTA ROGERS*

SAT
22
A man's mind plans his way, but the Lord directs his steps.
—*PROVERBS 16:9 (RSV)*

I was asked to become the new chair of the personnel committee for my church, but I felt nervous and unsure about accepting. *What if I can't handle it? What if I do something stupid and make a fool of myself?*

Then I remembered a birthday party I'd attended when I was six. The party was run by older kids, who announced that we would play "Egg Hop." They placed eggs in a random pattern on the floor, then took all of us younger kids into the next room. They blindfolded my best friend, told her she had to walk through the eggs without breaking any, then led her into the other room and closed the door. Soon we heard howls of laughter from the older kids. I looked down at my new patent leather shoes and began to shake. I couldn't get egg yolk on those shoes, I just couldn't! The older kids came back for their next victim. More laughter from the next room. Another victim. More laughter.

When the older kids came for me, smirking and dangling the blindfold, I burst into tears, sat down on the floor and refused to budge. No amount of cajoling could persuade me to change my mind. Finally, they led me into the next room to show me the floor: no eggs! All the fun and laughter had come from watching the blindfolded participants tiptoe carefully through nonexistent obstacles.

That's what I was doing now, worrying about problems that might not exist. After sending up a prayer for courage, I called the outgoing chair of the personnel committee and stepped out in faith. "Okay," I said, "I'll give it a try."

Lord, today I will set aside my fears and move forward with confidence, relying on Your guidance. —*MADGE HARRAH*

SUN

23

First go and be reconciled with your brother; then come and offer your gift. —*MATTHEW 5:24 (NIV)*

At a church potluck awhile ago, older parishioners were asked to share childhood memories to help us younger parents strengthen our families. An elderly Greek lady, Helen, told us that every Saturday evening her family had prayed special prayers ending the old week and starting the new. Most importantly, they asked forgiveness of each other and their Father. "Only then did I feel ready to go to church the next day," Helen said.

Their Saturday ritual seemed only an interesting old custom until a few weeks later, when our family attended the Liturgy at a Romanian Orthodox monastery in southern Michigan. At one point during the Liturgy, the clergy embrace and ask forgiveness of each other, then bow to the congregation, asking the people to forgive them. When they had finished, the woman in front of me turned to the lady next to her and whispered, "Forgive me, Mom." Her mom asked her for forgiveness in turn, and they hugged each other. Then, before receiving Holy Communion, I noticed each nun go to the abbess, bow and ask forgiveness, then turn and bow to all the other nuns.

Looking at my husband Alex across the heads of our children, I mouthed the words, "Forgive me."

"I do. Forgive me, too," he whispered. We reached behind the kids and gave each other's hand a squeeze.

Now, before our family receives Communion each Sunday, we ask each other's forgiveness. Sometimes we think of specifics, like "Forgive me for losing my temper and shouting at you," or "Forgive me for not doing what you asked right away." At other times, nothing definite comes to mind, but we ask pardon for *any* ways we've wronged or failed each other, knowingly or unknowingly, and seal our reconciliation with a big hug. Cleansed of the past week's failures or irritations, we are renewed to start fresh another week "fighting the good fight of the faith."

Father, before I worship You today, help me be at peace with everyone. —*MARY BROWN*

MON
24

Strengthen your feeble arms and weak knees.
—*HEBREWS 12:12 (NIV)*

"Please make every effort to attend our upcoming high-school class reunion—it may be our final one," the letter said. But when it added, "Some of you have never attended any," I felt guilty.

Frankly, I'd never wanted to go. During my teenage years, I envied those who "had it all." *They* had the right clothes. *They* had friends galore, top grades, self-assurance. *They* were chosen for school plays, class officers, special projects—I was never even nominated for anything.

As I read the letter, scenes from those old school days surfaced on my mental screen: the demanding buzzer summoning us to the next class; the clash of banging locker doors; the rush of book-bearing classmates rounding the corridor where a winged Venus presided over one end and a bronzed Abe Lincoln over the other; the pep band playing "Oh, Johnny" and "When You Wish Upon a Star"; our cheerleaders jumping around in red and white outfits; the pain of our team's defeats and the dizzying triumphs of our victories.

Those memories were overwhelming; they made me even more determined not to attend. But my husband convinced me otherwise. "It might be your last reunion. I think you should go."

So we went, and I'm glad. Why? It proved therapeutic. I learned I had not been the only one who felt inadequate back then. Former classmates told me they'd envied *me*. "You lived on a farm! You had a Shetland pony to ride. A hay mow to play in. Now you're a writer. You've traveled a lot."

Father, forgive me when, even now, I envy others. You never meant for Your children to be like anyone else—You created each of us to be special to You. —*ISABEL WOLSELEY*

TUE

25

Cast thy bread upon the waters: for thou shalt find it after many days. —*ECCLESIASTES 11:1*

My friend Larry lives to fish. He wears T-shirts decorated with jumping bass, a hat stuck with fish hooks—he even carries a small boat atop his pickup. Larry thinks nothing of driving fifty miles to a special fishing hole, dragging the boat off the truck and relaxing on a lake for a couple of hours of catch-and-release fishing before driving back in time for work. He drapes lights shaped like trout on his camper trailer in the evening. And if you dine with Larry, well, you know what's for supper.

Many friends plan at least one fishing trip with Larry each summer, partly to rock in his camouflaged boat with their lines played out, and partly to enjoy his faith-filled conversation, for Larry is as much a philosopher as a fisherman. Though I don't even own a fishing rod, I've grown to treasure his earthy wisdom.

Not long ago, over cups of tea, I complained to Larry about my career path. "Maybe I'll have to move . . . or try a different field," I grumbled.

" 'Cast thy bread upon the waters,' " he quoted to me. I sighed in frustration. Today I needed answers, not quotations.

"And that's another thing," I fumed, "I've never understood that passage. Why on earth would anyone want to throw away good bread?"

"No, no," he chuckled softly. "Don't you see? It's bait. 'Cast thy bread upon the waters' means to draw the fish. Trust me, they'll come!"

I had thrown bread to the fish in nearby Sinks Canyon for twenty years; they leaped out of the water to snap at it. Larry was definitely on to something.

"So, you're saying that I should trust that whatever I have right now will draw whatever else I need later?" He grinned and tilted his fishing cap. Suddenly, the possibilities were limitless.

If Larry ever invites me to go fishing, I'll try it. I expect I'll learn about more than just a sport.

Lord, I begin to see Your wisdom in choosing fishermen as Your first disciples. —*GAIL THORELL SCHILLING*

WED

26

"I, the Lord, have called you in righteousness; I will take hold of your hand. I will keep you. . . ."
—*ISAIAH 42:6 (NIV)*

During a time of great difficulties in our family, friends continuously encouraged me, "Keep hanging in there. Hold on to God and His promises. He'll see you through." Like a terrified child, I clung to the Lord Jesus, but sometimes I felt my strength was slipping. I wondered how much longer I could hold on to God's hand.

At first, I saw my part-time job as a registered nurse as a good diversion. For eight hours in this other world, my own problems could disappear into the background.

One day after finishing my rounds, I checked on Mr. Jones. He was in the last stages of throat cancer, and he was blind. I found him propped up in bed, struggling for breath. He was starving, yet afraid of the pain of swallowing. I took his thin, veined hand in mine. "Nurse," he croaked in a hoarse whisper. "Like you're holding my hand, Jesus is holding on to me."

He motioned to the Bible lying on the bedside table, and I read from the place he had marked. "I, the Lord, have called you in righteousness; I will take hold of your hand. I will keep you."

A flush of joy washed over his face. "Yes! Yes, that's it. He's holding me."

Driving home that night, I thought about Mr. Jones's words. Could anything be worse than what he was living through moment by moment? Yet in his extreme weakness and pain, he'd found peace, strength—even joy. How?

Slowly, it dawned on me: It's not how hard we hang on to God's hand, but how tightly He holds on to us that counts.

As I contemplated this wonderful fact, peace replaced my panic. No matter what lay in the future, all would be well with me and my children as we are held safe in the hand of almighty God.

Thank You, Father, that when I stumble and fall, I am upheld by Your loving hand. —*HELEN GRACE LESCHEID*

THU
27
They have ears, but they hear not. . . .   —*PSALM 135:17*

Several years ago I went through a difficult period. My husband was retiring from the Navy after twenty-two years, and we were in a time of transition. The future seemed uncertain, and Larry and I both were experiencing anxiety.

At the same time, my aunt came from Indianapolis to visit my grandmother here in Richlands, North Carolina. With her she brought a gift for me from my cousin, whom I very seldom see or hear from. There was no way Cheryl could have known that I was going through a tough time, but when I opened the package I found a small cloth angel with a wooden head and lacy wings. Attached was a little poem that read:

> *I'm a little coping angel, come to help you cope.*
> *When things are looking rather bleak,*
> *And you are out of hope,*
> *Then you will need a coping friend*
> *To chase those clouds away, to cheer you and be near you,*
> *And to brighten up your day.*
> *So through the trials yet to come, and trials always do;*
> *Remember I'll be by your side, just looking out for you.*

When I called to thank Cheryl for her kindness, I asked how she could have known I needed such a gift. She told me that God had prompted her to send it.

Now the little angel hangs above my work station as a daily reminder that I, too, can be a messenger of God's love, but only if I'm willing to open my heart and let Him lead me.

Lord, help me tune my listening ear to You, that I might be of service to others.   —*LIBBIE ADAMS*

FRI
28
Impress them on your children. . . .
—*DEUTERONOMY 6:7 (NIV)*

At 3:00 A.M. in the bedroom of my father's house in the mountains, a crash of thunder shook me awake. In a voice nearly drowned by the sound of heavy rain drumming on the roof, my ten-year-old son John said, "Why did Grandpa just drive away?"

Alarmed, I jumped from bed and searched the empty house until I found a note on the dining room table: "Gone to the emergency room."

Dad had been suffering from a severe virus. Now my heart pounded thinking of him driving off alone into a violent thunderstorm. John and I hastily dressed and ran through the soaking rain to our car. As we wound down the driveway, John asked, "Are you sure you can drive in this?"

I answered, "I'll go as slow as I need to and I'm praying."

When we arrived at the emergency room, I was relieved to find Dad's white car parked safely in the lot. He was in the examination room, being fixed up with a prescription. As we were leaving, Dad ran into a friend of his whose husband was suffering from a serious lung infection. As Dad introduced us, I recognized the worried look in the woman's eyes as the same call to prayer that I had felt in the thunderstorm.

It was a simple exchange. I asked the woman if I might pray with her. She nodded. I put my hand on her shoulder and said a short, quiet prayer for her husband's successful treatment.

Several days later, while we were driving back home, John asked, "Why did you pray with that woman from the hospital?"

"Well, John," I answered, "she needed it, just like all of us."

In the midst of the thunderstorm and in the emergency room, I had nearly forgotten that John was with me, watching what I did. During those pre-dawn hours, my son had been observing, remembering and evaluating my prayer habits. How many times had he been watching when I slogged my way through an emergency without stopping to pray? How many worried people had he seen me pass without offering a hand to grab on to in prayer?

Dear Father, today make my prayer habits ones that will invite others into closer communion with You. —*KAREN BARBER*

SAT
29

A fountain of gardens, a well of living waters. . . .
—*SONG OF SOLOMON 4:15*

My wife and I left our home in the high desert for a day hike in the mountains one hot summer day. We drove north of Silverton and walked up a trail that was lush compared to the arid area around our home. Dramatic climatic changes occur within an hour's drive in western Colorado.

I spent the first hour of our hike mentally apologizing to God for ignoring the wonderful work He had done all summer. The unusual rains that brought us mud and mosquitoes also brought the most stunning display of wildflowers I have ever seen.

When we arrived in a meadow above the timberline, I wondered about Christ's forty days in the desert. Had He spent forty days in His Father's wilderness on this side of the globe, it might have been forty days of admiration, not preparation.

Not much is known of Jesus' first decade as an adult. I like to think that He spent ten years touring His Father's world. Did He sit at the convergence of a dozen melted snow streams, surrounded by floral rainbows? Did waterfalls tumble from mountain peaks on three sides? Did He admire the variety of colors vying for attention? Did the cool mountain breeze expose wave after wave of fire-red paint-brush, purple bellflowers, burgundy queen's crown, white saxifrage and columbines of all hues?

If so, the years must have flown by. And I can see how He could have scoffed at Satan's three temptations after my day in the mountains. It is easy to resist offerings from hell when you've had a glimpse of heaven.

Dear God, thank You for giving us such beauty on earth that we can imagine what heaven will be like. —*TIM WILLIAMS*

SUN

30

Thine eyes are upon all the ways of the sons of men. . . .
—*JEREMIAH 32:19*

Before my son Harrison was born, I'll have to admit that all the fuss about babies mystified me. Just exactly what could reasonably intelligent and sane people gain from the company of a tiny human who divided his or her time between eating, sleeping and crying?

Of course, the minute Harrison entered my world, I started to think very differently. Suddenly, I couldn't wait to get home from work to see what the little guy was up to. My wife Candy and I would express our amazement at each and every move Harrison made in his first few months of life.

Amazement aside, Harrison's arrival also brought a fair share of trials and tribulations. During his first weeks of life, he demanded constant attention. And just when he began to sleep through the night, we had to rush him to the hospital for an emergency double hernia operation. After the surgery, he needed an apnea monitor while he slept. After several weeks, with the doctor's permission, we took him off the monitor, and fatherhood started getting easier.

One night the phone rang as I was playing with Harrison in his room, and I went to the next room to pick it up. I knew that Harrison was safe; Candy had done an excellent job of baby-proofing his room. But during the few minutes I spent on the phone, Harrison began to wail.

I walked to the edge of the doorway and peered inside. There was Harrison, as safe as could be, turned away from the door so that he couldn't see me. He didn't know I was there watching him. He had no way of knowing everything was all right.

I stood there in awe, knowing that the same way I was watching over Harrison, God watches over me every second of the day. There are times I feel lonely or deserted; there are certainly times when I'm afraid. But God is watching. Everything is going to be just fine.

Father, all is well, knowing that Your eye is set upon me.

—BROCK KIDD

My Days of Prayer

1 _____

2 _____

3 _____

4 _____

5 _____

6 _____

7 _____

8 _____

9 _____

10 _____

11 _____

12 _____

13 _____

14 _____

15 _____

16 _____

17 _____

18 _____

19 _____

20 _____

21 _____

22 _____

23 _____

24 _____

25 _____

26 _____

27 _____

28 _____

29 _____

30 _____

July

Because there is one bread, we who are many are one body, for we all partake of the one bread.

—*I Corinthians 10:17 (RSV)*

S	M	T	W	T	F	S
	1	2	3	4	5	6
7	8	9	10	11	12	13
14	15	16	17	18	19	20
21	22	23	24	25	26	27
28	29	30	31			

THE PRAYER THAT IS ALWAYS NEW

Our Father. . . . *Give us* this day our daily bread.
—*MATTHEW 6:9, 11*

As I was saying the Lord's Prayer several years ago, I was struck by two words: *Give us.* How late in the prayer it comes, this very first request for our own needs—halfway to the end! Since the words Jesus gave His disciples were the pattern for the entire life of prayer, He must have been telling them, "Your own needs must always come second."

That certainly hadn't been my order of business! My prayers usually led off with a cry for help: "*Give* me the words to write her," when Maude's husband died. "*Protect* Andrew on his trip." "*Guide* the doctors during Fran's surgery."

Jesus has different priorities. Start by honoring God, He tells me. Hallow His name. Pray for His kingdom. Seek His will. Spend half your prayer time—the first half—putting the Father first. Jesus was all too aware of the wrenching human need He was sending His disciples to confront. Yet He didn't tell them, "Here's how to ask for God's aid in difficult situations." He said, "Worship God."

So I set out to follow this model. It is a tough discipline when the need is urgent! The very first week of the experiment, the prayer chain at our church learned of a college student—a parishioner's daughter—threatening suicide. *Make her answer her mother's phone calls, God!* I wanted to cry. *Have the dorm staff force her door open! Get her boyfriend to apologize!*

Instead, using the sequence of the Lord's Prayer, I made myself start, not with the problem, but with God's all-sufficiency. I concentrated on the greatness of His name. I asked for His kingdom to come everywhere on earth, including that dorm room; for His will to be done in all situations, not this one alone.

And as I followed Jesus' pattern, a curious thing happened. The panic was gone. I found myself offering my intercessions while focusing on the nature of God, forever working toward the very best. The prayers of many people were in fact answered when the student at last picked up the telephone and spoke to her mother.

Looking at our need through the lens of God's love: That must be why, in the prayer Jesus taught, the words *Give us* come so late.

Our Father, come first in my prayers and actions today.

—ELIZABETH SHERRILL

TUE
2

But one thing is needful: and Mary hath chosen that good part, which shall not be taken away from her.

—LUKE 10:42

My husband's business trip happened to take us near Mount Rushmore in South Dakota's Black Hills. Since we had heard all our lives about the four gigantic presidential faces chiseled in the mountain, we made a little side trip to see them for ourselves. Maybe it was the fact that it was nearing the Fourth of July, or that the day was all blue sky and sunshine, or that a youth choir had traveled a long way from home to sing patriotic songs in its shadow, but the magnificence of Mount Rushmore overwhelmed me.

George Washington, Thomas Jefferson, Abraham Lincoln, Theodore Roosevelt—each seemed to be staring straight at me from his lofty perspective. Especially Washington. Caught by his demanding "give it your best" gaze, I had no trouble picturing his soldiers following him anywhere.

Visiting Mount Rushmore that day, I learned something new about the carving of the mountain. Severe funding problems had threatened the project in 1930. The commissioners created a "school children's fund," asking each South Dakota grade-school child to contribute a dime and each high-school student a quarter. Imagine the disappointment when the campaign that year yielded only one thousand seven hundred dollars toward the hoped-for ten thousand dollars. It seems there was a new fad sweeping the country just then, a gadget called a yo-yo. The basic model cost a dime; the larger, fancier one a quarter. For a child, the choice between inspiring faces set in stone and a bit of fun on a string was really no choice at all.

I wonder sometimes about my own choices in life. Am I reaching for the rock-solid things that will endure beyond the moment? Or do I too often grab for what's merely fashionable? I hardly ever see a yo-yo anymore, but I do know of an incredible mountain in South Dakota that draws thousands of admirers every year.

Jesus, may I always make my choices under Your steady gaze.

—CAROL KNAPP

WED

3

And the elders, said, We are witnesses. . . .   *—RUTH 4:11*

In July, my cousin Pam Banta drove her father, my ninety-six-year-old Uncle Howard, from Oberlin, Kansas, to Colorado to spend a week in the family cabin next door to our house. It was a delight for my husband Robert and me to watch Uncle Howard enjoying this family vacation spot so much. And what wonderful stories he told of life with my grandparents and their six children when they came here in the early 1900s! How we laughed when he told us about all eight members of the family crowding into their Model T, bumping along over washboard roads, staying overnight unexpectedly at a farmhouse because of a flash flood and spending an hour waiting for a herd of cattle to cross the road. That trip, which now takes six hours, then took three days!

Though he's thinner and looks more frail than when I last saw him, Uncle Howard still plays golf, walks every day and was glad to do a bit of hiking with us. His short-term memory is failing, but there's certainly nothing wrong with his long-term memory. He has changed my idea of what it is to grow old. It's true that many people do lose their physical and mental abilities as they age, but being with Uncle Howard showed me that there's one thing most older people keep all their lives—the memories of their youth. What a treasure is stored there for younger generations who take the time to ask, "What was life like when you were a child?"

O Holy One, may I never avoid spending time with my elders for lack of something to talk about!   *—MARILYN MORGAN KING*

THU
4
Forever, O Lord, your Word stands firm in heaven. Your faithfulness extends to every generation. . . .
—*PSALM 119:89–90 (TLB)*

If ever you need a shot of spiritual adrenaline to give you confidence in the enduring promise of America, visit the Library of Congress in Washington, D.C. Completed in 1897, its breathtaking sculptures, murals and paintings trace our cultural heritage and represent every aspect of civilized life and thought. It is the official repository for copyrights; its shelves hold what is claimed to be "approximately the entire current product of the American press"; its research resources are among the best in the world. The Latin inscriptions in the family corridor of the main entrance capture its essence: *Litera scripta manet* (The written word endures); *Liber dilectatio animae* (Books, the delight of the soul); *Efficiunt clarum studio* (Study, the watchword of fame); and *In tenebris lux* (In darkness, light).

For me, visiting the library was a pilgrimage. Most inspirational were the quotations lettered above the symbolic sculptures in the west gallery of the Rotunda. Religion, holding a flower in her hand representing God revealed in nature, has the inscription: "What doth the Lord require of thee, but to do justly, and to love mercy, and to walk humbly with thy God?" (Micah 6:8). History, holding a mirror turned backward to reflect the past: "One God, one law, one element. And one far-off divine event, To which the whole creation moves" (Tennyson). And most remarkable, Science, holding a globe of the earth in her left hand, and in her right a mirror, held forward so all may look into her images of truth. Hard-nosed Science, with her traditional demand, "Prove it to me before I will believe," has above her statue Psalm 19:1: "The heavens declare the glory of God; and the firmament sheweth his handiwork." Proof enough!

With tears in my eyes I paused and reflected, thanking God for the enduring faith of our forefathers, indelibly inscribed in the halls of the Library of Congress.

Almighty and all merciful God, through the witness of those who have gone before us, and with prayers for those who will come long after us, continue to bless America. —*FAY ANGUS*

FRI

5

A cheerful heart is a good medicine, but a downcast spirit dries up the bones.　　　*—PROVERBS 17:22 (RSV)*

I poked my head apprehensively through a hospital door where I could hear the tick-swoosh of kidney dialysis machines. A series of strokes and complications with diabetes had left my friend not only needing dialysis, but also blind. I dreaded the visit; my own medical problems and depression gave me little space to be supportive. King Solomon's proverb, "A downcast spirit dries up the bones," had taken over my life, and Barbara would need more encouragement than I could give.

A nurse spotted me. "Is this where I can find Barbara Martin?" I asked.

Hearing my voice, Barbara cheerfully called, "Brenda, I'm over here!" I was so shocked at the joy and excitement in my friend's voice that I couldn't help but smile as I approached.

"Look, see what I brought you!" she exclaimed, accepting my kiss, and from a bright purple lunch pack she produced a half-dozen chocolate covered cookies, sprinkled in red, white and blue speckles. "Happy Fourth of July!"

"But how—?"

"Bill had to do the baking," she interrupted, referring to her husband, "but I did the dipping. And my daughter helped with the sprinkling."

I was so surprised that I could hardly blurt out my thanks. Barbara had spent her whole life cooking and baking and making all kinds of chocolate candies, but I'd assumed her blindness and other troubles would put a stop to that. Clearly not!

Never have six hours passed so pleasantly. We chatted and visited, and when she overheard another patient ask a nurse where he could meet people, Barbara invited him to our church. When he agreed, I marveled at my friend. Her cheerful acceptance of where life had put her was like a ray of hope in my own dark place.

I go back often now. Barbara thinks I do it for her. I do it for both of us. A cheerful heart is good medicine!

Dear Lord, help me to accept what I cannot change in my life. And, like Barbara, help me to find new ways to meet my limitations and be a blessing to others wherever I am, and in whatever circumstances I may find myself.　　　*—BRENDA WILBEE*

SAT
6

"But the Counselor, the Holy Spirit . . . will teach you all things, and bring to your remembrance all that I have said to you." —*JOHN 14:26 (RSV)*

I woke, weeping, from a dream about a life long ago, when my children were young and I was their gallant knight. But alone in the darkness at 3:47 A.M., I was only an old man dreaming of the past.

Then I remembered that Jesus said He would send the Holy Spirit to be with us as Counselor, to teach us and *remind* us of what Jesus had taught. So I prayed, "God, I'm lonely and miserable. My faith has apparently lost its power, and I can't remember what to do!"

The words formed in my mind: *What would you tell someone else to do in this situation, Keith?*

"I'd say something like, 'I, too, have awakened in the dark, feeling lost many times over the years. And God has always helped me through.' "

What happened? What did He teach you to do?

"Turn on the light, and get out of bed. Then *do* something! Even God would have trouble guiding a stationary object. You've got to be moving to get guidance. So get up."

What next, after you get out of bed?

"Well, I go into the kitchen and brew a cup of herbal tea. Then I sit down at the breakfast table and go through the Twenty-third Psalm, reminding myself that God has helped people for thousands of years—even through 'the valley of the shadow of death.' And then I say a prayer of commitment."

Anything else?

"Well, the rest doesn't sound too spiritual. But I need to let some time pass for God to do His work on my fearful feelings. So if I still can't go to sleep, I may read a novel, the sports section of the paper, a magazine about travel or anything that points me toward the future—where my midnight demons do not live. And by the time I've acknowledged Him as Lord and taken a few small steps out of 'the land of shadows,' I usually even feel some peace."

Lord, thank You for Your Spirit, Who reminds me of what I need to know. Amen. —*KEITH MILLER*

SUN

7   After this manner ye shall offer daily, throughout the seven days. . . .   —*NUMBERS 28:24*

So much of life is made up of routine. I get up and out of bed each morning, prepare breakfast, get washed and dressed and ready for work, pause for my morning quiet time, and then on to the office or, on Sunday, to church. Although the word *routine* has a negative connotation, the routine in my life can be a real positive because it gets me out and about so I can contribute to our Guideposts ministries, be involved in my community, and participate in the affairs and activities of my church.

The day's routine takes me out of myself and into the concerns and interests of other people. And it's amazing what I'll find happening in my community if the focus isn't just on myself. My church here in Pawling, New York, is a great example. Christ Church, a white-steepled interdenominational church, stands across from my home on Quaker Hill. This small community church offers a remarkable number of programs and activities that are made possible because people's churchgoing routines have given them the opportunity to use their imaginations, their talents and their interests to do things for others. We have an outreach program at the local prison for women, with whom we do crafts. Sometimes we make late-night runs into the city to feed the homeless. And our radio program broadcasts our services throughout the Hudson Valley.

You can find a like opportunity in your community if you look for it. You'll find an exciting way of living out the Christian experience day by day if you make helping others a part of your regular routine.

Lord Jesus, help me use the routines of my life to grow daily in Your image.   —*RUTH STAFFORD PEALE*

MON

8   To every thing there is a season, and a time to every purpose under the heaven. . . .   —*ECCLESIASTES 3:1*

"I've given up driving my car," my old friend said, "and, you know, it was one of the most difficult decisions I've ever had to make. We Americans love our cars and take them for granted as almost indispensable in our lives. When the time comes to hang up your keys, you feel a tremendous sense of loss, as if your life is severely limited. It left me with a real sense of depression."

"You seem to have gotten over that," I said. "How did you do it?"

"I turned to the Bible, as I often do with a problem, and found myself reading Ecclesiastes, where the preacher says that there's a time for everything. 'A time to be born, and a time to die . . . a time to weep, and a time to laugh . . . a time to keep, and a time to cast away.' Those words are thousands of years old, but in their majestic cadences you can almost hear the clock of the universe tick. They made me think that even where driving a car is concerned, there is a time to stop, and a wise person must accept that necessity without feeling deprived or depressed. So that's what I've been trying to do."

"Good for you," I said, and hoped that someday I would be equally wise.

Father, grant me the wisdom to know when the time is right for hard decisions. —*ARTHUR GORDON*

TUE

9 Thou shalt not steal. —*EXODUS 20:15*

I'd built up quite a nice little collection of pink packets of sweetener in the clear glass sugar bowl on my kitchen counter. Oh, it wasn't that I couldn't afford to buy them; it's just that whenever I was in a luncheonette or coffee shop, there they were, and I'd pop one or two—or three—"extras" in my purse or pocket.

One night Betsy, a longtime friend, visited for a cup of coffee after work. Picking up one of the pink packets, she commented, "Hey, that's funny! This has the name of a diner on it!"

Turning slightly red, I babbled something about running low on supplies. But when she picked up the next one and it had the name of a different diner on it, she teased me, "My dad used to call that 'dime crime.'" As my face flamed, she continued thoughtfully, "I've done my own share of 'dime crimes.' Why, I remember my sister haunting the library for the next two Mary Poppins books and the librarian telling her that somebody was keeping them way overdue. It was me—I'd shoved them under the bed. I was too lazy to return them."

Hmm. I thought of the times I'd been "too tired" to return books

on time—had someone else been waiting? "But I don't *steal*," I
protested.

"What about the time you fibbed and told Fira [the Russian
woman I tutor] that you had a "touch of flu"?

"I guess I committed 'time theft,' " I admitted.

"The commandment says, 'Thou shalt not steal,' " Betsy pointed
out. "It doesn't say, 'Except sweeteners' or 'except time.' "

I laughed. "You're right."

When Betsy left, I "went straight." I bundled up my stolen pink
packets for the battered women's shelter and decided to *purchase* all
my artificial sweeteners from that moment on. Then I called Fira to
schedule an extra session.

**God, have I committed any "dime crimes" lately? If so, let me take
action to make amends today.** —*LINDA NEUKRUG*

WED
10
"See how the lilies of the field grow. They do not labor or
spin. Yet I tell you that not even Solomon in all his
splendor was dressed like one of these."
—*MATTHEW 6:28, 29 (NIV)*

When I was a child, my family lived in a city, not a big one, but a city
nevertheless. Outdoors I played on concrete, and the only time I saw
a tree was when we took a bus to a small park. Then we moved to a
suburb where some of the roads weren't paved and trees were everywhere. I was thrilled!

Next door to our house was an empty overgrown lot just waiting
for a builder to come along. To me it was the most beautiful garden
I had ever seen, filled with bushes, grasses and flowers of every color.
I didn't know they were weeds—"stinkweeds," the neighborhood
kids called them. I thought they were the kind of flowers people
picked to give to someone they loved, and I picked a huge bouquet
for my mother. As I carried it home I heard some of the kids making
fun of me, although I didn't know why.

My mother must have heard them because she met me at the
door and opened her arms wide to receive the bouquet. "What beautiful flowers!" she said in a voice loud enough for the kids to hear.
Then she hugged me. When she closed the door, she said, "We must

give them some water right away." She found a vase and arranged the weeds as if they were the rarest flowers in the world.

Eventually I learned to tell the difference between a weed and a flower, but to this day I have a deep affection for weeds. I got that from my mother, who cared more about the meaning than the price of things. To her, my wild bouquet told her that I loved her, and that's what mattered.

Lord, help me to see Your love for this beautiful earth in the wild things You have made.　　　　　　　—*PHYLLIS HOBE*

THU
11　　The tongue of the wise brings healing.
　　　　　　　　　　—*PROVERBS 12:18 (NAS)*

My children grew up with a very noisy, critical mother. I didn't talk; I lectured. And they didn't listen; they argued. So when my twin sons approached their late twenties, I told God I was willing to do anything to be able to communicate effectively with them. He gave me a radical idea: *Keep your opinions, warnings, lectures and I-told-you-so's to yourself. And don't pry.*

One scorching July day, I heard the squeak of brakes from the driveway and hurried outside. It was one of my sons. He didn't visit often. He stumbled out of his truck, crying so hard that I wondered if he'd been in an accident. I hadn't seen him cry that much since he was about ten. Now his broad shoulders shook uncontrollably and his tears formed tiny puddles on the pavement. I reached up to hug him, and even though he towered over me, he crumpled onto my shoulder, his tears soaking my shirt. He let me hold him awhile, then lifted up his head and said, "You haven't called or fussed or nagged or told me how wrong I am. You haven't said *anything* at all!"

Four small words formed in my melting heart, scurried through my astonished mind and reached my trembling lips: "I love you, son."

He looked me right in the eyes, sniffed loudly, nodded once and hugged me so hard I couldn't breathe for a moment. Then, arms tightly around each other, we walked toward the house.

Thank You, Father, for teaching me how to use my tongue—wisely. Amen.　　　　　　　　　　—*MARION BOND WEST*

12

Breaking bread in their homes, they partook of food with glad and generous hearts. . . . —*ACTS 2:46 (RSV)*

In July 1942, when Ruby and I were engaged, I left her and my teaching job in East St. Louis, Illinois, to accept a position at the Rock Island Arsenal, about two hundred and fifty miles away. It was wartime, and I wanted to help with the war effort.

Only one restaurant in Rock Island would serve African Americans, and it was closed on Sundays. Then, within weeks of my arrival, it closed for good. I didn't know how to cook, so I was forced to depend on the lunch cart that came through the arsenal every day. My kindly landlady felt sorry for me, but she was elderly and a widow. Food rationing made it difficult for her to offer me meals or teach me how to cook. But all was not lost. My landlady found me a two-room apartment that I furnished as a first home for Ruby and me. I even bought a new stove!

Ruby and I married in September, and I hurried back to work in Rock Island the same day. Ruby joined me one week later. When I returned home from work on the evening shift and mounted the stairs that first day, a wonderful aroma greeted me. I entered the apartment, and Ruby sat me down at the table and served me hash brown potatoes and golden veal chops. It was truly a feast, my first real meal in weeks.

As I savored that heavenly meal, I offered a quiet prayer of thanksgiving for Ruby, our new home and that deliciously prepared meal. Even now, fifty-nine years later, the memory remains. I was then, as now, truly blessed.

Comforting Father, thank You for the evening when You joined our hearts at that tiny table. —*OSCAR GREENE*

13

"Blessed are the dead who die in the Lord. . . . they will rest from their labor, for their deeds will follow them." —*REVELATION 14:13 (NIV)*

I look at the familiar exit sign and feel the lump in my throat grow larger. It has been nine months since I last made this five-hundred-mile round-trip. Nine long months. I pull off the interstate and take the back roads to the small town where she lived. Her house, now owned by strangers, is ill-kept: Trash litters the yard; the shrubs have been pulled up; and one window in the back porch is broken. I push down on the gas, remembering the meticulous way Mother kept everything, and turn toward where I know I'll find her.

The old cemetery where she is buried is small. I park my car between two huge trees and reach into the backseat for the dozen roses I've just bought. Mother's grave is easy to spot, flanked as always by bouquets of purple silk flowers. I stand at the grave. It is a beautiful day . . . birds, sun, corn swishing in the field next door.

As I brush a few leaves from her grave and place the flowers, I read the stone: AT REST IN HEAVEN. It's easy to imagine my mother in heaven. But at rest? That's harder. She was always working, organizing church dinners, visiting shut-ins, creating missionary lessons or cooking for just about everyone!

I stoop to kiss her gravestone and, on impulse, pull out one of the roses. I'll take it back with me and place it on my desk at work; not as a reminder of Mother's death, but as a tribute to her life—a life of service well-lived and worthy of emulation.

Help me, Father, to live my life in response to Your voice. Let me leave a legacy of holy work, done with diligence and joy.

—*MARY LOU CARNEY*

SUN
14   **And ye shall seek me, and find me, when ye shall search for me with all your heart.**   —*JEREMIAH 29:13*

The rector opened the Sunday-morning service by welcoming the parishioners and also the visitors and tourists, always well represented in a large city church. Then he added a third category to his welcome. "Those of you who are here church-shopping—we are very glad to have you with us." For a moment I hardly registered his words. Then I thought with dismay, *Do people shop for churches the way they shop for a lawn mower? How soon will* Consumer's Report *judge some congregation or other to be a "best buy"?*

As the organ launched exultantly into "All Hail the Power of Jesus' Name," I thought about shopping with my daughter for her forthcoming wedding. She wanted everything to be the best she could find at a price we could pay. She worked tirelessly on the Internet and in the library to find good information and track down promising leads.

It was all a part of her joy in her fiancé and their future together. It was moving to watch and to be a part of it.

Why then was I so bothered by the idea of church-shopping? The phrase was just shorthand for the work and loving attention that many people put into finding a church community in which they could both worship and grow most fully, a place where they could volunteer their talents and check in with God on a regular basis.

I looked around the church that I had come to regard as my spiritual home. I, too, had shopped to find this church. And my joy in finding it outweighed discovering the biggest bargain in the finest store.

Help us, Lord, as we seek to find a spiritual home and to do our best in Your service.   —BRIGITTE WEEKS

THE PRACTICE OF PRAYER

MON	*Positive Prayer*
15	Ask in prayer, believing, ye shall receive.

—MATTHEW 21:22

One of my daughter Keri's assignments when she was in the second grade was to create a poster that would introduce her class to the study of nutrition. For days she searched through magazines; she cut, she pasted, she drew. Finally, she unveiled her work: a silhouette of a man formed by a colorful collage of fruits and vegetables, breads and meats. Across the bottom of her poster, she wrote these words: "You are what you eat."

As in nutrition, so in prayer: "You are what you pray." Once we clean house and rid ourselves of bad habits, grudges and our other shortcomings, once we surrender all our negatives to God, a void forms. To fill that void, we need to practice Dr. William R. Parker's third point of successful prayer: "Make Prayer Positive."

During your designated prayer time, immediately upon waking in the morning or when you lay your head on your pillow at night, pray positive prayers. Throughout your day, hold on to positive thoughts, wholesome images, hopeful ideas. "Ask," Jesus said, "and you shall receive." You are what you pray!

Like Keri, painstakingly cutting pictures of broccoli and carrots and brussels sprouts from a tall stack of magazines, you can choose a set of positive traits that will eventually define the new you. Do you hanker to be an optimist? Do you want to be known as generous and admired as one with a kind heart? Pray for those traits. Do you want to be remembered by your smile, your compassion for others, your listening skills? Practice those habits. Surrender any negative inclinations directly to God and replace them with affirmative thoughts. Be kind. Look for good and acknowledge that good.

Pray positively. *Be* positive. You are what you pray!

Father, I want to be beautiful for You! Help me believe in the best self I am becoming.   —*PAM KIDD*

TUE
16

Amaziah was twenty-five years old when he became king.... He did what was right, but sometimes resented it!   —*II CHRONICLES 25:1-2 (TLB)*

Teachers have to do a lot of things they don't want to do. When our college dean asked me to teach American literature next fall, I felt like crying. *Oh, no,* I thought, *anything but that! I loathe fiction! This is so not me.*

My wife tried to console me. "I know you don't like fiction, but that could be a plus. You might bring something unique to the class, something a starry-eyed poetry peddler might not think to do."

"Yeah, right. How about if I burn the textbook in front of the class?"

I fumed for weeks, but as the summer wore on, I reconciled myself to the duty with the following thoughts:

1. I might actually like the course. I'm not always the best judge of what I might like or hate. Many of my favorite foods, like pizza and soup beans, were foods I first detested, then grew to love. I remember reading about a student who was forced to take a history class he didn't want. Turns out he loved it so much, he changed his major and eventually became an award-winning history professor.

2. I will learn something. Who knows? Reading Longfellow's poems might make me a better writer, and wading through Emerson's essays might improve my thinking.
3. There is honor in doing a difficult task, whether it's emptying bedpans in a nursing home or trimming office expenses because of budget cuts.

Right now, bedpans sound really good, compared to fiction! I wish I could do this job with a passion, but with God's help, I will at least do it, however reluctantly. It's all I know to do. Pray for me!

Lord, I know You understand what it's like to face distasteful duties. I'll need Your help with this one, more than ever.

—*DANIEL SCHANTZ*

READER'S ROOM

In July 1999, I received a letter from a woman claiming to be my sister. The letter had been forwarded through Social Security. Apparently, my father, whom I hadn't seen or heard from for fifty years, had remarried and had two other daughters beside my sister and me.

My first thoughts were that this was some kind of joke. Why, after fifty years, would she decide to make contact? I would have to think about this before replying.

The day after I received the letter was July 29. The Scripture in *Daily Guideposts* for that day was "Rejoice with me; for I have found the piece which I had lost." I immediately opened my *Women's Devotional Bible* to Luke 15 and was drawn to the story on the following page about a sister dying and a new "sister" coming into her life. There was then no doubt in my mind that God had spoken to me and that the letter I received was real.

I contacted my "new" sister by e-mail. We now correspond regularly and hope to meet each other's families this year.

—*JOSEPHINE MCCONNELL, LAKE CARMEL, NEW YORK*

^{WED}

17

Incline your ear, and come unto me: hear, and your soul shall live. . . . —*ISAIAH 55:3*

I had three-year-old John's wrist firmly in hand as we walked home. It was the end of a hot, sticky day, and we'd gone out to our local Indian restaurant to relax in the air-conditioning. The kids ate well and were generally good, but John refused to keep his voice down at the end of dinner, and I had to take him home.

Up the street we trudged, John wailing and screeching. I smiled and greeted at least a half-dozen neighbors as I pulled John along. Regardless of my I-have-it-under-control exterior, I was seething inside. *We don't get to go out to eat often, but we did today because the heat was so beastly. Why couldn't John appreciate what a treat this was? Why couldn't he behave?*

The child in me wanted to shout, "Why do you have to ruin everything?" while the adult in me whispered, "Come, Holy Spirit, give me the words to handle this with love." My anger hissed, "When will you grow up?" but my love for my son sang, "Please, Holy Spirit, show me the way."

We marched into the apartment, and I brought John over to sit on the sofa with me. His turmoil was waning; mine was still chugging along at an alarming speed. I held him silently for a moment as I sent up one last plea for help. I waited. Then I opened my mouth to speak, and out came words and thoughts that were certainly not my own.

"I can tell you're growing up, John, because you're able to calm yourself down so much more quickly than you used to. I'm so pleased at how your self-control is improving."

My son seemed to grow an inch before my eyes. He smiled and snuggled against me. "I'm sorry I was naughty, Mommy. Next time I will listen better."

Lord, wherever my spirit is troubled, speak to me through Your Holy Spirit, and give me a listening heart. —*JULIA ATTAWAY*

THU
18 "Let your hand be with me, and keep me from harm so that I will be free from pain. . . ."
—*I CHRONICLES 4:10 (NIV)*

This year, my birthday fell on a regular workday, so I took the day off, just as I've done for the last several years. "Why?" asked a co-worker who is many years younger. "When you become an adult, isn't your birthday just like any other day?"

"Actually, I have this thing about birthdays," I told her. "I see them as God's gift of a once-a-year day to celebrate the person He's created each of us to be, and an opportunity to pause and consider where we are in the process of becoming that person."

She rolled her eyes, so I continued to defend my birthday theory. "It's a day when you're supposed to have a private birthday party with God."

"How?" she asked.

"I like to find a nice quiet place outside. Sometimes it's at the table on our back patio, or on top of a rock by a stream in the mountains, or on a bench in the shade at a nearby park. I take a notebook and my Bible. I read and reflect back and look forward and talk to God and listen to Him, asking Him where we are in my growing-up process. I always end by writing a birthday prayer, filled with 'thank-you's' for past blessings and 'pleases' for future ones. Then I tuck the prayer in my journal or Bible so I can read it several times during the year. Later in the day, I like to celebrate with my family and friends."

She gave me one more roll of her eyes before turning and walking away, as if my birthday tradition sounded a bit odd to her. But when her birthday fell on a regular workday a few weeks later, she took the day off, too.

Father, thank You for my once-a-year birthday and the opportunity to celebrate with You.
—*CAROL KUYKENDALL*

FRI
19 O Lord, thou hast searched me, and known me. Thou knowest my downsitting and mine uprising, thou understandest my thought afar off.
—*PSALM 139:1-2*

"Come here, Marty," I say with practiced nonchalance.

Marty, my yellow Lab, is curled up under the coffee table in a tight ball, as if to make himself as small as possible and therefore somehow less visible, if not altogether invisible. He wears a doomed expression and refuses to return my gaze. The question I can never answer is this: How does he know when I am going to give him a bath?

For some reason this dog—who will joyously propel himself into a freezing lake in the dead of winter and practically refuse to come out—profoundly dreads the prospect of a quick, lukewarm bath. Through the years, I have learned to disguise my nefarious intentions. I don't put the towels and shampoo out where he can see them. I don't start running the bath water. I don't say the word *bath;* I don't even spell it out to my wife Julee when she asks what I'm up to. I conduct all the necessary preparations in complete secrecy. And still, he always knows.

How, Lord?

For some reason, I've never gotten an answer to that prayer.

Today I get down on all fours, rub his head, look at him and say, "It's okay, Mar-Mar. I'll be fast."

His liquid brown eyes look straight back at me as if to say, "Let's get it over with." No, not "as if." That *is* what he means. A spine-tingling sense of awe comes over me. I absolutely understand what this animal is thinking!

And then Marty is up, moving slowly like a prisoner going to the gallows. By the time I get to the bathroom, he is sitting in the tub, waiting.

Lord, maybe some day You will tell me how Marty knows he's getting a bath. In the meantime, thank You for the relationships we have with our animals . . . and for the miracle of communication.

—*EDWARD GRINNAN*

A GRAND CANYON JOURNEY

The Grand Canyon of the Colorado River is one of God's supreme masterworks—a place where every stone proclaims its Creator's glory. Since Rhoda Blecker's first trip twenty-five years ago, she has become a Grand Canyon regular, and this week you'll find out why, as you join Rhoda for the rafting ride of a lifetime.

—THE EDITORS

SAT
20

Day One: To Stretch the Spirit
Then shall the lame man leap as an hart, and the tongue of the dumb sing: for in the wilderness shall waters break out, and streams in the desert.   —ISAIAH 35:6

My journey into the Grand Canyon began, improbably enough, in a hospital bed in Los Angeles. Three days earlier, on Thanksgiving eve, I had found a lump in my breast. With visions of my mother's death in 1955 after metastatic breast cancer devoured her liver, I demanded surgery ASAP, and was scheduled for a Monday morning trip to the operating room.

It was while I was waiting for that trip—unsure if I'd awaken with one breast or both—that I swore to myself I would take a very different trip, one I'd dreamt of since I was a child. No matter what, I would run the Colorado River through the Grand Canyon.

Slightly less than two years later, both my breasts and I found ourselves on a bus to Lee's Ferry, Arizona. It was 1976; not many people had yet run the river commercially. Many of my friends thought I was crazy, and two of them actually told me so.

"But you're going all by yourself," Lois said. "You won't know anybody else on the trip."

"I'm sure the outfitters know what they're doing," I answered her. "Besides, if you can't make friends on a twenty-two-foot raft, I don't know where you're likely to make friends."

Jerry said, "Well, personally, I have no desire to conquer nature."

I replied, "I don't want to conquer nature. I want to become a part of nature."

I wish I'd been smart enough to recognize what was pulling me into the canyon—a need for oneness, for the stretching of spirit that only wilderness can provide. And for me, true wilderness is desert.

It is not for nothing that Sinai was a desert mountain. It is not for nothing that a desert river is so special. In the mountains, a river belongs. In the desert, a river is a gift from God.

Lord, when I am in dry places, remind me of Your goodness by sending the blessing of water. —*RHODA BLECKER*

SUN

21 *Day Two: House Rock*
Moses said to the people, "Do not be afraid. God has come to test you. . . ." —*EXODUS 20:20 (NIV)*

The first truly scary rapid on the Colorado River is at mile seventeen, and rafters usually reach it on the morning of the second day of the trip. House Rock Rapids takes the entire river to the left and bounces it off a cliff so that it flows back to the right in what golfers call a dogleg.

Because the Colorado is a big river, House Rock is a big rapid. It looks frightening, long and powerful. Before we get to it, we've been through two other large ones, but they are among the smallest of the river's major rapids. Rafters from the little California rivers tend to goggle and swallow their spit when they see the size of those early rapids, but those of us who are Colorado River veterans wait until we get to House Rock before we start tightening the ties on our life vests.

House Rock looks dangerous. It's got three big holes—places where water pours down over a buried rock, creating a hydraulic that can impede a raft's forward progress, perhaps torque it, wash paddlers out, and generally throw a lot of cold water on what was hitherto a pleasant morning.

Those of us who've run the river before, however, know a secret about House Rock. It's a very forgiving rapid. Unlike some rapids later in the trip, House Rock lets paddlers make a lot of mistakes without exacting a penalty. We sometimes think that God put House Rock at mile seventeen to let us have a gentle taste of what the river will be like later, as if to help us develop our skills, to teach us how to paddle together in big water, how to dig hard, how to trust each other in a place that won't slam us if we're inept.

House Rock is one of those experiences that look scary, but that lead us through to calm water again.

Dear God, thank You for sharing the trials that strengthen me.
—*RHODA BLECKER*

MON
22

Day Three: Vasey's Paradise
"I will sprinkle clean water upon you, and you shall be clean...."   —*EZEKIEL 36:25 (RSV)*

Much of the water in the Grand Canyon is undrinkable. It's been contaminated by human and animal waste, and if we want to make any of it potable, we have to add chlorine bleach to it or run it through a very fine ceramic filter. Very soon we're tired of its stale, medicinal taste.

But at mile thirty-two is a source of sweet, pure water. It springs free of the cliffs and tumbles down to the river amid a riot of greenery. This double waterfall is called Vasey's Paradise, and by the time we paddle up to it on day five, we are longing to empty our canteens and refill them with the fresh, tasty, untreated natural water that dances, gurgling, down the rock face. Sometimes we camp upstream of Vasey's, at a place called South Canyon, and spend an entire night longing to get that final half-mile downriver to the source.

I'm always startled by the sudden appearance of a drinkable spring in the middle of the desert, where water can be expected to be brackish, polluted or just plain absent. The guides explain that this particular assemblage of rock layers places an impermeable clay high above the river, just beneath several layers of sandstone and limestone through which the water can filter downward, removing the impurities even more effectively than our ceramic filters do. Then the water moves along the clay and, cleansed, it springs out of the canyon wall into the air, gloriously white and sparkling.

We are the same as that water. We are tempered and chastened as we travel, and sometimes we need to be cleaned of the impurity we've carried along with us. God provides the permeable layers of prayer for us to percolate through, leading us deeper. Then when we're ready, we, too, spring forth into the air.

When the grime and grit of the world has gotten into my spirit, Lord, help me cleanse myself with prayer.   —*RHODA BLECKER*

TUE
23

Day Four: Rough Waters
"When you pass through the waters I will be with you; and through the rivers, they shall not overwhelm you...."
—*ISAIAH 43:2 (RSV)*

There is an unmistakable moment when a raft commits itself to a rapid, a small but clear nod of its snout or its prow. From that point on, there's no turning back. You just have to make the ride through the white water the best you possibly can.

Sometimes the moment passes unnoticed, especially when a rapid is one of the smaller ones, part of the Roaring Twenties or the Jewels, but there are some rapids that are so frightening that the moment of acquisition, the moment when the run becomes inevitable, is vitally important.

Bob, one of our boatmen, always said, "The most important moment of our run is the moment we leave the shore." He meant the river had a certain timing, and if you put in at the wrong moment, it can flip you. I understand that philosophy, but I never agreed with it. It has always seemed to me that as long as a few powerful strokes of oar or paddles will take the raft safely to an eddy at the rapid's head, not into the frothy white rooster tails and haystacks of the rapid, then we are not committed; we can still get away. But once the raft has made that small nod, and agreed to run the rapid no matter what, only then is it too late to turn back.

In really big water, I tighten my life vest and pull the straps tight to hold my glasses on before we leave the shore. When the raft makes its nod at the top of the rapid, I bow my head for a second and add an acceptance of my own—a prayer.

Lord, when I'm going through rough waters, help me to remember that You will steer me through. —*RHODA BLECKER*

WED
24

Day Five: Into the Stillness
The waters prevailed and increased greatly upon the earth; and the ark floated on the face of the waters.
—*GENESIS 7:18 (RSV)*

My favorite part of the Colorado River is the flat water between Elves' Chasm and Blacktail Canyon. A lot of paddlers don't like flat water because the current slows down, and if you want to move along, you have to work harder to accomplish it. Those who are adrenaline junkies (and the river gets its share of them) want the wild moments in the rapids, where the white water churns all around you, smashing the raft from the front and sometimes from the sides.

To me, the rapids, which are a relatively brief part of the trip, are punctuation marks between the texts of the longer, quieter stretches.

The stretch between Elves' and Blacktail (mile 116 to mile 120) is magical. The water is still—except for an occasional riffle that adds a gentle sighing to the cry of the ravens and the liquid call of the canyon wrens—so still that the reflection of shoreline, walls and sky make a perfect duplicate of the scene through which we float. It feels as if we're floating on them, their uneven beauty smoothed to let us drift along. Sometimes we sing, and the towering walls echo the sound back at us as if we were in a cathedral, gathering our music in its buttresses, singing along with us.

Often we float in silence, absorbing the silences, the echoes, the natural tones of the canyon wilderness. I usually watch the reflections on the surface of the river, because it's my only chance to actually see myself floating in the sky.

God, thank You for silence and still water, and for a world of beauty reflecting Your glory.   —RHODA BLECKER

THU
25
Day Six: Fountain of Youth
Your youth is renewed like the eagle's.
                                        —PSALM 103:5 (RSV)

I know I'm supposed to be a mature, responsible woman. Yet every time my husband Keith and I go to the Grand Canyon, I find myself cavorting like a spring lamb. I scramble over rocks to the river's edge, splash around, engage in water or mud fights, laugh loudly, sing a lot at the top of my lungs. I do the kinds of reckless things that would probably embarrass or appall me back in Los Angeles.

For a long time I wondered what came over me on river trips to make me so entirely not myself. I determined to put a stop to this inappropriate behavior. And then one day, at Havasu Creek, on the beach just across the azure pool into which Beaver Falls cascades, I watched several women in their seventies jump from a twenty-foot ledge into the water and come to the surface laughing as if they'd been infected by my canyon madness.

When they swam to the beach and began toweling off, we smiled at one another, and I asked, "Is this the kind of thing you do at home?"

One answered teasingly, "I'm afraid there just aren't that many waterfalls in Omaha."

And the other said, "Oh, no, I would never!"

"What makes you do it here then?" I pursued, curious. "I mean, I do a lot here I'd never do anywhere else, too. When I get home, I always wonder how I could have been so childish, but then every time I come back, I do it all over again."

"But it isn't childish at all," the second woman said seriously, sitting down beside me and rubbing her gray-white hair. "It's child*like*."

I knew the difference instantly and realized I had forgotten it. To be childlike is to regain—even for a moment—that sense of wonder which is God's gift to a child.

I thanked her and got up to play in the water. Then I thanked God for sending her to me.

Lord, help me not to take myself so seriously, and remind me to make time in my life for childlike play. —*RHODA BLECKER*

FRI
26

Day Seven: The House in the Desert
And God said . . . "I set my bow in the cloud, and it shall be a sign of the covenant between me and the earth."
—*GENESIS 9:12-13 (RSV)*

In 1989 I led a Jewish group into the Grand Canyon for a thirteen-day run down the Colorado River. We held services at waterfalls beneath the soaring cliffs, did Israeli dancing on the beaches, studied Torah in the sunlight among the tamarisk trees, hiked, sang, played in the water and generally had a fine time. When it rained for several days, we saw flash floods and watched lightning illuminate the mesas high above us.

We called our little congregation *Bet BeMidbar*, which means "The House in the Desert," and our slogan was "Serving the Colorado River since Tuesday."

I'd worked hard for more than two years to organize the trip. I wanted to have a *minyan* (the ten people needed for many Jewish communal prayers) so that I could pray those prayers at Saddle Canyon, at Redwall Cavern, in Blacktail and Matkatamiba, below Deer Creek Falls, and in Fern Glen. My spirits soared when I could actually do all of those things.

And then, during our Friday night services two days before the end of the trip, something happened that raised the entire experience from our realm to a realm beyond us. The rain had stopped earlier in the afternoon, so the evening sky was filled with clouds scudding away before the wind. There's a point in the service where we all turn and look toward Jerusalem. As we turned, we caught our breaths. There, painted across the canyon in a sweeping arch was a double rainbow, the golds glowing brightly against a darkening evening sky. The rainbows stayed, growing brighter, all through the service. Only when we were done and getting our dishes for supper did they finally fade away.

I told my husband that night, "You know, I spent two years planning this trip, arranging everything, but I couldn't have arranged the rainbow, the sign of the covenant. God did that."

Dear God, thank You for the signs You give us that Your promises never fail. —*RHODA BLECKER*

SAT

27

For our light and momentary troubles are achieving for us an eternal glory that far outweighs them all.
—*II CORINTHIANS 4:17 (NIV)*

When I complained to my neighbor that my petunias were not as prolific as hers, she told me, "You have to deadhead them, like this." She bent down to pinch a faded bloom from its stem. "Make sure you pinch it off low enough, or it will go to seed. If the plant thinks it has finished its life's work, it will quit blooming."

That afternoon my husband Leo, who hates to sacrifice so much as one faded bloom, watched in mock horror as I began to deadhead the entire petunia patch. "Oh, don't pinch that purple one off. Oh, ouch! Not that red one." He was clearly siding with the petunias. "Those poor posies. You're taking that blue one, too? Will you ever stop?"

I paid no heed. Within a few days, I drew his attention to the petunia patch, now loaded with dozens of jewel-toned flowers. He grudgingly acknowledged the benefits of deadheading once he saw the results.

Like those petunias, I have been enduring some "momentary light afflictions" myself. I surmise it's because I've been letting some of my gifts and talents go to seed. "Let the younger generation do it" is creeping into my mindset. And with less to occupy my mind, the inclination is to focus on the physical: *Oh, ouch, Lord. My back is so stiff today. And yesterday my feet hurt. And I hope I'm not getting a cold. And this pain in my elbow is something else.*

God seemingly pays no attention to my ailments, but goes right on deadheading.

Is this ever going to stop, Lord?

His answer is unexpected, but effective. Along comes an offer to teach Sunday school. A request for a patchwork quilt. A plea for homemade jam. A challenge to take photographs for church bulletins. Before long I am in full bloom again, the aches and pains of aging all but forgotten. After all, my life's work is far from finished.

Lord, help me remember that momentary afflictions here on earth are only the buds of an eternal bouquet. —*ALMA BARKMAN*

SUN
28

The centurion answered him, "Lord, I am not worthy to have you come under my roof; but only say the word, and my servant will be healed." ... When Jesus heard him, he marveled, and said ... "Truly, I say to you, not even in Israel have I found such faith." —*MATTHEW 8:8, 10 (RSV)*

At church this Sunday, Aidan, our six-month-old next-door-neighbor, was baptized. Problem was, Aidan's brother Ryan was there, too, acting like a two-year-old, which he is. As Rev. Lucas read the Beatitudes, Ryan had his own attitude and crawled down the center aisle. Most of us found this terribly funny, but Ryan's parents looked terribly stressed.

My wife Sandee nudged me. "Barb and Kevin need a hand with Ryan," she said. And I had the aisle seat. So I picked Ryan up, and—miraculously—he became quiet. He stayed quiet through the whole baptism, right through the part where we renounce Satan and all his works.

Before Communion, I handed Ryan back to Barb. She said, "You're a saint."

Yeah, right. I am no saint. My catalog of sins is not only broad, it's deep. My wrongs require their own database, indexed by category. I wish I were kidding. My sins *are* great.

"You're a saint," Barb said.

But that's not the funny part. At the exact moment Barb was uttering those words, I was reciting a prayer in my head, a prayer I've known almost all my life: *Lord, I am not worthy to receive You, but only say the word and I shall be healed.*

Barb and Kevin needed a hand with Ryan. Sandee saw that and

sent me, closest to the aisle. And Ryan, for whatever reason, calmed down as I held his wonderful weight in my arms.

And this is how God makes saints of all of us—in our little missions; our small miracles; our tiny, remarkable ways. We are not worthy, but only say the word—"Barb and Kevin need a hand with Ryan"—and we shall be healed.

Lord, open my ears to hear Your healing Word. *—MARK COLLINS*

🦅

"Speak the truth to each other. . . ."
                                                    —ZECHARIAH 8:16 (NIV)

When our children were little, we often encouraged them to use words to communicate their feelings and wishes, instead of whining or acting out. In our life together, Harry and I still find that to be a useful reminder. We've been married almost a decade, and we agree that we have an unusually good marriage. We think that's partly because both of us put such a high value on communication. But in spite of that, we can still sometimes get cross with each other.

Recently, we traveled to Colorado Springs for several days of meetings. One of the things I dislike about staying in a motel is that the TV is usually given such a prominent place. At home we keep our TV in a closet and almost never turn it on. Maybe that's why it acted like a giant magnet when we opened the motel room door.

After a long day of meetings I just wanted quietly to read my book; Harry wanted to watch the evening news. I knew I couldn't concentrate with the TV on, so I headed into the tiny bathroom with my book and shut the door. With growing irritation, I struggled to concentrate. Was it my imagination, or was the TV getting louder? I put my fingers in my ears. My book slid to the floor. Finally, I burst out the door. "Harry, could you please turn that thing down?"

"I'm sorry, I didn't know you were in there trying to read. They just finished a piece that I knew you wouldn't want to miss. I turned up the volume so you could hear it better."

So much for our great communication. We laugh about that incident and consider it a good reminder of how easy it is to assume the other person knows what we're thinking. And of how important it is to use words.

My Father, I want to keep on learning and growing in my ability to communicate with those whom I love. —*MARY JANE CLARK*

TUE

30

If a person lives to be very old, let him rejoice in every day of life. . . . —*ECCLESIASTES 11:8 (TLB)*

My friend Violet, in her late seventies, has been a published poet for many years. But suddenly she stopped writing, and when I asked her why, she said, "Oh, who cares what an old lady like me has to say?"

Living in a youth-worshiping society, I can easily understand her thinking. As I'm firmly ensconced in middle age, I sometimes wonder if I'm past my peak of creativity and accomplishment. But a newspaper article I recently ran across has made me think again.

It seems one of the hottest trends in home decorating is using the wood from old Southern tobacco barns for flooring. This wood is as much as two hundred years old, the original trees a century older than that. What gives the wood its value is its age and all the character that shows on its weathered surface: the knotholes, the scratches and the particularly colorful patterns seared into the wood as a result of the tobacco curing process. According to the article, people are paying twice as much for tobacco-barn wood because it has a rich history that new wood can't match.

When I shared this news with Violet, she said with twinkling eyes, "Well, I guess I've got that kind of character and the weathered surface, too!" And the next time I saw her she read me her latest poem.

I believe God created me in His own image. While my looks have changed over the years, that doesn't lessen my value to Him or to anyone, as long as I continue to use God's gifts as well as I'm able. Then, as with the aged wood of the tobacco barn, each new experience adds a little bit more color and character to the rich patina of life God has given me.

Loving Creator, help me always to treasure the priceless gift of life You have entrusted to me, and help me to use it well.
—*GINA BRIDGEMAN*

WED
31

And he shall turn the heart of the fathers to the children, and the heart of the children to their fathers. . . .

—*MALACHI 4:6*

During my last two summers of high school, I spent idle hours pelting golf balls across a driving range and honing my short game on the practice green. Away from my boarding-school classmates, I had a handful of golfing buddies I enjoyed playing with, but jousting with them from tee to tee couldn't compare with the times I played with my father.

I'd wake from a late-morning slumber and call him at his office: "Dad, can you play golf today?" He would hesitate, then promise to call back. Minutes later the phone would ring; the answer was always yes. When we'd tee off and when we'd have lunch were the only uncertainties.

Now that I'm grown, I can't imagine how my father managed to cancel or rearrange his appointments to accommodate my whimsical desire to play golf. I know that the golf itself was not the attraction; it was simply the joy of being together.

I'm a father myself now, and my four-year-old son William often says, "Daddy, let's play!" He usually says it when I'm heading out the door, sitting down to pay the bills or trying to get through the newspaper. Like my father, I hesitate; my list of chores and responsibilities seems never-ending. But then I remember those golfing days with Dad. "Okay, son," I say. "Let's play."

Lord, help me to use my time to enrich the lives of those around me.

—*BILLY NEWMAN*

My Days of Prayer

1 _____

2 _____

3 _____

4 _____

5 _____

6 _____

7 _____

8 _____

9 _____

10 _____

11 _____

12 _____

13 _____

14 _____

15 _____

16 _____

17 _____

18 _____

19 _____

20 _____

21 _____

22 _____

23 _____

24 _____

25 _____

26 _____

27 _____

28 _____

29 _____

30 _____

31 _____

August

If two of you shall agree on earth as touching
any thing that they shall ask, it shall be done for
them of my Father which is in heaven.

—Matthew 18:19

S	M	T	W	T	F	S
				1	2	3
4	5	6	7	8	9	10
11	12	13	14	15	16	17
18	19	20	21	22	23	24
25	26	27	28	29	30	31

THE PRAYER THAT IS ALWAYS NEW

<table>
<tr><td>THU

1</td><td>Our Father. . . . Give us this day our daily bread.
 —MATTHEW 6:9, 11 </td></tr>
</table>

I was learning to start every prayer by worshiping God, following the model of the Lord's Prayer, when I noticed something else about this verse. I had seen that not till halfway through the prayer was I allowed to bring up my own concerns. And which concerns, in this model prayer, was I told to focus on? The needs of *this day* alone. "Pray," Jesus says, "about the chores and choices of the next twenty-four hours only."

What about long-term issues? I thought.

I remembered an Ann Landers column about reader mail. In the ten thousand letters sent her each month, she wrote, a single question appeared most often: *What if?* "What if I lose my job?" "What if a loved one dies?" Illness, crime, even asteroid collisions—her mail overflowed with fearful possibilities.

I remembered how superior I'd felt to these anxious souls. *It's silly to waste energy on things that might never happen! My worries are real ones!* Or were they, I wondered now. I glanced back through my prayer journal at the problems that had gobbled time, energy, sleep. And every one of them was firmly rooted in the future.

The whole of the Lord's Prayer has become more meaningful as I direct it toward the next few hours. "Hallowed be thy name in my life *this day*." "Thy will be done in my life and in the lives of those I'm praying for *this day*." "Forgive me my trespasses *this day*."

Some of this day's legitimate concerns, of course, may involve preparing for the future, even the distant future—but in day-sized chunks, in quantities I can handle. God alone, the words "this day" tell me, can handle the days to come, held in His safekeeping till they do.

A *Daily Guideposts* reader recently sent me a prayer of St. Augustine that I've made my own:

Our Father, keep me from stain of sin, love me, guide me, lead me, just for today. —*ELIZABETH SHERRILL*

2 He wakens me morning by morning, wakens my ear to listen like one being taught. —*ISAIAH 50:4 (NIV)*

After driving through a game reserve in South Africa looking for animals all day, we arrived at camp just in time to pack snacks for a night ride. I called to my eight-year-old daughter Elizabeth to change into warm clothes. She and her friend Danie were busy filling squirt guns.

"But I don't want to go on the night ride," she wailed. "I want to stay and have a water fight with Danie. We've been planning it all day!" I insisted she get ready, and she stomped off to her room, wailing protests.

I went in and explained. "I understand you had a long day in the car, and playing with Danie sounds much more fun right now. But that's something you can do every day we're here. Tonight may be the only chance you'll have in your whole life to see animals in the wild at night. I think you'll be very sad tomorrow if you choose to miss it just to do something you can do any other day."

Somehow Elizabeth pried herself away from the camp fun and came with us. Elizabeth still talks about the luminous eyes peering at us from trees, the elephant at the watering hole, the hyenas circling our vehicle.

The next morning I woke early and pondered what to do before the alarm went off. I considered writing postcards or finishing a novel. But then I smiled, remembering Elizabeth's decision the previous evening. *I can write postcards or read later. But this will be my only chance today to spend time alone with God.*

How often I waste these precious, quiet, moments on things I can do at other times during the day. Whether in the morning or during a lunch break or late at night, these pauses to pray or read His Word add up to a "once in a lifetime" chance to grow closer to God.

My Lord, help me take every opportunity to be with You.

—*MARY BROWN*

I will praise thee; for I am fearfully and wonderfully made: marvelous are thy works. . . .   —*PSALM 139:14*

I grew up outside the city limits where my favorite farmyard pets were Bantams. So when my husband Lawrence and I visited the New York State Fair one hot summer afternoon, he said, "I know you like to hang out with chickens, so wait for me here in the poultry building while I find us sodas and sandwiches."

"Fine," I answered. I'd just spotted a demure little hen whose every row of black-edged feathers was in place, and I couldn't wait to stick my fingers through the cage wires and caress her beneath her beak. "*Pawk, pawk*," I said to her.

"*Pawk, pawk*," Biddy answered back

Biddy and I were both *pawk-pawking* up a storm while I idly wondered if, on Noah's Ark, Mrs. Noah had had a favorite pet and, if so, perhaps it had been a Bantam—the long-ago predecessor of this very hen. Suddenly I became aware that a wide-eyed boy, five or six years old, and his mother, eyebrow raised, were taking it all in. *Good grief, what they must be thinking! People talk to dogs, horses, flowers. But to a chicken?*

To cover my fluster, I said to the boy, "Bet you don't know where a chicken's ears are."

"Aw, chickens don't have ears."

"Sure they do. How else can they hear?"

Mother and son gave their full attention as I gently pulled back a tiny round tuft of feathers an inch behind each of Biddy's eyes. "These hinged-at-one-side trapdoors cover her ear canals."

Just as they left, Lawrence returned, lunch in hand. He laughed as he told me, "Too bad you're not around more often to teach kids important things—like where a chicken's ears are."

Father, the more I see of Your wondrous works, the more I realize how "fearfully and wonderfully" You've made everything in this universe.

—*ISABEL WOLSELEY*

SUN

4

But true praise is a worthy sacrifice; this really honors me. . . . —*PSALM 50:23 (TLB)*

The personal journal I've kept for nearly thirty years began as a challenge. I'd been grumbling about my circumstances, so a friend suggested I write down one thing, every single day, for which I was truly thankful. Even though the first entries were simple, it sometimes took me quite awhile to write, "Thanks, God, for a good night's sleep" or "I praise You for keeping us safe during the hail storm." Later, I began to praise God for answered prayer: "Thank You for Patrick's finding just the right job . . . for guiding the doctor's hand during my neighbor's eye surgery . . . for giving me the right words for today's speech." Gradually the journal became a record of my walk with God. Looking back, I clearly saw His guiding hand, His presence and His leading in every circumstance, whether joyful or difficult.

I was browsing through last summer's entries when the one for August 4 leaped off the page: "Thank You for the rain, but it wasn't as much as we needed." Whoa! That wasn't a prayer, it was a complaint! I read on and discovered a disturbing number of complaint-prayers. When I replaced my car after 197,000 miles, I griped about what I didn't get: "Thank You for the car, even though it doesn't have a trunk light." In response to a generous gift to the agency where I work, I'd written, "The money will help, but they could have given twice as much."

Something was wrong with those entries because something was wrong with my relationship with God. During the difficult times, it was easy to recognize God's blessings and give praise. But as my life became more stable, I'd begun taking His loving care for granted.

My recent entries are more honest. Yes, I still grumble and complain. But day by day, God is helping me develop the thing that was missing in my previous prayers and in my life—a thankful heart.

Lord, let me honor You with the praise that comes from a truly grateful heart. —*PENNEY SCHWAB*

MON

5   Ask, and it shall be given you; seek, and ye shall find; knock, and it shall be opened unto you.   *—MATTHEW 7:7*

My wife Beth and I were walking down the beach, the tide swirling softly around our feet. Lost in thought, I glanced up to see an old man meandering toward us, gray head bent down, holding a metal detector in front of him.

"Look at that old fellow," I said to Beth. "How would you like to spend your days uncovering tin cans and a few nickels and dimes?"

As we passed the man, I called out, "Had any luck today?"

Stopping, he grinned and motioned for me to come over. He held out his hand; a large diamond ring and a gold cross and chain were cradled in his palm. With eyes sparkling, he said, "I've had a great day!"

"How often do you find diamond rings like that?" I asked.

"Well, I've been doing this on and off for a year now, and I've found three diamond rings, one emerald ring and all sorts of necklaces and earrings. My wife doesn't laugh at me anymore. No sir, she ushers me out the door with coffee and a kiss every morning!"

As Beth and I said good-bye and ambled on down the beach, I began to wonder where I, too, might buy a metal detector.

There are a lot of buried treasures in my own life that I have never attempted to uncover: the desire to paint; a longing to write fiction; an urge to help the abandoned street children lost in cities around the world. Yet, I have not done these things because of the fear that I might appear foolish or come up empty-handed.

The joyful grin of the old man on the beach challenges me to try anyway. If I want to find, first I have to seek.

God, give me the courage to dig deeply into life and unearth the treasure You have already given me. Amen.   *—SCOTT WALKER*

TUE

6   For we are unto God a sweet savour of Christ . . . the savour of life unto life. . . .   *—II CORINTHIANS 2:15-16*

Without a doubt, my favorite tree is the aspen. On midsummer days when the woods are perfectly still, without even the whisper of a breeze, somewhere within the canopy of the aspen, a leaf or two will catch a small breath of heaven-sent air and quiver. Heart-shaped, they balance like ballerinas on slender dainty stems and dance in counterpoint to the stillness of the forest. I often sit under a towering pine and challenge myself to find a moment when the aspen does not quiver. Incredibly, in all my years of watching, this has not yet happened.

Now I know why I love the aspen: It's a visual reminder of the constant quivering of my own heart. God knows, I'm most grateful for all that He has given me: a secure home, a loving husband, family and friends who bless my life. Still, deep within me there is a small breath of apprehension that keeps my heart aquiver for all tomorrow's "what ifs." Worries about the grandkids growing up, with prayers for their safekeeping and godly living; concerns about the golden years my husband and I now cherish, with thanksgiving for health that keeps us moving and doing (although I must confess it now takes us twice as long to do half as much); and anticipation of that final stroking of God's hand that will lead us home, with the apprehensive question, *Which one before the other?*

The constant fluttering of my heart once confused and bothered me. No more; I now embrace it. The aspen tree has helped me understand. Like the perpetual dance of its heart-shaped leaves, my quivering heart is a celebration of life; a celebration that, even in the middle of tranquil stillness, catches a breath from heaven and dances with a never-ending rhythm.

Thank You, Lord, for the breath of heaven that keeps our hearts dancing.   —*FAY ANGUS*

WED
7
And I will put my spirit within you, and cause you to walk in my statutes. . . .   —*EZEKIEL 36:27*

I had a tiff with my husband Lynn yesterday. Not a big one. At least it didn't start out that way. We needed to go somewhere and do something, and I didn't want to go. So I said so.

He said, "Okay. I'll go by myself."

That made me feel guilty, which made me defensive, which then made me angry. So I said some more stuff. Then he said some more stuff. And suddenly the tiff didn't have much to do with the original problem about going or not going. It escalated into a review of all the little irritations we'd both been holding on to for the past several weeks. Unfortunately, I have a pretty good memory for those irritations.

As I got myself more and more tangled up in my words, I knew eventually I was going to have to apologize in order to let myself out from under the mess I'd started. I hate that feeling, so I tried to ignore it by storming out of the house to take the dogs for a long walk. When I came back, I found Lynn working in the garage and feebly apologized, but this morning, as I drove to work, I still carried a lingering feeling of regret.

"Bob," I said to a man who works in our office, "you always seem so calm, regardless of the circumstances. Do you ever get mad at someone and say things you wish you hadn't?"

He considered the question for only a moment. "Not very often," he said. "I just learned a long time ago that it's not worth it."

It's not worth it. Such a simple answer. Such a profound truth.

Father, when I'm headed toward a silly tiff again, help me to remember it's not worth it.   —*CAROL KUYKENDALL*

THU
8

[Jesus] arose, and rebuked the wind, and said unto the sea, Peace, be still. And the wind ceased, and there was a great calm.   —*MARK 4:39*

Not long ago, a hurricane swept by our Florida place, and though it was more than a hundred miles out in the Gulf of Mexico, the lost beach that I surveyed later testified to the strength of wind and waves.

My most memorable storm-on-the-water encounter came one summer when Shirley and I and two of our sons, Christopher and Daniel, were houseboating on the upper Mississippi River between Minneapolis and St. Louis. Late one afternoon, I sensed that a storm was brewing and headed for port. The Mississippi is a pretty big river, and we had several miles to travel to safety. Anxiously, I pushed the throttle to the max, hoping to outrun trouble, but every minute the sky drew darker and the wind stronger. Our flat-bottomed houseboat pitched up and down like a cork. By the time a marina came into view, rain was pelting down so ferociously that I could hardly see. Finally, we neared shore, but a gust of wind suddenly threw us forward and we came within a hair of ramming the dock. Somehow I got the bucking boat straightened in the nick of time and close enough for the boys to tie up. Inside, dry and secure, I breathed a sigh of relief and a silent prayer of gratitude.

Afterward, I told a veteran boater, who had ridden out the storm mid-river, about my near collision with the dock. "The safest place in weather like that is on the water," he explained. "All you need to do is drop anchor, point the bow in the direction of the wind and trust your boat."

I've thought of his advice often when storms of a different kind have buffeted my life. Sometimes I've tried to outrun them or battle them alone without success. But they've all abated when I've trusted my Anchor—the One Who, as William Cowper wrote, "plants his footsteps in the sea, and rides upon the storm."

> Calm us with this truth, Lord;
> Though our boats are small and the sea grand,
> You hold us secure in the palm of Your hand.
>
> —*FRED BAUER*

FRI	For God so loved the world, that he gave his only begot-
9	ten Son, that whosoever believeth in him should not
	perish, but have everlasting life. —*JOHN 3:16*

I'd spent a week touring the museums, churches and historic sites of London. I was filled to the brim with conflicts and wars fought in the name of Christianity by kings, queens, bishops, archbishops, popes and generals. Great names were committed equally to opposite causes. Some on opposing sides were buried in the same place, like Queen Elizabeth I and Mary, Queen of Scots in Westminster Abbey. After a week of sightseeing, the things for which all these people had fought ran together in one great river of uncertainty. Who was right? Who was wrong? Where did I fit into this pageant of conflict and betrayal?

I took respite in tiny, picturesque Brockenhurst in the New Forest. I trudged up a sleepy, narrow street with shuttered houses and flower-filled window boxes. I climbed stone steps into the cool, shady shadow of an eighteenth-century brick country church. A neatly kept, flower-bordered path led me to a plot with weathered tomb-stones. The writing on most had faded to a blur. But one was still legible:

STEPHEN OLDEN
AGED 35 YEARS
DIED NOVEMBER 5, 1876
BELIEVING IN JESUS

Stephen Olden's bones were beneath my feet, but his spirit was alive in the words on the stone that said what mattered most. And standing in this humble, out-of-the-way place, far from the places where history had been made by the great ones of the world, I again found my footing—believing in Jesus.

Lord, You alone are my rock, my salvation. —*SHARI SMYTH*

SAT

10

Honor the Lord with your substance and with the first fruits of all your produce. . . . —*PROVERBS 3:9(RSV)*

Charlie, Texas, has a population of about a hundred and twenty, mostly farmers and fruit growers. Once a year, if and when the crop comes in, the Charlie Peach Festival draws five hundred to six hundred people from the surrounding towns to eat homemade peach cobbler and peach ice cream, courtesy of the hardworking folks who run the orchards. People drive for miles to watch the ice-cream crank-off and the pea-shelling contest, and to join in a little bit of country fun. The festival under the shade trees is like stepping back in time.

Charlie is about fifteen miles north of my home in Wichita Falls, and we city folk continue the trek to Charlie's fruit stands throughout the summer to buy fresh-picked produce. When it's really hot and the orchard owners are tired of sitting at their roadside stands, they leave little cigar boxes out alongside the baskets of sweet, juicy fruits and vegetables with signs that say, HONOR SYSTEM. PAY FOR YOUR PURCHASE HERE.

There's always money inside the cigar boxes. That's one of the best things about Charlie, I think: Along with the old-time country fun, people there still think we're all neighbors who care about one another, and we can be trusted. It's a nice feeling, sweeter even than a Charlie peach.

Father, help me always to bring out the best in people by expecting the best from them. —*MARJORIE PARKER*

SUN
11 The Lord will bless his people with peace. —*PSALM 29:11*

My wife Rosie, our son Ryan and I drove to Onekama, Michigan, this past summer. I was to speak at a camp about two hours north of Grand Rapids on a lake that empties into Lake Michigan. I had spoken at the camp the year before, while our friends Carl and Phyllis were there, but this time we would know few, if any, of the people—almost a hundred families—who would be there. I was worried about how we would be received, and I was particularly concerned about how Ryan would do in this new environment.

When we arrived, we found that Carl and Phyllis had been there the week before and had left us a wonderful note of encouragement. "Don't forget we're praying for you," they said. Then, before we could get settled in, a couple who had been at the camp the year before greeted us joyfully. They began to introduce us to others, and soon our fears disappeared.

Finally, at lunch one day, one of the younger couples came over and told us how much they appreciated our ministry that week. That day and the rest of the week, the Lord blessed us with His peace. And I'm sure that Carl and Phyllis's prayers were a big part of the reason why.

Lord, no matter how great my fear, You are able to give me peace. When my spirit is troubled, help me to keep on praying and believing.   —*DOLPHUS WEARY*

MON
12 For ye yourselves are taught of God to love one another.
                              —*I THESSALONIANS 4:9*

Standing at the rail, I was waving as the *Caronia* pushed off from the port of Madeira. I looked down at the people onshore: local officials, their job done; merchants with their stands of native curiosities put away; a few interested souls drawn to see a big ship heading out to sea. They were waving, too. A little girl, no more than three, stood with her father, her arms moving vigorously, yelling something. I tried, but I couldn't hear what she was calling out.

"Good-bye, good-bye!" I shouted to her.

The *Caronia* pulled farther away. Laborers stopped in the middle of hoisting a load to salute us; a man waved from his little boat. All, it seemed, were communicating, and the passengers were doing the same. It's a joyful gesture, this waving, and a sad one, too.

I remember as a boy standing at an L&N railroad crossing and waving to riders as they sped by toward Nashville, Tennessee. I knew no one, but it didn't matter; I waved. Why? It could have been a longing to go with them to Nashville, or the need I felt to stay at home, or the amusement of making a split-second bond of friendship, or a heartfelt desire that God protect us, whatever our journey.

I remember standing on the rail of another ship, the *Maasdam*, as it was leaving St. Johns, Newfoundland. There is a very narrow channel for ships coming and going from St. Johns, with imposing hills on either side. A father sat with his daughter on a knoll nearby and waved at us. We were close enough to hear one another and the father called out, "Come back soon!" Perhaps the little girl in Madeira was saying the same thing; I like to think she was.

W**hat would it be like to meet the people we wave to, Lord? Make them loving friends.**

—VAN VARNER

TUE

13

He gathers the lambs in his arms and carries them close to his heart. . . .   *—ISAIAH 40:11 (NIV)*

As our old cat Minnie got even older, she had more and more ailments. In her sixteenth year, she suddenly developed fluid in her back feet and around her heart. Our vet worked out a formula of medications for her. Added to the things she already took for her tired old bones were five more prescriptions. Minnie balked at that much medicine and glared at me, refusing to take it.

We were both weary, so I picked her up and wrapped her in a favorite flannel sheet and sat down with her in the rocking chair. Only her tiny gray head stuck out of the blanket that covered her bony five-pound body. For a moment, she looked startled. Then she shut her eyes, relaxed her body and purred loudly. She almost looked like a kitten again. She was as calm as if I'd given her a tranquilizer. I rocked in the chair and sang to her as if she were a newborn.

After a while, I reached over and picked up some of her pills and the syringe of water. Gently, I pried her mouth open. She continued to purr, half asleep. I quickly squirted the water into her mouth, and she gulped it down as if she were a baby taking a bottle.

Minnie purred as I sang "Rock-a-Bye Baby," and all her fears dissolved in my arms.

Help me to remember, Father, that Your loving arms always wait to comfort me.   —*MARION BOND WEST*

WED
14

I heard the voice of the Lord, saying, Whom shall I send, and who will go for us? Then said I, Here am I; send me.
                                                            —*ISAIAH 6:8*

Our host in Rwanda was a senior government official who was educated in Europe and America. During the 1990s, as the trouble in his country deepened, he moved his family to America and became chairman of the math department of a major American university. He did everything he could to challenge the American government to take action before the horrible days of genocide, and when the tragedy came, the pain was almost too much for him.

Then General Kagame returned from exile to Rwanda to end the genocide and restore order. Before success was assured, he put out a call to all overseas Rwandans to return home to help rebuild their country. Our host read the general's plea in his university office and immediately went to the dean of faculty to resign his position.

The dean and all his colleagues began to argue with him about the insanity of wasting his life and talents by returning to a land where almost no resources were available and there was still a strong possibility that he would be killed. Finally, in exasperation, the dean said, "How can you leave this vital position to go into the unknown?"

"Dean," he replied, "if I leave here, you will have fifty applicants for my position within two weeks. If I do not go to Rwanda, there will be no one there who can do what I can do."

When I asked him how he was able to return home and work with so much confidence, he quoted Lamentations 5:21 (NIV), "Restore us to yourself, O Lord, that we may return; renew our days as of old," and said, "In one way, the awful difficulty of Rwanda's problems is a blessing. It forces us to acknowledge that only God can solve them. Only God can restore our nation, and this makes us hope and trust in Him."

Lord, I give You the broken places of my life today and expectantly wait on You to restore them.   —ERIC FELLMAN

THU

15

In thee, O Lord, do I put my trust; let me never be ashamed. . . .   —PSALM 31:1

On a mid-August morning at the State of Maine Writers' Conference, my friend June joined me at breakfast and said, "We missed you this morning. We had a great time!" I smiled weakly. Every year June conducted a poetry reading on the beach at 7:30 on Thursday morning. For three years I had avoided the reading, even though June and the conference director had pleaded with me to attend. I thought it would be embarrassing to have to sit on the beach and try to write poetry.

The next year, I made up my mind to overcome my embarrassment. I rose early and headed to the beach. I sat, pen and paper in hand, and as I fumbled for words, I looked at the ocean. It was peaceful, mirror-calm, the sun's rays spreading gold on the water. There were no seagulls, no insects, only a comforting breeze. I started thinking about the human needs all of us on the beach that morning shared: the need for affection, for achievement, for security and for acceptance within a group. I tried to convey all of this—the peace without and the neediness within—in my poem.

I left the reading feeling refreshed. Later, at the Friday-morning award ceremony, I was surprised to receive first prize for my poem. But I received a greater gift when I discarded my pride and joined that Thursday-morning family on the beach. All I needed to do was to accept it with thanks and appreciation.

Understanding Christ, thank You for standing at the door, waiting until I opened it and accepted Your blessing.   —OSCAR GREENE

READER'S ROOM

I have enjoyed *Daily Guideposts* now for several years. Knowing that each page relates a personal story makes the books extra special.

One story that stands out in my mind was written by Brenda Wilbee for August 31, 1998. August 31, 1958, was the day I was married, but after twenty-eight years my marriage, like Brenda's, ended. I related to her feelings of sadness as she prepared for her daughter's wedding, which I, too, had to do even as my divorce was becoming final. I can also rejoice, however, in how God saw me through it all. The wedding was beautiful, the years have passed, and God has given me a new life. As Brenda said, God can create "something new in me." I am thankful to Him for doing just that.

—*BEVERLY ANN SHARPF, TUALATIN, OREGON*

THE PRACTICE OF PRAYER

FRI

16

Receptive Prayer
Believe that ye receive them.... —*MARK 11:24*

"It seems like a lot of our prayers are being answered," one of the members of my Sunday prayer class remarked a few years ago. "Shouldn't we be keeping some sort of count?" So that day we pledged to acknowledge every answered prayer. Some are answered within an hour, some within a week. In other cases a year or more passes and then one day: "Guess what? My prayer was finally answered. And a unique answer it turned out to be!"

Sometimes the answers aren't what we want them to be. We ask for a healing; our friend dies. Even when our hopes are disappointed, we have to trust that God's field of vision encompasses a lot more than we can comprehend.

Dr. William R. Parker's fourth point of successful prayer moves us in an entirely new direction. "Make prayer receptive," he says. When you pray, believe. Trust that God your Father has heard your request and even at that moment is answering your prayer. Now act as if you believe—thank God that you will receive.

"Every prayer is answered," says Dr. Parker. Are you ready to stretch your faith that far? The world will tug at you, encourage you to doubt. But by committing yourself to the practice of prayer, you've begun to remove yourself from the darkness of doubt where unhappiness festers. You are, even now, moving away from the shadows and into God's circle of light where hope, joy, peace and contentment abound.

So ask your Father for whatever it is you want, then thank Him, because He is already answering your prayer. Live in expectation. Believe that His answer will come. You don't have to ask over and over. God heard you the first time. Trust!

Father, open my eyes as You answer my prayers. Let me embrace Your simplest answer. Give me a glimpse of the intricacies that lie in Your most complex answers. And even when I cannot see, let me believe.
                                                                    —*PAM KIDD*

SAT

17 A man's wisdom gives him patience; it is to his glory to overlook an offense. —*PROVERBS 19:11 (NIV)*

I was visiting Dallas to meet with cousins I love deeply but rarely see. We hugged, embraced, prayed and talked over old times. We discussed the new marriages, new babies and new adventures in our lives. We shopped, went sightseeing and then met for dinner at an Italian restaurant.

The hostess was gracious and seated us at our table. The waiter came promptly, poured olive oil into a saucer and promised to bring us hot bread. Shortly after he left, another party of about eight people was seated near us. Our waiter went to them, took their orders and quickly brought them warm bread. While we looked on, our waiter returned to the other table with a second helping of bread, while we continued to wait for our first.

Two of my cousins began to make excuses for the waiter. "He's really busy," said one.

"He's going to get to us eventually," said the other.

But another one of my cousins just wasn't having it. He leaned forward and said he was politely going to give the waiter a piece of his mind. "He has to see us. He's walking right by us," he said.

"There's no point in doing that," my cousin Lajuana said. "We'll just wait. We can just choose to overlook it." Soon other staff members brought bread, delivered our orders and even stopped to chat and laugh with us. Our hurt feelings were forgotten, and we enjoyed a wonderful dinner together.

Lajuana had learned that there's power and peace in choosing not to be offended. She knew—I'm still learning—that we can transform testy encounters into opportunities for mutual kindness. It's not easy, but the peace that results is reason to keep working at it.

Lord, help me to grow in Your image. Help me to choose peace and patience over taking offense.   —*SHARON FOSTER*

SUN
18

From one new moon to another, and from one sabbath to another, shall all flesh come to worship before me, saith the Lord.   —*ISAIAH 66:23*

Summer Sundays. Wherever I am on vacation, I look for a church on a summer Sunday. Get up early, slip out before breakfast, find my way to a place I saw that had a sign out in front saying, SERVICES AT 8:00 AND 10:00. I've worshiped on a beach with my feet in the sand. I've sat in an eighteenth-century pew beneath a stark puritanical pulpit. I've sung unfamiliar songs from unfamiliar hymnals and listened to musicians on out-of-tune pianos. Sometimes I've been asked to stand up and identify myself, other times I've sat silently among the congregation. But always I've been made to feel very welcome. "New York City?" people exclaim. "You sure do need our country air!"

Indeed I do. And I need to hear different preachers give the message; big-city churches have no monopoly on good sermons. The best messages can be found in little, out-of-the-way places with only a few people in the pews. I usually look for a church of my denomination, but it's invigorating to discover one from a different tradition.

Always I see the similarities shared: one faith, one Lord. What I like best, though, is being with people who believe in starting out Sunday with God. Then we scatter to the beach or the lake or the mountains.

"I'm just passing through," I explained to an elderly lady at one of the churches I visited.

"Aren't we all?" she responded wryly. How nice to stop for worship along the way.

I worship You, Lord, and praise Your name.   —RICK HAMLIN

MON

19   The heavens declare the glory of God. . . .   —PSALM 19:1

Flipping pancakes for fifteen over a smoky campfire; washing dishes in an enameled basin under the stars; sleeping on the ground, probably in a wet sleeping bag: Welcome to "roughing it" at its finest. Welcome to my favorite part-time job.

For several summers now, I've cooked for wilderness outfitters in spectacularly beautiful settings in the Wind River Mountains of Wyoming. With camp set up maybe twenty miles from the highway, we can count on solitude, wide open spaces and no running water. A two-hundred-and-fifty-gallon tank in the back of the pickup provides all the water we need. Logs offer rustic seating. A portable table in the tall grass becomes the kitchen. The natural splendor more than compensates for the lack of creature comforts.

Sunlight streaks the horizon salmon and gold when the camp boss rouses me from my tent around 5:00 A.M. to boil the first gallon of coffee. I blow on my numb fingers, for up here at nine thousand feet, the temperature plunges below freezing every night. No matter, I'm warmed watching the early sun glint off frosted buffalo grass and serene horses who swish their tails as they graze.

After breakfast, I pack lunches for the eager riders and wave goodbye as they clop down the rocky trail. By the time the sun climbs directly overhead in an impossibly blue sky, I've finished washing the breakfast dishes. Now comes the best time—Big Sky devotional cloud-watching.

The first day out, I began to read my devotional book, resting my head on a rolled saddle pad. Cicadas darted and clicked under lodgepole pines fragrant with hot resin. After a paragraph or two, billowing clouds, brilliantly white and edged with quicksilver, drifted by, distracting me. I rested the book on my stomach and just gazed; in fact, I never read another word for five days.

Out here, where God sees to it that devotions fill the whole sky, I've learned to save my book for town.

Lord of Creation, how great You truly are!
—*GAIL THORELL SCHILLING*

TUE
20   Blessed are ye that hunger now: for ye shall be filled. . . .
—*LUKE 6:21*

My husband Andrew is not a cook. I vaguely knew this when we were dating, but the degree of his culinary deficiency was made plain shortly before our wedding, when I helped him pack up his apartment. When I opened his kitchen cabinets, I discovered that was where he stored his collection of 1930s horror movies. We agreed to divvy up the chores: I'd cook; he'd wash the dishes.

This year, our son John, newly four, learned that his father is culinarily challenged. He immediately took charge of the situation. "Mommy, you're going to have to teach me how to cook, so that when I'm eight I can teach Daddy!" He's serious about it, too. Each night he comes into the kitchen, perches on the stepstool and asks what he can do to help. If there isn't anything, he commands, "Then tell me what you're doing. I need to know, so that when I'm older I can explain it to Daddy."

John is remarkably good in the kitchen, and a genuine help. As he plucks leaves of basil and smashes garlic to make pesto, I am rather in awe of his cheerful, matter-of-fact determination. I try to think of what I approach with the same gusto. Housekeeping? Not a chance. Motherhood? Perhaps. My faith? Now there's an interesting idea: If I were as focused on following Christ as my son is on knowing the names and uses of kitchen utensils, my whole life would be different. So would my family's.

Heavenly Father, grant me a hunger to know Your ways.
—*JULIA ATTAWAY*

WED
21
When He utters His voice, there is a tumult of waters in the heavens. . . . —*JEREMIAH 51:16 (NAS)*

There's a sinister smell in the air as I roll through the street on my red bicycle, and a dark shadow falls across my path. I glance up and see cumulus clouds climbing high in the eerie pink sky above the train yard. Beneath them are coiling black gargoyles with daggers of light in their bellies. A gray squall line races toward me like a long row of Brillo pads. A cold, invisible hand pushes me back, and I take the hint, turning toward home. My bike has wings, and my legs have engines.

Trash cans tumble through the street, and children run squealing to their porches. Faces appear in windows. Lights go out. Sirens sing in the distance. Young maple trees rock back and forth like happy dancers, their leaves hissing like ocean surf. A flock of blackbirds dashes from tree to tree, laughing as they go.

Needles of rain begin to stab my face, and I lick my lips. Mothballs of hail dance on the ground, and I feel as if I'm riding through a skillet of popping corn. Veins of light scamper across a charcoal sky, then—*Wham! Boom! Whump!*—thunder pounds me with the sound of heaven's mansions crashing together, and I let out a yelp!

I should be terrified, but I'm not. My fear is overwhelmed by happiness, and my eyes are wet with gratitude. For weeks we have prayed for rain, we melancholy farmers. At bedtime, before meals, from pulpits and in special meetings. And now—just in time—an utterance from the heavens.

How like You, God, not to panic when we do, but in one exhilarating hour of mercy, to send ten million drops of rain for every whispered prayer. Let it rain, Lord, let it rain, let it rain!

—*DANIEL SCHANTZ*

THU
22
"In my devotion to the temple of my God I now give my personal treasures of gold and silver . . . ."
—*I CHRONICLES 29:3 (NIV)*

Going to horse camp was the highlight of my childhood summers. Still too young to be boy crazy, I was horse crazy, and going to camp meant a reunion with my true love, a giant white gelding named Silver. This would be my fourth summer with Silver, and I could hardly wait to see him again. He was the biggest horse at camp, almost seventeen hands, and riding him was like flying an airplane, but outside, on the nose!

When I arrived at camp, I scanned the pasture, but I didn't see Silver. *Good*, I thought, *they must have him in the ring already! As soon as I unload my gear, I can ride!* But as the train of campers marched on, I saw the ring was empty, too.

Our favorite camp counselor, a girl we called Kansas, caught up to me as the other campers went on to choose their cabins. She took me back to the pasture to explain that Silver had died during the year. She pointed to a large horse at the far corner of the pasture, standing apart from the others, and said she knew it was sudden, but she was hoping I'd ride Sunny this summer.

Sunny was a new palomino, and he was a little skittish. He stamped once and shook his mane; he looked like he was made of sunlight. I was stunned for a moment, because he looked so much like a golden Silver. I turned to Kansas and whispered, "It won't be the same."

She put an arm around my shoulders and said, "It never is."

That night, I was awakened by a light so bright I thought it was morning—but it was only a little after midnight. Blinking, I pulled my boots onto my bare feet and stepped outside. The moon was so full and bright, like a silver sun. I had never seen anything like it in smog-choked Los Angeles. I looked across the trees, bright green in the white moonlight, and toward the pasture. The horses were quite still until Sunny raised his head. He looked silver in the moonlight. Silver. He turned and walked farther out in the pasture, disappearing into a tree's shadow. I looked up at the moon again, squinting in the bright light. *Thank You, God,* I prayed, *for letting me say good-bye.*

Dear Lord, thank You for the animals that share our lives.

—KJERSTIN EASTON

FRI

23

That which I see not teach thou me. . . .   *—JOB 34:32*

Shortly after we were married, Larry and I moved to a small house on Hargett Street in Richlands, North Carolina. We had a big backyard, so we decided to till up a plot of land and plant a vegetable garden.

Pretty soon I began to notice a neighbor, Mr. Herrior, standing in his yard under some huge shade trees, staring silently at us while we worked. Every day he was there, but he never said a word.

"I wish he'd find something else to do," I complained to Larry. "It's unnerving having him stare at us like that." But Larry wasn't bothered and just kept on working. As the weeks went by, our garden grew and flourished, and it seemed I could hardly keep all the vegetables picked and canned. I had learned to ignore Mr. Herrior, but his presence didn't irritate me any less.

Then one day I went out to finish picking the green beans. The vines grew thick and heavy on most of the row, but toward the end I came to a section where the leaves were sparse. There, to my great surprise, one very large, overripe green bean hung all by itself. I was stunned by the size of it.

That's when I caught sight of Mr. Herrior and felt a sudden tug at my heart. He was walking back toward his house—a lonely figure, old and unnoticed.

Well, it may be too late for the old bean, I thought, *but I can still do something about my neighbor.* Quickly, I picked up the bucket at my feet and went running across the yard. "Wait, Mr. Herrior! Wait!" I called to him. "Would you like some fresh green beans?"

Father, when I see more with my eyes than with my heart, help me to gain a new perspective.   —*LIBBIE ADAMS*

<hr>

SAT

24

Lo, children are an heritage of the Lord and the fruit of the womb is his reward.   —*PSALM 127:3*

I have two sons. Twins. Five years old. I love them.

I say this right up front, because I do love them, but I have to remind myself of that sometimes, because they are driving me stark raving insane, and they are driving my wife batty, and they are driving their sister to distraction, because they fight all day long.

The boys scream and yell and kick and spill things deliberately and batter each other with shrill voices and shout at their parents and slam doors and throw mud and throw books and break windows and threaten their sister with plastic swords and kick doors and run away into the neighbor's yard. All in all, they are making me seriously consider signing them up as cabin boys on a slow boat to Malaysia.

Yet they are our children, and miraculous gifts to me from the incomprehensible nursery of the Lord. Even when they catch the cat and spread peanut butter on her tail, I must chase after their holiness as desperately and energetically as the cat chases her buttery tail, for they are a one-time-only offer, and I said yes.

Dear Lord, thanks for the peculiar adventure of children, who are wondrous and mysterious, who make me gray and tired, and who lead me closer to joy than I have ever been before. *—BRIAN DOYLE*

SUN
25

You care for the land and water it. . . . you soften it with showers. . . .   *—PSALM 65:9–10 (NIV)*

During our summer vacations, our family often went to prayer services at the Benedictine Priory in Weston, Vermont. One sunny afternoon, we walked through a field to what remained of an old hay barn, where the Benedictines sat in a semicircle. Completely open on one side, the barn had a roof, but the crowd was so large that the overflow reached far out into the meadow. There was silence until Brother Gregory picked up a guitar and we began to sing psalms to the music he had written—songs that have become so beloved that we once heard one in Notre Dame in Paris.

But while Brother Gregory had become world-famous, it was clear to all that Brother Leo, the founder of Weston Priory, was the leader. In midlife, he had felt a call to leave his Benedictine home in Germany and start this new community. White-haired, quiet and frail, he watched everything with thoughtful eyes behind thick glasses. I often wondered if he ever smiled.

Suddenly, the sky grew dark and a furious rainstorm began. Some in the fields headed to their cars. We were under the roof, but I couldn't help thinking of the wet and muddy walk we would have ahead.

The singing ended. Brother Leo looked out at the rain and grinned. "What a wonderful surprise!" he said. "We do not think enough of the surprises of God. Too often we see them as interruptions that keep us from doing what we want. But they are really signs of His intervention in our lives. When the sun was bright, we did not think that the earth and its seeds were thirsting, even as we thirst, for His living waters. But now we will remember this storm with joy, when new flowers come. At times it may seem hard, but let us search for God in every surprise He sends us—however dark or sudden or unwanted."

On the walk back to our car, I actually thought the rain and the mud were wonderful!

God, keep my heart open to Your presence everywhere.

—*FULTON OURSLER, JR.*

MON

26 As in water face answers to face, so the mind of man reflects the man.   —*PROVERBS 27:19 (RSV)*

Our townhouse windows here in Minnesota overlook a beautiful, deep emerald pond rimmed with huge leafy trees. Having moved from the overwhelming natural beauty of Alaska, it means a great deal to me to have this corner of creation to look at.

Last autumn I watched the setting sun slant burnished copper across the feathered plumpness of Canada geese as they sought a landing on the quiet water. In the winter I tramped through the powdery snow layered on the frozen pond, discovering a tiny nest woven among the neatly creased crispness of wheat-colored reeds at the pond's edge. Spring's advent seemed to fling an array of excited birds about the pond, all eager to outshout one another. I listened with grinning ears to geese honking, ducks quacking, crows cawing, red-winged blackbirds yodeling—and wrote to my friend, "Imagine your worst fifth-grade classroom in stereo!" Soon there appeared on the lush lawn vigilant web-footed parents, herding downy goslings across the grass.

It is summer now. A warm wind bends the elegant cattails. At night, fireflies—a new source of wonder for me—wink around the pond like fallen fragments of the stars overhead. And today a graceful egret etched its gleaming white reflection in the shallow water, occasionally stretching double its long curving neck to lunge for an aquatic appetizer.

I thought of the proverb, "As in water face answers to face, so the mind of man reflects the man." I fancied that God saw my face mirrored beside the egret in the tranquil waters of the pond. And I hoped with all my heart that He saw reflected there my absolute enjoyment of Him and all that He has made.

Father in heaven, thank You for Your reflection in every season of Your creation. *—CAROL KNAPP*

TUE
27

We are the children of God . . . and if children . . . then heirs of God, and joint-heirs with Christ. . . .
—ROMANS 8:16–17

My relationship with my daughter has had a difficult beginning. My son Julian and I seemed to hit it off right from the start, but Noelle has always seemed a little leery of me. All the things that I did to entertain Julian when he was her age did nothing for her. Everything that made him laugh just left her bored. Julian would run to my arms when I came home from work; Noelle would just continue to do what she was doing. When I tried to kiss her, she couldn't be bothered.

I couldn't put my finger on why I had done so well with Julian and not with Noelle, until one day, quite literally, it hit me.

I got down on the ground, lay on my back and called to Noelle. She picked up her doll, came over and smacked me on the head with it. Then she jumped on me and laughed and giggled as we rolled around. She was insatiable. She couldn't get enough of her dad—on her level and with the freedom to have her own way. That night after her bath she hugged me, sat on my lap and kissed me, all the while glowing like a hundred-watt bulb.

These days, our evenings are like this: As soon as we finish dinner, I lie on the ground (I know, it's terrible for my digestion) and wait for Noelle to come and jump on me. I never wait very long.

Lord, thank You for the earthly gift of Your heavenly Son, Who came down to our level to lift us up to Yours. *—DAVE FRANCO*

WED
28

"Yes, in my early years, when the friendship of God was felt in my home." *—JOB 29:4 (TLB)*

My granddaughter Christy had completed her education, secured a good job and purchased a condominium. Now she was in the process of signing the final papers. I was visiting her mother Emily when she called with the news.

"Everything is signed," Christy announced proudly. "The service personnel are to go over in a little while to turn on the electricity. But I have an appointment at my office and can't be there. Could you go and unlock the door so they can get inside?"

Emily hung up the telephone and said, "Come with me, Mother. Let's go and attend to this for Christy." As we left the house, Emily picked up her well-worn Bible and slipped a marker into it.

At the condominium's front door, she paused with the key in her hand and said, "Wait a minute, Mother. There's someone I want to be the first to enter Christy's new home."

I stepped back as she inserted the key and turned the knob. As the door opened, she reached her Bible across the threshold and into the room. I silently joined in as she bowed her head in prayer. She thanked God for her child's opportunity to purchase a home, welcomed Him as the first guest and beseeched Him to stay and to bless all who would come there.

She paused, opened the Bible to the marker and read aloud the first words of Psalm 25: "Unto thee, Lord, do I lift up my soul, O my God, I trust in thee."

"God is here," she said softly, "and our prayers will help keep Him here always."

Dear God, how wonderful to know that You do dwell in my home and that I can put my trust in You. —*DRUE DUKE*

THU
29
Behold, the kingdom of God is within you. —*LUKE 17:21*

My wife Tib and I were driving through the southwestern United States, often stopping to admire the cactuses that thrived in the arid soil of Arizona and New Mexico. There were prickly pear and barrel cactuses and saguaro. But my favorite was a strange treelike plant, which at times soared twenty-five feet into the sky like a giant with his arms outstretched to heaven.

"It's a yucca," said Tib, who is our family naturalist. "Early settlers called it the Joshua tree because it reminded them of Joshua in the Bible, who pointed the children of Israel to the Promised Land."

It was a nice simile, but something was wrong. The arms of our desert Joshua were pointing every which way, sometimes toward the east, sometimes to the south, north or west, at times even downward.

Then I realized that the pioneer simile was a good one after all. For the land flowing with milk and honey is not "out there" somewhere. It is everywhere, for "the kingdom of God is within you," wherever the Lord is to be found. Over the years I have known rich people who are never satisfied, and poor people who are content because they have made their homes in the Promised Land. If you asked them to point to the Promised Land, they would be puzzled: "The promised land? Why, it's right here."

Father, help me understand that nothing can compare with living in Your presence.   *—JOHN SHERRILL*

FRI

30

And when we had taken our leave one of another, we took ship; and they returned home again.   *—ACTS 21:6*

When I attended parent/student orientation with our second son, Chris, at a university clear across the country, I thought I was an old pro at sending a child off to college. After all, our first son, Jeff, had been at college for three years. I settled complacently into my seat for a seminar entitled "Parenting through the College Years" and smiled wryly as the leader began by passing boxes of tissues down the auditorium rows.

The leader played an audio tape of a mother whose son was away at college. She talked about being in the grocery store, reaching for her son's favorite brand of yogurt and then pulling her hand back when she realized her son was no longer living at home. By now, my eyes were burning, and I needed one of those tissues.

After playing the tape, the leader asked for comments. A man raised his hand. "We've sent eight children off to school, and this is our last. Saying good-bye is something you never really get used to. I remember trying to play it cool with my third one. I casually said good-bye at registration. Then something made me turn around and look at my son. He looked confused, like he didn't know what to do next. I walked back to him and did what I'd wanted to do all along. I gave him a hug and said, 'I know you'll do fine.' Don't pretend when you say good-bye. Be sincere about what's in your heart."

As the group walked to lunch, I tapped the man with the eight children on the shoulder and confided, "The only reason I can muster the courage to leave my son here, so far away from home, is that I'm a praying person. I'm trusting that God will be with him. And I'm trusting that God will be with me, too."

Dear God, I can't possibly say this good-bye without Your help. Be with us both while we are apart. Amen. —*KAREN BARBER*

SAT
31
Be ye not as the horse, or as the mule, which have no understanding: whose mouth must be held in with bit and bridle.... —*PSALM 32:9*

For weeks, I'd been imagining myself riding horseback through the Big Sky country. John Wayne himself would have been impressed, seeing me riding proudly on my noble steed.

My father and I had been planning this trip to Wyoming for more than a year. After months of research and hours more surfing the Net, we chose Justin and Sandy Wright of Mule Shoe Outfitters in Pinedale to be our guides. We planned to meet up with the Wrights at the head of the trail that leads up to the Wind River mountain range. From there we would travel for several hours by horseback to the campsite that would serve as our home base for the week.

Once our plans were set, our deposits paid and our reservations confirmed, we had months to anticipate the exploits that awaited us out west. In the interim, I made sure we were equipped with plenty of film and a couple of extra disposable cameras. I didn't want to take any chances on leaving Wyoming without a stack of pictures to chronicle my mountain-man days.

At last, the big day rolled around and we were on our way. I spent a good deal of our travel time ribbing Dad about my superior horsemanship and assuring him that I would wait up for him at every mountain pass. Finally, we met up with our guides, who introduced us to the animals that would serve as our transportation during the coming week.

Dad was assigned a big brown mare. He really did look like a cowboy, sitting high in the saddle, a cowboy who was a quick draw with his camera. He joyfully clicked picture after picture of me, standing with a red face and a sheepish grin next to my "noble steed" and new best friend, Molly the mule.

Father, bridle my ego and give me good humor when the events of life rein me in. —*BROCK KIDD*

My Days of Prayer

1 _____

2 _____

3 _____

4 _____

5 _____

6 _____

7 _____

8 _____

9 _____

10 _____

11 _____

12 _____

13 _____

14 _____

15 _____

16 _____

17 _____

18 _____

19 _____

20 _____

21 _____

22 _____

23 _____

24 _____

25 _____

26 _____

27 _____

28 _____

29 _____

30 _____

31 _____

September

We are labourers together with God . . . .

—*I Corinthians 3:9*

	S	M	T	W	T	F	S
	1	2	3	4	5	6	7
	8	9	10	11	12	13	14
	15	16	17	18	19	20	21
	22	23	24	25	26	27	28
	29	30					

THE PRAYER THAT IS ALWAYS NEW

1 Our Father . . . forgive us *our debts*. . . .

—*MATTHEW 6:9, 12*

Our debts, or trespasses, come first in the Lord's Prayer, before the trespasses of others. Did He put the crucial issue of forgiveness in this order because accepting forgiveness can be harder than offering it?

The obstacle's on my side. His part was done on a Cross long ago, but I can still mope about for days under a cloud of self-accusation. It was Kathleen, a reader in Indiana, who showed me a way to appropriate what God so freely offers. She kept blaming herself after some uncharitable act, she wrote, even after she'd prayed for forgiveness. Kathleen decided that when she'd done something she regretted, she would ask God to give her three chances to do a kindness instead. "I've never seen a prayer answered so fast!" she said.

Ever since Kathleen wrote to me, I've used her prayer following my own misdeeds—and seen it answered just as swiftly. Just two days ago, for instance, I ducked into another aisle of the supermarket to avoid running into a woman I knew would stop me with a long-winded family update. Wheeling the cart out to my car twenty minutes later, I was sorry. Recently widowed, the woman lives alone; news of her family in far-off Seattle is her lifeline. First I asked God to forgive my lack of charity, then for three chances to do better.

Just seconds later, three parking spaces away, a woman dropped the sack of groceries she was lifting into her trunk. Together we retrieved rolling cans and mopped up a broken jar of salsa. When I got home ten minutes later, the phone was ringing. Did I have an address the church secretary had been unable to locate? "Sorry to inconvenience you," she said, but I assured her (truthfully!) I was happy to go look for it. And in the afternoon's mail came a plea for donations to a lupus walk. I wrote a check then and there.

They don't "earn" forgiveness, of course, these little motions of goodwill. That's the part that Jesus did. They're His assurances, that's all, that I've a part to play in the fellowship of all God's restored and forgiven children.

Our Father, what chance to serve will Your forgiveness provide today?   —*ELIZABETH SHERRILL*

MON
2

For the man who uses well what he is given shall be given more, and he shall have abundance....
                                          —*MATTHEW 25:29 (TLB)*

When I was a kid, I wanted to be four things when I grew up: a doctor, trapeze artist, airline pilot and writer. But then I discovered that I have no natural talent in math or science. I've never balanced my checkbook and never got higher than a C in science.

Trapeze artist? Dad built me a stellar trapeze in our backyard, and I organized neighborhood circuses every summer. But in seventh grade, when I grew to five feet seven inches tall and faced the fact that I'd inherited my grandmother's large bones, I knew my torso would never fly from wire to wire on a high trapeze.

The airline pilot dream lasted through high school when I took flying lessons and discovered I'm not at all adept mechanically. I still have trouble remembering which dipstick is the oil and which is the transmission fluid when I open the hood on my car.

My fourth career choice held more promise. In second grade mother gave me an old Smith Corona typewriter to play with, and I started writing with gusto. But by 1992, after writing more than forty thousand radio commercials, I asked myself, "Am I really happy doing this work?"

That's when a friend said to me, "Pat, don't take your ducks to eagle school. You can send your ducks to eagle boot camp, give them a little eagle hat, an eagle badge and an eagle T-shirt, but no matter how hard you try, those ducks will never become eagles. Maybe your real talent is something besides advertising writing."

I quit my job to stay home and write the kinds of things I wanted to write. I took a large pay cut, but my work, based on the real talent God gave me, suddenly became much easier and more joyful than anything I'd done before.

Will this be the year you decide to start that second career or go back to school to fine-tune the natural talent God planted in your heart and soul?

Thank You, Lord, for giving each of us one special talent that can make our work joyous. —*PATRICIA LORENZ*

TUE	Rejoice in the Lord, O you righteous! Praise befits the
3	upright. Praise the Lord with the lyre, make melody to him with the harp of ten strings! Sing to him a new song, play skillfully on the strings, with loud shouts.

—*PSALM 33:1-3 (RSV)*

Some moments last forever. Recently my parents celebrated their fiftieth wedding anniversary. Mum wanted to go camping at Manning Park in British Columbia, Canada, so that's what we did. We rented a couple of cabins and all of us—Mum, Dad, siblings and offspring, fifteen in all—met for a long weekend.

We had a wonderful time. My young nieces instigated a water balloon fight. My daughter-in-law went horseback riding and canoeing for the first time—and enjoyed herself. My older sister baked a huge ham for the celebration dinner. I sketched wildflowers and dared to jump off a suspension bridge into an ice cold mountain lake, surprising my children almost as much as myself. My son and Dad brought out their cameras to capture the beauty around us. My daughter staked out the hiking trails. We all hiked the alpine. We recalled old memories and, depending on the story, laughed or groaned. Some of us took long soaks in a bubbling hot tub.

My favorite moments, though, were the evenings gathered about the campfire. My youngest crouched over his guitar; the rest roasted marshmallows and gorged ourselves on s'mores. Blake strummed through the old camp songs and newer gospel songs. Soon three generations were singing God's praises.

All around us, the night fell softly. The wind mewed in the pines. Starlight twinkled from above. What is that verse from Browning's poem? "God is in His heaven—All's right with the world."

Thank You, God, for such moments as these, for the gift of family and for songs we can sing back to You. —*BRENDA WILBEE*

WED

4   The joy of the Lord is your strength.   —*NEHEMIAH 8:10*

This has been a year of adjustment for my family. My oldest son Drew graduated from high school and is now a student at Furman University in South Carolina, a long way from our Texas home. It's been hard for Beth and me to let go of our firstborn.

As Drew was packing his bags and preparing to leave, I called an old friend from my own high-school days, Kathy Fertig. "Kathy," I said, "I wasn't prepared for the grief I'm feeling. Did you feel this way when your boys graduated?"

Much to my surprise, Kathy laughed and replied, "Well, no, I didn't. I mean, I shed my share of tears. But mostly I felt excitement for them. I felt like a mother bird nudging her young out of the nest and enabling them to fly. This was the moment they had been raised for. This was what all of the love and efforts of parenting were all about. It really was an exciting time for me."

As Beth and I stuffed all of Drew's belongings into our van and headed east toward Furman, Kathy's words kept ringing in my ears. Slowly, I, too, began to feel more excitement than grief. This truly was the moment I had been hoping for and dreaming of for Drew. What an opportunity! And what a fulfillment of the toil and aspirations of generations.

Joy and sorrow are often intertwined, inseparable emotional twins. When this happens, we can choose which emotion will be dominant; whether joy or sorrow will rule the day and set the agenda for our lives. Talking with my friend Kathy helped me to see that I had some choice in whether my world was dark or bright, filled with happiness or pain. Her contagious upbeat attitude made all the difference in transforming a dismal trip into a wonderful time of celebration.

Lord, may I decide today to be happy and joyful. Amen.

                                —*SCOTT WALKER*

THU

5   A man hath joy by the answer of his mouth: and a word spoken in due season, how good is it!   —*PROVERBS 15:23*

I was at the office, and I felt like picking up the phone and calling my wife Rosie for one of those "just because" calls. The phone rang five or six times, and then the answering machine came on. I left a message, thinking that Rosie had just stepped out to run an errand and would call back in an hour or so. But when she did call back, she said, "You called and the phone beeped, but I was talking to my friend." Right away, I knew exactly whom she was talking about, the special lady who calls Rosie her "psychiatrist," because my wife has a wonderful way of just listening.

Rosie said, "I really didn't say that much. Most of the time I just listened. But when we got ready to hang up, my friend kept thanking me. 'But I didn't do anything,' I replied. She quickly reminded me that it's therapeutic to talk to someone who will allow her to 'just let it out.' 'There are times,' she said, 'when I say to myself that what I'm going through is very difficult, but if I can simply talk to my "psychiatrist," everything will be all right.' "

For years, Rosie has seen her ministry as helping me in mine, but lately God is showing her what a great ministry she has in the lives of others.

Thank You for Rosie, Lord. May I emulate her silent ministry to those who need to speak. —DOLPHUS WEARY

FRI

6

"I would fly away and be at rest; yea, I would wander afar, I would lodge in the wilderness." —PSALM 55:6–7 (RSV)

While attending college in Santa Barbara, California, I felt a deep inner restlessness. I dropped out of school with the idea of "finding" myself, but I really had no intention of going back. I wanted to escape—from school, from society, from the human race. So I packed my clothes and a sleeping bag, strapped it all on the back of my motorcycle and headed out into the desert.

I enjoyed swaying my bike through the curves of the foothills, but just outside Santa Paula, my rubber intake manifold developed a serious crack. I must have looked helpless, standing by the side of the road, staring at my motorcycle and holding the meager toolkit that came with the bike. Within minutes, another biker had stopped to help. He was a large man with a flowing black beard, weathered skin and a large silver earring. He rode a custom-made three-wheeled "motor trike" and carried a healthy assortment of tools. In a few minutes, we had patched the crack with some tape and a spare hose clamp, and I was speeding through the desert.

I got to the rim of Death Valley late that night, but the patch on the manifold was losing to the growing crack. The next day I met another lone camper in the valley with a pickup truck full of tools and odd parts. We managed to patch the manifold again with more tape, more clamps and a spare piece of pipe. By the time this repair gave out, I had sputtered north to Sacramento, where my friend Tony lived. We found the correct replacement part, and I was on my way.

But not back on the road to nowhere. My escape from responsibility hadn't lasted much longer than my intake manifold. I headed back to Santa Barbara and re-enrolled in school, eventually graduated and got on with my life. There are still times when I feel I haven't found myself, but I think I'm getting closer.

Lord, help me to find my truest self in loving others and in loving You. —*BILLY NEWMAN*

<hr>

SAT
7   "I, even I, am He who comforts you. . . ."
—*ISAIAH 51:12 (NAS)*

Despite all of our efforts and our vet's, Minnie, our frail sixteen-year-old cat, was becoming worse. Finally, one Friday evening early in September, she gobbled up an enormous amount of tuna for supper, took all her medicine without a fuss and asked to be let out on the porch. She tasted the recent rain, sat down and gazed out over the yard. She was having difficulty breathing; her back legs were still retaining fluid, and there was still some fluid around her heart and lungs. When she sauntered back inside and attempted to curl up for her usual nap, she couldn't lie down. She had to sit up, and even then her breathing was labored. I stayed with her until midnight.

At five the next morning, I lay down beside her on the floor and whispered, "Let go, girl. Please give up." But she hung on like a bulldog. I stayed with her until eleven. Not once did she shut her eyes.

Shortly after eleven, my husband Gene and I took her to the vet. When he saw her, we could see the grim truth in his face. Minnie needed his help—one last time. While Gene signed the papers, I unsuccessfully fought back my tears. We'd both planned to stay with her to the end, but we fled—desperately trying to avoid or, at least, delay our grief.

We drove home silently, mechanically wiping away the tears, staring straight ahead without talking. At home we quickly devised some all-day plans and went out again. But we were home again at seven. When we opened the back door, no faithful old cat sat waiting to greet us. In our minds, we could see Minnie again and hear her impatient *meow*. We looked at each other and saw the grief both of us had been evading, and fell crying into each other's arms.

When grief closes in, so do You, dear Comforter.

—*MARION BOND WEST*

<u>SUN</u>

8

Children's children are the crown of old men; and the glory of children are their fathers.   —*PROVERBS 17:6*

I recently saw a bumper sticker that read, IF I HAD KNOWN HOW MUCH FUN GRANDKIDS WERE, I WOULD HAVE HAD THEM FIRST.

As the overtaxed father of three girls under the age of ten, I smiled weakly at the thought. As I drove, I made some mental notes to myself:

When I become a grandfather, I will not be mean to my grandkids. I will, instead, realize how short the candle of childhood is and enjoy its brilliant flame. And I will quietly put up with my grown daughters' wide eyes and *tsk-tsks*: "He wasn't like that with us."

No, he wasn't. He was exhausted. He's trying to make up for it now.

When I become a grandfather, I will let my grandkids play music. Loud. And I'll dance, arthritic joints and all, to whatever pop-techno beat my grandkids like. ("Mommy, Granddad let me play my *Truly Trash* CD really loud!" "He did? I wasn't allowed to play my music above a whisper." I know. You're right. I was trying to catch a nap between helping you with your school project and correcting my own students' papers. What can I say?)

When I become a grandfather, I will allow my grandkids to vent their litany of parental misdeeds and mistakes. And then I will remind them that I was a parent once, and that I know what it's like, and if they could glimpse even a fraction of what their parents feel for them, how much they sacrifice, how they would gladly lay down their lives for their children. . . .

And I will do all of this because the first thing I'll do as a grandparent, the very first thing, the very, very first thing I'll do, is forgive myself.

Lord, thank You for indulgent grandparents and grateful grandchildren. And don't forget to bless the frazzled parents caught in between. *—MARK COLLINS*

<hr>

MON

9

"I will see the rainbow in the cloud and remember my eternal promise . . . ." *—GENESIS 9:16 (TLB)*

Midmorning, when the light is just right, my daughter's room is filled with hundreds of tiny rainbows, scattered across two walls and a section of the ceiling. They last for ten minutes or so, and she calls me in so we can bathe ourselves in the wonder, sometimes catching a few of the rainbows across our faces or in our hair.

The rainbows come from the light refracted through the many small crystal figures on the window ledge and the dewdrop prisms dangling from invisible threads here, there and everywhere. To expand the glory, our daughter continues to add more and more crystals to the decor of her room, the most recent being a double-strand necklace of aurora borealis purchased at a yard sale. The "Rainbow Room," as we now call it, is a beautiful reminder that we are enveloped and embraced by the promises of God.

It is extraordinary to me that God's first covenant, His promise to Noah that He would never again destroy the earth by a flood, was symbolized by the rainbow He set in the sky. The brilliant colors come from light shining through water—water symbolizing our tears and sorrows, turned into an arc of joy by the light, a symbol of God's glorious presence and power.

The rainbow has been called the "smile of God," meeting us where we are and leading us on with strength for today and hope for tomorrow. And standing in my daughter's room, bathed in rainbows, I believe it.

Help me look for rainbows, Lord. And when I find one, let it remind me that the brightness of Your loving presence is always with me.
—FAY ANGUS

TUE

10

Jesus said to them . . . "Stop judging by mere appearances, and make a right judgment." —*JOHN 7:21, 24 (NIV)*

New Yorkers have a largely justified reputation for being a pushy, impatient bunch, and to most people's way of thinking this translates as "rude." In my eighteen years of living in Manhattan, I have learned a surprising fact: To a New Yorker, being pushy *is* being polite.

At first, I didn't know what to think of this frenetic, elbow-to-elbow metropolis and its hurry-up citizenry. I recall ordering a toasted bagel at a busy midtown deli on my way to work one morning shortly after I moved here from my native Midwest. After the counterman tossed me my bagel, I tried to make a little small talk, passing a few innocent remarks about the new subway cars the Transit Authority had just put into service. All at once from behind me came a gruff, sarcastic bellow: "Next, already!"

I turned to find a line of people glaring at me. The man who made the remark rolled his eyes and crossed his arms. Red-faced, I grabbed my bagel and scurried off, shocked at the utter lack of civility.

I don't know when exactly the change in me occurred, but I remember the circumstances: I was waiting in line at the bank on my lunch hour while a customer chatted up the teller, and all at once I found myself wanting to bellow, "Next!"

I mean, I didn't have all day.

What I'd finally understood was this: In a big, crowded city, people have to act quickly and decisively, or the whole system will come to a grinding halt. What I initially mistook for pushiness was really a New Yorker's way of showing consideration to his fellow citizens.

It occurred to me the other day that I have lived here longer now than I have lived in any other place. And, yes, I'm more often in a hurry than not. But I try not to be in the kind of hurry I was when I arrived here—a hurry to judge people before I got to know them.

God, You've managed to surprise me yet again. You made me a New Yorker! —*EDWARD GRINNAN*

WED
11
So Jacob served seven years to get Rachel, but they seemed like only a few days to him because of his love for her.
—*GENESIS 29:20 (NIV)*

One day, not long after my wife Joy and I returned from Africa, I was asked to meet a couple who had spent many years there and wanted to talk about current developments. Although they were both Americans, the wife had been born in a tiny African village where her parents were missionaries. After returning to the States and meeting and marrying her husband, she traveled back to Africa with him and visited the village where she had been born.

When she told the people about their wedding, the village elders became upset and held a long council. They came to the groom and demanded a bride-price, as was the custom in their culture. The new husband wanted to make a good impression and asked what it was. "Two chickens and a crate of orange soda," he was told. He thought they must be joking and was about to laugh, when he saw how serious they were. Theirs was a poor village, and they had set what they thought was a high price for one of their most beloved daughters. With great solemnity, he bought the required items, took them to the council and received a joyous blessing.

As he told me the story, he took his wife's hand, and with a twinkle in his eye said, "I'd pay twice the price anytime, all over again." Perhaps there's something to be said for the idea of a dowry or a bride-price: After all, when you've paid dearly for something, it's a whole lot harder to take it for granted.

Lord, today let me tell the ones I love the most how much their gift of love means to me.
—*ERIC FELLMAN*

THU
12
Bright eyes gladden the heart. . . .
—*PROVERBS 15:30 (NAS)*

"Guess who came to visit me today?" My sister Zelma's brown eyes were dancing with delight.

As they had before she was diagnosed with cancer, I thought sadly. She hadn't had any upbeat moments since she was admitted to the hospital two weeks ago, so I was curious about who or what could have lifted her spirits this much.

"A little black dog!" she continued, not even giving me a chance to guess. "His name is Niichii—a Cree word for pal or friend. His owner Dennis brings Niichii into the hospital every day to visit patients. I've already asked someone to go to the pet store for doggie treats."

Niichii's visits thereafter were the highlight of Zelma's last days. About 1:30 P.M. every afternoon, Dennis walked quietly into Zelma's hospital room with the little Sheltie padding softly along behind him. Approaching the bed, Dennis lifted Niichii up so the little dog could lie alongside Zelma. She'd smile as she felt his warm nose nuzzling her hand for a treat. Soon Niichii and Zelma would both drift off to sleep.

Visiting with Dennis, we learned that severe diabetes had curtailed most of his activities, but not his willingness to be of help to others less fortunate. That's how he came to acquire Niichii the therapy dog. As providence would have it, Dennis and his wife Lucille lived just five minutes away from the hospital, so it wasn't long before Dennis and Niichii were both sporting volunteer I.D. cards, Dennis's on his pale blue vest and Niichii's on his dog collar.

Even though Zelma's strength waned and her ability to communicate grew less and less, we knew she was aware of the little dog's visits to her bed by the way she'd bury her hand in the Sheltie's long coat and smile faintly. Niichii, in turn, would lay his long nose on his paws, raise his eyebrows and look up at us as if to ask, "How is she today?"

She's comforted, Niichii. Comforted by you.

Lord, help me to take Your unconditional love to the people around me in their hour of need.
                                                                    —*ALMA BARKMAN*

FRI	Command those who are rich in this present world . . . to
13	put their hope in God, who richly provides us with everything for our enjoyment. —*I TIMOTHY 6:17 (NIV)*

One clear September evening, I drove, between sage-covered lumps of lava rock, into the Idaho desert on a two-lane roller-coaster road. The lava blowouts spoiled my view of an autumn moon climbing up the eastern wall of the sky.

The moon looked ten times bigger than it had the night before. I had watched from a sleeping bag on top of Antelope Mountain as it cruised across a sky full of stars. Now I wanted a picture. I kept driving as the moon escaped the horizon's grasp, and searched for a better view.

When I finally stopped, I found I had waited too long. The huge half moon that had been peaking over the eastern horizon had now risen high into the star-filled sky and shrunk into a small silver ball. Because I had waited, I lost the picture I wanted.

As I started again along the moonlit road, it seemed to me that I was doing the same thing with my life: I was waiting for something better. But God was offering me plenty to enjoy—two great daughters, a loving wife and a dental practice full of patients happy with my work. When I reached home, I stopped waiting for something better and started enjoying the blessings God offers every day.

Lord, cancel my "wants list" and open my eyes to the blessings You've already given me.   —*RICHARD HAGERMAN*

SAT

14

But God forbid that I should glory, save in the cross of our Lord Jesus Christ. . . .   —*GALATIANS 6:14*

Symbols are powerful things, full of meaning and truth. An old acquaintance who had been out of the country for a long time told me how stirred she was by the sight of our Stars and Stripes, a symbol of freedom. At a wedding I attended last week, the couple exchanged rings, symbols of their mutual commitment and love. And no symbol is as significant for Christians as the Cross, because it represents Christ's sacrifice and Resurrection.

I once heard a speaker say that believers can see God everywhere, while the faith-challenged can't see Him anywhere. The man said he saw crosses everywhere he looked—in ships' masts, in the panels of doors, telephone poles, garden trellises—"all reminders of Jesus' redemptive act for me."

All of this reminds me of a story someone related during the last Olympic Games. It was about two divers with world-class aspirations. They trained for hours every day, under the tutelage of a top coach, and often after hours by themselves. One diver, Al, a Christian, quietly shared his beliefs with Jim, who listened with interest but harbored doubts. One night, Jim couldn't sleep, and he decided to go to the pool. Though the complex was closed, he sneaked inside and made his way through the dark to the diving platform. Aided by bright moonlight, he climbed the stairs to the springboard, high above the pool, and prepared to dive. But something caught his attention and stopped him—the shadow of his body and extended arms on an adjacent wall. It formed a cross, a cross like the one Al said Christ had died on for our sins. In that instant, Jim bowed his head and accepted Christ.

While he was still in prayer, a custodian appeared and turned on the lights. "Don't jump!" he yelled.

Jim looked down; the pool had been drained that afternoon for repairs.

> Thank You, God, for that old rugged Cross,
> Which saves us from death, suffering and loss.

—*FRED BAUER*

THE PRACTICE OF PRAYER

SUN
15

Listening Prayer
Rest in the Lord, and wait patiently for him. . . .
—*PSALM 37:7*

When David and I were first married, we went as Presbyterian missionaries to the Appalachian Mountains. There we made friends with a remarkable man named Father Killian Mooney, a Catholic priest who had come to Harlan County to serve a mission parish. Every morning he rose at four o'clock and trekked to a quiet place behind the church. He stayed there and prayed till 8:00 A.M.—four hours of prayer at a stretch, every day.

As I struggle to maintain a positive prayer practice, I'm in awe of Father Mooney's power of concentration. I can see myself out behind that church, saying, "Okay, God, three hours and fifty-five minutes to go. What now?"

Recognizing my limitations as I set aside a time each morning to walk and talk with God, I take along some helpful guidelines from *Prayer Can Change Your Life* to get me in the groove. First, I center myself on God. I tell Him I appreciate the way He grows trees and fluffs clouds and paints the sky. Next, I tell God how very much I want to surrender to Him, to give all my problems to Him. I sigh, let go of the previous day's failures and give them to my Father. I reaffirm the person I wish to become and thank God that despite my lapses, I am getting better. And then I listen.

"Is there anything You want to tell me, God?" I ask.

A breeze ruffles my hair. There is a long silence. A leaf sails on the soft wind and lands at my feet. I pick it up. My mind clears. I have a sense of well-being.

"Is there anything I can do for You today, Father?" I ask out loud.

A list forms in my mind. *Check on Dot. Write a note to Ginny; she needs encouragement. Call and invite George to dinner.*

I turn around and head for home. It's going to be a great day!

Father, let me be as good a listener as I am a talker, as I commit myself to the practice of prayer. —*PAM KIDD*

MON

16

Let every one of us please his neighbour for his good. . . .
—*ROMANS 15:2*

When I was six years old, I decided that my mother was the most generous person in the world. Why? Because she let me lick the batter from the bowl and spoon when she baked sugar cookies. I couldn't believe that anyone would give up that privilege, and I secretly thought that when I was an adult, I would always lick the batter off the spoon when I baked cookies. I didn't care if I ever learned to drive or swim or dance, or did all the other things I thought of as adult, as long as I could lick that spoon.

Well, I am an adult now. At least, I can drive and swim and dance (though not very well). But when my nephews were visiting and we made chocolate chip cookies, I offered them the spoon and bowl to lick. I enjoyed seeing their eyes widen as they scraped off and ate every bit of that batter. And I enjoyed watching them eat it more than I would have enjoyed eating the sugary concoction myself.

So I decided to be generous a few more times that week. I carried my neighbor's groceries up to her apartment even though I was tired after a full day of work. Her glowing face more than made up for the effort. And I picked up the check after my friend Dana and I had coffee and cherry pie at a diner. When she asked why, I said, "Just because." And I felt great, even though my pocketbook was a little lighter.

So I'm going to ask God to keep showing me opportunities to be generous this week. In fact, I think I'm going to bake another batch of cookies with my nephews!

Thank You, Lord, for the pleasure of pleasing others.

—*LINDA NEUKRUG*

TUE

17 My days are swifter than a weaver's shuttle.... —*JOB 7:6*

The freeway shoots like an arrow of asphalt across an everlasting prairie. I've been on it seven hours—seven hours of sameness. My body feels as stiff as Pinocchio, and my eyes are melted gumdrops. In desperation, I get off the freeway and take old Route 54.

Immediately I am in another world, where every new mile is different from the last one. The ditches are a random madness of blue chicory, Queen Anne's lace and black-eyed Susans. I pass a rare elm tree, as majestic as a pillar in the Parthenon. Then a wind-blown willow. Then a pointed pine, and now a row of crimson sumac. On my right, a forest of green corn weaves over rolling plains, and wild sunflowers peek above the tassels.

I coast through small towns, ghosted by the coming of the freeway, yet still alive somehow. On a used-car lot sits a black '49 Chevy, like the one my brother Tommy drove to college, and my mind smiles with memories. At a yard sale, my wife eagerly loads up with old-town jewels and junk.

For the next few miles, a peaceful stream follows the route before mysteriously disappearing into a cemetery of white stones and black walnut trees. I slow down for a roadrunner and her babies, then brake for a construction flagman, who turns out to be a pretty blonde with a dandelion on her hard hat. I shut off the motor, and I'm stunned by the utter silence of the countryside. I step outside to stretch, letting the demons of fatigue out through my fingertips. The fragrance of freshly mown hay makes me inwardly sigh for my little dream farm.

When, at last, I ease back onto the freeway, I am a new man.

I need the speedways of life to make time, but I also need the slow ways, with their artful asymmetry. I need construction delays and interruptions. I need pleasant surprises and eyes full of beauty.

God, be my flagman and slow me down, so I can see the treasures I have sacrificed to speed. —*DANIEL SCHANTZ*

READER'S ROOM

In September 1991, my husband was nearing the end of an almost fifteen-month battle with cancer. He was facing his own death, and as a pastor and father, was trying to prepare his church and our family for the changes that would lie ahead. The September 13 devotional by Terry Helwig dealt with the fact that there are times in our lives when words escape us, and that sometimes when we wish to help someone, it's enough just to sit and hold his hand. I could by no stretch of the imagination know what my husband's pain felt like, nor could I imagine his view of what heaven would be like. I was losing my best friend, my pastor, my husband, and all I could do was to sit quietly with him and hold his hand. He died three weeks before his thirty-eighth birthday.

Your devotions have spoken to my heart during good times and bad times. Thank you for making a difference in my life.
—*JANET LOHR, JOHNSTOWN, PENNSYLVANIA*

WED

18

Your beauty should. . . . be that of your inner self. . . .
—*I PETER 3:3–4 (NIV)*

One of the fun things about editing *Guideposts for Teens* is that I get to have Christmas twice. I celebrate in December, of course, with everyone else, but I also get to immerse myself in the holiday when we do our December issue, months before the actual event. Which is why, one September day, I was tying bows on box after empty box for a Christmas photo shoot. Colorful paper gleamed on parcels of all shapes and sizes, trimmed with bright red ribbons, fluffy tulle and colorful stick-on bows. The presents were beautiful but empty—useless, really—except for the illusion of seasonal beauty they conveyed. There was nothing inside but air and space—no substance at all.

I thought about those packages the next day as I began my morning routine: walk off those calories on the treadmill; eat bran cereal; shower; wash and condition my hair; use moisturizer (lots!); apply just the right makeup; curl my hair; choose a fashionable outfit, complete with shoes and hat. Oh, yes, and try to find time to read a few verses in the Bible. Packaging—how much time I was spending on that! But substance? Where were the daily disciplines that would provide me with inner strength and wisdom? Disciplines such as prayer, meditation, reading. Maybe even fasting. Weren't these as important as the "beautiful wrappings" I invested so much in?

So these days I'm getting up earlier and working on the whole package—not just the outside wrappings and trimmings. I'm giving daily attention to the part of me that is *truly* important: what's inside.

Forgive me, Father, when I let the mirror be my measure of beauty and completeness. Help me to embrace the disciplines that will make me whole, inside and out.   —*MARY LOU CARNEY*

THU
19   Then shall thy light break forth as the morning....
                                                —*ISAIAH 58:8*

We were leaving the church after the funeral service for an old gentleman we had known for a long time. "It's a bit sad, isn't it?" I said to my friend. "We're going to miss him."

"I used to find funerals so sad," my friend said, "but not anymore. Not since I came across a phrase that changed my thinking about them altogether."

"Really?" I said "And what was that phrase?"

"Just eleven words: *Death is simply putting out a candle because morning has come.*"

"That's quite lovely," I said. "And very true. Who said it?"

"Wish I knew, but I don't. I tried looking it up once, but the source given was simply 'Anonymous.' All I know is that every time I go to a funeral, I remember those words and the sadness seems to go away. Perhaps you should try it yourself."

"I will," I said. And I have. And it does.

Father, guide me toward words of truth, regardless of who has spoken them.
                                                                —*ARTHUR GORDON*

FRI

20

For it has been granted to you on behalf of Christ not only to believe on him, but also to suffer for him. . . .
                                                —*PHILIPPIANS 1:29 (NIV)*

I am lying on the chair in the endodontist's office. My hands and arm muscles twitch involuntarily. My husband Andrew assures me that at a certain age it is actually pleasurable to have one's mouth thoroughly anesthetized and lie back with nothing to do for an hour, but I have yet to reach that stage of maturity. I am terrified.

I force myself to lower my shoulders, which are locked up by my ears. I wrinkle my brow and relax it. I take a deep breath and let it out slowly. These procedures transform my terror into a state of mere violent agitation. I decide I am too focused on myself, and will think about the Christians in Indonesia who are being martyred for their faith.

About ten years ago, I flew to Jakarta to help a friend who had just had a baby. In my imagination I travel back through the island of Java again, remembering the places I visited, the people I met and the churches where I worshiped. What must it be like to know that your house could be burned, your children killed, your life ended simply because you believe that Jesus Christ is the Son of God, Who died for our sins and rose again?

"How are you this morning?" interrupts the too-cheerful voice of the endodontist. "Ready to begin?"

I look at him carefully, distrustfully. I remember this: Although God may not want us to suffer, Christ sanctified suffering when He died for us on the cross. God can use my suffering for good if I unite it with His. Yes, I'm ready. I'm ready to lie back and do nothing for an hour, except pray. This tooth is for you, Indonesia.

Let me not be afraid of suffering, dear Jesus, knowing that it is a path marked with Your saving blood.
                                                        —*JULIA ATTAWAY*

SAT
21

A new heart also will I give you, and a new spirit will I put within you. . . .   *—EZEKIEL 36:26*

"I would like to apologize to you both—for being so know-it-all and distant while you were growing up," said my husband to his brother and sister, who are twins. I gasped, and under my breath said a nine-word prayer: "Oh, Lord, don't let this end in another fight." They are in their fifties now, but my husband Edward has never managed to have a constructive relationship with Janet and John, who are five years his junior. It had always troubled me, and I had made several unsuccessful efforts to help.

Now here we were, eating lunch in a pleasant New Hampshire hotel, and my husband was apologizing for behavior that he had never mentioned in our many years together. He rarely talks about how he feels, and I was genuinely shocked as he went on. "Will you forgive me?" he asked.

The twins, their eyes fixed on the tablecloth, were clearly taken aback and dealing with a flood of not-so-pleasant memories. John finally looked up and said, "I'm working on it."

Janet said only, "I agree with John."

Later that day John said to me, "Eddie seems so different some-how, his spirit is lighter." He looked at me questioningly.

I replied as truthfully as I could, "I think he is realizing that it is not too late to right a wrong or to ask to be forgiven. My guess is he's been listening to a voice stronger than either yours or mine."

Our visit concluded with photo-taking and promises of closer fellowship. As we drove home down the long highway, I thought to myself, *Every self-help book I've ever read says you can't change people. What do they know? People* can *change. But it takes more than self-help; it takes God's help.*

Lord, nothing is impossible when You are the peacemaker.

—BRIGITTE WEEKS

SUN
22

> But now in Christ Jesus ye who sometimes were far off are made nigh by the blood of Christ. —*EPHESIANS 2:13*

It was a beautiful Iowa autumn day. My husband and I, traveling on a business trip, stopped in Nashua to see The Little Brown Church in the Vale, made famous by the hymn "The Church in the Wildwood." There is an amazing story surrounding this place.

In 1857, when William Pitts was inspired to write his song, there was no church there. He imagined one while passing through town, waiting for his stagecoach to change horses. Then in 1859 an energetic young pastor, Rev. John Nutting, arrived on the scene, knowing nothing of Mr. Pitts and his song, and got busy trying to build a church. The Civil War slowed the project considerably, but eventually the church was completed. In the fall of 1863 Mr. Pitts accepted a teaching position in the same town, and to his utter astonishment, there was a brown church exactly where he had pictured one six years earlier!

We discovered a small clapboard country chapel, shaded by a grove of magnificent trees. Entering the simple sanctuary through a quaintly arched front door, we felt as though the faith and prayers of all those who had worshiped there still lingered in the air.

Sitting in a worn wood pew, September sun filtering from small panes of glass in the windows, I felt a longing to know the many generations of Christians who had gathered in this place. Here I was, sitting where they had sat, yet they were far away from me in time. Then my eyes found a plain wood cross on the wall behind the altar. A small gold crown encircled it. A rush of sheer joy engulfed me. The risen Savior has snapped the bands of time and death, and given eternal life to His people. There is a way to cross the years, and it is the way of the Cross.

Jesus, I long to meet You face to face, side by side with all the generations who have loved You. —*CAROL KNAPP*

FOR EVERY SEASON

MON
23

Be self-controlled and alert. Your enemy the devil prowls around like a roaring lion looking for someone to devour. Resist him, standing firm in the faith....

—*I PETER 5: 8–9 (NIV)*

Today is the first official day of autumn. Unlike summer and spring, this season often begins with great weather fanfare. Huge low-pressure systems sweep summer's heat off the northern parts of the map with fierce thunderstorms and wind; hurricanes and tropical storms inundate the southern coastal areas. This year, as fall arrived, my husband Bill and I found ourselves in Alabama with a tropical storm bringing torrents of rain inland in bands. But our son David was receiving his Army Aviator's wings and no storm could make us miss that.

We followed the storm to Topsail Island, North Carolina, where it blew out to sea. Yesterday, as I faced east, the warmth toasted my face and the front of my arms and legs. At my back, the northwest winds blew cool fall air over me. I was poised between seasons.

My prayer life is sometimes like that, too. After a season of hectic prayer and expectation, there will come a lull, a peace to stop for a bit, still mindful of the winds of the enemy, and relax into the warmth of the Father's love, still mindful that the winds of the enemy howl at my back.

Earlier this year, my prayer partner Ellen and I had been praying about an ongoing situation in her son's life. Week after week we pleaded, seemingly to no avail, for a breakthrough for him. One week, in the midst of our prayer storm, we both suddenly knew it was time to stop asking and just leave it with God. Despite the cold wind of the unsolved problem on our backs, we were content to rest in the warmth of the Son.

Lord, thank You for autumn—a respite from heat and a gift before the cold of winter—and for autumn rests in my prayer life. May I bask in the warmth of Your Son and still be vigilant in watchful prayer.   —*ROBERTA ROGERS*

TUE
24

The counsel of the Lord standeth for ever, the thoughts of his heart to all generations.   —*PSALM 33:11*

I love how parenting gives me opportunities for second chances: second chances to experience childlike wonder as I observe my children; second chances to read and learn something new from a classic children's book; second chances to discover how to love others well.

Recently, I've been getting a second chance to learn about building a loving relationship in marriage by observing my daughter Kendall and her new husband David. They communicate with a tender honesty and willingness to confront and work through their differences. For instance, when they tell each other, "I love you," as they often do, they go a step further and add "because." "I love you because you are strong when I'm not." "I love you because you make me laugh." "I love you because you know how to untangle the mess my mom makes on her computer."

Just the other day I got an e-mail from David, who was trying to encourage Kendall through the stressful task of looking for a job. "I'm learning what it means to comfort rather than antagonize, and support rather than be silent," he wrote. As I watch and listen, I'm discovering some second chances to tenderize similar places in my own marriage.

God gives us children to help them grow up, but I'm increasingly convinced that God gives us children to give us a second chance to grow up, too.

Father, help me keep my eyes wide open to the Divine discovery of second chances.   —*CAROL KUYKENDALL*

WED
25

Teach us to number our days, that we may apply our hearts unto wisdom.   —*PSALM 90:12*

Have you ever played this conversational game with friends: "If I knew I had only a year to live, what changes would I make in my life?" I'm glad I've had some practice in considering that question, because it's recently become a very real issue for me.

I'm feeling in excellent health just now, and for that I'm very grateful. But the reality of my particular variety of cancer is that long-term survival rates are very low. The possibility of a new metastasis popping up on the radar screens of my CT scans forces me to plan my life in very short blocks of time. Booking plane tickets or scheduling visits to faraway family or friends is difficult—I find myself unable to plan anything with much certainty beyond the next scheduled checkup.

One doctor friend suggested that I consider the six weeks until my next scans as a gift box of time, a gift to be opened with care, thoughtfulness and joy. None of us knows just how many days we'll have on this earth. It's so easy to get caught up in the urgencies of everyday life and miss what we know to be the really important things.

Recently I wrote in my journal, "Will I ever wake up in the morning and not appreciate our clean air and blue sky, the fragrance and beauty of the garden in bloom, the joy of [my husband] Harry's faithful loving? Probably. But I hope not. I'd like to be acutely aware of each day."

Maybe a whole year to consider making changes in the way we live is too long. My latest thinking is that every new stage of life (college, job, marriage, parenthood, retirement) should come with these instructions: "For maximum enjoyment, measure out in six-week increments."

O Lord of the moments, accept my thanks as I open the gift box of this day.　　　　　　　　　　　　　　　　　　　—*MARY JANE CLARK*

THU
26

Whatever you do, work at it with all your heart, as working for the Lord, not for men. . . . It is the Lord Christ you are serving.　　　　　—*COLOSSIANS 3: 23–24 (NIV)*

"What do you do?" I heard myself ask the father of one of my son Ross's classmates at Parent Night. *Ugh!* I thought. I detest that question because I never know how to answer. Usually I say, "First, I'm a mom, then I'm a writer." But sometimes, when I get through the first half of that sentence, the look in their eyes says, "That's not a real job." So I don't dare add to the list: I'm also a driver, a meal planner and cook, a teacher (of Sunday school), a photographer . . . you get the idea.

God has given me many abilities and fills my life with opportunities to use them. But at times they don't seem to be worth much in a society that measures success in dollars and cents. While my life consists of many jobs, I'm sometimes reluctant to claim as part of my identity the ones that aren't validated with a paycheck. Or I was, until my five-year-old Maria set me straight.

We were sitting at the kitchen table one afternoon after school, talking about what she might be when she grows up. As I caught up on the monthly bills, she sat with a pile of colored markers, carefully drawing picture after picture.

"I can do lots of things when I get big," she said, her gray-green eyes shining.

"Anything you want," I said.

"I can wear a pretty costume and dance on a big stage."

"*Ooh*, I'd like that."

"I can be a baby doctor or a dog doctor," she said, pushing a patch of sandy bangs from her eyes with her small, rainbow-streaked hand.

"I know what you can be when you grow up," I said. "How about an artist?"

"That's silly, Mommy."

"Why, honey?" I asked, puzzled.

"Because I already *am* an artist," she announced.

Instantly I understood what Maria was saying. Whatever she does, whatever she spends time working hard on, that's what makes her Maria. If God has given me a job and the ability to do it, however insignificant it might seem in the eyes of others, it's real work to Him. And that's an assignment I can do with pride.

Help me see beyond what the world values to what You value, Father. Then I will be a success. —*GINA BRIDGEMAN*

FRI
27

They that dwell under his shadow shall return . . . and grow as the vine. . . . —*HOSEA 14:7*

When my children were small, I was the magical elf of our pumpkin patch. In mid-August, when the pumpkin vines began setting on fruits about the size of apples, I would sneak into the garden with a nail, stick or barbecue skewer, and scratch each child's name on a baby pumpkin. The scratches made a thin mark, but didn't otherwise damage the fruit. Better yet, the tiny globes remained invisible beneath the broad, scratchy pumpkin leaves and my work went unnoticed.

Over the next few weeks as the pumpkins swelled and turned first ivory, then yellow, then brilliant orange, the scars would grow, too, stretching with the shell and forming a brownish welt. By harvest time each fifteen-pound pumpkin would be personalized with a two-inch-tall name—a source of infinite amazement and speculation.

After the first September cold snap, I would casually suggest, "Maybe we'd better go pick those pumpkins." My four children would rush to the dead garden and easily spot the orange pumpkins glowing like lanterns amid the leaves blackened and shriveled by frost.

"Mom," Tess would suddenly shriek, "it has my *name!*" The enchantment never failed. As the older children caught on, they still let Trina, the youngest, delight in finding her special pumpkin without spoiling my secret. Even when all the children were old enough to solve the mystery, they would remind Mom to "go name the pumpkins" as soon as they first bulged on the vine.

I haven't grown pumpkins for years now and half of my children have left home. Very often I wonder whether my relationship with God has made any difference in their lives. Did I pass on my faith—really and truly? Did I make an impact? Then I pause to consider the faint etchings on those tiny pumpkins—and know that in God's good time, for my children, too, there will indeed be a joyful harvest.

Lord of creation, thank You for the miracle of growth, in my garden and in myself.   —*GAIL THORELL SCHILLING*

SAT
28   Break forth into singing, ye mountains. . . .
                                        —*ISAIAH 44:23*

It's the last weekend in September, and my husband Robert and I are taking a long drive on Trail Ridge Road in Rocky Mountain National Park. It's been many years since I've traveled this gorgeous drive, with its breathtaking views of layer after layer of tree-decked mountains and snow-topped peaks. Scattered among the deep green pines are brilliant patches of sun-yellow aspens, their leaves shouting a final crescendo before bowing out to winter, the season that will

soon strip their branches to bare white. As Robert drives, we breathe in scene after scene of nature's most glorious beauty.

Suddenly now, the years roll back and I'm riding with my parents on this same drive. While they marvel at the beauty of each view as the road winds and turns, their young daughter sits in the backseat, restless and tired of being cooped up in the car. I really can't understand the point of such long drives without a destination, and wish I were back at the cabin climbing on the big boulders or gathering pine cones.

My parents have been gone for more than twenty years now, and today I see the mountains and trees as they saw them, with a deep sense of awe, as if I'm seeing this great beauty through their eyes.

I think I surprise Robert when I say, "I know what I can do! I can enjoy this for my parents, and for my grandparents, so long gone, who also dearly loved these mountains. I'll be their eyes, just for today!"

Great Creator, as I breathe in the beauty of Your creation, may I also enjoy it for the sake of loved ones who have gone before me.

—*MARILYN MORGAN KING*

SUN
29
And God blessed the seventh day and made it holy. . . .
—*GENESIS 2:3 (NIV)*

It was Sunday morning. I'd been out late the night before, and I had to drag myself to church. "If I didn't have to teach Sunday school, I would have slept in," I muttered to myself, slumping in the pew. The first few hymns dragged by; then it was time for the children's sermon. Snore.

"This box is so heavy," the leader said, pushing and pulling a blue box into the middle of the circle of seated children. "No wonder it's heavy," he said, lifting the lid. "Inside are all the days of the week and all the things I have to do on those days. In my office, I do projects and talk on the telephone. Afterward I run errands and come home tired. Saturdays I have to mow the lawn, weed the garden, wash the car. At night I often go out with friends. The hours can get heavy and tiring.

"But there's one day that's different. It's called the Sabbath. God hallowed it and made it special. He even made it one of the Ten

Commandments. On this day we push aside all the heavy things and come together as God's people to pray and hear His Word.

"When we do this, we are not only obeying one of the commandments, but we're making the rest of the week lighter and easier to carry," he said. Dropping a card marked "Sunday" into the box with the other days of the week, he picked it up and walked away with a light step.

I sat up and remembered why I was here: Not because I had to be, but to honor the day God hallowed, and in so doing, carry the blessing and peace of the Sabbath into the week.

Lord, help me to walk into Your house with gladness, putting aside everything but You.   —*SHARI SMYTH*

MON

30

For the word of God is quick, and powerful, and sharper than any two-edged sword. . . .   —*HEBREWS 4:12*

When I returned from Bible study one Monday evening in the fall of 1999, my wife Ruby said, "Your sister called. Aunt Ruth fell, and she's in the hospital."

I blinked and mumbled, "Not Aunt Ruth!" At ninety-nine, Aunt Ruth had seemed stronger than ever. She still had all her teeth and only used glasses for reading. Until she was ninety-five, Aunt Ruth had ushered at church; she drove her car until she was ninety-seven. By choice, she lived alone in a twelve-room house where she tended her garden, mowed the lawn and removed the snow.

Aunt Ruth grew up when schooling was optional and left school to help support her family. But she was always an insatiable reader, and she returned to school to earn her GED at age fifty-two.

She was always honest, and sometimes her words stung. When she saw my picture on the back cover of *Daily Guideposts, 1988,* she said, "I saw your picture, and I noticed the polo shirt you were wearing. The other men had on ties and jackets. I felt you would know better!" From December 1979 until September 1999, I wrote to Aunt Ruth each Tuesday. In 1996 she wrote, "I can't read your writing. I would have thought they would have corrected your penmanship when you were in school. It's too late now!" I gulped; from then on, I typed my letters.

Two days after my sister called, on our fifty-seventh wedding an-

niversary, Aunt Ruth died. We attended her funeral at St. John's Episcopal Church in Williamstown, Massachusetts, where she was baptized in February 1900, and where she attended church for ninety-nine years and six months.

Aunt Ruth's words may sometimes have been cutting, but they came from a kind heart. And for me, her words and her example were always a challenge to do better.

Dear Lord, thank You for Aunt Ruth. Help me also to be a beacon in a young person's life. —*OSCAR GREENE*

My Days of Prayer

1 _____

2 _____

3 _____

4 _____

5 _____

6 _____

7 _____

8 _____

9 _____

10 _____

11 _____

12 _____

13 _____

14 _____

15 _____

16 _____

17 _____

18 _____

19 _____

20 _____

21 _____

22 _____

23 _____

24 _____

25 _____

26 _____

27 _____

28 _____

29 _____

30 _____

October

Let my prayer be set forth before thee
as incense; and the lifting up of my
hands as the evening sacrifice.

—Psalm 141:2

S	M	T	W	T	F	S
		1	2	3	4	5
6	7	8	9	10	11	12
13	14	15	16	17	18	19
20	21	22	23	24	25	26
27	28	29	30	31		

THE PRAYER THAT IS ALWAYS NEW

TUE

1   Our Father. . . . forgive us . . . *as we forgive* our
debtors. . . .   *—MATTHEW 6:9, 12*

It was an old wound, but one that still smarted. Years ago, an editor published under his own name a piece I'd sent in to his magazine. When I asked him about it, he apologized profusely. It had been an oversight, he explained, in the pressure of production: "Please forgive me!" I didn't want to seem petty. "Of course, I forgive you," I said.

Over the years the story was reprinted here and there, always with that other name on it. And each time I saw it, a stab of resentment told me that my words of forgiveness had been only that—words. "It's the message of a piece that counts," I'd tell myself, "not who gets the credit." But that pang of resentment told me I was clinging to a grudge.

In my prayers, when I reached the words "as we forgive our debtors," that editor would sometimes come to mind, and I knew my reaction was out of God's will. This is the only verse of the Lord's Prayer that comes with a warning: "If ye forgive not men their trespasses, neither will your Father forgive your trespasses" (Matthew 6:15).

The editor had done his part—the part I'd always thought hardest when I'd been the one at fault. He'd confessed his mistake and asked forgiveness. But I had sidestepped the other half of the process. Wanting to appear the all-loving Christian unruffled by trifles, I'd rejected the hard work of genuine forgiving.

I was learning that it starts with a frank acknowledgment of the hurt. It was humbling to admit that something this small had caused me such distress, but when I saw the editor at a conference recently, I knew I had to do it. "It hurt me at the time," I said, "and because

I wasn't honest, it's gone on hurting." I asked him, in turn, to forgive my lack of candor, and asked God to give each of us the grace of true forgiveness.

Somehow the hug we exchanged seemed to come from the Father Himself.

Our Father, help me forgive not with the lips but with the heart.
—*ELIZABETH SHERRILL*

WED

2

A soft answer turneth away wrath. . . . —*PROVERBS 15:1*

My late husband Roland and I were married on the second day of the month, so every second of the month, he placed a love poem he'd written for me on my breakfast plate. He made sure that nothing else was ever scheduled on the second. Then, to conclude our day, he'd take me out to dinner.

But after one hundred and eighty poems and fifteen years together, he contracted Parkinson's. Yet even as his health declined, he remained a gentleman. And a gentle man.

That is, he did until one day when—in front of visitors, no less—he suddenly shouted, "You're taking care of me just to show off how good you are! Well, you're not!"

I was embarrassed, shocked, devastated.

I immediately phoned a counselor whom his doctor had recommended "just in case." She gently explained that when someone who has spent a lifetime in his or her own control no longer has control, that person often turns on someone close to him or her—usually the caregiver. Her advice? "Don't argue or try to reason. Just answer gently, confirming your love again and again." What relief I felt! I took her advice, and within hours Roland was his usual self.

After his death, I was asked to speak to a group of caregivers and I told this story. It was not easy to tell, but I sensed it was necessary. One in the group told me afterward, "I gave up a good part of my life to take care of my aunt, and near the end she treated me like dirt. I've carried anger about her for the past fifteen years. Now, finally, I think I can forgive her because I know why."

Oh, Lord, help me show compassion to those who are going through circumstances that are beyond their control. —*ISABEL WOLSELEY*

THU

3

I will all the more gladly boast of my weaknesses, that the power of Christ may rest upon me.

—II CORINTHIANS 12:9 (RSV)

This morning when I opened my eyes, I realized I had a cold. Not a crushing, debilitating one, but not a light, barely noticeable one, either. It was one of those colds that makes you feel as if you're stuck in low gear but not feeling quite wretched enough to stay in bed. The absolutely worst kind of a cold—the kind you drag around with you all day.

I groaned, reached for a tissue and staggered toward the bathroom, dragging my cold with me, hoping a hot shower might help. As the water beat down I thought of all the people Jesus healed—the leper, the blind and the deaf men. Even Lazarus, raised from the dead. *What about me?* I wondered miserably. This cold, I understood, would not be "miracled" away. It would be my constant companion for the next few days, at least. Nobody in the Bible had ever been miraculously healed of the common cold. *Why do You permit viruses, God? What were You thinking?*

All right, I finally resolved, turning off the water and groping for a towel, *this complaining is getting me nowhere.*

Yet it occurred to me, standing there dripping wet, that there are times when all I know to do is to moan and complain. In fact, complaining is the *only* thing that feels remotely good. Like now. I had complained my way out of bed and through my morning routine and, yes, I was feeling a bit better for it. Complaining actually took my mind off my cold. Who knows, I might just complain my way through the whole day.

Wiping the steam off the mirror, I smiled. "Thank You, Lord. I know it's not a very pretty form of praying, but I appreciate that You hear me out, grievances and all. I'll try to keep the complaining down from now on."

It was, after all, only a cold.

Teach me, Lord, to turn all my sufferings, big and small, into prayer.

—EDWARD GRINNAN

<table>
<tr><td>FRI
4</td><td>Command them to do good, to be rich in good deeds, and to be generous and willing to share.
—I TIMOTHY 6:18 (NIV)</td></tr>
</table>

My boyfriend Travis is a graduate student, working on his Ph.D. in chemistry. Near his university, a pharmaceutical company was closing its local research center and called the school's chemistry department with a generous proposition. Because the cost of packing, moving and insuring the equipment would be too high, they were willing to donate it all to the students. If the department sent their own trucks and elbow grease, they could keep anything they could carry out of the building.

When the first truck returned to campus, Travis helped to unload the first bin, packed to the brim with newsprint and glassware. Students descended on the bounty like piranhas. When the very first bin was unloaded, newsprint ripped, broken glass tinkled and bickering ensued. In a few short minutes, all that remained was an empty bin, some debris and a few dejected chemistry students.

The driver of the truck walked over to the group and wiped his hands on his jeans. "You here to help unload?" he asked one student.

"Yeah, but I guess we're too late," the student replied.

"Too late? No way!" Travis called from the truck. "There are seven more bins in here! And there are at least two more trucks on the way."

The driver nodded. "We need to unload this truck, so it can make another trip."

Wide-eyed, the group gathered around the truck and began unloading it bucket-brigade-style. Soon the truck was empty and on its way to fetch another load. The treasures from the first raid safely stowed, students began to trickle out of the building again. The commotion quickly resumed, but this time there were fewer sounds of glass breaking, and the shouting was to announce new finds:

"I found a Rotavap! Anyone need one?"

"I do!"

"Here, pass this over to John!"

"Hey, Travis, weren't you looking for a furnace controller? I found one for you!"

"Look! Here's a whole bin of flasks!"

What a change!

Lord, when good fortune comes my way, I know it comes from Your hand. Help me to cheerfully share Your gifts with others.

—KJERSTIN EASTON

SAT
5

Not that I have already ... been made perfect, but I press on to take hold of that for which Christ Jesus took hold of me.   —*PHILIPPIANS 3:12 (NIV)*

One Saturday, as I was clearing off a cluttered bookshelf, I came across the baby books I had kept for my two sons Greg and Jeff. I had recorded detailed information about each of them, noting everything from their first faltering steps to their high-school graduations.

I was young and inexperienced, and I felt inadequate as a mother. To compensate, I expended a vast amount of energy trying to become the perfect parent. I couldn't be perfect, of course, yet even now, browsing back through the books, I could feel the old lingering sense of guilt and regret.

Later that same day, while rummaging through a box filled with odds and ends from one of the bedroom closets, I came upon an envelope containing two little badges. The first one had been given to Jeff by his second-grade teacher Mrs. Parker. It bore a whimsical smiley face and a shiny gold star, and proclaimed in big black letters, "JEFF IS A GOOD LISTENER." As I looked at the badge, I remembered how hard second grade had been for Jeff, and how I had always seemed to be lecturing him about his behavior in class. Most days, I felt, I had been impatient and demanding.

Then I took the other little badge out of the envelope and turned it over in my hand. It had been unevenly cut out of green construction paper, and written on it in a child's scrawl was, "Momy is a good listener." I smiled. Here was my own personal badge of recognition, lovingly crafted by a seven-year-old, who obviously hadn't shared his "Momy's" opinion of herself.

Greg and Jeff have grown into fine young men. As for the "perfect parent," I've learned that there is no such creature. With God's help, I do the best I can, and in His grace He forgives me the rest. The real accomplishment is in learning to forgive myself.

Thank You, Father, that through Your love I can forgive all imperfections, even my own.   —*LIBBIE ADAMS*

SUN

6

And the Lord spake unto Moses face to face, as a man
speaketh unto his friend. . . . —*EXODUS 33:11*

We had started a new contemporary service at our church, and communion was different from the usual passing of trays down the row—
it was by intinction, or dipping the bread into the cup of wine. My
nineteen-year-old daughter Joanna and I were servers. She had the
cup, I the loaf. "Christ's body was broken for you, Annie," I said,
breaking off a piece of bread and handing it to the first teenager, as
one by one my church family (wearing name tags) came forward.

I was surprised at how emotional I felt as I said each name. Jesus'
sacrifice for the world suddenly became so intimately personal! I
found myself weeping as I looked into the faces of the young, the old,
the mentally and physically challenged. I was embarrassed by my
emotion, but just kept breaking the bread, amazed and awed at
Christ's redeeming love for each of us.

That communion experience also carried over into my Bible
study. God's promises in His Word are for each of us. And one way
I can claim them is by inserting my own name. For example, in Jesus'
words in John 16:27 (NIV): "The Father himself loves you, Marjorie,
because you have loved me." Try it! He knows you by name!

**Father, thank You for sending Your Son to suffer and die for me and
for all of us, each by name.** —*MARJORIE PARKER*

MON

7

The eyes of the blind shall see out of obscurity, and out of
darkness. —*ISAIAH 29:18*

The fall that John was three, he began to complain of headaches. At
first they were occasional, but gradually they became more severe and
more frequent. Our pediatrician was concerned but optimistic. "The
good news," he said, "is he shows no overt signs of neurological
problems. The first thing to do is see a pediatric ophthalmologist."

On the day of our appointment, John and I set out for the eye doctor. I'd given him nightly drops of bottled tears so he'd be ready for
the eye drops, and we'd talked about what was likely to happen. I was
somewhat surprised, therefore, when John turned and said timidly,
"Mommy, I'm scared."

"Why are you afraid, sweetheart?" I asked gently.

His face clouded up, and his chin quivered. "I can't tell you!"

"Sure you can, honey. The doctor isn't going to hurt you. She's going to see if your eyes are causing your headaches, so we can find out how to make the pain go away."

John blurted, "But, Mommy, I don't want glasses!"

I held him and stroked his forehead, trying to figure out what was the matter. My husband Andrew and I both wear glasses, so having them wouldn't be odd. And John had never heard anyone making fun of someone for wearing spectacles. What could it be?

"Sweetheart, what's scary about having glasses?" I asked.

"Oh, Mommy, if I had to wear glasses, I could never *see* anything ever again!"

It took a moment before I understood. The only times John has looked through glasses, he has looked through either mine or Andrew's, which of course make the world blurry to him. Naturally he thought that if he wore glasses, too, he'd lose the ability to see! No wonder he was scared. Restraining my amusement, I explained to John how glasses work.

The ophthalmologist pronounced John's eyesight perfect. We eventually learned that his migraines were allergy-induced. In the meantime, I learned something about the importance of stopping to look at things from another person's perspective.

Holy Spirit, open my eyes wide enough that I may see the best way to share Your love.
                                                        —*JULIA ATTAWAY*

TUE

8

And there was a rainbow round about the throne . . .
                                                        —*REVELATION 4:3*

At dawn, as I was readying my dog Shep for her morning run, there was a ranting *swoosh swoosh* sound as the wind rattled my windows. I could tell that the weather was bad, and stepping out the door, we were nearly blown away by the torrent. The rain, unrelenting, fought us harshly as we crossed the street to the park. I took off Shep's leash, generally a cue for a wild romp, but she stayed close to me, tail between her legs. Somehow we managed to travel our familiar route and got home, well-soaked.

At noon I could not believe the duration of the storm. It was still howling, and the rain still fell in sheets that left water ankle-deep in the streets. Then, around four, it calmed down at last and began to clear. "Come on, Shep," I said, and we headed out and . . .we stopped, and I stared. There, soaring across Manhattan, from the Hudson River to the East River, was a rainbow—no, two rainbows, shimmering their delicate colors for all, residents and visitors, to see. People on the sidewalk were looking up and pointing, amazed, exclaiming to men and women they didn't know, and cars stopped and their occupants got out to witness the wonder in the heavens.

The spectacle didn't last long, but its meaning has. I thought of the covenant God made after the flood that Noah endured, so much longer than the all-day storm we had experienced. I thought of thousands of New Yorkers suddenly talking with one another about something they all shared with delight. Most of all, I was grateful for the wild magnificence of nature, and for being permitted to participate in the beauty that crowned it.

I thank You, Father, for all Your manifestations that cause me to think of You.   —*VAN VARNER*

WED

9

Let no one seek his own good, but the good of his neighbor.   —*I CORINTHIANS 10:24 (RSV)*

"Madge, come back to the auditorium right now," called my friend Carolyn as she ran toward me down the school corridor. "They want you to play the piano for the evening program!"

My heart jumped with excitement at my classmate's announcement. That meant that the judges for the district high-school music competition had chosen my award-winning performance of Sibelius's "Romance" for additional recognition during the annual "judges' choice" concert! I hurried to find my music teacher.

"Will I have time to warm up first?" I asked. "That one run is so difficult—"

"Oh, you're not playing 'Romance,' " he replied. "They need someone to accompany Joanne when she plays her viola solo. Her accompanist has already gone home, and I told the judges you're good at sight-reading."

Accompany Joanne? But she was from a rival school!

"No!" I cried.

My teacher frowned. "This concert is not just about getting a high score during the contest. It's about good sportsmanship and sharing a love of music. I know you'll want to do your best for Joanne."

I felt sick with rebellion and disappointment. Still, once Joanne and I were onstage, I played as well as I could on such short notice.

Afterward, Joanne said with a sweet smile, "Madge, I've always admired your playing. Thanks for helping me out. I wish we could know each other better."

Warmth spread through me at her words. School rivalry was actually kind of silly, I decided.

"Good luck at the regional competition," I said.

"You, too," she replied.

Lord, today I will do the best work I can while reaching out to help someone else do well, too.   —*MADGE HARRAH*

THU

10

I will not leave you comfortless: I will come to you.
                                                        —*JOHN 14:18*

It was after midnight when, at last, Bob was sleeping soundly. His hands were not shaking. For four days since he'd arrived at the hospital, I'd stayed by his bed to grasp his hands when they began to shake from Parkinson's disease. I held them and spoke softly to him, and he would drift off to sleep. I ignored the fatigue that clawed at my strength and the ache in my heart at seeing him suffer.

When he began to breathe steadily, I removed my hands from his and stood watching the pain etched on his face. Oh, how I longed to gather him up out of that bed and hold him close to me! Tears suddenly streamed down my face; I rushed from his bedside and into the small bathroom. I must not let him see me cry!

I sank down on the toilet seat lid, buried my face in my hands and sobbed as quietly as I could. Before long, I felt a hand on my shoulder and heard a woman's voice asking, "Oh, my dear, what is it? What's wrong?"

In a whisper, I told her, "He's so sick! So very sick!"

She gathered me up into her arms. My convulsive sobs dampened the nurse's uniform she wore. I don't remember the words she spoke, only the gentleness of her voice, and the tender warmth with which she held me.

"I haven't dared to cry," I finally told her. "I mustn't let him see my eyes red or detect the upset from my voice! He's never been able to stand anything hurting me."

"It'll be all right," the nurse murmured, holding me until I could stop crying. "Come, let's sit down."

For some time we sat on the little fold-down bed provided for me, and we talked quietly. When I was finally composed, I asked her name.

"Betty," she answered, gave me a hug and was gone.

I did not see Betty again before Bob's death. But I will always know that she was a godsend that night when what I needed most in the world were some kind words, a shoulder to cry on and a warm hug.

Thank You, Father, for the angels in white who serve You through our hospitals. Let me also minister Your mercy every chance You give me.

—*DRUE DUKE*

FRI

11

"They shall not be ashamed who wait for Me."
—*ISAIAH 49:23 (NKJV)*

I know it's hard to believe, but college students can be a bit irritating. I am most impatient with my students' impatience. For example, I will give a written test, then collect the papers and head for my office. All along the way, students will hover around me:

"Do you have those papers graded yet?"

"Can you at least tell me if I passed?"

"Could you e-mail me my grade at work?"

"Grade mine first, okay?"

I suppose it bothers me so much because I grew up in the forties and fifties when patience was a way of life. Once I ordered a baseball glove, advertised on the back of a Wheaties box. The fine print said, "Allow six to eight weeks for delivery." Six weeks is an eternity to a child, but it taught me that the world of business does not revolve around me.

I try to be understanding, because today's youth were born into the age of vending machines, overnight mail, faxes, instant credit and microwaved meals. Patience isn't even on their list of values. They see patience as a weakness.

What enables me to tolerate my students is the knowledge that I can be just as impatient, especially when it comes to having my prayers answered. I fire off a round of prayers, then hover around God for days. "Do You have it worked out yet, God? Sometime today, maybe? Or tomorrow?"

I forget that the answers to my prayers may require timing, planning and coordination with others' prayers. The bigger the prayer, the more time it may take to work it out. I have to remind myself that God is not a vending machine and He isn't bound by an earthly clock. I may need to allow six to eight years for delivery, or even more.

Thanks, Lord, for the very special joy that comes only after waiting a long time for the things I want. —*DANIEL SCHANTZ*

SAT

12

When I am afraid, I will trust in You. —*PSALM 56:3 (NIV)*

I've been living with this "what-if" fear, which I sometimes think about in the middle of the night. When our children started leaving home and going off to college in faraway places, I began dreaming that someday, when they got married and settled down, they would live close enough so that I could be involved in the lives of my grandchildren. I imagined myself watching a grandchild perform in a preschool program or play in a soccer game, or making cookies for an after-school visit. As that season of life draws nearer, however, my adult children are still living in faraway places, and I've started to fear that things may not turn out the way I dreamed.

"I don't want to be the kind of grandma who has to carry little presents in her purse to coax her grandchildren into liking her when she gets off the airplane to visit," I whined to my husband Lynn recently.

"You're racing ahead of yourself," he told me gently. "Relax and trust God."

His words reminded me of a story in Corrie ten Boom's book *The Hiding Place*. She, too, dealt with "what-if" fears, and her father helped by asking her about riding to Amsterdam on the train.

"When do I give you your ticket?" he questioned.

"Right before we get on the train," she answered.

"Exactly," he reassured her. "And God in heaven does the same thing. He gives us what we need when we need it. So don't run out ahead of Him, Corrie."

Maybe my grandchildren will live within driving distance, maybe they won't. But that time hasn't come. I don't even have any grandchildren yet; the train hasn't pulled into the station. But while I'm waiting, I don't have to run ahead and squint to see the train way off in the distance. I can relax and trust God, knowing that He will give me whatever I need when I need it. He will give me my ticket when the train pulls into the station.

Father, I pray for greater trust to believe You . . . and act like I believe You.
—*CAROL KUYKENDALL*

SUN
13

"You shall therefore lay up these words of mine in your heart. . . . And you shall teach them to your children. . . ."
—*DEUTERONOMY 11:18–19 (RSV)*

A teacher was needed for the Sunday-school class for six- to eight-year-olds in our church. I hadn't taught small children in three decades, but when no one else stepped forward, I volunteered—reluctantly.

I felt out of place that first Sunday as I stepped into the small trailer behind the church—sort of like Alice in Wonderland. I seemed to be too tall, the chairs were too small and the children weren't eager to give me their attention. As hard as I tried, I couldn't seem to get through to them. As they rushed out of the room to head for church, I was certain I'd flopped.

I had the same experience the next Sunday. As I prepared for the third Sunday, I realized that I really hadn't asked for God's help. So I called on the Great Teacher. It was a desperate prayer: *I want to teach the children, Lord, but I want us to have a good time, too.* Then I prayed for each child by name: Bethany, Ava Claire, Emory, Aaron. . . .

The following Sunday, they all made eye contact with me. The girls gave me quick, shy smiles; the boys shared some of their misadventures of the past week. On Monday, as I began praying about the class, I added a P.S.: *I'd sure like a sign, Lord—anything—to encourage me as a teacher.* There was a postcard for me in Tuesday's mail. Painstakingly printed in large, downhill-slanting letters, it read: "To Miss Marion. I had a good time Sunday. I hope you did too. Love, Ava Claire."

Maybe I know a bit more now, dear Jesus, about why You tell us to become like little children if we want to enter Your kingdom.

—*MARION BOND WEST*

READER'S ROOM

I wish I could properly tell you how many times the inspirational message for the day has been just what the doctor ordered to help me through those twenty-four hours. In 1999, my husband Ken and I sold our beloved, big, old Victorian home in which we'd lived for forty-six years and where we raised our four sons. The words Eric Fellman penned for October 18 through 24 were beacons of hope as we went through some of the emotions and experiences he and his wife suffered through. Our phone would ring, and it would be son number two, Brian, saying, "Mom, did you read Eric Fellman's message today? It was just what you were worried about."

Thank you for *Daily Guideposts* each year and the love that splashes from each page.

—*BETTY HAUGHIN, BELLEVUE, PENNSYLVANIA*

MON

14   I have called you friends....   —*JOHN 15:15*

My fiftieth birthday was fast approaching, and I was planning the party of the century—okay, maybe the *half* century. But instead of a crowd, I opted for seven close friends: one from elementary school; one from college; business colleagues and shopping buddies; people who had known me forty-five years and people who had known me less than five.

We took the train into Chicago on a sunny October morning. I wore a white-beaded crown, courtesy of one of my friends, and carried a scepter with the number fifty on it. We window-shopped our way down Michigan Avenue as people smiled and occasionally even bowed to the "birthday queen." We ate lunch at an Italian restaurant. We saw a play. And every hour on the hour—no matter where we were—my friends all sang "Happy Birthday" to me. Finally, a huge white limo picked us up, and we ate our way home, feasting from a gigantic picnic basket packed by one of my friends.

But my favorite part of the day came when my friends all told "Mary Lou stories"—how each had met me and one memorable moment we'd shared. How surprised I was by the things they remembered, by the events they cherished!

"Once Mary Lou and I were almost killed by a sow in her barnyard." That was my friend Melva.

"Nobody can sniff out sale racks like Mary Lou!" said Lurlene.

"I remember when we lived in the dorm together," said Rachel.

As I looked around that circle, I knew that the real celebration here was not the fact that I had lived fifty years. It was, rather, a celebration of friendship, of kindred spirits who find each other and hold on for a lifetime.

Let us be generous, Father, with the best gift we can give each other—the gift of friendship. —*MARY LOU CARNEY*

THE PRACTICE OF PRAYER

TUE	*Persistent Prayer*
15	Perseverance must finish its work so that you may be mature and complete.... —*JAMES 1:4 (NIV)*

Our son Brock met his friend Ben Cannon when they were freshmen at the University of Tennessee. The first time Ben visited our home, our fourteen-year-old Keri was smitten—and the rest is family history. Keri was in college and Ben was living in Nashville, sharing an apartment with Brock, when our daughter came of age. I wasn't the least bit surprised when it happened: Keri and Ben had fallen in love!

But something was holding Ben back. He had a dream, and he would not let it go: He wanted to be a dentist. Three times he had applied to the University of Tennessee School of Dentistry. Each time he was rejected. "You played around as an undergraduate and your grades aren't good enough," Ben was told. So he enrolled in night school and pulled up his GPA. "Not enough science in your background." Ben rescheduled his working hours and took science courses. "Too many applicants. You're at the bottom of the list." Ben waited a semester, then applied again.

Finally, miraculously, the call came. Years of grueling course work followed, but Ben never wavered. He was soon one of the top students in the school, and four years later, Ben, by now our son-in-law, was invited to join one of the leading dental practices in the Nashville area.

At some point, you're probably going to become discouraged with your prayer pilgrimage. You may even go through a time when you feel like giving up. When that time comes, I hope you'll think of our Ben. Like him, you can turn your setbacks into opportunities. You can go back to God with that image of the person you want to become. God will meet you where you are. He'll hold your hand as you regain lost ground. He'll never, ever stop believing in you.

Father, let every hour of every day become a prayer that brings me closer to You and the new life that You offer.   —*PAM KIDD*

WED

16

Behold, God is my salvation; I will trust, and not be afraid. . . .   —*ISAIAH 12:2*

I woke up feeling crummy. "Oh, it's nothing," I said doubtfully to myself, but getting dressed for work I felt worse and worse. Then the internal dialogue began: *Should I call him? Suppose I need antibiotics? He'll just tell me to rest. It'll go away. No, he won't be there. No. Anyway, he won't call me back.*

Finally I did call, and got an answering service with those so-familiar words, "The doctor will call you back." Right. Maybe. This is the twenty-first century and this is New York City. Everyone leaves everyone else messages.

My skepticism was entirely misplaced. Less than five minutes later, the phone rang and I found myself talking to the doctor and writing down his instructions on my notepad. It so happened that I called him again several times during that long and hard winter. Without fail, without appearing in haste or irritated, he returned all my calls within minutes, not hours.

As I looked back, I experienced a feeling that I couldn't quite place at first. Relief? Gratitude? Repentance for my negative attitude? No, none of these turned out to be the strong and sustaining emotion I was feeling. It was a simple five-letter word: *trust.*

Help me, Lord, to continue to learn to trust in You and in those You have placed around me. —*BRIGITTE WEEKS*

THU

17 It is not good . . . to be hasty and miss the way.

—*PROVERBS 19:2 (NIV)*

Recently, my son Ross and I watched a terrific TV special highlighting baseball's twenty-five greatest moments. The one among them that has particularly stayed with me happened in game six of the 1975 World Series.

Boston Red Sox catcher and Hall-of-Famer Carlton Fisk hit a dramatic home run in the twelfth inning to beat the Cincinnati Reds, keeping alive the Sox's hopes of a Series victory. Fisk hit the shot straight down the left-field foul line toward Fenway Park's legendary wall, the Green Monster. After jogging a few steps from home plate, he waved his arms at the ball as if coaching it to stay fair—which it did—to win the game. (But the Sox lost the Series.)

It's not the home run, but Fisk's comments that were so poignant. Asked many years later about that night, he remarked that since it happened so early in his career, he thought he'd likely have more such moments. But that turned out to be his only World Series. The moment had passed so quickly, and was never to come again in his twenty-four-year career.

To me, that's an important truth about all of life. My daughter Maria asked if we could read a chapter of *Charlotte's Web* tonight. "It's late," I told her, "and I want to get in a load of wash." *There's lots of time to read,* I thought. But who knows? God has blessed my life with abundance, but not with any guarantees.

Besides, that exact moment with Maria will never come again. The days will pass in a blur and soon she and her big brother won't have time for me. What once seemed like an endless road, dotted with those "Mommy, watch me" moments stretching into eternity, will too quickly reach an end.

So I have to go now. I have a date with a girl named Maria and a spider named Charlotte.

Open my eyes, Lord, to the all-time great moments in my life, so I don't miss a single one. —*GINA BRIDGEMAN*

FRI

18 If ye shall ask any thing in my name, I will do it.
—*JOHN 14:14*

Four of us from our Victim's Impact Panel spoke to the people arrested for drunk driving this month. A highway patrolman gave details about several of the alcohol-related fatalities he had handled. I told them about working as an emergency medical technician at a car wreck where three young men were killed. Mary Jo, the president of our Mothers Against Drunk Driving chapter, spoke next. She told our forty listeners about her mother who was killed on Ute tribal land by a drunk driver.

San Jean was our last speaker. She is a courageous Ute woman who always begins by saying, "I'm here not to speak of the dead, but to speak for them."

The audience response varies from month to month. We didn't seem to be getting through to them on this night. San Jean's eyes were shut while Mary Jo shared memories about Jenny, her mother. San Jean's sister is the drunk driver who killed Jenny. I don't know if San Jean's eyes were shut out of respect for Mary Jo's mother or if she was praying. I know I closed my eyes and prayed for San Jean and Mary Jo. And I prayed that our stories would reach, and change, our seemingly unmoved audience.

When we finished, we met in another room to wait for the written comments. Before the people who were arrested are allowed to leave the courtroom, they have to fill out a comment sheet. The comments on that night were the best ever. We were mystified, but encouraged. I told my wife about it the next day—how we felt that our presentations are becoming more polished, and that is why we affected this group so much.

While I was talking to her, however, I remembered my prayer for San Jean and Mary Jo's mother. "It's the first time I prayed for help during one of these," I admitted.

Dear God, thank You for the times You hear my pleas for help. Now help me to make prayer my first, not my last, resort.

—*TIM WILLIAMS*

SAT
19

And be ye kind one to another. . . .   —*EPHESIANS 4:32*

When my neighbors Phyllis and Martin decided to get a dog, they knew exactly what they wanted: a small dog, female, young but not a puppy. They also wanted a dog who needed a good home. So they went to our local animal shelter and spelled out their needs.

A few days later they received a call from the shelter. A small, female, one-year-old dog had been brought in by a young couple who couldn't keep her because their working hours didn't allow them much time at home. Although it broke their hearts to give up the dog, they felt it was the only fair thing to do. When Phyllis and Martin saw her, they knew she was just the dog for them and took her home.

The next month they received a second call from the shelter. Another small, year-old dog—this one a male—had been brought in by someone who found it hungry and wandering along a road. "He's really nice and well-trained," the woman said.

Phyllis looked at Martin, and without a word they knew what each was thinking. "Let's just take a look," Martin suggested. They did and, of course, they adopted the dog.

Now and then, when I'm walking my dog, I meet Phyllis and Martin walking theirs, and they all look so happy—two little dogs who wanted a home, and two people who wanted their love. Sometimes, when we open our hearts, God has a way of filling them more abundantly than we could ever imagine.

Dear Lord Jesus, make me aware of all I have to share. Amen.

—*PHYLLIS HOBE*

ISLAND PILGRIMAGE

The tiny, windswept island of Iona, off the west coast of Scotland, has been a place of prayer and pilgrimage since A.D. 563, when the Irish monk Columba founded a monastery there from which he brought the Christian faith to the people of northern Scotland. Two years ago, Marilyn Morgan King and Robert King answered an inner call to make their own pilgrimage to Iona. Over the next eight days, they'll take us with them as they explore the island and come to experience God's power transforming their hearts.

—THE EDITORS

SUN

20

Day One: Setting Out

They that wait upon the Lord shall renew their strength . . . they shall walk, and not faint. *—ISAIAH 40:31*

It was cold, windy, raining. People all around us were putting on rain gear. We had none. Our paper lunch bags were rapidly disintegrating; the guides were asking medical personnel among us to identify themselves, "just in case." Here we were, my husband Robert and I, two unprepared Americans in our sixties, about to begin a six-hour pilgrimage walk in bad weather, over rocky hills and boggy valleys, with no assurance of safety. Yet some inner longing had brought us thousands of miles to this remote island off the coast of Scotland. Men and women throughout the ages had risked everything because of such a longing.

My own yearning started years ago when I read my first book about Iona, this small island that is known as one of the most deeply spiritual places in the world. Without knowing how or when it would happen, my heart had sensed I would someday make this pilgrimage. When I learned Robert had already been here and would love to return, we knew nothing could stop us.

How can I explain it? For us I think it was a yearning to express, in some concrete way, the spiritual journey both of us had been traveling separately all of our lives. Now, by the grace of God, we were pilgrims on the road together. Obviously, the trek would be more difficult than we'd expected. Would my blistering feet hold up? Would this drenching rain make us sick? What if one of us fell and broke a bone? Could we—should we—take the risk? I looked into Robert's eyes and saw the answer: "Yes! With God and each other, we'll make it!"

The spiritual journey is never easy. No one is ever fully prepared. Commitment to the journey is essential. I will go. Will you come, too?

> May the road rise to meet you;
> May the wind be always at your back;
> May the rain fall softly upon your fields;
> May God hold you in the hollow of his hand.
> *(A Gaelic blessing)*
> —*MARILYN MORGAN KING*

MON
21

Day Two: Women of Prayer
"Wherever the gospel is preached in the whole world, what she has done will be told in memory of her."
—*MARK 14:9 (RSV)*

The early morning shower had begun to subside when our small band of pilgrims made its first stop, in front of an ancient ruin. Jan, one of our two guides from the Iona Community, told us it was the remains of an Augustinian nunnery dating back to the twelfth century. The nunnery is as old as the abbey, where we started our journey, but unlike the abbey, it has not been rebuilt.

Jan told us that when she first came to the island, the Reverend George McLeod, the Scottish Presbyterian minister who founded the community, led the pilgrimage walk and didn't even stop here. She took this oversight as symbolic of the way women's contributions to the religious life have often been overlooked. Her words pierced my heart, for I had been to this island once before and I had not even noticed the remains of the nunnery.

Who were these women, generations of prayerful women, leading lives of simple devotion on this remote island? Like the woman who

anointed Jesus at Bethany, they did not seek recognition for themselves, but simply wanted an opportunity to express their deep personal faith. I need to find a way to value their spiritual contributions.

**Let us dream. Let us prophesy. Let us see visions of love, peace and
justice. Let us affirm with humility, with joy, with faith, with
courage, that You, O Christ, are the life of every child, woman and
man.** *(From a South African women's prayer)* —ROBERT KING

TUE
22
Day Three: Becoming the Body
Bear ye one another's burdens, and so fulfil the law of
Christ. —*GALATIANS 6:2*

"See that big mound on the horizon? That's one of the high places
on the island," said Jan. "Many people have settled there, from as
early as the Iron Age, seeking a high place for safety. Yet climbing can
also be treacherous. There will be many rocky hills on our journey
together, and the rocks can be quite slippery. It will be essential for
us to help each other as we climb, and also as we cross the swampy
bogs on the journey ahead." As we moved onward, our voices joined
in singing: "Alleluia, alleluia, alleluia."

I did all right at first, but at a steep place between two sharp rocks,
I struggled to get my footing and started to slip. At that moment, a
young woman behind me said, "Let me carry your bag for you!"
What a relief it was to hand her the canvas bag in which I carried our
two full water bottles! With her help, I made it to the top of the
mound.

Later, when we came to a boggy place, a long-legged man ahead
of us leaped across. *I'll never be able to make that jump!* I thought.
Then the man turned around and held out his hand to help the rest
of us make the long leap. Each time we came to a bog, first one man
and then another and another reached out to offer the same help.
Once I made a misstep and the swampy ground pulled the shoe right
off my foot! Immediately, a man reached into the muck, pulled out
the shoe and wiped it off with his handkerchief!

As we ascended the rocky hills, younger and better climbers
reached back to pull others up. A wondrous thing happened as peo-

ple offered, and others accepted, help. We who had been strangers in a strange land became a bonded band of pilgrims traveling together as one body.

> May I today live more simply
> —like the bread.
> May I today see more clearly
> —like the water.
> May I today be more selfless
> —like the Christ.
> *(Traditional Russian prayer)*
> —*MARILYN MORGAN KING*

WED
23

Day Four: The Bay of Turning the Back
They pulled their boats up on shore, left everything and followed him. —*LUKE 5:11 (NIV)*

It was decision time. The group would split temporarily at this point. Those who wanted to see the marble quarry would go with Alan, and those who chose to go ahead to St. Columba's Bay would continue with Jan and wait there for the first group. I went with Jan, to spend some quiet time at the bay. As I sat in silence on the grassy hill overlooking the heavily pebbled bay, with a gentle breeze softly blowing my hair and sprinkles of water cooling my cheeks, a deep peace entered into me. I was glad I had decided in favor of taking time for contemplation.

When the first group again joined us, Jan explained that St. Columba arrived on Iona on the day of Pentecost in 563, after losing a lawsuit brought against him in Ireland for hand-copying another man's Bible. He and his twelve monks climbed the high hill near the bay to confirm that they could no longer see Ireland. In this way, Columba turned his back on his error and began anew. Thus the name, "The Bay of Turning the Back."

As part of our meditation at this spot, we were asked to pick up two pebbles from the beach. We threw one into the sea as a symbol of something in our life we'd like to leave behind, and we brought the other back with us, as a sign of new commitment in our heart. The peace of this place deepened for me as I cast away the stone, turning my back on envy, and placed the stone of new commitment in my bag to take home.

What would you like to cast out of your life? Perhaps you'll decide to find a stone to represent it, and one to symbolize your commitment to your own spiritual journey, casting one away and placing the other in an important place. It will bring peace to your heart.

> **Bless to us, O God,**
> **The moon that is above us,**
> **The earth that is beneath us,**
> **The friends who are around us,**
> **Your image deep within us.**
> *(Traditional Celtic prayer)*
> —*MARILYN MORGAN KING*

THU
24

Day Five: Together in Love

For he has made known to us in all wisdom and insight the mystery of his will, according to the purpose which he set forth in Christ as a plan for the fulness of time, to unite all things in him, things in heaven and things on earth. —*EPHESIANS 1:9–10 (RSV)*

For me there was one real *Aha!* moment on this pilgrimage hike with my wife Marilyn. It came shortly after we had climbed a rather steep hill to reach the highest point on the island. From this vantage point you can see water all around. You know then that you are truly on an island. I remembered my first visit to Iona, and how separated from the world I felt, being on an island after having grown up in the Midwest, thousands of miles from the ocean.

But Jan, who was leading the meditation, did not focus on the sense of isolation that living on an island can elicit. Rather she pointed to the surrounding islands, barely visible through the mist. "These islands," she said, "are all interconnected. You may not recognize the connection, since it is under water, but it is nonetheless real. If you go deep enough, you will see that these islands are all part of a single landmass."

Her observations led me to reflect on my feeling of separation—and the deeper unity that underlies it. Since my marriage to Marilyn, I have come to appreciate, as never before, the spiritual interconnection of all beings. Our love has been a window into the divine

Love, a love that overcomes division and "unites all things in heaven and on earth." What divides us, I have found, is largely superficial, while the love that unites us is deep and all-encompassing.

> Across the barriers that divide race from race;
> Across the barriers that divide rich from poor;
> Across the barriers that divide people of different faiths;
> Across the barriers that marginalize so many;
> Come, Lord,
> And reconcile us through Your pain and tears
> for all the world. *(Iona* by Peter W. Millar*)*

—*ROBERT KING*

FRI	*Day Six: Rejoicing in the Lamb*
25	It is not the will of your Father which is in heaven, that one of these little ones should perish. —*MATTHEW 18:14*

On the west side of the island of Iona is a sheltered area shared by all the crofters (sheep-raisers) living on the island. Here all the sheep are free to graze together, the little lambs dancing and playing near their mothers. For me, one of the most delightful experiences of the pilgrimage was to watch the tiny woolly creatures cavorting around; they allowed us to come quite close to them. It reminded me of the little lamb I'd found within myself at a time of great pain in my life, the lamb that had accompanied me through Holy Week in *Daily Guideposts, 1993,* healing the broken places in my life. How could I have dreamed, during that dark time, that I would one day be blessed by marriage to my soulmate Robert, who now walks beside me on this spiritual journey?

As we were about to leave the area, one of our guides stopped to block a hole under the gate, just big enough for a little lamb to crawl through. "When lambs become separated from their mothers, they die," he explained. "The creatures of the earth are part of God's family, too, so we try to take good care of them, just as God cares for us." What a bright moment it was for me to be reminded of the Lamb of God Who continues to lead me on my spiritual journey through life!

Teach us, Lord, to walk the soft earth as relatives of all that live. *(Native American prayer)*   —*MARILYN MORGAN KING*

SAT
26

Day Seven: Facing Death
Though I walk through the valley of the shadow of death,
I will fear no evil: for thou art with me. . . . —*PSALM 23:4*

We are nearing the end of our pilgrimage. Our final destination, a small stone chapel overlooking the sea, is just ahead of us. But first we must pass through a graveyard. How appropriate! No spiritual journey would be complete that did not confront the reality of death.

This is no ordinary graveyard; it has been, from ancient times, the burial place of Scottish kings. Even Macbeth, made famous by Shakespeare, is said to be buried here. But so also are many of the local people, men and women who have worked the land, fished the sea, raised families and welcomed visitors to the island. None of the ancient graves are marked. And perhaps that is as it should be. For in death we are divested of our reputations: The humble and the mighty are one in the eyes of God.

When I retired a few years ago, I felt a deep sense of loss. The work that had given me my identity in the eyes of others was over. It felt like death to my ego, and in a sense it was. But it was also an opening to the Divine, a reminder that we are never really separated from God.

Turning to my beloved companion, I thought, *This journey is about letting go and trusting that the One Who has been with us all along the way will be with us at the end.*

> O God, give us Your shielding,
> O God, give us Your holiness,
> O God, give us Your comfort
> And Your peace at the hour of our death.
> *(Traditional Celtic prayer)*
> —*ROBERT KING*

SUN
27

Day Eight: Journey's End
I was glad when they said unto me, Let us go into the house of the Lord. —*PSALM 122:1*

Finally we came to the goal of our Iona pilgrimage, the oldest building on the island, a chapel built in the twelfth century. What a bedraggled lot we were, less than half the size of the group that had left the abbey that morning. Exhausted, many with stinging feet and aching backs, but all with overwhelmingly jubilant hearts, we entered the small chapel and stood in silence together. There, in the ethereal glow of the closing day, from somewhere within our group, a soft refrain began to rise, a refrain that had accompanied us throughout the day, "Alleluia, alleluia, alleluia."

What I have carried home with me, more than anything else, is the overwhelming sense of life as an ongoing journey into God's presence, on a road filled with pilgrims—laughing and crying, praying and singing, and sometimes just being silent together in love. As my husband Robert and I have relived our Iona experience, we have been acutely aware of the presence of *Daily Guideposts* readers walking beside us, as well as all those devout men and women throughout the centuries who have known the heart's longing for God.

Yes, the longing is still there. I think it may be God's way of drawing us home. So I'll continue to follow it as long as I live. Perhaps we'll meet on the way home.

> May you be an isle in the sea,
> May you be a hill on the shore,
> May you be a star in the darkness,
> May you be a staff to the weak,
> And may the power of the Spirit
> Pour on you, richly and generously,
> Today, and in the days to come.
> *(Iona* by Peter W. Millar)
> —*MARILYN MORGAN KING*

MON
28 "Let me teach you; for I am gentle and humble, and you shall find rest for your souls. . . ." —*MATTHEW 11:29 (TLB)*

I was tootling full-throttle along the 5 Freeway, commonly known as the Grapevine, en route from Pasadena to Bakersfield, California, when the grade suddenly became scarily steep. Hurtling downhill while trying to negotiate the curves had me on the verge of panic. It was difficult to slow down, and I wondered what on earth I would do in the event my brakes failed.

Enormous trucks were hogging the right lanes, their drivers trying to control their heavy rigs. Then I saw a sign: RUNAWAY TRUCK RAMP, 1/4 MILE. Sure enough, going off the freeway was a long exit ramp that tilted up toward nowhere. *Hmm, so that's how they handle it,* I thought.

The fact was, I needed a runaway ramp, not for the car, but for me. Lately my life had been getting more and more out of control. There was no way I could put the brakes on speaking commitments, deadlines, correspondence and household chores. Emotionally, I was frazzled, short-tempered and impatient. Spiritually, I was rushing through devotions hurriedly read but not meditated upon, and my prayers were sent heavenward on the run.

Late that evening, as I searched the Scriptures, I found these words of Jesus: "Let me teach you; for I am gentle and humble, and you shall find rest for your souls." I desperately needed that rest. I'd been reading the Psalms and the letters of Paul, but it had been a long time since I had opened my Bible to the Gospels, where the words of Jesus were highlighted in red.

I decided that the words of Jesus would be my spiritual runaway ramp, a place to begin prayerfully putting on the brakes and sorting out all the other out-of-control aspects of my daily life. I would let Christ teach me, and I would listen carefully to His voice.

Lord, it's so easy for me to go spiritually out of control in all the busyness of my life. Today and every day, quiet my heart with Your peace.
—*FAY ANGUS*

EDITOR'S NOTE: Four weeks from today, on Monday, November 25, we will observe the ninth annual Guideposts Family Day of Prayer. We want you to join us as we pray together as a family. Please send your prayer requests (and a picture, if you can) to Guideposts Prayer Fellowship, PO Box 8001, Pawling, NY 12564.

TUE
29
He that is of a merry heart hath a continual feast.
—*PROVERBS 15:15*

In my top desk drawer is an old buckeye that my grandfather gave me many years ago. "For good luck, buddy," I remember him saying. The buckeye is a brown nut similar to a chestnut. Its surface is smooth and hard. That old buckeye acts as a perfect stress-reliever. I roll it around in my hand and suddenly I think about my grandfather.

Pa was a big man, six-foot-four and barrel-chested, but he had the heart of a playful child. He would spend hours raking leaves, then pile them into a great mound and take a running leap into the pile, his big body scattering leaves everywhere. And more than once I'd seen him turn from some summer project to escape the heat with a quick dive into the lake—with all of his clothes on!

Food was another of Pa's great joys. He loved to cook, and he'd make wonderful things with cheeses and meats and vegetables, always delicious. Whenever he took me out to eat, he insisted on my ordering the most adventurous thing on the menu. While other five-year-olds were eating hamburgers from the children's menu, I was tackling a whole lobster or figuring out just exactly how to eat an artichoke leaf.

So here I am in my office, rubbing my buckeye and remembering. By now, almost everyone else has gone home. I look out the window and see a worker blowing the leaves off the city sidewalk and I know just what I'm going to do. In thirty minutes I'm home, out of my suit and into my jeans. "Harrison," I say to my ten-month-old (he's named after Pa), "how about coming outside with Daddy and raking some leaves?"

Father, keep my heart merry through the seasons so that someday my life will be remembered as a continual feast.   —BROCK KIDD

WED	Don't you think that God will surely give justice to his
30	people who plead with him day and night? Yes! He will answer them quickly!... —*LUKE 18:7–8 (TLB)*

You can tell a lot about a person by looking at the front of his or her refrigerator. My seventy-seven-year-old stepmother Bev has magnets on hers from some of the countries she and my dad have visited over the years. My busy son Michael and his wife Amy have large magnetic alphabet letters at the bottom of their refrigerator for their little ones, Hannah and Zachary, to practice their spelling words. My friend Sharon has hundreds of tiny magnetic words on her refrigerator, so her whole family can create sweet, goofy or sentimental poems.

My refrigerator is what reminds me to pray a dozen times a day, because the top two-thirds of it is a solid mass of four-by-six-inch photos. Everyone from one-hundred-and-one-year-old Great Aunt Peggy and ninety-five-year-old Aunt Helen to my two-year-old granddaughter Riley. My four children, their spouses, my other four grandchildren, my folks, brother, sister, their families, other aunts, uncles, cousins and assorted friends all hold a place of honor on my refrigerator.

One is a picture of Jane Knapp, a friend I've never met in person. She interviewed me by telephone on her small radio station years ago, and we struck up an immediate friendship. In 2000, Jane's e-mails were gut-wrenching updates about her cancer. One day, after months of chemo, I received this note from Jane:

"The doctor called a few minutes ago and told me that the PET scan results showed new cancers in my liver, kidney and lung. He said usually new cancers do not pop up at the same time, so I'm very discouraged, but have to keep believing in the power of prayer."

Jane's photo and all the others on that frequently opened door help keep my loved ones in my mind, heart and prayers many times a day, every day.

Lord, bless, protect and comfort every person whose face is on my refrigerator. And thank You, especially, for putting them into my life.
—*PATRICIA LORENZ*

THU
31
Since we are surrounded by so great a cloud of witnesses, let us also lay aside every weight, and sin which clings so closely, and let us run with perseverance the race that is set before us. . . .   —*HEBREWS 12:1 (RSV)*

The other day on television I heard an author discuss how he communicated with people who had passed through this life and were now "on the other side." He claimed to be able to bring messages from them to living friends and relatives. His listeners were astounded. Though Scripture warns us against trying to communicate with the dead, my Bible also tells me that we are "surrounded by so great a cloud of witnesses" (Hebrews 12:1, NIV). The picture I conjure up in my mind is of loved ones who have gone on to their reward, cheering us on, along with angels whose protection is spoken of often in God's Word.

And those angels are always nearby. Perhaps you have had an encounter where you were strangely saved from some precarious circumstances, or know of someone who has had an experience that defies earthly explanation. I heard of such an encounter recently, the central figure of which was a four-year-old girl named Kerstin.

The family had gathered at the hospital bedside of Kerstin's grandmother to keep vigil during her final hours. Kerstin's mother tried to explain that soon her grandmother's pain would be over. "There's no need to worry," she consoled.

"I'm not worried," Kerstin answered. "Grandma's got angels all around her."

The little girl's mother thought at first that her daughter's imagination was at work. "Are they flying?" she asked, attempting to draw Kerstin out.

"No," Kerstin said emphatically, "they're just standing beside Grandma, waiting to help her."

What was it the prophet Isaiah said about the restoration of David's kingdom? "The wolf also shall dwell with the lamb, and the leopard shall lie down with the kid . . . and a little child shall lead them" (Isaiah 11:6).

> Give us, Lord, the faith of a child,
> So that our doubts can be reconciled.
>
> —*FRED BAUER*

My Days of Prayer

1 _____

2 _____

3 _____

4 _____

5 _____

6 _____

7 _____

8 _____

9 _____

10 _____

11 _____

12 _____

13 _____

14 _____

15 _____

16 _____

17 _____

18 _____

19 _____

20 _____

21 _____

22 _____

23 _____

24 _____

25 _____

26 _____

27 _____

28 _____

29 _____

30 _____

31 _____

November

Rejoice evermore. Pray without ceasing. In every thing give thanks: for this is the will of God in Christ Jesus concerning you.

—*I Thessalonians 5:16-18*

S	M	T	W	T	F	S
					1	2
3	4	5	6	7	8	9
10	11	12	13	14	15	16
17	18	19	20	21	22	23
24	25	26	27	28	29	30

THE PRAYER THAT IS ALWAYS NEW

1

Our Father. . . . *deliver us from evil.* . . .
—*MATTHEW 6:9, 13*

The impression was so sharp I actually pulled the car to the side of the road. My husband John, on a business trip to California, needed prayer! I looked at my watch: 4:30 P.M. here in New York, 1:30 in Los Angeles.

Though I had no idea what the emergency was, I'd had too much experience with these nudges to prayer to ignore them. Like the time I'd "known" our granddaughter Sarah was in danger; at the very moment I prayed, I learned later, she'd fallen from the top of a jungle gym—and walked away with only a chipped tooth. Or the letter that came from my elderly friend Barbara Nelson saying she'd prayed for me for hours one day. Barbara had no way of knowing it was the day of my cancer surgery.

So I sat in the car, praying for John's safety. After about forty-five minutes, the urgency left me and I felt a tremendous peace. All evening I wondered what story of averted calamity he would have to tell.

When John phoned around 10:00 P.M., my time, however, it was to report an uneventful day. Where had he been at 1:30? Circling the Farmers' Market, looking for a place to park. No, no particular problems.

I hadn't told John over the phone about my overheated imagination. But when he got home, I mentioned the foolish episode. "I'm glad I was wrong about your being in trouble!"

John shook his head. "I'm not sure you were wrong," he said "That no calamity happened doesn't mean your prayer was wasted. It means it was answered."

I stared at him in silence. I was thinking about the tens of thousands of miles we drive safely each year, the illnesses we *haven't* had, the plane that *doesn't* crash. The disasters that *don't* happen to John and me, our family, our friends, people everywhere. I thought of the millions of voices joining each day in the Lord's Prayer. *Deliver us from evil.* And I thanked Jesus again for teaching us to pray.

Our Father, keep me obedient to Your prompting, whether I see all or only a fragment of Your providence.   —*ELIZABETH SHERRILL*

WHAT GOD HAS JOINED TOGETHER

SAT 2	Our Savior, Christ Jesus . . . has destroyed death and has brought life and immortality to light through the gospel. —*II TIMOTHY 1:10 (NIV)*

This past year was bittersweet because, while it was the year Joy and I celebrated twenty-five years of marriage, it was also the year her father, James D. Fickett, died after a long illness.

Death is a subject we like to avoid in our culture. Christians even invent euphemisms for it, like "passing away" and "going to be with the Lord." Through Joy and her family, I learned a lot about dealing with the meaning and the heartbreak of the death of a loved one. Here are three of the things I learned:

- Time with a dying loved one is invaluable. Joy's family was given the grace of a gentle process that took several weeks. She was able to travel from Virginia to California three times and be there for her dad's final moments. She had time for memories, healing old hurts and bonding more deeply with siblings than the years of living far from home had allowed.
- Funerals and memorials are for the living. My brother-in-law was asked to speak at his father's funeral. He came to me and said he didn't think he could do it and asked if, since I was trained as a

minister, I would speak. While I was willing to help, I encouraged him to speak about his dad also. He did, and was blessed beyond measure; his thoughtful words touched every listener's heart.

• Death is a reminder to cherish life. Ask yourself, "If I knew I was going to die next Tuesday, whom would I call or write or visit?" Then get out your calendar and schedule those calls, letters and trips. You will never be sorry.

Lord, for the gift of life I am deeply grateful; for the promise of new life beyond death I am joyfully hopeful; and in the cherished memories of those who have gone before I am richly blessed.

—*ERIC FELLMAN*

<table>
<tr><td>SUN</td></tr>
<tr><td>3</td></tr>
</table>

Upon this I awaked, and beheld; and my sleep was sweet unto me. —*JEREMIAH 31:26*

I have a sofa bed that has been put to good use over the years; in New York City, a hotel reservation is expensive and hard to get. Well, the old Varner Hotel is still in business, and my guests (I truly enjoy having them) are still coming. With the wear and tear of people and time on the convertible, I recently found it necessary to send it out for a new frame and a costly fabric redo. That should have made my visitors content but, alas, I long ago found that the noises outside bothered some of them. The traffic, the sirens, the buses that pick up passengers under my second-story windows made sleeping, they said, difficult.

"Difficult?" I replied. "What do you mean? I have no trouble. Why, in the background I hear the comforting buzz of Manhattan's melody. When it's time for sleep, I sleep." Until a Sunday morning not too long ago.

It was dark outside, and I was awake. I looked at the clock: 4:50. I tried to go back to sleep. No good. Slowly I began to sense that it was quiet, the kind of stillness that I remembered came at the top of a mountain in Switzerland, too high for the flight and chatter of birds. It was silent, all right—unearthly. Was it in Habakkuk that the Lord was in His holy temple? "Let all the earth keep silence before him" (Habakkuk 2:20). Quickly I got out of bed and hurried to the window. Both Central Park West and 81st Street were closed! Then I remembered: The city was preparing for the marathon. Now there were no sirens, no traffic, no buses, only signposts awaiting tired runners.

I went back to bed, but I couldn't sleep in silence, without the comforting sounds of the city. But the marathon comes but once a year. Maybe next year I can spend the weekend with a friend who always has Manhattan's melody humming outside.

Lord, I promise to keep silent before You when You are in Your holy temple. —*VAN VARNER*

<u>MON</u>
4
For with God nothing shall be impossible. —*LUKE 1:37*

As a volunteer caregiver in a nursing home, I was frustrated. Every time I tried to talk with Caroline, I seemed to alienate her. Her scant memory, eroded by Alzheimer's, curtailed any conversation I started. She seemed unnerved at having to remember what was said thirty seconds before. So instead of conversing, she wheeled her chair around the fourth floor, asking probing questions and giving orders. Her monologues always ended with a dead-end dismissal: "It's been a pleasure to see you. Let me know if I can be of any help."

Then one day, I stopped at a grocery store to pick up a few things on my way to the nursing home. A display of fresh-cut flowers caught my eye, and I thought I'd make one more attempt to get through to Caroline.

With the flowers in my hand, I stepped out of the fourth-floor elevator and walked to Caroline's room. She wasn't there. I glanced down the hallway; again, no sign of her. Finally, I found her in the TV room and presented the bouquet to her. Her face lit up; she leaned over to inhale the floral aroma. And then, rather than shoo me off as she'd been accustomed to doing, she graciously talked with me for more than twenty minutes.

The next time I came to see her, she was her old abrupt self. But before rolling past me down the hall, she stopped, smiled and reached out to take my hand. "It's nice to see a familiar face," she said.

Dear God, help me to remember that little things can make a big difference. —*BILLY NEWMAN*

TUE
5

Determination to be wise is the first step toward becoming wise! And with your wisdom, develop common sense and good judgment.
—*PROVERBS 4:7 (TLB)*

I was surprised to find a piece of paper with the heading MERTILLA TOWNSHIP: MILL LEVY FOR ROADS among the ballots I was given on Election Day. My husband Don and I had discussed candidates for judge and county commissioner while we drove the fifteen miles to Plains, our polling place, but he hadn't mentioned a mill levy. If there had been a story on it in the newspaper, I'd skipped it. After marking the other ballots, I scanned the mill levy petition. One thing was obvious: voting YES would raise my taxes. I checked NO without bothering to read the full text.

"How did you vote?" I asked Don on the way home.

"Yes, of course!" he told me, surprised that I'd asked.

"Well, I voted no!" I said. "Our taxes are already way too high!"

"Did you actually *read* the petition?" Don asked. "We'd pay less than fifty-five dollars each year—not much compared to getting that east road built up and graveled."

When we heard the results that night, the Mill Levy had been defeated—by one vote.

Were there other times I'd been uninformed about the issues and had neglected to pray for wisdom before casting my vote? I didn't have to go far into my memory. I'd supported an official whose views were hostile to the poor. I'd helped our church elect a leader without the skills to take us through difficult times. And because I didn't bother to learn about the Mertilla Township mill levy, our east road continues to be nearly impassable after a hard rain.

Lord Jesus, help me to vote with an informed mind and a compassionate heart, trusting that my choices will be pleasing to You. Amen.
—*PENNEY SCHWAB*

WED
6

A word fitly spoken is like apples of gold in pictures of silver.
—*PROVERBS 25:11*

"We writers are childish folk," Somerset Maugham once wrote, "and cherish a word of praise." True enough, but the hunger for approval isn't limited to writers. If there is one single characteristic that we all share, it is this yearning to be admired or appreciated more than we think we are. That is why a kind word banishes discouragement, at least temporarily. Sometimes it can actually heal a wounded spirit.

A compliment is often most effective when it deals with something surprising or unexpected. One day years ago I was with DeWitt Wallace, the founder of *Reader's Digest*. I admired Mr. Wallace greatly and would have been thrilled if he had offered any kind words about my writing. What he did say, at one point, was, "I've been noticing how you stand up straight with your shoulders back. I wish everyone did."

Well, I wasn't even aware that my posture was worth noticing, but the unexpectedness of Mr. Wallace's remark made me remember it to this day. It also made me realize how simple it is to look for attractive traits or qualities in people and remark upon them from time to time.

Golden words in pictures of silver? To the hearer, that's often exactly what they are.

Lord, teach me not to withhold admiration when it is deserved.
—*ARTHUR GORDON*

Catch us the foxes, the little foxes that spoil the vines. . . .
—*SONG OF SOLOMON 2:15 (NKJV)*

The catastrophes of life don't bother me as much as its minuscule miseries: nuisance paperwork; waiting in lines; wee worries that steal my sleep. I would rather be swallowed by a whale than nibbled to death by these minnows.

For example, I never liked school as a boy. I didn't mind tests and recitations, I was simply annoyed by a cramped desk, sun in my eyes and an overheated radiator. Most of all I was irritated by almost constant hunger.

So every morning on the way to school I stopped at The Corner Store and bought a small box of pretzels for ten cents. It was about the size of a paperback, with a cellophane covering that displayed the pretzels in mouthwatering rows. I would put this box in my desk, directly under the inkwell hole. Whenever my stomach complained, I would quietly fish a pretzel through the hole and slowly savor the salty treat like a lollipop. One box lasted all day, and it kept me from going berserk.

Now that I'm a teacher, I haven't forgotten how miserable school can be. I keep the thermostat adjusted and the blinds pulled down, and I always keep a wicker basket of pretzel sticks on my classroom desk for students.

The ten-cent solution can be applied to other miseries in life, I think. When faced with a long, tedious meeting, it helps to loosen my tie and take along a glass of ice water or a pocket full of jelly beans. My wife carries a paperback in her purse, for the times when I "run into the hardware store for just a moment." And sometimes she does her paperwork out on the porch, where she can feel a cool breeze and listen to the wind chimes.

Life is just too hard to let the "little foxes" spoil its sweetness.

Lord, show me how to soften the sufferings of life by making little adjustments.
                                        —*DANIEL SCHANTZ*

FRI

8

Immediately the boy's father exclaimed, "I do believe; help me overcome my unbelief!"
                                        —*MARK 9:24 (NIV)*

Throughout her months of cancer treatment, I had assured my dear friend Louise that God cared. But when she bravely returned to the job she loved, she discovered that in her absence it had been given to someone else. I began to doubt my own words of reassurance.

I suppose that's why I overreacted when my teenage son Chris admitted that he'd lost his wallet a month earlier and had been driving without his license. "I was kinda waiting for it to turn up," he mumbled.

"There's no telling what's under that mess in your room. Or in your car. Or even in your book bag," I lectured. "Go to the Department of Motor Vehicles and get a new license this afternoon!"

That afternoon I was surprised when Chris drove into the garage at the usual time. "I don't need to get a new license," he explained. "The weirdest thing happened. When I got to school, they called me into the office. Someone had put my wallet on the secretary's desk."

I stared at him, finding his story hard to believe. Why would a wallet that had been missing for a month turn up so mysteriously at school on the very day I lowered the boom? "Show me the wallet," I demanded.

"You don't believe me, do you?" he replied.

"Just show me the wallet."

Chris pulled out the wallet and opened it to show me his license. I went back into the house shaking my head. Suddenly, Chris's words, "You don't believe me, do you?" rattled into my dry and empty soul. An inner voice seemed to say, *As long as Louise was recovering uneventfully, you believed that God was there. Then things didn't turn out the way you thought they should, and you stopped believing. But sometimes the most unlikely stories are the very ones that turn out to be so wonderfully true.*

It remains a mystery how Chris's missing wallet landed on the school secretary's desk that day. Funny that it turned up just when I was most in need of finding my missing faith.

Lord, help me never to stop believing that You care.

—*KAREN BARBER*

SAT
9

"We must work the works of Him who sent Me, as long as it is day; night is coming, when no man can work."
—*JOHN 9:4 (NAS)*

It had been a hectic, fast-paced week. Rushing to complete my seminar notes, I glanced at my cocker spaniel Bucky furiously scratching at fleas. For more than a week I had intended to wash the pup, but something else always barked louder. Now I felt guilty and neglectful.

Gathering my notes, I snapped a leash on Bucky's collar and quipped, "If your master won't take care of you, maybe the vet will!" Harried man and flea-bitten dog jumped into my Jeep and roared off down the road.

As I arranged with the veterinarian to have Bucky groomed, I noticed a sign tacked on her office wall: "God put me on earth to accomplish a certain number of things. Right now I'm so far behind I'll never die." My wide grin became rolling laughter as I read that pithy message. Life is indeed hectic. We never get "caught up." Yet I'll never have the time to do all that I want to do. So I had better make wise choices.

This morning I've reviewed my three-page, single-spaced "to do" list. I've decided what is truly crucial and must be accomplished, and what can wait—forever, perhaps. Choices are what make life rich or poor, full or empty. Only God can do it all.

Dear Father, give me the ability to use my time wisely. Amen.
—*SCOTT WALKER*

<hr />

SUN
10
"Six days you shall labor and do all your work, but the seventh day is a Sabbath to the Lord your God . . . ."
—*EXODUS 20:9–10 (NIV)*

I was having Sunday lunch with friends, celebrating the baptism that morning of their daughter, when the waitress came in. "Emergency phone call for Mary Lou Carney," she said. My chicken salad stuck in my throat as I ran to the nearest phone.

"Honey," my husband said, the fear in his voice as clear as the phone connection. "It's Brett. He's been hurt."

Our son Brett has always been oblivious to danger, whether riding his three-wheeler or rock climbing, walking rafters in the houses he builds or driving his pickup truck on icy roads. "What happened?" I asked.

"Power nailer. He has a nail buried in his leg. He's in the emergency room now."

I headed for the hospital, praying all the way. *Please, God, let him be okay. Prevent infection. Help him bear the pain. Send a good surgeon.* But on another level, I was fussing at Brett. *Why did he have to work today? If he'd been in church, this wouldn't have happened.*

I rushed into the emergency room and was shown to a small, curtained area where Brett lay, a morphine drip hanging from his bed. A dent just above his knee made it clear where the nail—complete with brass barbs—was buried. All thoughts of lecturing him about keeping the Sabbath vanished as I took his hand.

Brett looked up and managed a smile. "Grandpa always told me not to work on Sunday."

I squeezed his hand . . . and bowed my head in gratitude to One Who never takes a day off from watching over His children.

You are faithful, O Father, even when we are not. Forgive us for stealing from Your ordained day of rest. Slow us down enough to bless us.
—*MARY LOU CARNEY*

MON
11
I will make every effort to see that after my departure you will always be able to remember these things.
—*II PETER 1:15 (NIV)*

We really celebrated Veterans Day when I was growing up. My father would put out the flag on the front porch, step back, put his hand over his heart and bow his head for a few moments. Then my parents would go to church to pray for all the friends they'd lost in World War II, and for all those whose lives were still darkened by the shadow that terrible war cast over a whole generation of Americans, a generation that saved the future.

World War II dominated my parents' consciousness. The day after Pearl Harbor, my father, a naval reservist, requested active duty but was turned down because of arthritic knees and stomach ulcers. We lived in Philadelphia at the time, and the Navy officer who rejected my dad said, "Maybe if the Japanese capture the Liberty Bell, we'll have to use you."

That didn't stop him from doing his part. My parents had a sleek little inboard motorboat they kept moored on the Delaware River, and on weekends when the weather was fair Dad would take it out into the Atlantic and patrol the shoreline, looking for German U-boats, Mom steering while Dad swept the horizon with his binoculars. Once, Dad thought he spotted a periscope and radioed the sighting to the Coast Guard—but it didn't come to anything and probably wasn't taken very seriously, since U-boats weren't known to lurk around the mouth of the Delaware. He took a lot of ribbing about that in later years, but Dad didn't care. He'd done what he could to help fight a war that he understood had to be fought.

Some people might think that Veterans Day isn't relevant anymore, but I think they're wrong. I'm going to make a real celebration of it again; I'll start by putting out the flag.

God, protect our nation and shed Your grace on us this Veterans Day.
—*EDWARD GRINNAN*

TUE
12
Fear not: for I have redeemed thee, I have called thee by thy name; thou art mine.
—*ISAIAH 43:1*

Our little Mary recently celebrated her second birthday. She now has a new litany she repeats a dozen times a day in her sweet, high voice.

"I'm Ma-ry Fran-ces At-ta-way. I'm a toddler. I'm two years old."

Cute as it is, there is something extremely important to her in this self-definition. The day before yesterday she looked stunning in her green velvet Sunday dress, with her strawberry-blonde curls tumbling down, and I said, "You look like a princess!"

She shook her head and solemnly replied, "I'm a toddler."

She is not a princess. She does not want to be a princess. She wants to be who and what she is: Mary Frances Attaway, a toddler who is two years old.

It strikes me that Mary is on to something that I as an adult sometimes forget. I fall, not infrequently, into the trap of thinking in terms of who I'd like to be, of the image I'd like to project, the person I'm trying to become or wish I had been. Mary is true to being the person God created her to be—she is who she is. As I hear her proclaim to her brother and sister, "I'm Mary Frances Attaway!" I marvel at her confidence in simply *being* Mary. Being Mary is what God asks of her, and that, in and of itself, is enough.

Surely God sees through my pretenses (even the ones to which I'm blind) to the Julia He created. Which causes me to wonder: Why, then, do I ask God to meet me where I want to be, rather than where He has placed me?

Lord Jesus, help me to die to self, that I may find my name written in Your Book of Life.   —*JULIA ATTAWAY*

WED
13

Making melody in your heart to the Lord; Giving thanks always for all things unto God. . . . —*EPHESIANS 5:19–20*

My husband and I are pushovers when it comes to cats, especially when it comes to our Siamese cat Shushi. She has spent a good part of her thirteen-year lifetime curled up at the foot of our bed. The trouble is that now, in her old age, she needs to be let out around four in the morning, and in our old age, it is becoming increasingly hard for us to get back to sleep once we've gotten up to let her out.

Every time we decide to get Shushi off our bed, she looks at us with wide blue eyes, opens her mouth and gives us a heart-tugging silent *meow*; a *meow* that is far more eloquent than the usual string of audible *meows* by which she lets us know it's time for chow or time to sit on a lap. My cat-talk friends tell me the silent *meow* should be interpreted as a polite protest or a plea for indulgence. Maybe with their cats, but not with Shushi. I know Shushi as well as anyone can ever pretend to know a cat. I take her silent *meow* as an expression of contentment and affection for those who care for her. It comes from so deep within her being that it has no audible expression.

Sometimes, wearing my husband's socks and his extra-large sweater, I cuddle up in a comforter these nippy early mornings and sit on the patio, my hands wrapped around a steaming cup of coffee. If I could purr, I would. In the quiet of the breaking dawn, before the hum of traffic, there comes from deep within me an overwhelming contentment, a spillover of affection for all God does as caregiver of my soul. The words I want simply are not there; all I have is my own silent *meow*. Looking up to a cloud-dappled sky, I offer it to God. Somehow, I think He's smiling.

When words fail me, loving Lord, please listen to the silent melody of my heart.
                                                                —FAY ANGUS

THU

14

Be prepared in season and out of season. . . .
                                    —II TIMOTHY 4:2 (NIV)

I've been doing a lot of thinking about my future lately. When we discovered that my cancer had metastasized to my lung, my husband and I found ourselves forced into a gargantuan research project. Books, the Internet, friends in the medical field, other cancer patients and survivors—all have been important resources, and our files of information are now several feet long.

I've also found myself exploring the very real possibility—no, the certainty—of my own death. One of the unexpected benefits of having cancer is that I'm motivated to look seriously at the issues of death and dying. I'm not morbidly preoccupied with it, but for me, it's been important to consider the end-of-life issues head-on.

We've gathered some information about hospice care. Our wills are in order, and we've completed Living Wills and other medical forms. For a variety of reasons, I'd like my body to be cremated. I drop ideas for my memorial service into a file folder: church bulletins with a favorite hymn circled, scraps of paper with scribbled Scripture references. And I'm considering having a going-away party to celebrate where I've been and where I'm going. If it begins to look like my cancer is winning the battle, I'd like to gather all my friends for a celebration while I'm still around to enjoy it.

It feels a little like planning for a trip. It's important for me to prepare myself for the journey, to make some decisions and preparations. But I'm not packing my suitcase and moving to the airport. I find I sometimes need to investigate that unfamiliar and somewhat uncomfortable place, but it's meant for passing through—I don't want to live there.

In the meantime, all that I have, all that any of us really has, is just this moment. And now it's time to go for a walk and enjoy the glorious sunset.

May I make thoughtful preparations, Lord, as I contemplate coming to You.
—*MARY JANE CLARK*

THE PRACTICE OF PRAYER

FRI
15
Praying for Others
We ... do not cease to pray for you. ...
—*COLOSSIANS 1:9*

The persimmon tree at the edge of our cabin causeway is heavy with fruit. Like a small miracle, it has survived the terrible deforestation of the year just passed. Over the spring and summer, I have watched in awe as the woods have staged a comeback of sorts. First came species of wildflowers I hadn't seen before. By summer most of the birds were back, and this fall there was enough foliage to offer a bit of color.

As I gather persimmons for a Thanksgiving centerpiece, small wonders of new beginnings push aside memories of the woodsman's saw. Good thoughts to take the place of bad. My thoughts fly to all the prayer habits that move me from life's disappointments toward the goodness that's always out there waiting to be claimed.

At the top of the list is "Praying for others." Each week I leave my prayer class with a sheet of paper that contains a prayer request from each member. It's virtually impossible to dwell on my own problems or feel sorry for myself when I'm praying for others.

"Pray for your enemies" is another good habit, not because I *like* to pray for my foes, but because I don't seem to have as many since I've been praying for them.

"Pray for the world." Mother Earth needs our prayers, as do the AIDS orphans in Africa, and all the people at home and abroad who are oppressed, hungry and homeless. Prayer has changed me and now I am using prayer to change the world.

As for that personal prayer list, I hope you will consider making one of your own. Tape your list to the dashboard of your car, to the bathroom mirror, the refrigerator, your bedside lamp. Make God's "very good" world even better, one prayer at a time.

Father, as I grow closer to You, I want to be one who helps others to find new life in You. Point me ever in the right direction.

—*PAM KIDD*

SAT

16

"Every one then who hears these words of mine and does them will be like a wise man who built his house upon the rock." —*MATTHEW 7:24 (RSV)*

Last year I took a walk along a familiar, beloved logging road cut through the middle of a tree farm in North Carolina.

The root systems of most of the trees were, of course, hidden below the forest floor. One old specimen, however, had grown at the top of the road cut along which I walked. Its roots were exposed, and I was fascinated to see its now-revealed secret life. Its taproot traveled downward looking for water, corkscrewing and burrowing, dividing and wrapping itself around a huge buried boulder.

This morning, I took the same walk again, but now my visit was a sad one, for a storm had ravaged the area. Weeks of rain had been followed by strong winds. Hundreds of trees had come down and were now strewn haphazardly across the forest floor like spilled matches. Almost without exception, the trees that had been felled by the storm showed root systems that spread sideways a few feet and then stopped. When the winds came, they had nothing to hold them up.

But my gnarled old tree, the one with roots that dug deep into the soil, the one that wrapped itself around a rock, that old tree still stood.

Father, help me to dig ever deeper and wrap myself around You, so that when the storms come I may still be standing.

—*JOHN SHERRILL*

READER'S ROOM

I am a nurse working with HIV-infected patients. I read the daily inspiration every morning and find I am able to face each day and see every challenge as an opportunity. Scott Walker's message on November 25, 1999, about a grateful heart being the root of contentment and peace is a tool I use in facing each day. I am exposed to anger, sadness, addiction and death, but I remain joyful inside because God always hands me a gift in the people I care for, and for that I am so very grateful. I would like to thank all the writers for each and every day of their personal sharing.   —*ANN HUBER, FALLSTON, MARYLAND*

SUN
17

As each has received a gift, employ it for one another, as good stewards of God's varied grace.

—*I PETER 4:10 (RSV)*

When class was over, the six- to nine-year-olds I was teaching in Sunday school all scrambled for the door at once. I was alarmed by their unruly stampede, but I didn't know what to do about it.

Then one Sunday I was surprised to learn that they all really liked one of the things I used in my lesson. It was a punch-out that folded into a small box with a different picture on each of its six surfaces. When I pitched the box to a child, he or she made up a story to fit the illustration. Because they seemed to like it so much, I said, "I'm going to give this box to one of you to take home. But you have to do something to earn it. When class is over, whoever remains quietly in his or her seat will get the box." I was certain they'd forget and dash out as usual.

When our time was up, I said matter-of-factly, "Class is over." No one moved. "You may leave now," I said. Again, they sat stock-still. "Okay," I said, laughing, "I'll think of a number and hold up that many fingers under the table. The one who guesses correctly gets the box." They thought that was fair.

As I was about to put my hands under the table, I noticed that Avie, a little girl sitting in front of me, had briefly bowed her head and folded her hands. When she opened her eyes, I whispered, "Were you praying?"

She nodded, smiling slightly.

"Would you like to tell me what you were praying about?"

She leaned over and whispered, "That I'd win the box!"

Amazingly, her guess was correct, and an enormous smile lit up her face as I handed the box to her. Still beaming, she gave it to the girl sitting next to her, along with a big hug. "I want you to have it, Bethany," Avie said. "I love you. You're my best friend!"

Lord, I'm beginning to see why You wanted me to meet these children.   —*MARION BOND WEST*

MON
18   Dear children, let us not love with words or tongue but
      with actions and in truth.   —*I JOHN 3:18 (NIV)*

I was right in the middle of one of my life's darkest moments. My mom and dad were splitting up after forty-two years of marriage, and I was on the phone with my mom pleading with her to reconsider. Suddenly, the fear and panic that I had been trying to conceal came flooding out, and I began shouting at her.

I don't think my mother ever imagined that I would raise my voice to her like that. "Please don't call me again," she said, and she burst into tears. After a few moments, she hung up the phone. I sat there, trying to comprehend what was happening. I felt my throat tighten, but I refused to cry.

Just then my friend Mark called to say hello. My voice betrayed my emotions, and he asked what was troubling me. After listening to my story, Mark was quiet for a moment or two. Then he asked, "Would you like me to pray with you right now over the phone?"

I know that the words he spoke in that prayer were more for God's ears than for mine, so I guess it's okay that I didn't hear a word of it. All I knew was my friend had the courage to step into a very personal, painful situation and be there with me in prayer. The dam broke, and I cried my eyes out. The pain was still there, but healing could begin.

After listening to my story, Mark could have done what I would have done, what I have done on so many occasions with friends who were experiencing tough times. But instead of saying, "I'll pray for you," and leaving it at that, Mark did something much more courageous—and much more meaningful. He prayed not just *for* me, but *with* me, in the midst of my hurt.

Lord, help me to be bold in the way I care for others.

—DAVE FRANCO

TUE

19 Honour thy father and thy mother. ...   —EXODUS 20:12

"It just seems like I'm always doing this. I'm always the one," Max says.

The women—Max, Theresa, Darlene and Ruth—sit in the circle we share every Tuesday morning. It is my discipleship class, a circle where we meet to pray, study and share our lives. The class is made up of all ages and both sexes. This group, however, is all middle-aged women—some more middle-aged than others.

The four women are discussing caretaking—providing comfort for relatives and elderly parents. Most times the women smile, but sometimes there are tears, and they feel overwhelmed and alone. Sometimes they are resentful of brothers and sisters, aunts and uncles who seem to be absent and not sharing the responsibility. The resentment doesn't last long, a momentary but necessary venting. Then Max, Theresa, Darlene and Ruth are back to stories of how they have grown and been blessed by their service. And of how they have learned not to judge those who are not caretakers.

"I wouldn't do it any other way," Max and Ruth agree.

"I was there at her side when my mother passed," Theresa says. "It was an honor." The other women nod in agreement.

Darlene, who has quit her job to stay home with her dying mother, thanks the other women for their wisdom and their generosity in sharing their stories. Their words strengthen her, she says. I watch and listen, blessed by their examples.

God, help me to show love and gratitude for all the caretakers in my life. —*SHARON FOSTER*

WED
20

God made the wild animals according to their kinds, the livestock according to their kinds, and all the creatures that move along the ground according to their kinds. And God saw that it was good. —*GENESIS 1:25 (NIV)*

The small waiting room at the veterinarian's office was crowded with animals and their humans, including me and my two big dogs, Roscoe and Chaucer. They were getting their nails clipped. The woman next to me held a Schnauzer on her lap. "Routine shots," she said. A balding man with a beard stroked his black mitten-foot cat. "Infected chigger bites," he said. One woman was silent, gently patting the top of a small animal crate, her foot swinging nervously. Finally, the balding man asked, "Is it a cat in there?"

"Yes, she's having kittens," the woman answered. "She's had two, but the third one won't come. She's been in labor all night. She was a stray. She arrived on my doorstep one night, pregnant. I named her Buffy. She's a calico. I'll have her spayed after this, but I'm keeping the kittens."

The room was now silent; all heads turned to the dark interior of the crate that hid Buffy. "She's so sweet and such a good mother to the two already born." The woman stopped and bent her face to the cage door. "Oh, she's had it! Look, here it is!" Carefully opening the door, she held up a wet, mewling little thing, the size of a hair ball, its mouth making sucking motions. We clapped, cheered and beamed at each other. I felt tears on my cheeks.

Why all this emotion? I wondered. *Is it for the woman who took in a homeless feline? For the triumph of the mother cat?* Yes and yes. But a deeper awareness showed itself on each face and in me. Awe. No matter how small the creature, birth is a miracle. As God ordained it so long ago.

Creator God, thank You for the daily miracles through which You renew Your creation. —*SHARI SMYTH*

THU

21

For this child I prayed. . . .   —*I SAMUEL 1:27*

I am walking down the street in the city, shuffling and shambling, in no particular hurry, in one of those quietly pleasant cracks that open in your day sometimes, when you are finished early with one appointment and not yet due for the next. Suddenly, for no particular reason, I have a vision of my daughter at college. This vision doesn't make much sense; my daughter is eight years old and a decade removed from higher education.

But instead of grinning at the goofy vision, I stand there near tears, for I find that I cannot even imagine my daughter so far away in space and time. I cannot bear even to think of a time when she will be out of the house and living in some ragged, poster-populated dorm room with two sagging couches and a guitar just slightly and tellingly out of tune, and an open textbook in which whole passages are highlighted in alternating yellow and pink with notes alongside in blue, and one roommate on the phone and one asleep and one mooning over a boyfriend.

That day will come, and maybe by then I'll be able to handle it. But for now, I resume shambling through the city on the way home, where I will find my little daughter, and kiss her.

Dear Lord, thank You, most sincerely and heartfully, for daughters, but especially for eight-year-old daughters, growing up, but still at home.   —*BRIAN DOYLE*

FRI

22

He gathereth together the outcasts. . . . He healeth the broken in heart, and bindeth up their wounds.
          —*PSALM 147:2–3*

I was nine years old, being hustled out of our farm home and into my grandparents' car just as a stern-looking official drove up, sprang out of his Model A, quickly nailed a quarantine sign reading SCARLET FEVER in bold, black letters on a yellow background to our front door and then, just as quickly, jumped back into his car and roared off.

Of course I felt sorry that my little sister had this contagious disease. I felt sorry Mom was quarantined, too, to take care of her. I was sorry my father was relegated to being the go-between—leaving food, medicine and other necessities on the porch, bunking in the barn because he couldn't go in and out of the house either, lest he risk contaminating others with whom he came in contact. And I felt sorry for myself. I hated being shunted to Grandma and Grandpa's place. They baked cookies and tried to make me happy, but they were Methuselah-old to my eyes.

Worst of all, everyone had heard about the quarantine sign on our door, so my school classmates avoided me. "My folks said to keep away from you. We might catch it." I was in fourth grade, and this was my first experience of being shunned. Even my teacher said, "Sit in this special chair up here by me." At recess I stayed in a corner of the playground, watching other kids having a good time, until Pearl came and shyly asked, "Want to play jacks?"

Pearl was the class outcast. All the rest of us girls had short, permed hair; Pearl's was straight and long in a waist-length braid. Pearl was just . . . *different,* and, well, it simply wasn't cool to be associated with "Pigtail Pearl." But during the six weeks that elapsed before the SCARLET FEVER sign was removed from the door and our family was free to come and go again, Pearl and I became best friends.

Thank You, Father, for the experiences that teach us compassion.
—*ISABEL WOLSELEY*

SAT	Epaphras, who is one of you, a servant of Christ, saluteth
23	you, always labouring fervently for you in prayers, that ye may stand perfect and complete in all the will of God.

—*COLOSSIANS 4:12*

My wife Rosie has begun to develop friendships with women outside of Mississippi through e-mail. It's been an adventure with some exciting rewards.

Recently, one of Rosie's new friends announced that she and two other women were going on a mission trip, and she asked Rosie to be a member of their prayer team. Rosie immediately began to pray for her friends; she felt so blessed to be able to have a small part in furthering God's work overseas. She then quickly e-mailed her friend to say yes to the request. Even though she could not go physically, she would have a special part in their work through her prayers.

"Dolphus," Rosie told me, "it's a great joy to intercede for others, but it's especially gratifying that these ladies trust me to be a part of their circle of prayer. I'm learning that God can use our prayers to do His work in the world, no matter who or where we are."

Although I knew that my wife was a wonderful prayer warrior, I was amazed that through the Internet she could be called on to help believers half a world away.

Lord, thank You for new ways of coming to know Your people's needs. Let me always be quick to respond to a request for prayer.
—*DOLPHUS WEARY*

SUN
24

Whatever is true, whatever is honorable, whatever is just, whatever is pure, whatever is lovely, whatever is gracious . . . think about these things. . . . and the God of peace will be with you. —*PHILIPPIANS 4:8–9 (RSV)*

A friend of mine seemed so serene in the face of the "midnight dragons" (the problems and pains) of life. I asked her what she did to silence the dragons. "I quit feeding them!" she told me. "I quit nursing the lizards—my doubts and fears—while they're small, and that keeps them from becoming those huge, fierce dragons."

I made a conscious effort to do the same, and it helped. But from time to time an emotional lizard would appear that I couldn't seem to avoid feeding. Finally, one sleepless night, I cried out to God, and a memory came into my mind. I was a boy, and my mother was telling me, "What you put in your mind on a regular basis is what you will become in a few years, or even a few months."

So I began to memorize Bible passages that would, if I really lived them, change me into a strong, confident man of God. One was Paul's admonition from Philippians 4:8. I added the Twenty-third Psalm, the thirteenth chapter of First Corinthians, the Beatitudes and others.

Yesterday someone in our prayer group asked me, "What are you feeding the lizards these days?"

I smiled and said, "You'll never believe it, but the 'food' I'm putting in my mind now is the Word of God."

"Do the lizards eat it?"

"Gosh, no, they *hate* it."

My friend smiled and asked, "Then whom are you feeding the Word to?"

"Um, " I said, thinking about that, "I guess I'm feeding the angels God sent to free me from my fears."

Thank You, Lord, that, as we put the best things in our minds, You can bring us Your peace. Amen. —*KEITH MILLER*

MON
25
In every thing by prayer and supplication with thanksgiving let your requests be made known unto God.
—*PHILIPPIANS 4:6*

About twenty years ago, a faulty air conditioner started a blaze that severely damaged a wing of the Guideposts building in Carmel, New York. We had to find temporary working space for the people whose offices were burned, so the room in which we held our weekly Prayer Fellowship was pressed into service. The piano got shoved into a corner; the tables and chairs where we'd sit and read the prayer requests that had been mailed in to us were stacked up one on top of the other. It looked as though our Prayer Fellowship would have to be postponed until we could find a suitable room. That's when I discovered just how important that time of prayer was to all of us.

At 9:45 on the Monday morning after the fire, men and women appeared from various departments to pray as usual. It didn't matter to them that there was no place to sit in comfort; they sat where they could, on file cabinets and desks. Mostly, they stood. The important thing was to be together, to pray for those friends out there who were struggling with family, money or health problems, grief or any of the other troubles that can beset us.

For more than five decades now, we've started our week with prayer: for our work, for one another and for the hundreds of readers whose letters come to us each week. No one is required to attend the prayer time, and yet they do. And today, in addition to our faithful staff, five hundred volunteers will join us for our Family Day of Prayer to pray for the more than twenty thousand requests we've received.

In our troubled world, there is a need for healing that only God can meet. And in this twenty-first century, as always, prayer is still our best help.

Lord, on this Guideposts Family Day of Prayer, I pray for the needs of the whole Guideposts family. Bless us, heal us, comfort us, strengthen us and, most of all, keep us close to You.

—*RUTH STAFFORD PEALE*

TUE
26 They must enjoy having guests in their homes and must love all that is good. . . .   —*TITUS 1:8 (TLB)*

During the 1950s when I visited Grandpa and Grandma Knapp in Blandinsville, Illinois (population six hundred), I was amazed at the number of drop-in visitors they had. In the winter, they'd visit in front of the coal stove that plunked and hissed in the middle of the living room. In the summer, neighbors walked over to sit a spell in the porch swing. Grandma would bring out the pitcher of lemonade and an extra chair or two from the dining room so everybody could sit down.

Every day they came: old farmer friends who'd retired like Grandpa and moved into town; shopkeepers on their way home from work; the preacher from the local church; the town librarian.

In 1998, when my youngest child went off to college and my home became an empty nest, I wondered what had happened to that custom of drop-in-anytime hospitality. Why is it that we think we need a week to prepare for guests, and that we must have every nook and cranny in our homes white-glove-inspection clean, and that we must feed our visitors elaborate meals every time they come to visit?

I decided right then to encourage everyone I knew to stop in anytime. Whenever I saw my friends or neighbors or acquaintances, I'd say, "Stop in anytime! I mean it. If my car's in the garage, I'm home. So stop in."

Well, people started doing it. Now, three or four times a week I get a surprise visit from someone. I'm not expected to have the house clean or food prepared. Usually I just boil water for tea, pour lemonade and pass out graham crackers, if that's all I have on hand. And without all the stress and fuss, my guests and I can just visit our fool heads off, enjoying every glorious minute.

Thank You, Lord, for the gift of hospitality and, most of all, for the amazing variety of interesting people You've brought through my front door. —*PATRICIA LORENZ*

WED
27
You know the grace of our Lord Jesus Christ ... so that you through his poverty might become rich.
—*II CORINTHIANS 8:9 (NIV)*

As a refugee child in postwar Europe, I often pressed my nose against a store window yearning for the colored candies I saw displayed there. My mouth watered, but I had no money; I had to trudge back empty-handed to the overcrowded refugee camp with its porridge, potatoes and bread.

Later, as an immigrant high-school girl in Canada, I felt my deficiencies keenly:

I couldn't speak English, I couldn't hit a baseball and I didn't fit in socially. I felt too impoverished even to make friends.

I carried this inhibiting mentality into adulthood until I realized the meaning of God's grace: that Christ Jesus became poor so that I might become rich in Him. As I studied the promises of grace in the Bible, I began to see that God's blessings, although undeserved, were for me, too. Over time, I exchanged my "have-not" attitude for grace-glasses and I began to see the riches scattered throughout each day: pine branches laden with glistening snow; hot cups of tea shared with a friend; reading a good book by the fireplace; an amaryllis in bloom on my windowsill. Graced by Christ's presence and His bounty, I no longer felt like an outsider yearning to be let in, but like a child who's discovered that the whole candy store belongs to her Father.

To celebrate my discovery, I gave myself a middle name: Grace. **G**reat **R**iches **A**t **C**hrist's **E**xpense. Every time I write it, it's a reminder to me and a witness to the world of the generous nature of God, Who desires to lavish His favors upon us if we will but believe and receive them.

Father, thank You for this grace-day. Help me, like Jesus, to be a grace-giver.　　　　　　　　　　　　—*HELEN GRACE LESCHEID*

That I may publish with the voice of thanksgiving, and tell of all thy wondrous works.　　　　　　—*PSALM 26:7*

Every year at Thanksgiving, my mother's boss gave her a large turkey, so she was the one who brought the cooked bird for assorted aunts, uncles and cousins to devour at Aunt Paul's house in Brooklyn.

When we arrived at Aunt Paul's on Thanksgiving afternoon, Mom would join the crowd of cooks in the kitchen, while my cousins and I filled up on candies, nuts and other goodies. It was a wonder that we had any appetite left for dinner.

But appetite I certainly had, for turkey and the trimmings. Especially the trimmings, including Mom's wonderful stuffing, made of corn flakes, olives, celery, onions, butter and spices from a recipe she claimed to have found on a corn flakes box. I would have been happy to eat turkey and Mom's stuffing every day for a solid month. But no one else felt that way. So one year the aunts got together, and Mom was instructed to deliver the uncooked turkey to Aunt Frieda or Aunt Naomi. They could be trusted to stuff it safely, if heavily, with bread and liver stuffing. The family was delivered from corn flakes stuffing. And I was heartbroken.

Mom's been gone for twenty years now, but I still long for her stuffing. Every time I tell people about it, though, I'm greeted with puzzlement, or even revulsion. My wife Julia had the same reaction when I told her the story. That's why I was surprised, a few weeks before Thanksgiving last year, to see an e-mail on our computer from a cereal company. Not knowing for whom it was intended, I opened it. "Dear Mrs. Attaway," it read. "We have checked our records from the 1950s, but we were unable to locate the stuffing recipe you requested."

Julia stuffed our turkey with challah bread and chestnuts. She loves it, and it's delicious. But to me, knowing she had been willing to forego it so I could again taste my mother's stuffing, it was as sweet as manna from heaven.

Dear Lord, thank You for food, family and friends, for blessings without number. And especially for the memory of my mother's stuffing. —*ANDREW ATTAWAY*

FRI

29

In that day shall there be upon the bells of the horses, holiness unto the Lord; and the pots in the Lord's house shall be like the bowls before the altar.

—*ZECHARIAH 14:20*

"I don't think I could do it," a friend commented. "I'd be too embarrassed to ask people for money."

"It doesn't embarrass me," I answered, "because I'm not begging, but giving others the opportunity to support one of my favorite ministries." I'd always wanted to do more than write a check to the Salvation Army, and this year I found the time to lend a hand. My job was tending one of their famous red kettles and ringing a bell outside a supermarket. I served four hours once a week from before Thanksgiving to Christmas.

Hundreds of people dropped gifts into my kettle, for which I usually responded, "Thank you. Merry Christmas and God bless you." And I got to answer many questions about the Salvation Army's mission—helping in emergencies around the world, feeding the hungry, sheltering the homeless, and providing services for the abused, ill, lonely, poor and imprisoned—all in the name of Christ.

I also got a history lesson from Salvation Army employees. I knew that William Booth was the inspiring founder of the Salvation Army, but not that he began his ministry by feeding soup to the poor out of an iron kettle on the streets of London. It was a San Francisco follower of Booth's, however, who first used a kettle to collect money. In 1891, Captain Joseph McFee, wanting to provide Christmas dinner for the area's poor, set out a pot at the Market Street ferryboat landing, and passengers willingly contributed. Today, people all over the world place donations for people in need in cauldrons marked with the long-used motto "Sharing Is Caring."

Once, when I was young, I marched in Uncle Sam's Army. Now

356 · NOVEMBER 2002

I'm too old for military duty, but just the right age to help the needy. And, God willing, I'll be back at the same station next year, unapologetically ringing a bell for the Army that serves them.

> Teach us, Lord, that
> In stooping to ease another's plight,
> We all stand taller in Your sight.

—*FRED BAUER*

30

And he took the children in his arms, put his hands on them and blessed them. —*MARK 10:16 (NIV)*

The theater was packed with squirming, fidgety and chattering children. My husband and I should have realized that seeing an animated film on a Saturday afternoon might mean that we'd be surrounded by little ones. "Do you want to leave?" I asked. "We still have time to go to another movie."

"No, let's stay. Maybe they'll quiet down," Roy replied.

I wasn't so sure. I'd had an exhausting week at work. School had just started, Open House was near and I was still trying to learn all my students' names. *I came here to relax, not to be around noisy kids,* I thought.

I watched a little boy run up and down the aisle, wriggling to get out of his father's grasp. I shook my head. I was definitely not used to children this young anymore. My youngest was seventeen; I taught history to eighteen-year-olds. We had no grandchildren yet. I felt like we were in a foreign country.

The film started and, amazingly, the children stopped squirming and fidgeting and settled down to watch. Every now and then I'd hear a child whisper loudly, "Daddy, what was that?" or "Mommy, did you see that?" The preshow chaos turned into ninety minutes of giggles, spontaneous applause and peels of laughter. I caught myself laughing loudly right along with the children.

I left the theater feeling rejuvenated. The film had been funny and entertaining, but it was the presence of the children that really lifted my spirit. My grandmother used to say that being in the presence of a child is like sitting with the angels. So until the time is right for grandchildren, I guess I'll be going back to the matinee.

Thank You, Lord, for the laughter of children.

—*MELODY BONNETTE*

My Days of Prayer

1 _____

2 _____

3 _____

4 _____

5 _____

6 _____

7 _____

8 _____

9 _____

10 _____

11 _____

12 _____

13 _____

14 _____

15 _____

16 _____

17 _____

18 _____

19 _____

20 _____

21 _____

22 _____

23 _____

24 _____

25 _____

26 _____

27 _____

28 _____

29 _____

30 _____

December

Ye are no more strangers and foreigners,
but fellow-citizens with the saints, and
of the household of God.

—Ephesians 2:19

S	M	T	W	T	F	S
1	2	3	4	5	6	7
8	9	10	11	12	13	14
15	16	17	18	19	20	21
22	23	24	25	26	27	28
29	30	31				

A TIME FOR GIVING

Christmas is a time for giving and receiving gifts. But in the busyness of the season, it's sometimes too easy to lose sight of the reason for our giving—the wonderful gift God has given us in Christ. This Advent and Christmas, Rick Hamlin shares the Christmases in his own life that have helped him understand the meaning of our Christmas gifts.

—THE EDITORS

SUN

1

First Sunday in Advent

They presented unto him gifts; gold, and frankincense, and myrrh.

—MATTHEW 2:11

The anxiety begins just after Thanksgiving, about the time all the stores put up their Christmas decorations and the first Christmas cards arrive. I start asking myself, *What will I get Carol for Christmas?*

Let me make something clear here: We're not big spenders at Christmas. It's not the small box from Tiffany's or the big one from Saks that she would like or I would consider. The commercialism of the season appalls me. That said, I'm a late convert to gift-giving. The joke goes around the office, "So, Rick, what are you going to get Carol? Another frying pan? A pot holder?" One of my best friends once bought his wife a new hubcap for Christmas. A hubcap! She wasn't exactly thrilled.

What both my friend and I have learned is that a gift is only right when it shows how much you've thought about the recipient and consider what really pleases her. So at Christmastime I go into places I know nothing about: a store that only sells soap, a hand-thrown pottery shop, a boutique filled with beautiful scarves. I cringe when a salesperson discovers my ignorance. But that's part of the process— learning about things my wife likes.

You might say it's the thought that counts. I'd go further than that. The wise men traveled hundreds of miles to give the Christ Child gold, frankincense and myrrh. I take a subway, a bus and clippings of ideas I've culled throughout the year. The right present has a long journey attached to it. One that puts you in the ranks of those who realized that a little child could be an uncrowned king.

Lord, give me patience and understanding at this gift-giving time of year. —*RICK HAMLIN*

THE PRAYER THAT IS ALWAYS NEW

MON
2   Our Father . . . thine is the kingdom, *and the power*, and
      the glory. . . .   —*MATTHEW 6:9, 13*

As I concluded the Lord's Prayer this morning, the word *power* took me back to an afternoon in England.

The Community of St. Clare is a contemplative order in Oxfordshire whose chief work is prayer. I'd been corresponding with one of the nuns, but Sister Susan Elizabeth Leslie and I had never met. So when my husband and I went to England in August 2000, the convent was the first place we went. How, I wanted to ask this veteran prayer warrior, could she spend her days interceding for human griefs and still keep her own spirit unburdened?

Sister Susan met us in the doorway of the convent, a merry-eyed woman in a black habit, who enfolded us each in a bear hug. The joy in her face told me she'd learned how to lift the weight of the world's woes without breaking under it.

Yes, she said over mugs of tea in the kitchen, the requests for prayer that poured in day after day were wrenching. A crippled child, an estranged son, abuse, divorce, death, homelessness. "What a privilege it is to be allowed to carry these burdens!"

"But how do you keep them from crushing you?" I asked.

"Oh," she said, with a smile that made little of the labor of prayer, "we let Jesus carry the heavy end."

It was His power, not the sisters' own, she reminded me, that brought about the wonderful answers to prayer that also arrived with the daily mail. "When we remember how weak we are, the job gets easy."

Jesus, to Whom the Father gave the griefs of the whole world and the power to redeem them—the secret of the life of prayer.

Our Father, as I lift my prayers to You today and always, let me trust the heavy end to the power that never fails.

—*ELIZABETH SHERRILL*

TUE	Then saith he unto them, My soul is exceeding sorrow-

TUE
3

Then saith he unto them, My soul is exceeding sorrow- ful, even unto death: tarry ye here, and watch with me.
—*MATTHEW 26:38*

As I sit at my desk on a crisp, cold December morning, the sun is rising, burning away the mist of dawn. This is the first hard frost we've experienced in temperate central Texas.

Outside my study window is a large tree newly devoid of leaves. Perched on a limb are four small birds, young mourning doves, I think. Somehow I have awakened before the birds, a novelty for me, and I sit quietly watching them.

I don't remember ever seeing birds asleep before. The doves are tightly huddled together, a thin hoarfrost coating their wings. With heads and beaks tucked into the down of their puffed breasts, they lean against each other for warmth. Though they will compete for seeds at my bird feeder in a few short minutes, for now they are one nestled body, a unity of feathered warmth and safety.

For a moment I reflect on the breakfast I just shared with a friend at a local diner. Arriving in darkness, we sat together, heads bowed in conversation, quietly sipping cup after cup of steaming coffee. He had recently lost a child, a wound that will never fully heal. We needed each other's warmth in the midst of a world that can freeze your heart to stone. As the sun rose, we parted. But for a little while, we were one, held close by concern and love for each other.

Sometimes the best thing I can give is my presence. It's not important that I find words to say; wisdom is often found in shared silence. Before dawn in the winter, it's enough to feel the warmth.

Dear God, I do not have much to give, little wisdom to impart. But I can give my presence to those who are cold and alone. Help me to do so today. Amen. —*SCOTT WALKER*

WED
4

For the things which are seen are temporal; but the things which are not seen are eternal. —*II CORINTHIANS 4:18*

Our children Ross and Maria love to watch home videos of when they were very small. Maria, now seven, especially enjoys seeing her twelve-year-old brother as a baby. They laugh at how he waddles around and falls down or chases the dog and squeals. The last one they watched, of Ross's third birthday, is a favorite.

"There's the big bug," Ross said, watching himself unwrap the year's best-loved gift. "I wonder what happened to that thing?" While the kids laughed about a boy who'd wanted a big, ugly bug for his birthday, I felt a little sad. All he'd wanted that year was a toy bug, and we searched everywhere for the right one. But now, like so many other things that once mattered so much, it had disappeared, either given away or settled to the bottom of a junk drawer.

"All those treasures forgotten," I said to my husband Paul, thinking that I don't need more reminders that my kids are growing up.

"Yeah," he said, "but remember how much that ugly bug meant to him? That's what matters."

As I thought about it, I understood. No matter how much our children may have loved a special toy or stuffed animal, those things simply don't last. The gifts that matter are the ones we can't hold in our hands. Love, trust, joy, faith, self-confidence—the gifts I have prayed for God to help me impart to my children—those are the things Ross and Maria hold on to tightly and take with them everywhere they go.

Now when I find those former treasures in the junk drawer, they serve as gentle reminders that while my children are growing up, they're not abandoning their real treasures, but taking along the best of all we've given them.

Teach me, God, to enjoy the passage of time as another of Your eternal gifts. —*GINA BRIDGEMAN*

364 · DECEMBER 2002

THU 5

If possible, so far as it depends upon you, live peaceably with all. —*ROMANS 12:18 (RSV)*

For seventeen years I was a union member, and in 1965, I was the first African American chosen for promotion to management in my company. I was involved in labor disputes, and I worked hard to prove that the choice had been a wise one.

In 1969, the union went on strike for 102 days. I was forced to cross the picket line, but I was torn. Our supervisor warned us to form car pools and ride together if we were going to cross the picket line. When I saw the men who worked for me on the line, I waved to them, but they turned away.

Then came a zero-degree morning when our plumbing malfunctioned. There were no replacement parts in the house, so I had to head for the hardware store, go home to fix the plumbing and drive to work alone. As I neared the plant, I saw the pickets circling like angry bees. Fear raced through me, and my hands turned cold. I closed my eyes and said, "Lord, help me to keep my peace. Help me to remain silent no matter what."

The picket captain glared, and the pickets circled faster as I approached the line. What would they do? The picket captain stepped back and nodded to the pickets. All at once they removed their hats, placed them over their hearts and sang, "We shall overcome. We shall overcome someday!" They parted and I drove through, thanking God with each hum of the car motor. They had gotten even, but their humor had saved the day.

Dear Lord, thank You for the goodwill that keeps the peace when our differences are serious and our tempers rise.

—*OSCAR GREENE*

FRI 6

Ye shall have a song, as in the night when a holy solemnity is kept. . . . —*ISAIAH 30:29*

When I was a new widow back in the eighties, I often awakened in the middle of the night, unable to go back to sleep. Then I discovered Moody Broadcasting's all-night program, *Songs in the Night*. Feeling as though I were the only person in the world lying awake, I listened intently, holding my radio. Sometimes I even sang along—inevitably off-key.

Now I'm remarried, but I've begun to awaken again some nights around three. I know that music at 3:00 A.M. would disturb my husband Gene, so the radio is out. Recently, though, Jimmy Bamberg, a friend who is a minister of music, told a small group of us, "If you wake up and can't sleep, sing to the Lord. He'll love it! It doesn't matter if you can't sing. He just longs to hear from you."

Even from a tone-deaf person? I wondered.

"Go a step further," Jimmy continued with a smile. "Make up your own songs for Him."

The next time I awakened at 3:00 A.M., I discovered that I could sing in my heart or my spirit without making a sound. Singing silently, I could even sing on key! *"Holy Spirit, Thou art welcomed in this place. . . ." "Lord, I lift Your name on high. . . ." "Savior, like a shepherd lead us. . . ."*

I began to anticipate my bouts of insomnia. During one session, a few words I'd never heard before slipped into my thoughts. I sang them without making a sound:

> *How can it be that Calvary was just for me?*
> *I didn't know You loved me so, You had to go*
> *Endure the shame and bear the pain to clear my name!*
> *At last I see that Calvary was just for me.*

Oh, Father, maybe at last I belong to a choir! Maybe there are lots of us singing You songs in the night.   —*MARION BOND WEST*

SAT	"Even to your old age I am He, and to gray hairs I will
7	carry you. . . . I will carry and will save."

—*ISAIAH 46:4 (RSV)*

It was my wife Julee's turn to buy the dog food, but I was sorry I hadn't taken the chore on myself. When I came in, breathless and sweaty, from my Saturday morning double workout at the gym, I saw two bags sitting on the kitchen counter: one "active" formula for Marty, our frenetic Lab, and another marked "senior." The vet had been suggesting senior dog food for our nine-year-old cocker spaniel Sally Browne.

Call it denial, but I refuse to think of Sally as aged. Dogs are around too short a time as it is. To me, Sally would always be a puppy.

I looked at her now, sitting patiently at my feet, waiting for me to dole out lunch. Not so long ago, she'd have been leaping and barking hysterically. I looked into her expectant eyes, still bright but beginning to be eclipsed by cataracts. It was harder for her to get up in the morning these days. Once, a little rattle of the treat can and she'd be out of bed like a shot. She rarely chases after Marty anymore when we play ball, content to sit quietly and give an occasional bark of encouragement, or maybe caution, almost dignified in her bearing.

I filled her bowl and set it on the floor. Sally indiscriminately gobbled up her food, oblivious to its geriatric formulation or its implications. *I bet you think I'm not quite as much fun as I used to be either, girl?* I mused. Maybe that was the point. We were both getting older. Sally, at least, was handling it gracefully. Was I? Or was I projecting my own fears and denial on to her?

Well, perhaps just a little. And maybe I should slow down a little at the gym. After all, in dog years I'd be about two hundred. I could just relax, enjoy being a little older and a little wiser, and a little more dignified, like Sally Browne.

Lord, help me to resist the foolishness that I can stay young forever, and let me not forget that as I grow older I grow closer to You.

—*EDWARD GRINNAN*

A TIME FOR GIVING

SUN	*Second Sunday in Advent*
8	**Every man shall give as he is able....**

—*DEUTERONOMY 16:17*

My mother-in-law was an alcoholic. She loved her grandchildren, but her addiction made it hard to express that love. Every fall, for a dozen years, we went through the same heartbreaking scenario. In September she would call Carol and ask, "What can I get the boys for Christmas?" Carol gave her mother lists of things the boys liked and sent her samples from catalogs. She went so far as to suggest an 800 number to call with the exact item number of the Lego or Playmobil toy or football jersey.

Finally, about a week before Christmas we would get another call. "I'm so sorry," my mother-in-law would say, "I just haven't had time to get anything for the boys. Let me send you a check. You get something nice and put my name on it." Because we wanted the boys to know their grandmother loved them, we obliged. But it was painful.

Then one summer she did something very brave. She went into a rehab program and stopped drinking. That fall there were no calls from my mother-in-law about what the boys wanted for Christmas. No matter. We were busy rejoicing in her recovery. What we didn't know is that her body hadn't really recovered from the ravages of her disease. After only three months of sobriety, she had a massive stroke and died two days before Thanksgiving.

That December was a sad one, full of regrets. What if she had stopped drinking earlier? What if we had urged her into rehab years ago? We asked ourselves a thousand "what ifs?" Then, before Christmas, a big package arrived in the mail. Carol looked quizzically at the return address. It wasn't from a mail-order company she knew, and a phone call to California assured her that it hadn't come from my family. When she opened the box she discovered a present for the boys, ordered by their grandmother. The one present my mother-in-law had bought before she died. A gift that meant more than words can tell.

Lord, help me give in return for all I have received.
—*RICK HAMLIN*

MON
9

There are different kinds of gifts, but the same Spirit.
—*I CORINTHIANS 12:4 (NIV)*

My family never had a real Christmas tree, though I asked for one every year. "Too many pine needles in the carpet," Dad would say. "The sap will get everywhere. The tree will turn brown and the cats will go crazy," my mother would add. As a result, we've had many unusual Christmas trees through the years.

One of my favorites was Grandma Ellen's antique aluminum tree, with its rotating colored spotlight. Our holiday guests would comment on the shiny silver tree, looking rather puzzled, and ask Mom where she found it. The year we moved, there wasn't room to set up a tree amid all the boxes, so we decorated my dollhouse's Christmas tree. Finally, last year, just as I put the final glass ball on our almost-normal-looking artificial tree, it tilted wildly. I caught it just in time, star a-wobbling, and Mom came to the rescue, sticking the base in a large bucket of kitty litter. "Watch out for that last ornament," she said. "It's a doozy." But every year, no matter what the tree looked like, we would gather around it and sing and celebrate Christ's birth.

This Christmas was the first on my own, and I vowed I would have a real tree—a normal tree. My roommate and I piled into her family's station wagon and went to look for the perfect tree. She, a wise and experienced tree-huntress, found it immediately. Once we had it decorated, I sat back and inhaled the pine scent. *At last! A real Christmas tree,* I thought. I enjoyed finally having a living room that looked just like a Christmas card. But something was missing. Without my family there to celebrate, it also *felt* like a Christmas card—flat.

Then I visited my parents' home for the holidays, and my Christmas spirit was renewed. Their tree this year? My brother's seven-and-a-half-foot-tall contrabass saxophone strung with twinkle-lights and festooned with candy canes and Christmas cards. My brother played carols on the Christmas tree, Dad and I worked on the lights, and Mom fed us cookies and found more ornaments. It might have looked strange from the window, but it was our family tradition, and it was good to be home.

Father in heaven, thank You for reminding me that, under any circumstances, celebrating Your Son always creates a picture-perfect scene.
                                                        —KJERSTIN EASTON

TUE
10

And she brought forth her firstborn son, and wrapped him in swaddling clothes, and laid him in a manger; because there was no room for them in the inn.
                                                        —LUKE 2:7

There's a woman who stands at the corner of a busy intersection during the morning rush hour. She holds a sign that reads, HOMELESS. PLEASE HELP. GOD BLESS.

I've steered my beat-up minivan through that intersection enough times to have a nodding acquaintance with her. Sometimes I give her change, sometimes not.

On this particular day, I had nine-year-old Faith with me. As we came to the woman's corner, I rolled down my window and dropped some change in her paper cup.

"Who's that pretty girl with you?" the woman said, smiling at Faith.

"That's my daughter," I said. Faith was half-smiling; mostly she looked scared.

"Oooh, she's a good one. You take care of her, you hear?"

"Yes, ma'am," I said. Mercifully, the light turned green, and I drove on.

"Who was that?" Faith asked.

"A woman I see at the corner most mornings. Did you see her sign?"

Oh, yes, she had, because now Faith was crying very, very hard.

I offered some kind of lame reassurance—some clichés about social service agencies and temporary homelessness.

"I just feel so sad," Faith said through her tears.

Even in its dilapidated condition, my minivan was probably more comfortable than wherever that woman had slept last night. My van had heat. It could keep the wind at bay. My car was better than her home, and my nine-year-old saw through my trite little pep talk to that awful, singular truth.

So, Faith, here's my answer to your unasked question, in the form of an unasked-for prayer:

Lord, some things are unspeakably sad. I try to help in some small way, but sometimes it just gets to me. Help me to remember the good that can come out of the sad: People who have no place to stay—only a manger—make it work, somehow, and they grow and live and absolutely change the world forever, and ever. Amen.

—*MARK COLLINS*

WED
11

"Would it be any gain to him [God] if you were perfect?"
—*JOB 22:3 (TLB)*

I was playing darts recently with my friend Joe. We took a couple of practice turns and then started a game. After the first set of darts, I began to add up my score. "Oh, no," Joe interrupted, "the only thing that counts is the bull's-eye." I pointed out that other parts of the target had numerical value, too. But Joe persisted. "If you hit a bull's-eye, you win. Nothing else matters."

Seems a bit silly, doesn't it? But I realized during the next week that I, too, was afflicted with "only the bull's-eye matters" mentality. If I couldn't walk five days a week, why bother with three? If my stitches were going to be uneven, why even try to learn to knit? If I couldn't sing a solo, why take part in the Christmas cantata? But if close doesn't count, then why do they number all those circles on targets?

So I'm trying harder to find joy in *striving* for perfection, not just in *attaining* it. To enjoy the effort, not just the successes. It's going to take some practice for me, but I'm determined not to give up.

Maybe I'll call Joe and we'll play a game of darts.

Only You, God, are perfect. Thank You for not keeping score of the many times I miss the mark.
—*MARY LOU CARNEY*

THU
12

I pray that out of his glorious riches he may strengthen you with power through his Spirit in your inner being, so that Christ may dwell in your hearts through faith....
—*EPHESIANS 3:16–17 (NIV)*

One late November day my neighbor Jean and I spotted each other outside raking leaves and headed across our yards to chat. Jean mentioned that last weekend she had attended her niece's baptism. "You know," she confided, "it was weird being at church, hearing those prayers, when we don't believe in God."

I couldn't think what to say. She talked on about how she and her husband long ago decided that God doesn't exist. Although they both grew up in churchgoing families, they are raising their young children with no faith. I listened with a heavy heart as she described their family life, empty of all that anchors mine—no church, no knowledge of God's love, no prayer, not even grace before meals.

A few days later my daughter Elizabeth burst in the door from kindergarten, excited about the Christmas season. Suddenly, her voice filled with concern. "Mom, Cathy says her family doesn't celebrate Christmas! They don't believe in God. How can that be?"

Before I could find an answer, she looked up from her cookies and milk and declared with determination, "Mom, I'm going to pray for Cathy to get to know Jesus. I'm really going to pray that this Christmas she learns that God loves her, and she'll believe in God!" She paused right then to pray, and every mealtime or bedtime the next few weeks we prayed for Cathy's family and for Jean's family.

We continued our prayers during the year, and we've seen encouraging signs of God at work in Cathy and in our neighbors. And a new family tradition was born: Each Advent we make a concentrated effort to pray for those who need to know God. Perhaps you'd like to think about the people in your life and join us.

Dear God, please shine Your light in hearts that do not yet know You. Please come to those who have not yet received or found You.
—MARY BROWN

FRI
13

"I will never fail you nor forsake you."
—HEBREWS 13:5 (RSV)

For several months I've felt far away from God, even though I've been praying more than ever. At times it feels as if He's actually working against me. Oddly enough, it doesn't bother me too much because of something I learned from flying airplanes.

My flight instructor always emphasized the importance of trusting my instruments, instead of "flying by the seat of the pants." In one lesson, he put a hood over my head so that I could see only the instrument panel. He then put the plane through a series of maneuvers. "Now," he said, "straighten 'er out." Honestly, I thought the plane *was* straight and level, but the gauges said I was in a thirty-degree bank and a ten-degree dive.

Then there was the time I was headed west to Kansas City in a thick summer haze. Or so I thought. When I peeked at my compasses, they both said, "You are headed for New York City at one hundred and twenty miles an hour."

What is true of flying is true of living. Feelings deceive. Perceptions get scrambled by fatigue. Judgment is contaminated by lusts and wishful thinking. Politicians and advertisers confuse me. My peers do things I question, and I begin to doubt myself.

So last night I opened my Bible and checked my instruments. I came across a passage that said, " 'I will never fail you nor forsake you.' Hence we can confidently say, 'The Lord is my helper, I will not be afraid; what can man do to me?' " (Hebrews 13:5-6, RSV).

That's good enough for me. I trust my Compass, and I'll try to keep on trusting God, even when I don't "feel" Him.

Father, I'm glad my faith is built on something more stable and reliable than emotions. Help me trust Your Word more than my nervous system. —*DANIEL SCHANTZ*

READER'S ROOM

On Thanksgiving Day 1994, my Aunt Peg passed away after a long illness. She had been a strong Christian influence in my life and one of God's encouragers to me. She was one of the people I would talk to about the decisions I was faced with, and whom I would ask to lift me up in prayer.

That year, Aunt Peg had left each member of the family a copy of *Daily Guideposts* as a Christmas present. That started a tradition for me, and through many of the decisions I've struggled with, *Daily Guideposts* has been an encouragement.

Although *Daily Guideposts* cannot take the place of my Aunt Peg, I believe she left me a new friend and encourager. Her wise counsel still comes to me through the experiences of the *Daily Guideposts* writers.

Thank You, God, for the gift of Aunt Peg and the gift of *Daily Guideposts*. —*C. DONN TIPTON, SARASOTA, FLORIDA*

SAT

14

God has given each of us the ability to do certain things well. . . . —*ROMANS 12:6 (TLB)*

Come mid-December, for as long as my children can remember, Aunt Bess has spent nearly a week, early morning till late night, stirring and fixing, shaping and baking cookies and other scrumptious Christmas treats: butter tarts, fudge balls, spritzes, jumbles, shortbread, lemon bars and—one of our favorites—caramel pecan popcorn. Those of us who manage to finagle a trip to her kitchen sit there munching, our cheeks puffed out like hamsters, eyes blinking with culinary bliss.

"Now you just get your hands out of that bowl," she'll snap. "I know you—you take more than your share of the pecans, so's that popcorn looks real skimpy!"

Every year, Aunt Bess says with absolute finality, emphasized by a stubborn glint in her flashing green eyes, "I am *not* doing this again. Y'all hear! For sure, I am *not* doing it again." She seals this pact with herself by brushing back whisps of tawny red hair, kicking off her shoes and sitting down with a tall glass of peach iced tea.

But year after year, just days before Christmas, she comes calling with enormous trays tied with puffy green bows, the cookies carefully arranged to radiate like the rays of the sun from a center pyramid of mouth-watering fudge. She won't taste even one cookie. "No—they are for *you*! Now serve me some tea!"

Christmas week, right on cue, Aunt Bess gives us what no one else can: the gift of herself, hours of time, with love stirred in, year after year after year.

Thank You, Lord, for the gifts You have given me that I may give to others. And when I think I have nothing to give, remind me that the greatest gift I can give is the year-round gift of a praying heart.
                                        —*FAY ANGUS*

A TIME FOR GIVING

SUN
15

Third Sunday in Advent
Behold, the angel of the Lord appeared unto him in a dream, saying, Joseph, thou son of David, fear not to take unto thee Mary thy wife. . . .   —*MATTHEW 1:20*

Carol was six months pregnant with our first child that December, the year we saw Advent through new eyes.

When I sat in the pew and heard Bible lessons about waiting, I wondered what our child would be like. What sort of gifts would he have? Who would he take after in our family? As an expectant father I had my own set of worries: Would I be able to make enough to support a child? Would I be patient enough as a father? What if I had a kid who wanted to play catch every night? I was terrible at baseball.

After the service people would smile at Carol and say to me, "Aren't you excited about having a baby?" Scared to death was more like it. Then, one Sunday, the lesson was about Joseph and how he was ready to walk away from Mary when he discovered she was pregnant until an angel in a dream reassured him, "Fear not." The rest he had to take on trust. The trip to Bethlehem, the visits from wise men and shepherds, the hurried escape to Egypt—the Christmas story wouldn't have happened if Joseph hadn't trusted God.

So I promised I would trust God.

When William was born, I managed to find the energy to get up in the middle of the night when I had to, and in those first few years of parenthood we were always able to pay the bills. When he grew old enough to want to throw a ball after school, I learned how to throw one, too. Now as he enters his fourteenth year, I confess I have a whole new set of worries. What if he falls in with the wrong set of kids in high school? What if I can't afford college? What if he does poorly on his entrance exams? Then I remember: "Fear not." It's a gift I could use every Advent.

Thank You, God, for the gift of faith.

—*RICK HAMLIN*

MON

16   Thanks be unto God for his unspeakable gift.

—*II CORINTHIANS 9:15*

It was very difficult for me to find the Christmas spirit this year. The stark images of hatred, war and poverty I'd experienced in Africa made the commercialized American celebration seem trivial.

The worst moment came when a friend asked me to play Santa Claus at a party his two little girls were giving. "We put on this party every year and have Santa come and tell the story of Jesus," my friend pleaded. "It's the only chance many of these children and their families have to hear about the real meaning of Christmas."

That noble purpose did little to reduce the embarrassment I felt as I walked to their door dressed in a red suit and a phony white beard. But then the door opened, cries of "Santa's here!" filled the house, and forty kids all wanted to sit on my lap at once. When they quieted down, I told them that Santa brings presents because God gave us a very special present on the very first Christmas. Jesus came to bring love, hope and peace on earth, goodwill to men.

I thought I was doing pretty well until one pint-sized skeptic asked, "Is that really true, Santa?"

Suddenly, his question became my question. *What happened to peace on earth in all those places where suffering is so terrible?* As a moment's hesitation gripped me, I looked into the children's expectant eyes and saw the answer. If we could teach our children to understand fully the truth of Christmas, they would make a difference all over the world.

So I said, "It's the truest story in the whole world. Santa gives presents because Jesus came, and I want you to do the same. Give your mom and dad a hug, do something nice for your little brother or sister and, after you open your toys on Christmas, go to your closet and pick out a toy to give to some little boy or girl who didn't get any this year."

My little inquisitor thought about it for a minute and then replied with great solemnity, "Yes, sir, Santa."

Lord, help me to do my part to make the peace and love of Your kingdom present right here and right now. —*ERIC FELLMAN*

THE PRACTICE OF PRAYER

TUE
17

The Fruits of Prayer
The peace of God, which passeth all understanding, shall keep your hearts. . . .   —*PHILIPPIANS 4:7*

I've already checked most of the names off of my Christmas list. Beyond our immediate family, there are several friends at church, a few neighbors, the postman, our garbage men, all accounted for. Yet this year's best present is one I've given myself. I hope that you have received this gift in equal measure: the faithful practice of prayer and the one-on-one relationship with God that follows. We wrap most gifts in paper and tie them with ribbons, but this new habit of prayer can't be contained. It spills out into everything we do.

Any day now, you may find yourself on a Christmas mission to a nearby mall. Driving along, you'll experience a heightened awareness of God's presence. You'll turn off the radio and talk to Him, and it will feel as natural to you as picking up the phone and calling a friend. Maybe you'll even belt out a carol or two. And then you'll tell Him how good it is that He thought of Christmas, and you'll thank Him for the people you love and the joy ahead. You know you can tell Him anything, and when you park the car, if you have a sudden urge to dance through the empty parking garage, you'll dance. You'll give gladly to the bell ringer at the entrance to the mall. And when you walk down the crowded aisles of the stores, you won't think of what you don't have or what you can't afford; you'll think instead of the people all around you, these beautiful human beings with tell-tale traces of God our Father on their faces.

A sense of pure peace will descend around you—"the peace that passes understanding" that you've heard about in Sunday morning sermons—and you'll laugh deeply, then walk on with a smile, praying for the same peace for each person you meet. Prayer has truly changed your life.

Merry Christmas!

You give us peace, Father, and joy and love. Thank You.

—PAM KIDD

18

God loves a cheerful giver.   *—II CORINTHIANS 9:7 (NIV)*

Shortly before Christmas that year, Helen phoned. There was an urgent tone in her voice. "Can you folks come to see me tonight?"

"Is something wrong?" I'm afraid there may have been a hint of resentment in my voice. Helen was an elderly widow, housebound and lonely, whose one delight was to round up visitors for cake and coffee. At the moment, however, I was immersed in Christmas preparations for the family and had no intention of taking time to visit.

"No," she admitted, "there's nothing wrong."

"Then we'll come when we can," I told her.

She phoned the next day, and the next. And, finally, she used the one ploy on my husband Leo that never failed. "If you don't come, I guess I'll just have to throw out this big chocolate cake."

"We'll be there!" I heard him say.

We had scarcely brushed the snow from our boots on her welcome mat when Helen thrust an awkwardly wrapped Christmas present toward me. "I'm sorry I couldn't wrap it any better," she said. "The arthritis in my hands, you know." Sitting down in her big easy chair, she leaned forward on her cane, watching me closely as I opened the parcel.

My response was utter surprise and delight. A cookie jar in the shape of a big white porcelain kitten! "How did you know that I've wanted an unusual cookie jar for years and years! Did Leo tell you?"

"No, he never said a word. I guess Somebody bigger whispered it in my ear. I could hardly wait to give it to you. That's why I kept calling every day."

Helen laughed heartily when I confessed my impatience with her. Then, still beaming with joy, she got up and hobbled out to the kitchen to prepare the cake and coffee.

She's gone now, but the kitten cookie jar sits in a place of honor in my kitchen. It not only reminds me of Helen, but of a God so close that He can "whisper in your ear" the perfect present for a friend.

Father, this Christmas, attune me to those things that would bring genuine joy to others, and help me deliver them with cheer and goodwill. *—ALMA BARKMAN*

THU

19

Grace be with you, mercy, and peace, from God the Father, and from the Lord Jesus Christ, the Son of the Father, in truth and love. *—II JOHN 3*

It is Christmas Eve, and five of us file into church. My daughter Charlotte says in her practical way, "Take the end seat, Mom. You'll be the only person who has to get up." The others nod their heads in agreement. This is the place I would wish to be on Christmas Eve, but I am honest enough to realize that my family is here mainly to please me. For a moment, I wonder deep down whether I should have left them to their DVDs, VCRs, PCs and other acronymic pursuits. Never mind, it *is* Christmas.

The overflowing church is glowing with candles and flowers. The handbell choir is ethereal and the children's choir irresistible. The organ fills the air with the sound of trumpets, and we launch into "Hark, the Herald Angels Sing."

When the appropriate moment comes, I rise to go forward for Communion. It's a big church, so I have a ways to walk. I'm almost at the chancel steps when I feel a touch on my arm. I turn in surprise. There, right behind me, is Daniel, my baby, but now a grown man a head taller than I. We kneel together at the altar rail and receive the bread and the wine. As we rise and move to the side aisle, Daniel puts his arm around me and whispers, "I love you, Mom."

No moment in any church at any time was more holy—or more joyous.

Thank You, Lord, for the touch of grace, sent without fanfare and received with gladness. *—BRIGITTE WEEKS*

FRI

20   Blessed are the merciful: for they shall obtain mercy.
—MATTHEW 5:7

The other night my wife Pam and I attended a dinner here in Savannah, Georgia, for friends and veterans of our Eighth Air Force. We'll remember it for a long time because sitting side by side were Charles Brown, an Eighth Air Force bomber pilot during World War II, and a German fighter ace named Franz Stigler.

On December 20, 1943, on a raid over Bremen, Brown's B-17 was shot out of formation and, badly crippled, plunged almost to the ground with the tail gunner dead and four other crew members wounded. It was trying to limp home when Stigler in his Me-109 spotted it. The German fighter closed in, but when he saw that the bomber was helpless, he elected not to shoot it down. He tried to persuade Brown with gestures to land his plane and surrender, but when Brown ignored him and kept going toward England, Stigler finally just saluted him and let the Americans go. Many years later, a grateful Brown located Stigler, who was living in Canada, and the two became friends. Now, amazingly, here they were together.

In my own days with the Air Force, I wrote many stories about combat in the skies, and there was plenty of endurance and heroism to write about. But I never encountered an episode in which the dominant element was compassion. The Americans didn't want to publicize this story during the war, and on the other side, Stigler told us that night that he might have faced a firing squad if his Nazi superiors had learned what he had done.

In 1943, Franz Stigler's decision to spare his enemies' lives was a tiny pinpoint of light in the darkness of war. And today, after all these years, it is glowing still.

Father, teach us, in the words of the old spiritual, "to study war no more."
                                                    —*ARTHUR GORDON*

SAT
21

My voice shalt thou hear in the morning, O Lord; in the morning will I direct my prayer unto thee. . . .
                                                    —*PSALM 5:3*

"Ten o'clock and I'm already behind," I muttered. Not a single gift wrapped; cookies for the neighbors just a lump of dough in the fridge; too late to send cards and letters to arrive on time. And this afternoon at four, my first granddaughter would be baptized. I was hosting the dinner afterward and had only just slid the ham into the oven. The casseroles weren't made, the house was a mess—and the kids were still sleeping!

"Up and at 'em, boys!" I rolled Tom and Greg, both sixteen, out of bed. The racket woke up Trina, thirteen, who had given her bed to company and slept on the sofa. Over cheerless bowls of cereal, I recruited my morning help.

"Tom, you can vacuum the living room. Trina, please unload the dishwasher. Greg, you can empty the trash and clean the small bathroom. I'll peel the potatoes for the casserole."

My children wearily gathered dishes and slouched off to their assignments. Satisfied that we were proceeding on schedule—*my* schedule—I returned to the potatoes.

A few minutes later Greg reappeared. *Maybe he can't find the sponges or cleanser.*

"Mom, what's the date today?"

"December twenty-first. Why?"

He showed me the spiral-bound desk calendar with a prayer and inspirational thought for each day that we kept by the bathroom sink.

"Oh, I just need to fix this. It says August seventeenth." He turned the pages, grinned and sauntered off, reading the prayer for the day.

I paused in my potato peeling and considered the bathroom . . . toothpaste splatters on the mirror, wet towels on the floor, clutter on the counter. And the first thing Greg focused on was a *calendar*?

And a prayer—a perfect way to start a messy project and a busy morning!

Thank You, Lord, for children who remind me of what is truly important. —*GAIL THORELL SCHILLING*

A TIME FOR GIVING

SUN
22

Fourth Sunday in Advent
He that giveth, let him do it with simplicity. . . .
—*ROMANS 12:8*

It used to make me so frustrated. As a child, whenever I asked my dad what he wanted for Christmas, he said, "Just give me a hug and a kiss." And when I asked my mom, she said, "Why don't you make something nice?" It didn't seem fair because when I went to the stores clutching the few quarters in my pocket, I could spot all sorts of things that looked a lot nicer than any picture I could draw. I admired a vase all shiny and pink, and there was a framed picture of a forest with trees that, unlike mine, really looked like trees. And if I had enough money I could buy my dad something really useful, like socks or a new belt.

Alas, I didn't have enough money, so instead I made a dog out of clay that could work as a paperweight, and another year I made a tissue-paper collage of angels singing "Hark, the Harold Angels Sing!" (spelled just like that) and crafted an ornament out of papier-mâché that had a miniature Nativity scene inside. These I dispensed with hugs and kisses, but I couldn't help thinking those items from Woolworth's would have been more impressive gifts. Maybe when I was older I could buy Mom a scarf and Dad some handkerchiefs.

Since then I've been able to afford belts and handkerchiefs and scarves and the proverbial new tie that my father always requests, but when I go home at Christmastime it's the handmade gifts that are still displayed: the "Harold Angels" singing, the papier-mâché Nativity scene, the paperweight pooch. It's not just that they came from the heart, but they also came from the hand. That's why I tell my own children, "Make me something nice." A gift of creativity is meant to be shared. It can last forever.

Thank You, God, for the gift of creativity. Help me share mine.

—*RICK HAMLIN*

FOR EVERY SEASON

MON	
23	My days have passed, my plans are shattered, and so are the desires of my heart. —*JOB 17:11 (NIV)*

Here it is, the first day of winter, the day with the least amount of sunlight in the year. As a child, I often pondered how the shortest day of the year and the longest could be only three days apart, for Christmas Eve was surely the longest, most excruciatingly slow day I ever knew. Would I or wouldn't I get that most coveted gift? For most of my childhood that special gift did, indeed, appear on schedule.

Now, as an adult and a praying Christian, I know that when I deeply desire something, it is usually my very earthbound self that wants it. But sometimes the desire is there because my loving heavenly Father puts it there. One March, when I saw a house in Virginia for sale on the Internet, I immediately knew I had to go see it. When I walked in the door, it was as if warm arms opened to me and said, "Welcome! You are home!"

Then came the "longest day," the wondering wait. It seemed impossible for us to purchase the house. I prayed all through the next year that the Lord would put to rest the recurring desire in my heart. It would dim from time to time, but never fade. The house went under contract to another buyer. The deal fell through. Then the house was taken off the market, and I relinquished the dream. My husband Bill and I made new commitments to our church and to our community in Maryland.

Then, suddenly, Christmas came—only it came on Good Friday, when neighbors called and asked if we would be willing to let visiting friends look at our house. It was not—had never been—on the market. But it had been renovated, so we tidied up a bit and said, "Sure!" To our astonishment, in twenty-four hours our house was sold.

A week later, Bill and I sat in a restaurant in New Market, Virginia, as our realtor filled out the contract for us to purchase what was now so obviously a gift from the Lord, planned far ahead, given in His way and time.

Dear Lord, help me to rest in the plans and places You have for me in this new season. —*ROBERTA ROGERS*

A TIME FOR GIVING

TUE
24

Christmas Eve

For unto you is born this day in the city of David a Saviour, which is Christ the Lord.   —*LUKE 2:11*

The gifts began arriving on the first of December. Little things that appeared in unexpected places. A Christmas ornament, small Nativity figures, candy, oranges, a short booklet of devotions. And with each gift came a note, sometimes with a Bible verse, sometimes with a typed word of appreciation, and always signed, "Your Christmas elf." My friends Jim and Wendy didn't know who the giver was, but soon their children were peeking out of windows, hoping to catch the elf in the act.

It would have been easy to find the elf if he or she left the gifts at the front door in broad daylight, but this elf was secretive. The first arrived in the still of the night to be discovered with the morning paper. Others appeared on a desk at the office, on a car seat in the church parking lot and even in a nursery-school cubby. "Who do you think it is?" they asked each other every evening. It had to be someone who knew them well enough to put the gifts where Jim and Wendy would discover them. And it was someone who appreciated all Jim and Wendy had done for their community.

Finally, on Christmas Eve, Wendy figured it out. She found her clue in the minister's message: "Christmas arrives in the still of the night with little warning. A stable, a small provincial town, an undistinguished couple. The greatest gift of all hardly called any attention to itself. God's own Son born in a manger."

"It was you!" Wendy exclaimed to her pastor after the service.

"How'd you guess?" he responded, as he sheepishly fished the final present out of his pocket, a figure of the Baby Jesus in the manger for the Nativity.

"Your sermon," she said. "It gave you away." But as she thought about it, his giving in secret *was* the sermon. "Merry Christmas," she said.

"Merry Christmas!"

Father, prepare my heart for the gift of Your Son. —*RICK HAMLIN*

A TIME FOR GIVING

WED
25

Christmas Day

And the shepherds returned, glorifying and praising God for all the things that they had heard and seen. . . .

—*LUKE 2:20*

There comes that time on Christmas Day when all the gifts are given, brunch is consumed, the guests have left and there is nothing more to unwrap. In my family we go to our little stockpile of presents and take a mental inventory. *Who was it that gave me that nice blue sweater? That tie will go well with my brown suit. I must tell my parents that the towels are perfect.* The boys inspect their books while Carol fantasizes about a recipe in her new cookbook. Then as I put on the CD I was given, Timothy looks up from his new board game. "Dad, do you want to play Risk?" he asks.

"Sure," I say. William joins us for the game, as Carol settles in with the novel that her sister sent. We roll the dice and are soon absorbed in strategizing over the territory on the Risk board. As I listen to the music and hear Carol turn pages in her book (and listen to Timothy agonize over how to conquer Asia), I think about how grateful I am to have this family, to have this apartment for a home, to have friends and family who care enough about me to send gifts.

It's not the presents that have made this a fine Christmas Day. It's this time together, lounging on a winter's afternoon. It's being able to savor it without having to rush to the office or read my e-mail. It's hearing Carol chuckle in the armchair and watching the boys beat their dear old dad. Sure enough, busyness will return, but this day has reminded me of all the things I have that can't be wrapped up. That feels like my holiday gift. And for that I thank the good Lord.

Dear God, let me savor every day as though it were Christmas.
—RICK HAMLIN

THU
26
We will remember the name of the Lord our God.
—PSALM 20:7

I used to feel sad the day after Christmas, when the festive decorations abruptly disappeared from the stores and the radio stations quit playing Christmas carols, because I wasn't ready to pack Christmas away. So I created a few of my own post-Christmas traditions to make the celebration linger longer.

I started by identifying the parts of Christmas I like best. I like our tree, but hardly have time to appreciate it before Christmas. So now, in the days right after Christmas, I get up early in the morning when the house is quiet and dark, turn on the tree lights and snuggle down on the couch with a cup of coffee. I savor the silence and solitude, a snippet of time when I'm not distracted by my list of before-Christmas responsibilities.

I love the music, so I continue playing my favorite carols until I've had my fill, which is at least through New Year's and sometimes whenever it snows, even in February. Who says we have to stop playing the music we like, especially when the words are true all year 'round?

I like the memories we make, so I take lots of pictures and add them to the Christmas photo book that I keep on a shelf near my desk. That way, I can reach for it whenever I want a "Christmas moment," even if it's July.

My favorite part is the love that flows from the celebration of Jesus' birthday, so after Christmas, I pick out one decoration that I won't pack away. Last year, I chose a leaded-glass manger scene, which I put on the kitchen windowsill. When the morning light shines through it, I remember that Jesus' love is alive and real today and every day.

Lord, help me make the Christmas celebration linger longer in my home and in my heart.
—CAROL KUYKENDALL

FRI

27

And that every tongue should confess that Jesus Christ is Lord, to the glory of God the Father.

—PHILIPPIANS 2:11

The hotel on my block, I'm sad to say, has taken on airs. There's a new canopy leading to the street, and blue window awnings, and elegantly uniformed doormen to maneuver the revolving door. The lobby, which has been expanded and paneled in oak and filled with luxurious furniture, is not the only thing that has been expanded: The rates have taken on airs, too. But, for me, the sorriest thing is that, alas, they've gotten rid of the coffee shop and the jumbled crew who ran it.

It had the look of the thirties, with art for sale on the walls and, at this time of year, a pathetic little Christmas tree at the entrance. I had my dinner there once, maybe twice, a week, and I was often the only customer. I'd sit at the counter and they'd bring me dinner without asking: a cup of the soup *du jour* (the split pea was my favorite); toast, buttered; ham steak (usually) with potato and vegetable; rice pudding for dessert.

The boss was Greek, and as a rule he had his dinner and left for home, which meant that either Rumi or Roni, who exchanged shifts, was in charge. They were Muslim brothers, and they came from Pakistan. Eugene, the short-order cook from South Carolina, never took a vacation, and the smiling busboy, Rene, from Puerto Rico, spoke no English and resolutely spurned my efforts to teach him. Since I came from Kentucky, we were all regular New Yorkers.

I remembered each of them at Christmas with a little money tucked inside a Guideposts greeting card that carried the story of the birth of Jesus according to Luke. This to Rumi and Roni was nice, but to them Jesus was just a prophet. Every year I'd talk to them about Christ, the reason for the holiday, while they told me about the month of Ramadan, their days of atonement.

Well, nothing will be the same this year. I do wonder if Rumi and Roni will think again of Jesus, Jesus the Messiah.

I miss them all, Father. Please watch over them with special care.

—VAN VARNER

SAT
28
What is man that thou art mindful of him, and the son of man that thou dost care for him? —*PSALM 8:4 (RSV)*

Growing up, I often heard the story of my mother's lost Shirley Temple doll. Given to her during the Depression, it was much treasured. But her grandmother wouldn't let her play with it lest she break it. When I was in high school I decided to find my mother another Shirley Temple doll. But in every antique shop I searched over the years I invariably found nothing and left with my name on yet another list. Then one summer day, just a few years ago, I got a call.

"Don't sell it!" I shouted into the phone, yanking off my gardening gloves and kicking off my boots. "I'll be right up!"

The doll was in mint condition. I bought her on the spot. But during the long months between summer and Christmas, when I would surprise my mother, I did some research. To my dismay I discovered that there were over fifty different kinds of Shirley Temple dolls! What was the chance I'd found the right one?

I don't know who was more surprised when Christmas finally rolled around, my mother or I. She stared down into the opened box. "My doll!" she whispered, and I nearly burst into tears. I'd found the right doll after all.

"But, oh . . ." my mother said all of a sudden, hands poised frozen over the doll, "I might break her." After sixty years, my mother was still hearing her grandmother's admonition.

A few moments went by. Then my mother very gently lifted Shirley Temple from the nested box, and carefully let us all "play" with her.

Thank You, Lord, for caring about the little things, like finding the right lost childhood doll. —*BRENDA WILBEE*

SUN
29
A word spoken in due season, how good is it!
—*PROVERBS 15:23*

You can scarcely open a magazine or a paper these days without spotting cartoons showing fat little New Year cherubs wearing wraparound scarves emblazoned with "2003." Every year these cute infants remind me that many babies will be born during the upcoming months and it makes me wonder what kind of citizens they'll become.

I was born into a loving, secure family, yet as I grew up, I was painfully shy elsewhere. Doubtless I'd still be shy had it not been for certain people. People like Mrs. Blair, who noticed this backward child had no part in the Sunday-school Christmas play and told the chairman, "Isabel can be another angel in the heavenly host." That's how I got to wear a tinsel halo and a well-worn sheet for a gown and appear onstage with the other kids.

Then there was Mr. Smith, who bent down to my eight-year-old height and said, "With those big brown eyes, you'll have lots of boyfriends some day." His words stayed tattooed on my memory when classmates were swooning over each other and I was still hoping one of the "neat" guys would notice me. Ten years passed before one did, but Mr. Smith's words kept me from despair.

And "Miss Lulu," the college Latin teacher. I detested Latin, but it was a required course for a journalism degree. One day after I'd translated a difficult passage, Miss Lulu said, "That was excellent!" I ended the course with an "A" because of three words from her.

So as a new year begins, I remember—and am thankful for—all the Mrs. Blairs, Mr. Smiths and Miss Lulus who saw potential and knew how to instill confidence and self-esteem in a young and immature girl.

Dear Lord, You've told us You have given Your children different talents, but all of us have one ability in common: We can encourage one another.
                                                              —*ISABEL WOLSELEY*

MON

30

Jesus . . . departed again into a mountain himself alone.
                                                              —*JOHN 6:15*

In this small mountain village where my husband Robert and I live, many of the residents are summer people. Our good friends the Kramers left for California at the end of September, the Actons left for Arizona a couple of weeks ago, and one by one many of our other neighbors are disappearing, their summer places tightly closed for the winter. The village lake is dotted with skaters now, while in summer its banks were lined with people fishing, families picnicking and frequent weddings held in the gazebo on an island at its center. The main street looks practically deserted, with only two small businesses still open.

Though we miss our friends and the neighborhood get-togethers that are part of summer life here, we're not lonely. We keep in touch with our families and close friends by phone or e-mail, and God's beautiful creation keeps us company. This morning, I can gaze out at Mount Dewey through the window by my desk and enjoy its snow-covered, Christmas-card pines. Large, fluffy snowflakes are slowly, gently falling, as I sit inside our cozy house. Robert is baking bread and the scent surrounds me like a hug. Tonight we'll sit by the fire and read to each other. Then we'll end the day with our nightly prayer time by candlelight.

When I'm lonely, O God, I'll find gratitude in simple things, reach out to distant loved ones and spend time with You in prayer.

—*MARILYN MORGAN KING*

TUE
31

In whom we have redemption through his blood, the forgiveness of sins, according to the riches of his grace.

—*EPHESIANS 1:7*

As I stand on the threshold of another year, I wonder about the strength of my commitment to the faith to which I so vocally pledge allegiance. Am I guilty of more lip service than heart service? Maybe you sometimes share the same feeling, especially when falling short of Christ's high calling. I don't know about you, but I miss the mark every day—often by a mile. The only thing that keeps me from giving up is His promise always to forgive me and love me even when I foul up egregiously. That's grace.

I'm not sure I completely understand grace. I know it's an unmerited gift from God, but I believe it requires a childlike faith really to grasp its scope, its full dimension, its measureless majesty—a faith like that of a five-year-old girl named Jeanie whom I recently heard about. Her baby brother Philip had developed a rare blood disease and needed a blood transfusion to stay alive. Only Jeanie's blood was a match.

When asked if she would give her blood to save her brother, Jeanie at first looked puzzled. Her parents patiently explained the procedure and the importance of her gift. Finally, Jeanie seemed to understand and agreed. The next day at the hospital, the little girl lay down on a cot and watched intently as a nurse placed a needle in her arm and turned on the blood-extracting pump. Jeanie's mother sat at her daughter's side, holding her hand reassuringly. After a few minutes, Jeanie motioned to her mother to come closer. She had a question: "When," she whispered into her mother's ear, "am I going to die?"

Obviously she had misunderstood the nature of the procedure, but her commitment to her brother was total. She was ready to give him anything he needed, including her life. In the year ahead, we need to remember that that is exactly what Christ did for you and me, and act accordingly.

> Remind us, God, when we forget:
> Love so amazing, so divine—
> so deep, so wide, so tall,
> Demands from each of us
> our life, our soul, our all.

—*FRED BAUER*

My Days of Prayer

1 _____

_____

2 _____

_____

3 _____

_____

4 _____

_____

5 _____

6 _____

7 _____

8 _____

9 _____

10 _____

11 _____

12 _____

13 _____

14 _____

15 _____

16 _____

17 _____

18 _____

19 _____

20 _____

21 _____

22 _____

23 _____

24 _____

25 _____

26 _____

27 _____

28 _____

29 _____

30 _____

31 _____

FELLOWSHIP CORNER

It's been quite a year in the lives of our fifty-eight *Daily Guideposts* contributors, full of sunshine, but with a shadow or two as well. And they're waiting to tell you all about it in the Fellowship Corner, our annual family get-together. We've got a chair waiting for you, so pour yourself a cup of tea or a glass of milk and get ready for a good, old-fashioned visit, as our contributors share some of things they've discovered as members of our family of prayer.

LIBBIE ADAMS of Richlands, North Carolina, says, "As always, this past year brought changes. I went back to school to become a certified phlebotomist and then took a job at a gynecologist's office in Jacksonville. I enjoyed the work and loved the patients. But in the fall our son Greg and his wife Kim had their first baby, and suddenly all my well-laid plans for work fell by the wayside. One look at Lindsay and I knew I wanted to stay at home with her when Kim returned to her job as a nurse. It has been a happy decision for all of us, and my hours with Lindsay bring tremendous joy and wonder to my life. I have learned anew how incredible it is to witness the miracles of a growing baby as they unfold one after the other. My husband Larry and I still keep busy with our doghouses and storage buildings business, but we find time to camp, too, and spent the month of July in Berne, Indiana, in our travel trailer. We have family there who always greet us with open arms and shower us with such love. Every year, we find that our time with them is more precious. I also find that God is ever faithful, and I give thanks as I constantly see His hand at work in my life and in the lives of those I love."

"Although I used to belong to a large church, I mostly prayed alone," reports MARCI ALBORGHETTI, now more settled in her Stonington, Connecticut, home after living in the capital city Hartford for two decades. "Now I find myself more often praying with others who are part of my everyday life." Many joint prayers resulted from her *Daily Guideposts, 2000* series "Unlooked-for Blessings" on living with the gifts of cancer. "I received about one hundred responses to the series, and this correspondence truly was a form of prayer. I also pray more with people in my daily life: my companion and best friend Charlie, friends in crisis, Guideposts writers and editors with whom I correspond, my parents. So 'Praying Together' is really an appropriate theme for me this year!" Marci is thrilled with her book *The Miracle of the Myrrh*, a children's and family story about what might have happened to the Magi's three gifts to Christ. She also authored a series of devotionals called *Practical Meditations for the Compassionate Christian*. Book signings, readings and appearances also have taught her to "pray together" . . . sometimes with people she's never met before.

FAY ANGUS writes, "After a lifetime of phone calls, letters, and much begging and pleading, my cousin from Australia finally came to visit me in Sierra Madre, California. It was the first time we had met, and it turned out to be an astonishing confirmation of family traits that had us, like two genetic peas in a pod, liking the same things, saying the same things and suffering through bouts of bronchitis that we found had plagued both of us for as long as we could remember. Our fathers were born in China, children of missionaries who preached the good news of the gospel of Christ. Trenna, who has never been to China, speaks better Chinese than I, who was raised in Shanghai. She said grace in Mandarin with singsong inflections, ate with chopsticks and shocked the grandchildren into wide-eyed awe as she burped the loud *chi-boala* (satisfied) of thanks after a meal . . . all this with an Australian accent! We did the length and breadth of California in a whirl to remember. Still pleasantly exhausted, I will never quite recover and, frankly, I don't want to. *G'day!*"

"Changes and challenges have marked our year," writes *Daily Guideposts* editor ANDREW ATTAWAY of New York, New York. "At home, Elizabeth, John and Mary always seem to be growing out of their shoes and clothes and into new interests, new skills and new ways of relating to Julia and me and to one another. And then there's the new baby expected at the time *Daily Guideposts, 2002* goes to print in July

2001—just who will he or she be? At work, it's a constant challenge to improve our ministry to our whole *Daily Guideposts* family. All of these challenges are opportunities for prayer. But my deepest experience of praying together this year was at the celebration of the life of Mary Jane Clark in Durango, Colorado. Mary Jane's courage and faith, and the love showered on her by family and friends, spoke eloquently of the God Who transfigures our pain with the power of His Resurrection."

"It's hard to describe what life is like around our house," writes JULIA ATTAWAY of New York, New York. "Though it's somewhat akin to a great fireworks display: loud, colorful, exciting and sometimes mind-boggling." With a new baby expected in the summer of 2001 and John officially entering the Attaway homeschool in the fall, the semi-orchestrated chaos is likely to continue. "Praying together with three small children is always a challenge," Julia comments, "but it is a challenge that always bears fruit. I can't imagine life without my kids or life without prayer. It is prayer that holds us together, because it is through Christ that we are united."

KAREN BARBER of Alpharetta, Georgia, writes, "Since Gordon and I have three sons, people used to ask if we would try again for a girl. I always said, 'No, I'll just wait for a daughter-in-law.' Finally, this year, Leah joined our family by marrying our oldest son Jeff, who is in the Air Force in Colorado Springs, Colorado. We took a hilarious family trip through a wild animal park where huge water buffalo, zebras and even giraffes stuck their enormous heads right through our car window to be fed. I was impressed how Leah held her own against a buffalo with a tongue as long as her forearm, so I guess she'll do just fine with her new brothers-in-law Chris and John. I also finished a book entitled *Surprised by Prayer* [available from Guideposts Books]. It was challenging to make prayer a priority in my busy life, so I decided to start an experiment to record one hundred answers to prayer. Fifty-one days later when I wrote down the hundredth answer, I realized that looking for answers to prayer had changed me. During the course of the experiment, I became more systematic in praying and expanded my definition of the word *answer.* In the past, I had assumed getting an answer meant God would resolve my problems, but now I realize that getting an answer also means getting a response. Many of the one hundred 'answers' were actually new insights, directions and thoughts on how to handle my life better."

"The highlight of the past year was a family reunion, the first time in eleven years that our family had all been together," writes ALMA BARKMAN of Winnipeg, Manitoba, Canada. "In anticipation, my husband Leo and I hauled extra bedding out of closets, converted the rec room into sleeping quarters and stocked the freezers with home baking. Soon there were sixteen of us crowded around the picnic tables in our carport, eating, visiting, laughing and slapping mosquitoes. Over the next five days, many special moments were captured on film— Grandpa and little Ellis enjoying a big slice of watermelon, three giggling granddaughters showing off their nail polish, two young grandsons pestering their teenage cousins, four siblings hamming it up for the camera. Looking at the collage I made featuring the best candid shots of each family member, I also see how God has faithfully answered our prayers on their behalf. No parent could ask for more."

"The very day I heard that the theme for this year's *Daily Guideposts* would be 'Praying Together,' reports FRED BAUER of State College, Pennsylvania, and Englewood Beach, Florida, "I received a letter from a woman who had been diagnosed with non-Hodgkin's lymphoma, the cancer for which I was successfully treated a couple of years before. 'I prayed for you when I heard of your problem,' she wrote. 'Now I need your prayers.' I answered immediately that I would add her name to my prayer list. I can't count the number of times I've traded prayers with people in the worldwide *Daily Guideposts* family." Speaking of family, Fred and his wife Shirley are on the threshold of a golden wedding anniversary. To celebrate, they may take the whole family on another excursion like the one they made recently to Germany. "There were eleven of us on the trip," Fred says. "Children and mates and grandchildren—the latter of which are growing up. Jessica is heading off to college at Penn State, and her brother and sister are fast approaching the next phase of their education. Our four kids and three grandkids are a never-ending source of joy to Shirley and me. God is good."

"It's been a really full year for my husband Keith and me, all of it tied to communities of people to whom we are not related, but with whom we often share prayers," says RHODA BLECKER of Los Angeles, California. "We stay in close touch with the monastery, exchanging messages and gifts of love all year long. Our congregation, *Shir Ami*, which means 'the People who Sing,' started to talk about moving out of space we've shared with another congregation for three years and seeking our own facility, though it's still in the talking stage. Our *havurah* [a group of friends in the congregation] had the first of several upcoming weddings in the second generation, and we're looking forward to another in June. Oh, and we had a granddaughter born in January, two weeks before the birth of a great-granddaughter, which was kind of stunning for people who never actually had any children of their own. It's strange not to be actually tied by blood to our grandchildren, but then we are tied by love and prayers to them, and to all the other people who are so important in our lives."

A recent commitment this year reflects the *Daily Guideposts, 2002* theme "Praying Together" for MELODY BONNETTE of Mandeville, Louisiana. "I accepted an invitation to meet with fellow teachers before school to pray together. What a difference it has made! The peace and joy I receive from my prayer time with my colleagues is indeed contagious. My students even behave better!" Praying *with* others has inspired Melody to pray *for* others more often. "As a volunteer at the National D-Day Museum in New Orleans, I meet lots of people, especially veterans. When they arrive for the tour, I always find a moment to silently pray for this extraordinary generation of men and women who served us so courageously." Big news on the home front, too. Daughter Misty and her husband Indelethio are expecting their first baby. "My husband Roy and I are thrilled at the prospect of our first grandchild!" writes Melody. Other family members are doing well. Kristen is a student at the University of New Orleans and Christopher is now a firefighter. Kevin, a high school senior, is counting the days until graduation.

"Our calendar is always packed," says GINA BRIDGEMAN of Scottsdale, Arizona, "and what's on the schedule is bound to involve either school, church, Scouts or music." This year Gina and her husband Paul gave in to the inevitable and turned their living room into a music room. Both Ross, 12, a seventh-grader, and Maria, 7, a first-grader, play the piano and electronic keyboard. Ross plays trombone in his school's jazz band, and Paul plays the guitar. "I sing along," Gina says, "but mainly I'm their best audience." Highlights of the past year: Paul won two theater awards for scenery he designed at Grand Canyon University; Gina began teaching Maria's Sunday school class; Paul became an assistant scoutmaster for Ross's Boy Scout troop, and the two went on a weeklong camping trip to Yellowstone National Park. "I enjoy our busy life," Gina says, "but my favorite moment of the day comes when I'm tucking in Maria at night and she asks with her little voice, 'Will you pray with me, Mommy?' Sharing our desires and our thanks together has a power that makes me feel as though I'm kneeling right at the feet of the Lord."

"We have just returned from our annual family retreat at a nearby Romanian Orthodox monastery," says MARY BROWN of East Lansing, Michigan. "Mark, 8, said the best part was making a snow fort in the woods, Elizabeth, 13, loved the nuns' delicious cooking, while my husband Alex and I treasured the rest and quiet. Yet it is the time we spent praying together that refreshed and nourished us best. As we prayed in the chapel services and absorbed the monastery atmosphere of unceasing prayer, we came home renewed in our commitment to carve out times to pray more together. It's a challenge! Besides meals and bedtime, whether we're driving down the road or chatting at the kitchen table, when something comes up—like when Alex and I try to make a difficult decision or when Elizabeth told us a school friend was diagnosed with leukemia—we're trying to pause right then and ask God for help. In between volleyball and basketball practices, piano and flute lessons, concerts and games, the oil that keeps our relationships running more smoothly and gives Alex and I more patience to parent a turbulent teen and a feisty 8-year-old is our prayer together."

"How could so many eventful things be packed into one year?" asks MARY LOU CARNEY of Chesterton, Indiana. This year daughter Amy Jo was married—in between thunderstorms—at a flower-decked park. Then she and her new husband Kirk embarked on a honeymoon cruise of the Mediterranean. Amy continues her law school studies at Valparaiso University. Son Brett kept those power nailers going as he built two more duplexes. He also bought his first snowboard. "I just know his guardian angel has gray hair!" jokes Mary Lou. Husband Gary was busy with his excavation business, but he and Mary Lou managed a few weekend getaways, including one to New York City. This year also saw the closing of *Guideposts for Kids,* the children's magazine that Mary Lou edited for more than eleven years. "It was sad to see it go, but we've been able to launch two great new Web sites: www.gp4k.com for kids and www.gp4t.com for teens. What a challenge—and privilege—to utilize technology to minister to today's youth!" Prayer, too, has become more important in Mary Lou's life. This year she participated in her first spiritual retreat, attending a prayer seminar at St. Meinrad Archabbey. "My mother had a battered, framed sign that always hung in our home. It said, 'Prayer changes things.' And in this year of change and challenge, I've found it's true. Prayer changes me!"

MARY JANE CLARK and her husband Harry of Durango, Colorado, have embarked on a new and unknown phase of their journey together. After two years of battling cancer, they are recognizing that, barring divine intervention, Mary Jane has begun saying her final good-byes to their six children, her parents and siblings, and many friends. "My energy is diminishing every day, but I would like to thank the *Daily Guideposts* readers who have taken the time to write to me. It means a lot. My best to all who are praying for us here." The Clarks' almost twelve years of married life together have been wonderfully exciting and adventurous, spanning the globe from Kenya to a small town in Colorado.

"While the way ahead is often frightening and uncertain," says Mary Jane, "we are confident that God's presence goes with us."

On April 1, 2001, we received an e-mail from Harry Clark. Here is an excerpt:

The most extraordinary person I have ever known went home last night, Saturday, March 31, 2001, at 11:35. She left us quietly, as [her son] Ethan held her hand. . . . The depth of our sorrow is a reflection of the happiness she brought to our life, the joy and exuberance we shared.

MARK COLLINS, father, environmentalist and teacher, is known as "the guy with the car" in his Pittsburgh, Pennsylvania, neighborhood. His otherwise unremarkable 1990 Nissan Stanza has an unusual paint job. "I wanted to cover up the rust spots with a little paint," Mark says, "but the spot primer made it look worse." Mark remembered that his wife Sandee had once painted their closet door using nothing but kids' handprints. So he gathered up Faith, 10, Hope, 9, and Grace, 5, and *violà!* The Stanza was soon covered in multicolored handprints. "A lot of heads turn," Mark says, laughing. The real lesson, however, came from his eldest daughter. "You let us be creative," Faith said. "You showed us how it's okay to be yourself. That's so cool." Mark shakes his head at her words. "That wasn't my intent," he says. "I was trying to cover up rust, and she gleaned some insight that I never saw. Maybe that's how Faith works sometimes. You're just trying to do your job, to survive another day, and then this life-lesson—made out of your own hands—shows up right in front of your eyes."

BRIAN DOYLE is the editor of *Portland Magazine* at the University of Portland in Oregon. Brian's essays have appeared in *The Best American Essays* anthologies of 1998 and 1999, and in the *Best Spiritual Writing* anthologies of 1999 and 2001. He, his wife and their three children pray together by seeking hilarity, small birds, gingersnaps, and the bones of fish on the vast and teeming shore. The spiritual highlight of their week is a Sunday dinner filled with pasta, hubbub, chaos, laughter and a sense that a family webbed with love is ridiculously larger than its constituent parts.

"I never cease to be amazed at the blessings God sends my way!" writes DRUE DUKE of Sheffield, Alabama. "Maybe some people would say they are 'just happenings.' But I feel His love when they come. For instance, today I phoned the drugstore for a refill on a quite expensive prescription I have to take each day. When the young man delivered it, I found the cost charged was considerably less than it had been in the past. Feeling a mistake had been made, I called the druggist, who told me, 'We're just trying to save you some money.' What a blessing in my now limited income! In so many ways the blessings flow. Because my vision has prevented my driving a car for a number of years, my church recently presented me with a list of names and telephone numbers of twelve ladies on whom I can call at any time to take me anywhere I need to go. I've had to use the list, and their willing and happy accommodations are also a blessing from Him. I had dreaded facing 'special' days I always shared with my late husband Bob. But my daughter and grandchildren have made certain that some—if not all—of them are with me here at home or at my daughter's home in Huntsville on birthdays, Thanksgiving, Christmas and the like. Again, such blessings! These and the warmth of old and new friends so brighten my life that they keep me humming the beloved old hymn, 'Count your blessings, Name them one by one; Count your many blessings, See what God hath done.' "

KJERSTIN EASTON is a graduate student in electrical engineering at the California Institute of Technology in Pasadena. In her free time, she continues singing with small jazz groups on and off campus and has started taking guitar lessons. Her cats Nickel and Antimony have a new favorite sleeping spot: the fuzzy inside of her empty guitar case. Most of the time, however, she's in the lab. As part of Caltech's Collective Robotics research group, Kjerstin hopes to earn her Ph.D. "Collective robotics is an exciting research field," she says. "I work with a swarm of robots, where the individual robots' achievements build on other robots' efforts. The idea is to get the robots to complete a complex task as a group, as social animals do in nature. I've seen how this works in prayer, too. Whether through e-mail connections with far-off friends or in a small prayer circle, praying together makes an impossible load seem lighter." This year brought major challenges for Kjerstin. She was diagnosed with a chronic rheumatoid disease, and her family lost some dear friends and relatives to other illnesses. She also faced the qualifying exams for her doctoral program. She gives God and her loved ones credit, though. "Taking it to the Lord in prayer is much easier when you have friends and relatives to help you carry it there."

ERIC FELLMAN and his wife Joy live in Falls Church, Virginia, where they are very active in the National Prayer Breakfast, one great example of "praying together." In the last two years they have visited thirteen countries as part of a group of friends who visit international guests to the prayer breakfast in order to pray with those guests in their home countries for the people and needs of their regions. They have seen firsthand how prayer is a powerful force to change the hearts of people. All of this emphasis on prayer has challenged them to look more deeply into their personal prayer lives, especially as it relates to family. With two sons, Jason and Nathan, graduating from college last year and entering the job market, and another, Jonathan, trying to figure out how to focus his college career, petitions for grace and mercy come high on the list!

"Joyful, joyful! I am so grateful for my life and for all the lives that are touching mine this year," says SHARON FOSTER of Glen Burnie, Maryland. "My daughter Lanea continues her graduate school program, and my son Chase is close to entering his last year in high school. I give thanks for them continually. It has been more than a year since I heeded the call to write full-time, and I've now completed three novels: *Passing by Samaria, Ain't No River* and my latest, *Riding through Shadows* (Multnomah). The writing has made it possible to meet some of you at book signings. I am just completing my first year in a three-year discipleship program at my church. It has brought me wonderful opportunities to pray, study and experience fellowship with a small group of believers. It is a wonderful opportunity to be able to share my life and thoughts with the *Daily Guideposts* family, to be connected to a body of people committed to praying together and encouraging one another. All of your cards and e-mails have blessed me. Many of them have brought tears to my eyes. Thank you for embracing my family and me."

"My wife and I have gotten better at spontaneous praying," says DAVE FRANCO. "It doesn't matter if we are at the mall or in a restaurant or in the car. When we remember the needs of others, we just take a moment to pray together right where we are. No more, 'remember to pray for . . .' reminders from each other. It's added a dash of spontaneity to our faith. A little impulsiveness concerning our faith has come to feel rather good, actually." Dave lives with his wife, his five-year-old son and his two-year-old daughter in Solana Beach, California, having left New York City after eight years. "Who knows, maybe this coming year we can add one more spontaneous element to our faith. I'd love for our kids to grow up to be bold and impulsive about their Christian lives. Quick to love, ready to care, reflexively giving. I hope their mom and I can be good examples."

ARTHUR GORDON of Savannah, Georgia, writes, "For my last birthday, some tongue-in-cheek friend gave me a button sticker to wear: 'Over the hill is the age when Father Time catches up to Mother Nature!' There's a lot of truth in that, reflected in the number of prescriptions and doctors' visits that seem to become necessary as time goes by. A more cheerful yardstick is the appearance of yet another edition of *Daily Guideposts,* filled as always with warmth and humor and faith in the goodness of life and of people. And it's fun, once again, to be a part of it. For my wife Pam and me, travel has always been an exciting and colorful part of our lives. That, too, has been limited lately by health considerations. But still there are internal explorations to be made and new insights to be discovered right in our own backyard. Perhaps some items for future pages in *Daily Guideposts* are waiting for us there. In the meantime, we send our love."

For OSCAR GREENE of West Medford, Massachusetts, the year was a busy one. He finished his final three-year term with the Medford Cultural Council, which grants awards to local artists and performers. During Lent, he attended the four Sunday services of the University of Life. Each month he lunched with former co-workers, and later with his doctor, now retired. There were visits to Maine to attend his church choir and his Bible study outings on the beach. Oscar was asked to convene the public library's "Coffee & Books" when the leader fell ill. In August, he served as resident consultant at the sixtieth State of Maine Writers' Conference at Ocean Park. In September, Oscar and Ruby privately acknowledged their fifty-eighth wedding anniversary. On visits with his son, Oscar feels the warmth of praying together when the family joins hands and offers grace.

"For a long time," says EDWARD GRINNAN of New York, New York, "my wife Julee and I prayed to find just the right house." Last year they found it, a weekend place just off the Appalachian Trail, outside Great Barrington, Massachusetts, in the Berkshire Hills. "We'd been visiting the Berkshires for years, but this is the first house we've actually owned. Up till now, we were strictly apartment-renting urbanites." So were their prayers answered? "Yes, we are in love with the place. But that doesn't mean we stopped praying. Now we pray *for* the house . . . the leaky roof, the flooded driveway, the eaves that were torn off in a blizzard. Owning a house means Julee and I never run out of things to pray about together!"

"This year was full of prayers at the Hagerman house," writes RICHARD HAGERMAN of Wendell, Idaho. "There were prayers for inspiration as I prepared and presented sermons to some small churches whose pastors needed time for vacations and training. There were prayers for help as I planned the 'rough copy' for our church's monthly newsletter and a short meditation for our choir every Wednesday night. There were prayers for guidance as I led a devotional-writing clinic to a group of writers who named themselves WOW (Writers of the

Word). There were prayers for healing as my wife Dot had a separated little finger tendon reattached, and I had a second hip replacement. There were prayers for intercession as our granddaughters stepped into the worlds of business and college life. And there were prayers of thanks and praise as the Lord kept the promise of Psalm 91:15 (NIV): 'He will call upon me, and I will answer him.' "

"There are two times a day that we pray together as a family," says RICK HAMLIN of New York, New York. "At dinner and at bedtime. And it's funny how we'll sometimes get them confused. More than once have I wanted to start out grace by saying, 'Jesus, Tender Shepherd, hear me,' or listening to the boys say their prayers at bedtime, I've mentally thanked God for all my blessings. Dinnertime is when we give thanks, and bedtime when we ask God for protection. But there's no reason it couldn't be reversed. What I appreciate is the feeling of well-being that comes when we put ourselves in God's care. I continue teaching Timothy's Sunday school class, the fifth- and sixth-graders, and they keep me on my toes. Tim, Carol and I all sing in various choirs at church, so sometimes poor William is all alone in the pew. Tim entered sixth grade last fall, and Will is in high school. I enjoy my duties as managing editor at *Guideposts* magazine and am especially grateful for the time I pray with our readers at Monday morning prayer fellowship. My faith is continually lifted by reading the requests of those who have suffered so much more than I have and whose faith has remained constant."

"Life here in New Mexico continues to be exciting for Larry and me," writes MADGE HARRAH of Albuquerque, New Mexico. "He finally retired, but he still goes to the lab to do consulting work when he isn't gardening, flying for Civil Air Patrol or working in his home office. Meanwhile, in my office at the opposite end of the house, I write on my temperamental computer. ("Fatal Error" messages? Surely they could have named it something else, like "Non-Life-Threatening Temporary Setback.") Our children and grandchildren are doing well. They all live nearby and we often get together for family feasts. Before each of those feasts, we join hands in a circle and pray, and at those moments I feel overwhelmed with joy and gratitude for the blessings God has granted. Trips to our mountain cabin in southern Colorado also bring various members of our family together, such as when eight of us traveled there for the weekend this past summer, only to find no electricity and a freezer filled with rotten meat. The bad news: I'm the one who had to clean it up while everyone else huddled outside and gagged. The good news: After we buried the spoiled meat behind the cabin, the bears did not come and dig it up. As we head into a new year, I'm looking forward to whatever adventures lie ahead and depending on God's love to see us through."

PHYLLIS HOBE of East Greenville, Pennsylvania, writes, "During the four years my stepfather was in a nursing home, I used to bring my dogs Suzy and Tara to visit him. He had lived with us for six years and missed them very much. With the administrator's permission, I would bring the dogs in, one at a time, and visit with Dad in the reception room. They loved it, and so did he! And so did some of the other nursing home residents. Now that Dad is no longer with us, I decided to continue my visits with my dogs because they were able to bring smiles to so many faces. I connected with some pet therapy groups and I'm learning the ropes about visiting hospitals and other nursing homes. We have a little more training to do, and then some certification, but I think we'll have some very meaningful visits ahead of us."

"My life has been transformed in the past year," says BROCK KIDD, "and a lot of that change was powered by prayer. I was offered the opportunity to enter the ground floor of a start-up financial services company right here in Nashville, Tennessee. The offer was a dream come true, but I had a family now. *Should I take the chance?* At that point, prayer was practically my primary occupation, one delegated to family and friends as well. When I sensed that God was directing me toward my new employer, I felt that all those prayer partners had helped me get there. When my wife Candy and I were blessed with a beautiful baby boy named Harrison (after my grandfather), prayer took on a whole new meaning. I'm not sure I could handle the responsibility of fatherhood without the help that comes from prayer. Candy and I pray for his health, his safety and his happiness. And we're not too proud to ask for all the prayers we can get as we try to raise Harrison to be a good person. With all this change, my dependence on prayer has grown exponentially, as I learn to strike the proper balance between family and career."

PAM KIDD of Nashville, Tennessee, says, "Prayers—we don't talk enough about the ones that get answered. My daughter Keri's husband Ben Cannon graduated from dental school last June. One of Nashville's favorite dentists, Dr. John Douglas, asked Ben to join his practice. His office is a five-minute drive from our house, and Keri and Ben's first home is even closer. In addition, Keri is living out her dream as a therapist for children and adolescents. My son Brock and his wife Candy also live nearby and make sure little Harrison visits often. My husband David and I returned to Harare, Zimbabwe, along with Ben and Keri, in June. We traveled all that distance to see Joan, our 'Tea and Bread Lady,' move into a new facility, which is a sort of miracle gift from our Hillsboro Presbyterian Church family. That same generosity has allowed us to provide a salary for Joan so that she can work full-time serving the street children and AIDS orphans of Zimbabwe. Just two years earlier, I stood in downtown Harare, with my heart ripped apart, and watched this one lone saint scraping together tea and bread for hoards of hungry street children. I had nothing other than a prayer to offer: 'God help her.' I defy anyone to see this progress as anything other than answered prayer!"

MARILYN MORGAN KING and her husband Robert spent three weeks in England and Scotland, including a very inspiring pilgrimage to the Isle of Iona. *Daily Guideposts* readers were very much with them on that pilgrimage, which they've recreated for you in the special series "Island Pilgrimage." In June, they attended granddaughter Saralisa's dance recital and hosted the annual family birthday picnic in Kearney, Nebraska. They also visited Marilyn's son John, who will receive his master's degree from the University of Illinois in May. Daughter

Karen has reconnected with her high-school sweetheart, and they are developing a wonderful relationship centered in their shared Christianity. Son Paul continues to work for the *World Herald* and to be a super father to the six children who still live at home. Marilyn has recently started reading through her journals (all sixty-eight of them!), which span the past twenty-five years. "It's a fascinating and very rewarding life review!"

ROBERT KING has continued to build a life in retirement. During the past year he traveled to England and Scotland with his wife Marilyn, introducing her to some places he knew from an earlier time in his life and discovering some places he hadn't known. He returned to the college where he had previously served as dean for a ceremony honoring the president with whom he worked for seventeen years, and took the occasion to reconnect with friends from that period of his life. Robert's major accomplishment was the completion of a book, which will be published sometime next year, exploring the spiritual lives of two important religious thinkers, one Christian and the other Buddhist. The most exciting development, however, was becoming a grandfather for the first time and getting to know his lovely granddaughter Shaley as she begins to discover the world around her.

"I have ridden on the great strong wings of prayer all year," writes CAROL KNAPP from Lakeville, Minnesota. "It was prayer that gave Terry and me understanding when our daughter Kelly—wanting 'a story to tell'—eloped with Brett before the Easter wedding that was in the works! What joy to celebrate with them instead at a beautiful reception and reenactment of their vows on Easter afternoon. It is also my pleasure to pray with and for our other children. Tamara teaches a multi-handicapped classroom while raising two toddlers and expecting a third child. Phil is working to achieve excellence in bodybuilding and in Bible study—wanting to 'always be ready' to support his faith in Christ. Brenda is enjoying her senior year of nursing and falling in love with her 'dream man,' who takes her rock climbing, fishing and skiing in Alaska's outdoors. She has promised us she will not elope! Most recently, prayer enabled me to board the next plane

FELLOWSHIP CORNER • 409

to Alaska to give comfort to my dear friend Mary, whose only child was killed in a tragic accident. Prayer—to borrow a line from 'Joyful, Joyful, We Adore Thee'—allows our hearts to 'unfold like flowers before Thee,' so that God's powerful, compassionate touch reaches every hurting place."

 CAROL KUYKENDALL of Boulder, Colorado, says, "After four straight years of celebrating our children's engagements and weddings, we seem to be in a temporary lull for major family mile-stones, which is giving my husband Lynn and me the opportunity to celebrate some of the blessings we might otherwise take for granted. We celebrated good health as we stood on top of a fourteen-thousand-foot peak in the Colorado Rockies, and thirty-four years of marriage as we snooped around Santa Fe, New Mexico. And spending more time squinting at our computer screens, we also celebrated challenging jobs that help us stretch and grow. We thank God for protection from so many things that could have happened but didn't—like a near-miss car accident—and for His provision as we look forward to a once-in-a-lifetime two-week trip to Italy next year. Our grown children still live far away—in Portland, Oregon, San Francisco and San Diego, California—even though I keep praying that they'll come home one day ('home' is where your mom lives!). But in the meantime, I keep remembering what I recently heard about prayer: 'We go to God in prayer, not to get a hold of an answer, but to get a hold of God.' "

 "Praying together with two friends on a regular basis this past year has brought comfort and won-derful results," writes HELEN GRACE LESCHEID of Abbotsford, British Columbia, Canada. "I've seen each of my five grown children protected in faraway places and working hard to make a dream come true. Esther and Geoff, who have three chil-dren, are missionaries in Senegal, West Africa. David lives in Toronto, Ontario, and added a degree in medicine to his Ph.D. in molecular biology. Elizabeth and Teddy are planning a business venture, possibly in Australia. Cathy and Eric work in Toronto as an occupational therapist and financier. Jonathan and Cheryl are both

university students in Kingston, Ontario, in medicine and in education, respectively. I've also had personal dreams come true: publishing two articles in the Canadian edition of *Reader's Digest* and seeing my book *Lead, Kindly Light* into its second printing with a future German language edition."

PATRICIA LORENZ of Oak Creek, Wisconsin, writes, "The lifestyle of a single, self-employed woman in her fifties in America has to be one of the best. The freedom to work when I feel like it, to come and go and do as I please, is delicious. I travel frequently, thanks to the standby passes I get from the six airline pilot friends who use my house as their Milwaukee-area 'crash pad.' I put having adventures ahead of making lots of money as a priority in my life. Whether I'm traveling across Wisconsin in my little red car or flying to Florida to house-sit a mile from the Gulf of Mexico, each trip is an opportunity to see old friends, make new ones and get in all my prayers. After praying that my son Andrew will graduate from Arizona State University this year (and thus end sixteen straight years of having kids in college!), and for my other three children and their spouses and my five grandchildren, I start in on all my other relatives, friends and acquaintances. I love watching how the Lord answers each prayer. It's a wonderful life!'

This was a year of the Lord teaching ROBERTA MESSNER of Huntington, West Virginia, about receiving presents. "I've long loved everything about gift *giving*—the planning, the shopping, the wrapping," she says. "But when my sister bought me an antique blue graniteware salt box to add to my collection, I found myself gasping at the extravagant gift and exclaiming, 'For *me*?' " That, too, was the compelling message of Holy Week Roberta discovered anew as she was writing the series "At the Point of Our Pain" (March 23–April 1, 2002) for our readers. "I spent a lot of time in prayer asking the Lord to bring experiences to mind that would best highlight the many emotions of Holy Week," says Roberta. "And as I reflected on my life, all I could utter at His matchless Gift was, 'For *me*?' I want every *Daily Guideposts* reader to know that Christ died as if they were the only person in need of the gift of salvation."

KEITH MILLER and his wife Andrea, both writers, speakers and consultants, live in Austin, Texas. Their three daughters and their families all live in Texas. Several of their seven grandchildren are exercising their wings, preparing to leave their nests. One is already in California, and another is planning to go to college this year. The "Granny and Granddaddy Summer Camp," with the whole family for a few days each summer at a dude ranch, is the family highlight for Keith and Andrea. "I am excited about a book I am writing," Keith says. "It's a look at the New Testament message of Jesus from the point of view of what the disciples must have experienced hearing Jesus for the first time. The book will describe how God's radical command for us to love God and other people with all we are can really change our inner lives and our relationships. We are also praying that we can take people on an adventure in cyberspace to learn how to love. I am very grateful to be so excited about this work."

LINDA NEUKRUG writes, "This year, I moved—not to my beloved hometown of Brooklyn, New York, but just ten minutes from where I lived before in Walnut Creek, California. After a decade and a half here, I've still not adjusted to bank tellers knowing me and greeting me by name. I am still working part-time in a large bookstore and enjoying finding books for customers who say things like, 'I don't remember the title or the author, but it was on the radio a week ago.' I also help the events coordinator when authors come to town. I've discovered that the size of the crowd depends more on the weather or what game is on TV than the popularity of the book. I am glad to report that there were no earthquakes this year, but I've stocked up on candles in anticipation of the 'rolling blackouts.' I try to accomplish a new goal every year, and this year, I am nervously learning to drive a stick shift. I would like to thank my faithful correspondent Lorraine Sylling, whom I know only through the pages of letters, for being so upbeat and encouraging. I still believe in this quote from Eleanor Roosevelt: 'Prayer is a working instrument that does certain things, just as a pencil writes and a knife cuts.' I ask each morning, 'Please, God, help me be a better person today than I was yesterday.'"

BILLY NEWMAN, a new member of the *Daily Guideposts* family from Atlanta, Georgia, writes, "My wife Nan introduced me to *Daily Guideposts* eight years ago. Since then, these daily devotionals have been an active part of our lives. Several years ago, I felt called to help people live a life closer to God. I seriously considered going to seminary for a clerical career but eventually realized that this was not in God's plan. Slowly, I began to understand that I should fulfill this call, not by reshaping myself, but by using my God-given talents of photography and writing. This past year has been exciting and challenging. I wrote stories and captured images for various publications as a way to do God's work. Now, this edition of *Daily Guideposts* opens up another year, a year filled with new opportunities."

"I come from a family of scribblers, actors and artists," says FULTON OURSLER, Jr., editor-in-chief of *Guideposts* magazine from 1992 to 1999, founding editor of *Angels on Earth* and formerly deputy editor-in-chief of *Reader's Digest*. His articles have appeared in many magazines, including *American Heritage* and *Esquire*. His father Fulton, Sr., author of *The Greatest Story Ever Told*, also had careers as a magician, broadcaster, editor, playwright and columnist. His mother Grace Perkins Oursler was an actress and novelist, and became *Guideposts* magazine's first executive editor. His sister April Armstrong, a theologian, is the author of many books, as was his brother Will. Fulton lives in Nyack, New York. His wife Noel Nevill Oursler is past president of the Helen Hayes Performing Arts Center and currently president of Rockland Center for the Arts. They have five children: Theresa, a public-health nurse and editor of a mycological newsletter; Tony, a noted video artist; Mark, a lawyer; Carroll, a former art editor at *National Geographic;* and James, assistant to his father.

MARJORIE PARKER and her husband Joe are adjusting to an empty nest as their younger daughter Sarah adapts to her freshman year at Texas Tech. Sarah counts on her older sister Joanna, a senior at Texas A&M , for helpful advice, and Marjorie and Joe are counting on God to lead them through this new stage in their twenty-nine-year marriage. Their "nest" will be altered in another way, too: They'll move back to the country to the family ranch near Byers, Texas, where they lived for nineteen years before moving to Wichita Falls. "We've been praying together for more than a year about our upcoming move," writes Marjorie. "It's comforting to know God is in control and already has a plan for this new chapter in our lives." Marjorie is marketing two children's books and continues to write on a freelance basis, work in Bible study fellowship and teach the high school Sunday school class with Joe. She's looking forward to having more time to write and enjoy country life, and Joe is happy to have his bedtime hour back under his control and not a teenager's!

"My life is especially exciting these days," writes Guideposts chairman and co-founder RUTH STAFFORD PEALE of Pawling, New York, "because of the birth of two new great-grandchildren. Amelia Peale Berlandi was born on February 21, 2001, and Ruth Williamson Ehrhardt was born on March 27—blessed additions to the six great-grandchildren already in the Peale family! It's wonderful to welcome new babies into the family circle, and I'm very fortunate to have these two dear ones and their parents—and their grandparents!—living within close proximity of my home, so I can share in their joy. Also, my own birthdays keep adding up. I celebrated my ninety-fifth with colleagues, family and friends in New York City. I have a lot to be thankful and joyful for today and every day!"

ROBERTA ROGERS writes, "So many prayers this year! In the same month that *Is That You, Lord?*" was published, a series of miracles enabled us to buy our 'dream house' in the Shenandoah Valley. Our move weighed more than twenty thousand pounds, mostly books and paper! We love our new town of New Market, Virginia, and the people we have met here. Two months later, my husband Bill's mother, who is 94, came for a visit and decided to live with us. Then my mother, who is 92, moved from Connecticut to live eight miles from here. I have been learning the role of caretaker with much prayer. How thankful I am for the mountains that surround us—the views restore my soul daily. No daughters-in-law yet, but three of our four sons have brought home dear girls for us to meet. Tom remains in Atlanta, Georgia; Peter on Cape Cod; John near us; but David has gone to Korea for eighteen months to fly Apache helicopters. How much I appreciate the e-mails, notes and prayers from you, dear readers! Thank you."

This summer, DANIEL SCHANTZ and his wife Sharon visited Dan's parents in Elkhart, Indiana. His father Edward is a retired minister in the early stages of Alzheimer's. Virginia, mother of their six children (Dan is number two), cares for Edward at home. Sharon's mother Ruth Dale lives across town and takes care of herself. She still hangs out the laundry, walks her errands and carries on a telephone ministry of encouragement. Dan enjoys playing with his grandchildren Hannah, Rossetti, Silas and Abram. And he enjoys nurturing his garden. "The hollyhocks were gorgeous this year," he says. Dan likes to take walks in the country, where he is able to pray out loud as he walks. "Without my prayer walks, I couldn't face all the changes in my life."

"People take sabbaticals for study, travel and rest—why not one for family?" asks GAIL THORELL SCHILLING, who this year lives beside Merrymeeting Lake in New Hampshire with her daughter Trina, 15. "Since moving to Lander, Wyoming, twenty-three years ago, I've often wished that I could share Christmas with my New Hampshire relatives and Sunday dinners with my parents. My year here lets me do both. I'm also near enough to offer support as my parents reluctantly begin a move to assisted living." Though her "noncareer" move has satisfied a lot of longings, it has created as many more. "Just keeping in touch with sons Tom, 17, and Greg, 18, in Los Angeles, and daughter Tess and granddaughter Hannah back in Wyoming has caused major meltdown for my phone card. It's hard to be so far away from my children, even for just a year. I'm still trying to learn to let go and trust God to keep an eye on them—especially when the line is busy."

"I've kept a personal journal for nearly thirty years and a prayer journal for ten years," writes PENNEY SCHWAB of Copeland, Kansas. "It's a privilege and a joy to look back and see how God has answered prayer—and see how often those prayers were answered because people prayed together. The growth in service and witness of United Methodist Mexican-American Ministries, where I've worked for sixteen years, is attributable to prayers from faithful Christians. My husband Don and I continue to enjoy our grandchildren, Ryan, David, Mark, Caleb and Olivia. Don's latest home improvement project was creating a large recreation room in our basement, so the kids would have more room when they visit. I'm grateful for my family, and also for the family of *Daily Guideposts* readers. Since I wrote my first *Daily Guideposts* devotional in 1979, I've continued to be inspired and strengthened by prayers from readers."

On two recent trips to England, ELIZABETH (Tib) SHERRILL of Chappaqua, New York, had the privilege of staying at Winfield House, the American ambassador's residence in London, as a guest of the ambassador's wife Linda LeSourd Lader. Linda is the daughter of longtime *Guideposts* editor Len LeSourd. Tib says that seeing Linda, her husband Phil and their two daughters filling this important post so effectively made her think back to a years-long experience of *praying together.* "Once a week, Len, his wife Catherine Marshall, my husband John and I would meet to pray for our seven children—four of theirs and three of ours—seeing them through the crises all families know, from infancy through marriage." Tib wished Len could have lived to see his daughter in her current role, "but I know he's cheering her on from heaven," she says.

Guideposts Roving Editor and constant traveler JOHN SHERRILL used to claim he would never go on an organized tour. No more! Last February, with snow piled three feet deep in his Chappaqua, New York, driveway, John and his wife Elizabeth flew to La Paz, the southernmost tip of Mexico's Baja California. There they boarded the *Wilderness Adventurer* to go whale watching in the Sea of Cortez. "Sure enough," John reports, "in small dinghies we got so close we could almost touch these awesome mammals." But the tour also included the delights of going back to college. University professors from various fields gave lectures not only on whales, but on the history, geology and ecology of Mexico. "Does anyone," John says with a smile, "want to go on a cruise with us next winter?"

"This year I owned up to problems in my marriage," says SHARI SMYTH of Nashville, Tennessee. "When Whitney and I separated, failure hung on me like a neon light. But burning brighter were the prayers of God's people. They prayed for me when I was too down to pray for myself. They opened their arms and embraced me—and Whitney—exactly where we were. We reached out for help, and today we're back together. We love each other. Our marriage is mending. Part of the glue is the discipline of praying together every day. And what can I say of the year apart? I, in an apartment, finding a job, learning to make it on my own after thirty-two years, uncertainties swirling from all around. The first thing I now appreciate is how others manage with heavier loads than I have to carry, especially single mothers whose children are with them. The second thing is God is faithful. I didn't sink. Our four children, scattered, but connected by phone, mail and love, have been supportive. I'm proud of them all, but this year, especially Jon, who took a break from work to travel for two months in India. He and friends covered the whole continent, including hiking in the Himalayas. They're back. And so are Whitney and I. Relief and joy."

"Talk about answered prayers—ten years later," writes VAN VARNER of New York, New York. "It was exactly that many years ago that a Colombian painter friend, Antonio Acosta, died. His will stated that I should manage his exquisite, decorative, large collection. I, however, was the wrong person to handle this, with little knowledge of the highly competitive art market. I tried, unsuccessfully. I even created a twenty-four-page booklet with reproductions of selected works. No go. After ten years of having the paintings in storage, good friend Silas Mountsier suggested that I keep them at his spacious home, and that is where Bruce Pane saw them, exulted in them and arranged a huge showing where they are being offered for sale to benefit a worthy charity. Doubt? I did have some, maybe a lot. But on two matters I am confident: that Antonio's work will be seen and appreciated just as I am sure that my prayers, and those of others, have been realized. I should never give up, never."

"As I reflect on our *Daily Guideposts* theme of 'Praying Together,'" writes SCOTT WALKER of Waco, Texas, "I realize that this past year has indeed been a time of increased prayer for me and my family. My son Drew has left home for the first time to attend Furman University. Beth and I have discovered a new level and quality of prayer when, as parents, we now pray for a son who is on his own. I am increasingly aware of how important prayer is in the sustaining care and love of my family and friends. I also turned fifty years old this year, a time for personal reflection and meditation. I thank God for the marvelous gift of a half-century of life that He has given to me. And as I look toward the future, I ask God, perhaps more fervently than ever, for guidance, wisdom and the ability to make wise decisions. Without prayer, I cannot navigate the future years of my life. Finally, I am thankful for all of the *Daily Guideposts* readers whom I have been able to meet and correspond with this year. It is good to know that true family extends far beyond blood relatives. I am grateful for the bond that is created through sharing together a common devotional life by reading *Daily Guideposts*. Through this little book, thousands of people are praying for each other. This is a source of comfort and strength for me."

DOLPHUS WEARY, his wife Rose and their son Ryan live in Richland, Mississippi. Dolphus reports many exciting changes over the past two years. "Rosie and I celebrated thirty years of marriage, Danita graduated from medical school, Reggie completed his first full year living outside our home and fully employed, Ryan is in the eighth grade, and Rosie accepted the position of executive director of REAL Christian Foundation, an additional opportunity God has given us to support ministries to the rural poor in Mississippi." Dolphus was appointed by the governor of Mississippi to serve on the State Flag Commission, whose purpose was to recommend a new flag design to the legislature. The challenge of this task, as well as many others, has caused Dolphus's prayer life to increase. This task has also caused many people in Mississippi to pray more earnestly. It has especially been true with Mission Mississippi at its regular prayer breakfast. Every Tuesday and Thursday morning, these gatherings rotate between a dominant white church one morning and a dominant black church the next time. This is a real opportunity for the body of Christ to get together across the barriers of race and denomination to pray.

BRIGITTE WEEKS finds it hard to realize that she has been editor-in-chief of Guideposts Books (now Book & Inspirational Media) for almost seven years. This is the sixth year she has written for *Daily Guideposts.* "During these years, I've moved, my children have grown up and I've learned an enormous amount about writing, prayer and people." She says that improved health and a wonderfully creative period in the life of the Book Division have made the birds sing. "We've published moving stories about God's work," she says, "as well as original mystery novels, animal tales and our twenty-sixth *Daily Guideposts.* The books are my literary children, and as for my biological and adopted children, my eldest son Hilary is becoming a real businessman, traveling far and wide. My daughter Charlotte is now both a romance editor and married. And my youngest, Daniel, moves between the stage and a restaurant in the dual careers of so many famous New Yorkers—acting for the soul and waiting tables to sustain the body."

MARION BOND WEST of Watkinsville, Georgia, writes, "Shortly after having our beloved sixteen-year-old cat Minnie put to sleep, I discovered a mama cat with four kittens living in a huge pipe in a nearby field. It's been healing just to be able to buy cat food for them. Of course, they are totally wild and scamper away terrified when I drive up to leave food daily. I long to communicate to them, 'I wish you knew how much I care!'

Lately, I've been wondering if God experiences the same feelings when we flee from Him. The children in the first- and second-grade Sunday school class that I taught this year enabled me to remember that prayer is simply talking to God—when you're certain there's no unforgiveness in your heart. Thank you, Ava Claire, Bethany, Aaron, Emory, Daniel and Matthew."

This year finds BRENDA WILBEE of Bellingham, Washington, teaching composition at the community college, writing a new series of novels on Narcissa Whitman (a missionary who was the first white woman to cross the Rocky Mountains), and pursuing a degree in graphic design. "I am absolutely enchanted by this rapidly evolving technology. Right now I spend much of my time in front of the computer, pleased to have at last found a nontoxic medium for my artistic expression. My daughter Heather and her husband still live nearby. My oldest son Phil and his wife are in Seattle. Blake, my youngest, in his last year at Wheaton College, continues to travel the world with various mission organizations and spends his summers at the local Christian camp where he serves in multiple capacities. One of these days he will take off for good, and Heather, Phil and I shall have to travel to Africa, I guess, to see him. The biggest news this year? I turn fifty. I think this is unfair because I still haven't recovered from turning forty."

TIM WILLIAMS, a carpenter and firefighter from Durango, Colorado, is a first-time contributor to *Daily Guideposts*. He and his wife Dianne have two grown sons, Patrick and Ted. "I write three stories a week for www.InspireE.com, an e-mail writing venture I began two years ago," says Tim. "It's a challenge to write that many inspirational stories for my readers. Being a husband, the father of two adopted boys, a volunteer firefighter and emergency medical technician, a victim's advocate for Mothers Against Drunk Driving, and a youth Sunday school teacher provide me with more than enough stories." *Daily Guideposts* contributor Mary Jane Clark helped Tim with his first stories for the devotional book. "I'll miss the guidance Mary Jane gave me this year. She improved my writing, but even more, she improved my life."

Although ISABEL WOLSELEY and her new husband Lawrence Torrey were both in their 70s when they married, they're finding life contains new and exciting events. One of these adventures was driving from their home in Syracuse, New York, to McPherson, Kansas, to attend Isabel's high-school class reunion, her first after more than a half-century. Isabel says, "I learned I was not the only one during the teenage years who'd felt bashful and not part of the 'in' crowd, so going was a therapeutic experience." On their return home, they stopped in St. Louis, Missouri, where they ascended the city's famous Gateway Arch. "Everything went well in our claustrophobic, space-capsule-sized cubicle, which clanked and jerked 630 feet to the summit, until one of the five passengers in the cramped quarters verbalized my thoughts, 'What if a cable breaks?' " Isabel and Lawrence are expecting to leave for Papua New Guinea with Wycliffe Bible Translators. While waiting, Isabel gives several talks a month to church and civic organizations. "One of these groups is a type of hospice, as my late husband Roland was a hospice recipient, and I cannot say enough good things about those who serve in it."

SCRIPTURE REFERENCE INDEX

AUTHORS, TITLES AND SUBJECTS INDEX